The Market E...
and Chi...

Chief Editors:
Gao Shangquan, Liu Guoguang
and Ma Junru

FOREIGN LANGUAGES PRESS   BEIJING

First Edition　1999

Home Page:
http://www.flp.com.cn
E-mail Addresses:
info@flp.com.cn
sales@flp.com.cn

ISBN 7-119-01402-1

© Foreign Languages Press, Beijing, China, 1999

Published by Foreign Languages Press
24 Baiwanzhuang Road, Beijing 100037, China

Distributed by China International Book Trading Corporation
35 Chegongzhuang Xilu, Beijing 100044, China
P.O. Box 399, Beijing China

Printed in the People's Republic of China

Contents

Preface

Li Tieying

In 1993 some sixty well-known economists from home and abroad were invited to attend an international symposium of "The Market Economy and China" sponsored jointly by the State Commission for Restructuring Economy, the State Bureau of Foreign Experts Affairs, and the Chinese Academy of Social Sciences. Extensive and penetrating discussion were held on theory and practice, operative mechanisms, governmental functions, reform of enterprises, construction of the legal system, and other challenges facing China during its transformation to a socialist market economy. The organizers of the symposium have compiled the papers which were presented into the book—*The Market Economy and China.*

China is a large country with a population of 1.2 billion, uneven economic development and a generally low economic and technological development level. It is a very complicated and enormous project to establish a socialist market economy in such a large country as China. We are therefore faced with some arduous tasks. Only if we take Deng Xiaoping's theory of building socialism with Chinese characteristics as guidance, emancipate the mind, and practice and explore courageously with the spirit of seeking truth from facts, can we accomplish this glorious task entrusted to us by history.

During socialist modernization construction and reform and opening to the outside world, we should emancipate our minds and courageously absorb and draw on the experience of all the achievements of civilization, including all the advanced operation modes and management methods reflecting modernized production laws in the capitalist countries. We should also firmly resist degenerate things and thereby reflect innate socialist characteristics.

We should not deviate from the practice of reform and opening up while studying the new modes in theory. The economic management modes and systems of various countries develop along with economic development. We should proceed in all cases from China's basic conditions. It is those basic conditions that determine China's diversified economic sectors, the publicly owned economy as the main body with various forms, the important position of rural areas in economic development, the important role of the government in cultivating markets, adjusting the industrial structure, reducing differences between regions and preventing polarization; and also assure that we are building socialism with Chinese characteristics and establishing the new socialist market economic system.

The modern enterprise system suits the needs of the socialist market economy, because it includes distinct property right, explicits responsibilities, and separates functions for government and enterprises, and scientific management. We should actively explore effective forms of realizing public ownership based on the distinct ownership of state-owned properties, and the property right of corporate enterprises. All enterprises should strive to establish a modern enterprise system.

The advantages of the socialist system compared with the capitalist system mainly lie in higher productive forces and the realization of social justice which is impossible for the capitalist world. High efficiency, social justice, and common prosperity are the basic characteristics of the socialist system. However, socialist equality and justice do not mean egalitarianism. The "big-pot" and "iron bowl" only sacrifice efficiency, preventing the realization of real justice.

We should uphold the principle of giving priority to efficiency while giving consideration to justice. The principle of giving priority to efficiency is reflected in primary distribution; and adhering to the principle of to each according to his work, and more pay for more work reflects the principle of giving priority to efficiency. Social re-distribution embodies the principle of justice, and the government adjusts excessive differences caused by primary distribution through tax revenue, social insurance and other means, preventing polarization with the premise of guaranteeing efficiency, and realizing common prosperity.

Justice is reflected not only in distribution and consumption, but also in equal competitive conditions and opportunities during production and circulation. Justice is reflected not only in the quantity of distribution, but also in opportunities. Society should provide all people with equal competitive opportunities. Therefore, we should strive to establish standard market competitive order and operational mechanisms, such as a strong legal system, and guarantee the real unification of efficiency and justice in market competition.

The development of the socialist market economy also involves periodicity. Differing from capitalist society which changes radically, the socialist market economy will enter a new stage every few years. We should strengthen research into the developmental laws of economic periodicity, and establish a statistical indicator system precisely reflecting new economic operating mechanisms and indicating economic development.

At present we are confronted with rapid reform and development. Reform leads to rapid development and only through reform can the deep contradictions and problems restricting the rapid and sound economic development be solved. The objective of reform is to achieve development, and its success or failure is determined by practice. We must study accelerating reform under rapid economic development and its complicated economic relations, and master the high technologies controlling the national economy.

Closely related to the establishment of the socialist market economy are the relationships between reform, development and stability, between the transformation of governmental functions and the operational system of enterprises, macro control and market mechanisms, central and local governments, urban and rural reforms, economic development in east and west China, the economic structural reform and the reform of science, education, culture and public health, and the construction of a sound legal system. And we must solve these problems. I hope economic workers will study these problems in a thorough manner and put forward realistic and proposals. I also sincerely hope that overseas experts and scholars will continue to consider China's reform and opening up and put forward more and better suggestions.

Foreward

The 14th National Congress of the Communist Party of China (CPC) set the objectives of establishing the socialist market economy, and the Third Plenary Session of the CPC 14th National Committee put forward concrete objectives and procedures for the construction of the socialist market economy, marking the further acceleration of China's reform and opening to the outside world and confirming that the socialist market economy had entered a new stage. When China plunges into the practice of a market economy, *The Market Economy and China* has become available for readers.

This book is a collection of theses by many well-known Chinese and foreign economists, such as world-famous economists Lawrence R. Klein, professor of Economics at the University of Pennsylvania, U.S.A., and recipient of the 1980 Nobel Prize in economics, and Merton H. Miller, professor of Economics at the University of Chicago, U.S.A. and recipient of the 1990 Nobel Prize in economics. From September 18 to 20, 1993, an international symposium of "The Market Economy and China" was convened in Beijing by the State Commission for Restructuring Economy, the Chinese Academy of Social Sciences, and the State Bureau of Foreign Experts Affairs. Over 60 experts and scholars from the mainland of China, the United States, France, Japan, Australia, the Republic of Korea, Taiwan, and other countries and regions, as well as international organizations such as the United Nations Program, the World Bank, the Bank of Europe, and the Ford Foundation attended the symposium. There were extensive and penetrating discussions on theory and practice, operational mechanisms, governmental functions, reform of enterprises, construction of the legal system, macro regulation and control, and challenges confronting

China during its transformation to a socialist market economy. Jiang Zemin, president of China, met with the foreign participants and made an important speech at the symposium. Li Tieying, member of the Political Bureau of the CPC Central Committee, and minister of the State Commission for Restructuring Economy, met with all participants and attended the opening ceremony. The participants expressed excellent opinions of the points made on several important issues in President Jiang Zemin's speech, many of them substantiating their own theses, and some participants submitted written suggestions on other issues discussed by President Jiang Zemin.

To help readers gain a comprehensive understanding of these papers, the organizers worked very hard compiling the theses carefully into this collection. Of course, the viewpoints expressed in these articles do not necessarily represent those of the compilers.

From the theses of the foreign experts, readers may see that China's step-by-step reform was widely praised and the establishment of the objectives of the socialist market economy has strengthened confidence in national and international economic circle in the prospects for China's reform and opening to the outside world. We believe that guided by the Resolutions of the CPC Central Committee on Certain Issues on the Establishment of the Socialist Market Economic System, a new socialist market economic system will be preliminarily established by the end of this century. By that time Chin's economic development will have entered a new stage. Of course, during the process there will be many problems to be studied, and some new problems will emerge. However, we will surely attain our objectives so long as we persist in our objectives and unite around the Party Central Committee with President Jiang Zemin as its core, guided by Deng Xiaoping's theory of building socialism with Chinese characteristics.

November 20, 1993

Taking a Market-Oriented Direction and Pushing Forward in a Gradual Way
—The Basic Experience of China's Economic Reform

Gao Shangquan
Former vice-minister of the State Commission
for Restructing Economy and executive vice-president
of the Chinese Society of Economic Restructuring

Fifteen years have passed since China began economic reform. Over the past decade or so, reform has been a keynote of the country's social and economic life. It has penetrated into almost every aspect of the nation, from rural areas to cities, from coastal regions to the interior, from the non-state-owned economy to the state-owned economy, from the small-scale to the large-scale, from the economic field to the fields of science, education and politics, and it has realized universally acknowledged achievements. Looking back on the recent reform and summing up its experience, one finds that one strategy which China has employed is to gradually increase the proportion of market mechanisms in its economy, taking a market-oriented direction and pushing forward in a gradual way.

I. Taking a Market-Oriented Direction: Basic Achievements of Reform

One of the reasons China has been able to obtain success in economic reform is that it has adopted a strategy of taking a market-oriented direction and pushing forward in a gradual way. China's reform has undergone four stages: During the first stage, which started at the end of 1978 and ended in October 1984, reform was first implemented in the country's rural areas with great success; and reform was also conducted in cities on a trial basis by granting more autonomy to enterprises. In the second stage, which extended from October 1984 to September 1988, the focus of reform shifted from rural areas to cities, and reform was carried out in all fields. The third stage, which lasted from September 1988 till the end of 1991, was highlighted by the government's effort to rectify the country's economic environment and economic order to create better conditions for deepening reform. Comrade Deng Xiaoping's important speeches made during his tour of southern China in early 1992 marked the beginning of the fourth stage. Following Deng's instructions, the 14th National Congress of the Communist Party of China set up the economic reform target for building up a socialist economic system, which, in turn, has quickened the reform and opening to the outside world and has pushed it to a new stage.

Profound changes have taken place in China's economic system since reform began:

—The old structure of the country's economic ownership has been altered. While publicly owned enterprises still contribute to the bulk of the nation's economy, various other economic forms including collectively owned, privately operated and foreign-invested enterprises have emerged, and they have coexisted and developed well together with state-owned enterprises. In 1992, 48.8 percent of the nation's total industrial output was produced by state-owned enterprises, 38.2 percent by collectively owned enterprises, and 13.4 percent by foreign-invested enterprises, privately owned enterprises and individuals. Of the total retail volume of social commodities, state-run commercial enterprises account for 19.3 percent, the collectively owned enterprises, 27.9 percent and individuals, private owned enterprises and foreign-invested enterprises, 30.8 percent. The rapid development of the non-state-owned economy and the non-publicly owned economy has injected new vigor into our nation's economic life.

—Operational mechanisms of state-owned enterprises are now being transformed and gradually pushed into the market under the principle of separating government administration from enterprise management and ownership from operational autonomy. Various forms of reform have been conducted in state-owned enterprises with emphasis on granting them more operational autonomy. Ninety-three percent of the country's publicly owned industrial and commercial enterprises have adopted various forms of the contract system in production and operation. A number of enterprise groups have been established in order to combine production elements in a reasonable way. Some of the medium- and small-sized state-owned enterprises now have been either leased, transformed, or sold. In recent years, various forms of stock systems have been introduced into a great number of state-owned enterprises. By the end of 1992, more than 3,700 enterprises with stock systems had been set up throughout the country, of which, shares of 92 such enterprises are now on the stock exchanges in Shenzhen and Shanghai.

—Prices of commodities are now determined largely by the market, rather than by the state. Today the government has abandoned its control of the prices of most commodities. At present, agricultural products purchased with prices fixed by the state account for less than 15 percent of the country's total; only 10 percent of the nation's industrial consumer goods, and 30 percent of production materials are sold with prices fixed by the state. Meanwhile, various markets including securities, foreign exchange, labor, technology, and land markets have been developing at a high speed.

—Direct interference in the nation's economy by the government, largely by administrative means, is now gradually being replaced by indirect control chiefly by economic and legal means. The rigid economic system whereby production targets, investment, projects, and materials used to be under the direct control of the state has been shattered. As a result, production targets ordered by the government have decreased drastically. Before 1979, more than 95 percent of the country's total industrial production was turned out at the order of the state, a figure which has dropped to only 7 percent now. Proportions of production materials allocated by the state and commodities purchased according to the state plan have also decreased. Meanwhile, financial and monetary policies now play a much more important role in the country's economic life.

—While distribution according to work still dominates the social distribution system, many other distribution forms have now appeared. A new social insurance system is taking shape. The government's policy encouraging people to become rich through honest labor and allowing for differences in incomes to a reasonable extent has greatly mobilized the enthusiasm of workers.

—Opening to the outside world has greatly accelerated China's domestic reform and development; and a multi-layer, multi-form, and omnidirectional open setup has taken shape. By the end of 1992, the number of foreign-invested enterprises had reached 84,000 with an agreed investment of US\$ 58.7 billion and an actual investment of US\$ 11.2 billion. In foreign trade, China will conduct its import and export trade according to international practice and the regulations of the General Agreement on Tariff and Trade in order to expand economic and technological cooperation with the outside world and compete in the world market. The changes in China's economic system have tremendously improved social and economic life. Over the last 15 years of reform, China's gross national product has continued to grow at an average annual rate of 9 percent, national power has been obviously strengthened, and the life of the people has improved remarkably. Moreover, reform has greatly emancipated the mind of the Chinese people. With the spirit of finding truth from facts, the Chinese people keep searching in practice and have advanced reform step by step.

II. Pushing Forward in a Gradual Way: A Successful Experience

Instead of applying "shock therapy" to its economic system, China has adopted a step-by-step strategy. The essence of this strategy is that no reform measure will be carried out on an overall basis or be applied to the whole country until it has been tried in a given place and certain conclusions have been drawn. To ensure the success of reform, the government has set up a number of experimental sites throughout the country. These experimental sites designated by the government, either in a city, a county, or an enterprise, are responsible for the trial of various forms of reform measures. The following facts illustrate how reform has been carried out under this strategy: Reform was first implemented in the rural areas, then gradually carried out in cities; even when the focus of reform had shifted to cities, it was first tried in the special economic zones, then in coastal areas, and then in the interior. Market mechanisms were first introduced into rural industrial enterprises, privately operated enterprises, and foreign-invested enterprises, then gradually introduced into the state-owned economy. Reform was first carried out in a small way, such as granting state-owned enterprises more autonomy in production and operation, then was conducted on a large scale by gradually reforming the planned economy and the fiscal and financial systems. This method of pushing forward economic reform in a gradual way is a creation of the Chinese people. It is also a result of their persistent searches in practice.

Price reform is a typical example illustrating how reform has developed gradually. Price reform has always posed difficult problems in every country. It is also one of the first difficult problems we have met in economic reform. The Chinese government and economic circles both recognize the importance of price reform since they know that unless price is determined by the market, market mechanisms will not be brought into full play, competition among enterprises will not be conducted on a fair basis, and optium deployment of resources will not be materialized. They also understand that price reform must go together with market cultivation, though price reform is something that can be done quickly whereas market development will take a long time. They understand too that price reform requires financial strength in order to guarantee that the interests of the masses will not be hurt during the course of price reform. Price reform will exert varying impacts on different industries and products, and some industries or the production of some products require large investments, a long production term and high technology. The market cannot keep balance after the government abandons the control over the price, a fact which will result in inflation. Because of this understanding, the government has avoided adopting the method of lifting price control on all commodities at once, but has adopted a positive and prudent price reform policy, under which price control on commodities in different sectors is lifted at different times. Though China has a heavy task in price reform, it has already passed the crucial period.

Why has China adopted the strategy of gradual reform? If we answer this question generally, we can say that the present reform in China is the country's second revolution, aimed at fundamentally changing the country's economic system. This is a creative undertaking never attempted by our predecessors and has no model to follow; therefore, it must be done in a gradual way. But there are some other more profound reasons for the choice of this strategy:

First, reform needs time to win the understanding and support of all the Chinese people, therefore it must be pushed forward in a gradual way. Though people will ultimately benefit from reform, still the interests and power of some people will inevitably be adjusted to a certain extent. Therefore reform needs time to win the understanding and support of society. This is especially true for reform measures involving the adjustment of the people's interests. Therefore, such reform measures, before fully being carried out, must first be experimented with and gradually accepted by the people. Only when people understand these measures can they support them. Otherwise, reform will be very difficult, and it may even destroy previous achievements.

Second, the adoption of this strategy has something to do with the economic system itself. Every part of the economic system is closely linked with every other. If we want to reform the whole system, we must find the right point to make a breakthrough. When we start reforming a particular part of the system, we have to consider what impact it will exert on the other parts. The experience drawn from the past 15 years of reform tells us that reform should first be made on the softest link in the system rather than the most crucial and difficult parts. For example, reform of state-owned large and medium sized enterprises is of great importance, but it poses many difficulties. Therefore the government has chosen a roundabout way by first forcefully developing the non-state-owned economy in an attempt to form a group of competitive economic entities outside the state-owned economy and keep pressure on them to make fundamental reform of the state-owned economy possible. It is hard to imagine that reform of the state-owned economy could be carried out without such a strategy.

Third, the choice of the strategy for pushing forward to a gradual way is determined by the complicated national conditions existing in China. China has a large population, a vast territory, and unbalanced economic development. As economic development varies from region to region, conditions for reform also differ to a great extent, making it impossible to push forward reform at the same rate everywhere. Some regions may develop a little faster, while others may lag behind. This is quite natural.

Fourth, this strategy accommodates political needs. Reform in China requires a stable political and social environment. Radical reform measures inevitably surpass social endurance and cause social turmoil, hindering reform. China is a big nation with a population of more than 1.1 billion people. Stability is now the number one task confronting the nation. Therefore, the choice of any reform method must take stability into consideration.

III. A New Starting Point for Reform: Building up the New System of a Socialist Market Economy

China has set up economic reform targets for building up a socialist market economy. The target is undoubtedly the continuation and development of the past 15 years of reform which has taken a market-oriented direction, pushing our country's reform onto a higher stage. Building a socialist market economy means establishing an economic system in which public ownership is internally integrated with a market economy, and market mechanisms play a fundamental role in the deployment of resources. This is accomplished with positive and effective macro adjustment by the state in an efficient and equitable manner at the highest level.

To build a socialist market economy, we must first absorb and draw on the successful experiences of foreign market economic practices and abide by the general laws of a modern economy. These experiences are as follows: All commodities and production factors must enter the market, and market mechanisms must play a fundamental role in the deployment of resources; the relationship of property rights is clear, and enterprises are legal entities which have real autonomy in their operations and are themselves responsible for gains and losses; the government exercises indirect participation in economic activities mainly through economic means; economic relationships are legalized; a unified and open domestic market is connected with the international market in an organic way, and economic activities are conducted according to international standards and practices. The socialist market economy must also reflect the essential needs and the basic aspects of the socialist economic system and must accommodate the basic conditions of our country.[1] The socialist market economy must adhere to public ownership, and public ownership should integrate with the market economy. Otherwise, the vigor of public ownership will not be brought into full play, the value of state-owned assets will not be preserved and increased, and the public-owned economy will not be expanded and strengthened. Therefore, the basic form of public ownership must meet the needs of a market economy. The basic conditions of our nation demand the diversity of economic ingredients in a market economy. The development of the rural areas occupies an important place, and the government must play an important role in developing the market, adjusting the production structure, shortening the gaps among various regions, and in preventing division into two opposing extremes.

Establishing the socialist market economy is a complicated and systematic project. Building the main frames of this system involves the following steps:

—To establish a modern enterprise system in which the property rights of enterprises are clearly defined, and enterprises have operational autonomy and are themselves responsible for gains and losses, and competition among them are conducted on a fair basis. Various kinds of enterprises, regardless of their form of ownership, should all be established and registered according to law. They should have the right to the actual possession, use and disposition of their assets. Reform of state-owned enterprises should be conducted first by clarifying the relationships of property rights, enterprises in the sectors in which competition is fierce should be transformed into limited-liability companies with different types of shareholding systems. At the same time, the distribution structure of state-owned assets should be actively and positively adjusted according to the laws of a market economy and the characteristics of different industries, so long as the value of state-owned assets can be increased.

—To establish a modern market system with sound market regulations, complete organizations, and standardized behavior. Price controls on the vast majority of commodities and production factors should be lifted so as to form a mechanism in which price is mainly determined by the market. A complete commodity market system and production factor market system should be formed. Monopoly in different economic sectors, regional blockage, and departmental division should be erased. Various economic forms, different styles of operation, and numerous channels of circulation should coexist. Domestic and foreign trade should be interchangeable, and domestic market should be connected to the international market. A unified and open market should be formed. The primary tasks in market construction at the present stage are to open markets for various production factors, determine their prices at a reasonable level, and put an end to the situation in which there are double systems for determining the prices of production factors.

—To establish a system in which the macroeconomy is managed and indirectly adjusted mainly through economic policies and economic levers in an attempt to promote economic balance and the optium organization of the economic structure. Economic management and regulation institutions with reasonable structures, clear duties, and high efficiency should be established accordingly to meet the needs of a market economy. At present, transformation of the government's duties and functions and establishment of a macroregulation system are seriously lagging behind, severely hindering the construction of the socialist market economy. Breakthroughs must be made in the following three areas: The present financial contract system must be reformed, and a standardized tax distribution system should be implemented clearly defining the rights of the central and local governments. Monetary system reform should be accelerated, macrocontrol mechanisms of the central bank need to be perfected, and commercial banks should be operated as an enterprise. Establishment of a new investment system, in which investment is mainly made by enterprises on their own and their management, conducted according to different categories, should be speeded up.

—To establish a social security system with unemployment, support for the aged and medical insurance as its main elements. A new type of social security system must integrate a social security mechanism with a social stimulating mechanism. Priority should be given to the establishment of a unified institution for the management of national social security, and a unified policy should be mapped out and management and supervision of the social protection system should be strengthened. Nonadministrative social insurance organizations should be set up, the collection and use of social security funds and efforts to preserve and increase their values should be conducted strictly according to law in order to reduce loss and the waste of funds.

Building up a socialist market economy is a very difficult task. In the main, China can only push forward with reform in a gradual way. "Shock therapy" will not be used. But this does not mean that no rapid and large steps will be taken. When conditions for some reforms are ripe, when some reforms must be accomplished, fast and bold steps will be taken at certain times. It is quite obvious that reform in the present stage is very different from that of the past 15 years. Now reform has entered a most difficult stage in which some deep-seated problems must be solved with determination. If it takes us a long time to determine to solve them, losses may be great. Therefore, we must discover the right direction for tackling these problems, and grasp the present opportunity to take significant steps to accelerate the transition toward the new system of a socialist market economy.

What Do Our Economists Know Now About Transition to a Market System?

L. R. Klein
Professor at the University of Pennsylvania
and winner of the Nobel Prize in economics

I. Polar Extremes and Transition Dynamics

In 1978 China embarked on an important and ambitious program to shift from detailed and strict central economic planning to a liberalized system of market pricing. Some years later, the former Soviet Union made similar shifts, but with different practical implementation. There is no doubt that the Soviet leaders were impressed by China's progress by mid decade, and this influenced their decision to enter a transition phase. At the same time, other countries in the Council for Mutual Economic Assistance (CMEA) embarked on programs of economic liberalization, and after the breakdown of the Soviet political system in 1988-1991 each European member of CMEA went its own way toward transition. In some respects a number of developing countries, especially in Latin America, began to restructure their economies and also entered transition phases that had some of the same characteristics that appeared in transforming socialist economies also but had other characteristics that unique to their own special situations.

Economists around the world soon began to think about transition techniques and policies. They almost always said that this process was without precedent, so that there was little historical experience on which to draw for guidance. They noted that there was, however, a great deal of historical knowledge about the transition from capitalist systems, with varying degrees of market performance, to centrally planned socialist systems. The subject of this paper is to examine what we now know about the reverse process: the transition from a centrally planned economy to a market economy.

It should be remarked that by the time the Soviet transition began there was already some knowledge about China's transition experience. At an economics meeting in Budapest in 1985, a leading Hungarian economist was asked to Moscow to participate in a discussion about economic reform for the USSR and CMEA associates. When he returned to our meeting in Budapest, the Hungarian economist told me that the Soviets were more impressed by, and more interested in, China's economic reform than in those that had been implemented in Hungary.

It is very questionable to depend on what works in one country's economy and apply the same processes to the economic environment of another country, yet country-to-country comparisons are often used in economic analyses. Some lessons and experiences can be transplanted, but first we ought to look at the issue from a theoretical viewpoint. To begin with, let us look at the polar extremes. At one end we have the tightly controlled system of central planning, and at the other end the free market of competitive capitalism.

The central planning extreme was theoretically based on Marxism-Leninism, although those two thinkers had much more to say about capitalism and imperialism than about socialist planning. But their concepts of the labor theory of value influenced social accounting, which is a planning tool. The theory of complete state (public) ownership of the means of production (capital) was used to organize the details of goods output and labor input, and rigidly set the prices of individual goods. Inflation could not arise because prices were not allowed to change except by administrative decision. There was, however, hidden or repressed inflation. The result was excess demand. In the USSR, public debt was financed by printing paper money. Since prices could not rise very much, if at all, the visible aspect of inflation was long queues, waiting lists, and the hoarding of money. In the USSR this gave rise to the "ruble overhang."

13

Key projects, building, and the military establishment all flourished because the plan allowed it. These planned economies were largely closed internationally, except for intra-CMEA trade at negotiated or fixed prices, frequently in barter terms.

This system produced a great deal—art, music, scientific achievement, athletic prowess and many other things—but it delivered living levels that were not up to world standard.

In theory, intelligent central planners, equipped with powerful computers, should have engendered better economic results, but they did not do so, and probably had an inferior grasp of how the entire economy functioned.

At the other extreme we have the theory of a completely competitive economy in which each household and each firm pursue their own interests, optimize their patterns of consumption, and maximize profits. Individual nations participating in this sector of the world economy are assumed to continuously optimize their behavior in a completely free-trade environment among countries.

The French economist Walras theorized that such an economy could be described by a system of simultaneous demand and supply functions for all the goods and services available in the economy.

$$S_i = f_i (P_1 ... P_n) \qquad \text{supply functions}$$
$$D_i = g_i (P_1 ... P_n) \qquad \text{demand functions}$$
$$i = 1, 2, ... n$$

Through the equating of all supplies and demands

$$S_i (P_1 ... P_n) = D_i (P_1 ... P_n)$$
$$i = 1, 2, ... n$$

The n prices could be determined. This is called market clearing, because supplies are equated to demands, and the price system accomplishes this by finding that set of prices

$$P_1, P_2, ... P_n$$

that satisfies these equations.

This formal mathematical statement needs a great deal of elaboration. First, we can contrast this view with that of detailed central planning in two respects. Under central planning, there is generally an excess of demand. In practice, this was easy to observe. Theoretically, the equating of supplies and demands in all markets is the same as finding the price vector that makes all excess demands equal to zero.

Define

$$E_i (P_1...P_n) = D_i (P_1...P_n) - S_i (P_1...P_n)$$

The set of prices that makes $E_1, E_2...E_n = 0$ is the same as the set that makes $S_1 = D_1, S_2 = D_2..., S_n = D_n$. Market-clearing prevails under the price system, and this means that excess demand is eliminated. Also, the market is, in theory, cleared for all services as well as goods, but under strict socialist central planning many services are considered non-productive, and criteria are developed mainly for material products.

We should judge the properties of the market system in its most favorable light to establish its features. This system of equations of market clearing does not provide a solution for the absolute level of prices, rather, it determines only relative prices. There are many ways of looking at this feature, but one convenient way is to write

$$P_i = \frac{P_i}{P}$$
$$P = \Sigma w_i P_i$$
$$\Sigma w_i = 1$$

In other words, the individual prices are ratios of goods or service prices to the general price level, P, which is a weighted average of individual prices.

In classic economic theory, the general level of prices, P, is assumed to be proportional to money supply M, which is determined by the central monetary authority. The classic rule at the polar extreme is for the market economy to let relative prices be set by market clearing, and the absolute level of prices be set by monetary control. The rate of change of P is a measure of inflation; therefore the monetary authority determines inflation, while the market determines relative prices.

This is an attractive intellectual proposition because it means that the market acts as an automatic (analog) computer, while the central planning authority must operate the computer, and then only in an approximate sense. The silent market analog computer operates efficiently as an "invisible hand."

Finally, there is one other intellectual property of the market solution, namely, if all the supply and demand equations that make up the system are based on optimal, individualistic behavior by households and firms, the solution to the equation system can be shown to exist in a mathematical sense and to be (Pareto) optimal for the entire economy in an economic sense. Pareto optimality is not a strong property, but it has some attraction. It says that the equilibrium solution for the equation system defines a set of prices and quantities for all the economic participants such that the system cannot be moved to another position without making some economic agent worse off.

While this property has a certain degree of attractiveness, it has a major deficiency in the sense that the solution is not unique. For every distribution of wealth or initial holdings among society's agents there is such an optimum, and the market system does not tell us how the distribution should be selected; i.e. the solution is optimal, subject to the choice of wealth distribution. For the socialist planned economy, the central planners can select a socially equitable (not equal) distribution.

In addition to the fact that the market clearing solution provides no information about either inflation or wealth distribution, it is based on very restrictive assumptions:

(i) free entry/exit in all markets

(ii) equal access to economic information for all

(iii) rational decision making by all agents

(iv) absence of monopoly or monopsony power

(v) absence of natural disturbances (weather, physical environment, climate, etc.)

(vi) full employment of people and resources

There should be no interference with a smooth working economy. Also, it is a static system with an equilibrium solution, but the economy is rarely in equilibrium, and the transition process that we are studying involves the dynamics of imbalance. What happens during the transition is likely to be far removed from either of the polar extremes.

The socialist planned economy rarely, if ever, functioned as assumed in the polar extreme. Incentives faded after a vigorous early start; equitable distribution of wealth gradually became more and more inequitable; corruption was prevalent; technical change warranted fresh prices that did not appear; and people were dissatisfied in comparison with what other countries had achieved.

The conditions for efficient functioning of the market economy did not prevail; income distribution deteriorated in recent years; the business cycle introduced a lack of stability into the system; unemployment reached intolerable levels and persisted for long periods of time.

Neither system functioned according to its best theoretical case. In fact each of the two main economic systems functioned in practice as a mixed economic system. There are planning and socialistic aspects of most economies that regard themselves as primarily capitalist market systems. Similarly, there are market and private capitalist aspects to socialist planned systems. Both systems are imperfect in their actual implementation, and it becomes a matter of judgment where they will finally end up in any transition process. There will ultimately be socialist and market capitalist elements, simultaneously, in any practical system. And the outcomes are yet to be determined. The practical question facing the world economy at this time is where the former centrally planned economies will come to rest as the transition process runs its course. The market economies have their own transitions, but they are changing less actively than the economies in transition from "plan to market."

II. The Concept of Market Socialism

Oskar Lange, A. P. Lerner, and Fred M. Taylor argued more than 50 years ago that it would be theoretically possible to introduce market pricing into a socialist economy—one in which there would be widespread state ownership of the means of production. They based their analysis on a famous paper by E. Barone, who showed with General Walrasian methods that a rational solution for prices in a market economy would exist, in a mathematical sense, even if the means of production were socially owned and if the economy were guided by a central planning board. The board, however, would not fix prices and would respect market solutions.

Actually, the rule for practical application of a central planning board can be stated simply. In markets where there are surpluses, prices should be lowered, and in markets where there are unsatisfied demands, prices should be raised. The board should keep changing prices until all markets are cleared.

The concept of market socialism had been challenged by Ludwig von Mises and Friederich von Hayek, among other conservative economists, as being illogical. They stated that it would not be possible to find rational price calculations for capital goods in a socialist society. It is now accepted that market socialism is theoretically possible, but many modern economists, especially those following or working closely with the transition in the former CMEA economies, dismiss it as uninteresting and inferior to private ownership with market clearing. They do not want to modernize or liberalize socialism; they want to remove all socialist aspects during the transition period and aim for a system that resembles typical OECD (Organization for Economic Cooperation and Development) countries as much as possible. For them, one of the most important steps in the transition period is to privatize, i.e. convert state enterprise to capitalistic enterprise owned by individuals or groups of individuals, either domestic or foreign.

They are simultaneously introducing a market system and selling or distributing state-owned enterprises to private persons. It is their opinion that privately run enterprises are always more efficient than state-run enterprises. Issues of social equality, justice, or wealth distribution play little role in their thinking.

Another approach based on a different set of values and

attitudes would be one that takes the theoretical structure of market socialism seriously and follows more closely along the lines of a mixed economy objective.

It is not only in socialist economies that restructuring is taking place, but also in several developing countries. State-owned enterprises for infrastructural activities (energy, sanitation, transport, water, communication) are being privatized. These economies were mixed, with a relatively strong bias toward state ownership and operation; therefore privatization is being recommended as a step for shifting the balance in the mixed economy in the direction of more private ownership. In many cases, state ownership has gone beyond infrastructural activities. Many financial and some industrial or primary sector marketing activities are state operated.

Privatization with market clearing is being introduced quickly and on a large scale in both former socialist and developing economies. In some cases it is now proceeding smoothly, often after a turbulent and disruptive period of slow production, rising unemployment, and high inflation. The proponents of such transition strategies often proclaim that there is no other way to proceed.

There are, however, viable alternatives. China's case was recognized before the middle of the 1980s, and it followed a very different pattern. Agriculture and small-scale enterprises were being freed-up or liberalized. There was some degree of privatization, but that was not the centerpiece. Market pricing and personal decision-making in some sectors were the important features. The stated objective was to modernize by instituting market socialism, not by moving in a sudden, massive direction toward private ownership.

Agricultural output responded almost immediately and registered above-average growth for most of the decade of the 1980s. Similarly, service output—frequently small scale—also grew rapidly in this period, mainly at double-digit rates. After the impressive gains in agriculture and service related activities took hold, manufacturing then grew strongly.

When Western economists came to China in large numbers

after 1978, it was generally noted that agriculture would have to rise at about 3 or 4 percent annually just to feed the huge and growing population. By 1981, agricultural output was rising by 7 to 13 percent annually. This was the initial spurt reflecting liberalization of the sector. It now appears that agricultural expansion has settled down to a growth rate of 3 or 4 percent, but now services and industry have become the main sources of growth. In the early years services were quite outstanding, but now the extremely high growth rates are based in the industrial sector. Not every year has been a good year, but most have, and the average growth rate since 1978 has been at the top of the world list of national economic performance, when measured by output growth. From 1978 to 1991, the average annual growth rate (in constant yuan) was 8.7 percent. The 1992 figure was even higher, 12.8 percent. Population growth has been less than 1.5 percent; so the per capita performance is also very impressive for the world's most populous nation. The latest figures, with industry growth at more than 20 percent, are clearly not sustainable. The policy problem is to moderate the pace of growth so that it can endure along with the transition goal of step-by-step gradualism. This is in direct contrast to the shock-therapy policies of some former CMEA countries.

Following the economic liberalization of agriculture and small enterprises, the next step is to modernize activity in large state-owned enterprises. An important aspect for this step will be to bring technology to a higher standard. This can be done in many ways, but the importation of foreign capital, the formation of joint ventures with foreign entrepreneurs who use modern methods, and the steady upgrading of the educational establishment at all levels—elementary, high school, and university—are all being done in a step-by-step process.

III. Transition Criteria

An economy in transition should not immediately initiate the process of reaching its ultimate goals; it should first try to achieve a certain degree of macroeconomic stability. In the former CMEA countries, for example, an alternative route could have been to stabilize the economies in an overall sense and then set about restructuring.

Macroeconomic stability can be characterized by:

(1) Restraining inflation—preferably kept well under 10 percent;

(2) Maintaining high-level employment;

(3) Maintaining strong output growth—not necessarily as strong as China's, but certainly above 5 percent;

(4) Keeping the income/wealth distribution equitable;

(5) Providing basic social services for the population;

(6) Building up the country's infrastructure;

(7) Keeping the balance of international payments near equilibrium (current account near zero);

(8) Keeping the internal fiscal balance near zero; and

(9) Keeping the money supply under control—on a moderate growth path.

These are not easily attainable targets, but they imply that the public deficit should not be monetized, and that the deficit should be kept small to ensure that it can be financed without straining the economy. This refers to both the internal and the external deficit. If the economy can be kept on a strong expansion path, and there are enough cases where this has occurred to know that it can be done, then job offers will exist in large enough quantity to keep unemployment from rising rapidly.

The emphasis on rapid privatization with market clearing is likely to make the income/wealth distribution highly unequal in a quick fashion; this is to be avoided because cooperation of all people working together is needed to make the system function well, both during and after transition. A noted feature of many of the successful developing countries in Asia is that they have maintained fairly equitable income/wealth distributions.

The infrastructure contributes to smooth-working industrial and agricultural sectors. Rapid transportation, instant communication, healthy work forces, well educated work forces and many other population attributes stem from good infrastructures. The elimination of bottlenecks and the overall enhancement of the infrastructure will lead to strengthened productivity and sharpened competitiveness of industry. These things should be put into place as soon as possible, with higher priority than economic restructuring, such as privatization.

Generally, these criteria are falling into place in the Chinese strategy of development, but not on a wide scale in either Eastern Europe or the former Soviet Union. The realization of these criteria provides a calm environment in which to introduce reforms, some of which are likely to be quite unsettling.

IV. Some Transition Procedures

It is easy enough to call for the achievement of the various transition criteria mentioned in the previous section, but it is quite another thing to devise practical procedures that will help to realize these criteria.

Of the economies using shock-therapy (quick resort to market clearing, large scale privatization, rapid exchange depreciation) very few had begun, by 1992 or 1993, to realize macroeconomic gains. There are always some winners and many losers, giving rise to inequities in the distribution of income, but total GDP fell at the beginning in all the CMEA countries. By 1992, Poland had started to recover at a very low rate, and East Germany, assisted by massive transfers from West Germany, also made small gains. There was, however, widespread unemployment and serious inflation, except in Germany. The Czech Republic also made gains, but only after separating from Slovakia, where output declines are substantial. Where there have been economic gains, improvement was modest and has yet to prove itself, but the main result has been inflation, unemployment, external and internal deficit, and output decline, as well as increases in crime.

The most impressive aspect of China's reform, restructuring and liberalization is that it took place without putting the economy through a major recession. It proceeded gradually—not by shock-therapy—and then not only grew, but expanded in world record proportions.

What are some of China's more noteworthy procedures, techniques, and other transition features?

(1) The goal has been a mixed economy, with some private ownership, private decision making and some state ownership, in other words, market socialism;

(2) Implementation of openness for trade and technology;

(3) Creation of special economic zones (SEZs);

(4) Sequencing of economic reform prior to political reform;

(5) Introduction of modern economic education;

(6) Gradual geographic distribution of economic gains; and

(7) The absorption of quantitative methods from econometrics and statistics in preparation for application to economic planning.

Market socialism The major transitions in Eastern Europe and the Soviet Europe and the Soviet Union were distanced as far as possible from market socialism. This was immediate and adopted without hesitation. The transition has not yet produced impressive results for income, production, employment or trade. The experience with inflation has been mixed, but far more often it has been an unfortunate experience rather than a good one. It remains to be seen whether some impressive economic results are achieved, but it is likely that the outcomes will vary greatly from country to country.

It is often said that the CMEA countries had no option. But had they thought about the issues carefully during the 1980s, some steps for a more gradual transition could have been put into place because all the countries involved had China's example to study, long before the CMEA systems broke down.

Openness All the countries involved in transition economics want to participate in multilateral organizations, and many do, in fact, belong to such organizations. There are still some applications pending for GATT membership, and acceptance into this world trading body will be important for the development of export-import relationships on a multilateral basis.

Openness is important for more than direct trade enhancement, it is also important for facilitating capital flow. Most of the transition economies are badly in need of international capital import, not only to finance straight-forward activities, but also to facilitate the transfer of technology. Joint ventures with foreign partners, licensing agreements, and other mechanisms for transferring technology are some of the most important elements for transition economies in their move toward advanced technologies once they have developed a good flow of modern, standard economic activities.

Every economy that has tried to be self-sufficient has lagged in economic development; therefore openness is a necessity.

Special economic zones   A particular form of openness is the attempt to attract international business to a transition economy through tariff concessions, subsidies, special rights in protected areas, and by furnishing ample resources for transportation, telecommunications, and whatever business facilities are needed for contemporary practices worldwide. One attraction of the special economic zones is the provision of inexpensive labor and available raw materials.

Some form of special economic zones has worked well for Taiwan, Israel, Korea, Mexico, and other economies that are now expanding. The special economic zones in China are just beginning to yield rewards and appear to be excellent growth vehicles.

Economic and political reform   Transition economics is full of slogans with limited analytical content. One has been that economic and political reform are inexorably tied together and must be simultaneously introduced. There are many exceptions to this slogan.

There is much to be said for stabilizing and improving economic conditions upon entering a transition phase. Once economic stability has been attained, detailed economic reforms can be introduced, and they should be followed by political reform. This pattern will not be suitable in every instance, but it does seem to work where it has been carefully introduced.

It may be true that eventually economic and political reform will go together, but this is an area where individual conditions will dictate the pattern to be followed. Large-scale political reform in the Soviet Union (glasnot) did not seem to pave the way for effective economic reform (perestroika). Economic reform amid a turbulent situation has yet to appear. In Yugoslavia, prospects seem extremely poor for economic reform, and will never compensate for the dead.

Modern economic education Very few transition economies were open to modern economic ideas before the 1960s, though in some countries modern economics was taught to representatives from the CMEA affiliates. During the late 1960s this process began, and during the 1970s there was a steady flow to major universities and research centers. I personally had students and visiting scholars from the USSR, Poland, Czechoslovakia, Yugoslavia, and Hungary. The number was not large but it was well placed, developing a corps of scholars and researchers in modern economics.

In China, the process was different. Contact was made in 1979 by a team of economists from the United States representing the ACLS, SSRC, and NAS. In 1980 there was an econometric workshop, and after that an entire program covering many aspects of economics. The case of China was of unusual significance because modern economics was little known there for at least 30 years. The "cultural revolution" silenced those who had studied in the international community prior to the Liberation; therefore an entire generation of modern economists had to be created, and this was accomplished during the 1980s. "Shock-therapy" would have been disastrous in this period, and the gradual, step-by-step process was extremely well suited to China.

Economic analysis, economic thought, and economic methodology were developed in step with the modernization of the economy. This gave appreciation, understanding, and meaning to the transition.

Geographical distribution It is natural that large urban centers, ports, financial centers and other key areas be liberalized first since they can absorb the ideas of modernization more readily. After economic changes become established in these principal areas, they then can be installed throughout the country, to areas that have been less in touch with the outside world.

In the Chinese transition, this has taken the form of developing coastal areas first, together with the center of government.

The special economic zones took time to construct and become operational. They later moved to other areas, away from China's east coast. All the while, agriculture was being reformed on a nationwide basis.

The final step will be to locate infrastructural facilities throughout inland areas and to develop business gradually in the inland and west China, realizing a full geographical range.

Quantitative methods It is one thing to teach and absorb ideas from the general subjects of modern economics. It is quite another thing to teach the specific methods of econometrics and of general statistical method. That is, to a large extent, to give interpretation to the transition economy and its eventual targets. It is important to convey the meaning of the very idea of a price system. As was mentioned above, an econometric workshop was held in 1980, and from this experience the tools for economic planning in the form of data banks, computer software, model building, simulation studies for policy formation, and many other methods of implementing the concepts of modern economics transpired.

The fund of quantitative information in China was meager in 1979. The gradual buildup of time series samples, cross-section surveys, special indicators and many other information systems that are vital to intelligent economic planning needed to take place. To have done this on any basis other than gradual development would have created chaotic conditions and provided only an inferior information system. The introduction of modern economic thinking went hand-in-hand with development of useful quantitative information systems.

Russia and other republics of the former Soviet Union are at a great disadvantage in not having suitable information. The situation is different in some of the Eastern European countries; they had reasonable information systems in a few cases, but even in the best of circumstances the complicated introduction of market systems and privatization were rushed into immediate implementation without appropriate documentation or information. Again, this is a situation in which gradualism is much more preferable.

V. Measuring China's Transition Program

There are two special aspects of macroeconomic accounting that figure prominently now in the transition process. The first aspect is to shift from material product accounting, derived from Marxist views about value, to the system of national accounts according to UN standards and now used by most countries. Such aggregates as GNP and GDP are produced by the SNA (system of national accounts).

China now estimates GNP or GDP with due allowance for service activities as well as material product activities. China, like the United States and many countries in the former CMEA, including Russia, are adopting the SNA framework. This provides a better picture of economic activity, especially because increased service activity is part of modernization. In 1979, when US economists established formal contact with Chinese economists, the material product system (MPS) was being used, but in connection with participation in Project LINK, Chinese model builders followed the best Western practices by estimating more modern concepts like GNP or GDP. Actually, the same shifts in social accounting were taking place in Eastern Europe in Poland, Hungary, Czechoslovakia, East Germany, Yugoslavia, and the USSR. By now, Western social accounting concepts are quite familiar to all countries experiencing economic transition.

An added degree of complexity is introduced, when we consider comparisons among countries. This is an old problem for economists which has recently caught the fancy of the general public as a result of the striking results achieved in China. If China's GDP is measured in international prices, based on "purchasing power parity" for exchange rate conversion instead of contemporary market exchange rate, it turns out that China's GDP looks much larger than people had expected and shows the possibility for moving up the international ladder more quickly than was anticipated. China is so populous that many already foresee it becoming the largest economy in the world.

Among economic statisticians, comparative measurement between countries has a long tradition. The present newsworthy estimates about China emanate from a research team that had its origins more than 40 years ago. The first study was undertaken jointly by Milton Gilbert and Irving Kravis. They were primarily interested in comparing European economies with that of the United States after World War II. This research was extended by Irving Kravis at the University of Pennsylvania, the same Irving Kravis who was on the team of visiting economists in China in 1979. While in China, he collected some 100 prices and set about to measure China's GDP per capita on a scale that set the United States as an index value of 100.

His first estimate, in 1980, was that China's GDP per capita was about 13 percent of the corresponding US figure—about the same as that for the Philippines, and approximately double the figure for India. This figure was challenged by many economists, both inside and outside China. Nevertheless, Irving Kravis held his ground; he had been through similar criticism with Hungary for rating that country much higher on a PPP basis than in one using market exchange rate conversion.

The abundance of consumer services available at nominal and very low cost were the source of some of the mark up from conventional to PPP-based figures. Now that statistical offices of several international bodies such as the OECD, IMF, the World Bank, and the UN all use PPP-based figures for various international evaluations, people have begun to accept the concept that China, for example, is very prosperous and tending toward rapid progress, as in the case of Japan vis-à-vis the USA.

Kravis's comparative valuation from China in 1980 may have been higher than the figures that are prominent today—with China at less than 10 percent of the USA figure. It is difficult to be confident about point estimates in these measurements; the original Kravis estimate and that of his colleagues who now maintain the system, Robert Summers and Alan Heston, are somewhat higher than the figures of the IMF or the World Bank, but research scholars believe in the soundness of their procedures and stand by their higher estimates.

Many observers are so impressed by China's transition economy that they are inclined to accept even higher valuations than those suggested by the multilateral organizations. It is evident that purchasing power parity valuation can raise the level of GDP per capita through accounting for many low cost goods and services for consumers, basic food, rent, medical care, e.g. It is less evident that the rate of change will also be effected, but in China's transition period many new services and low-cost consumer goods can be introduced year-by-year as the economy modernizes, and this process can contribute to elevated growth rates as well as higher levels of GDP per capita.

Establishing a Socialist Market Economic Framework

Liu Guoguang
Vice-president of the Chinese
Academy of Social Sciences

China has enjoyed dynamic economic development for over a decade since adopting the policies of reform and opening to the outside world. From 1979 to 1992, the annual average growth rate of the gross national product was 8 percent. After readjustment during 1989-1991, the economy entered into another stage of rapid growth with the growth rate reaching 12.8 percent in 1992. In the first half of 1993, the growth rate rose to 13.9 percent with an increase of over 20 percent in total industrial output value for the past 12 consecutive months. In general, strong momentum still exists in the Chinese economy, and it is estimated that the growth rate of 1993 will reach about 13 percent.

However, with the economy developing at a very high speed, some problems emerge which demand solutions. These problems include:

1. Investment in fixed assets expanded on too large a scale. The whole society's total investment in fixed assets in the first half of 1993 increased by 61 percent over the corresponding period of the pervious year. After adjusting for inflation, actual expansion was still 34 percent. Also, the investment structure of fixed assets is not quite rational, with too many small and repetitious processing projects.

2. Infrastructure facilities are apparently inadequate to support economic development. Since 1992, railway freight capacity was able to satisfy less than 60 percent of demand. In the first half of 1993, this figure dropped to 40 percent. At the same time,

the supply of raw materials and energy falls far short of demand.

3. The financial sector also faces some disorder, with too much new currency being issued and widespread irregular inter-bank loans and unauthorized funds collection. Real estate, development zones, stock and securities markets are obviously over-heated while large amount of funds are idle.

These problems are reflected together in rocketing prices. In the first half of 1993, the national living cost index rose by 12.5 percent, and as much as 17.4 percent in the 35 large and medium-sized cities over the same period of the previous year. Furthermore, prices for production materials rose by even larger margins while the general price level in the first half of 1993 was 30-40 percent higher than the previous year. And the inflationary pressure accumulating over recent years has now begun to make itself felt. Under these circumstances, the Chinese government has adopted a series of timely measures including raising the interest rate beginning late June 1993 to strengthen macrocontrol of the national economy. These measures started by rectifying financial order and discipline aimed at preventing large fluctuations of economic development, sustaining the stable and coordinated development of the national economy, and providing a more favorable environment for deepening the reform. Over the past two months, macroeconomic control measures have achieved some initial results. However, we must bear in mind that the present contradictions and problems in Chinese economic life are rooted in "institutional bottleneck." That is to say, although China has experienced 15 years of reform and development and set as its goal the establishment of a socialist market economic system at the 14th National Congress of the CPC, the old system has only been initially dented and its weaknesses have not yet been eliminated. The new system is still under gradual construction and has not yet begun to play its full role. Both the old and new systems are now operating, creating continuous conflict and friction. The slow pace of reform in some areas has affected the normal operation of the economy. Thus, the only solution to the present contradictions and problems is to seize the current opportunity to deepen the reform and to expedite the establishment of a socialist market economic mechanism. China's research organizations and relevant government departments are all studying ways to design and build a socialist market economic structure. In my opinion, the following points deserve greater attention:

First is the creation of a new enterprise system. The traditional Chinese enterprise system is the product of a highly centralized planned economy. During more than a decade of reform, enterprises have gained some autonomy as a result of policy adjustment; however, the traditional enterprise system itself did not change. In order to expedite a market economic mechanism, priority must be given to cultivating market subjects. That is, enterprises making decisions on their own and taking full responsibility for their profits and losses. The traditional Chinese enterprise system has a non-corporate structure and organization with abstract state-owned property rights. As facts repeatedly demonstrate, to achieve fundamental changes in the operating mechanism of enterprises, the relations between property and ownership must be sorted out and a modern enterprise system must be established to meet the needs of the socialist market economic system. That is to say, the emphasis of enterprise reform must be transferred from the policy of granting enterprises greater decision-making power and more preferential terms to the creation of a new enterprise system. The basic concept of this new enterprise system is to build genuine corporate entities. Then enterprises will be given property rights over their assets as legal persons. Separation will then be completed, in a modern sense, between the ownership and rights of operation. On this basis, enterprises will be responsible for their operations as well as profit and loss. Modern companies are typically incorporated enterprises. According to the actual conditions prevailing in china, most of the enterprises should be transformed into limited liability companies, and a small number of them shareholding companies when conditions are ripe. Stricter limitations must then be made on companies issuing shares. Even for those enterprises which are not ready to introduce the shareholding system, new operational mechanism should be created to separate their business operations from government administration. Change of the enterprise system is, in fact, a restructuring of property rights. Such transformation will surely deepen our understanding of and enable breakthroughs in ownership relations. First, dominance of public ownership does not necessarily mean ownership by the state. Second, the dominant position of public ownership and the piloting role of state ownership should be formed in the process of competition. Third, all forms of property mix with and infiltrate each other. As more and more businesses come into being with mixed forms of ownership, and will become increasingly difficult to categorize according to ownership. The situation in which policy is made according to the nature of ownership must thus be changed. Fourth, it is not necessary to have a required percentage of state ownership of enterprises, rather different approaches can be taken in different sectors of the economy.

The second essential is to develop the market system while normalizing market regulations. Over these years of reform and opening, China has achieved some bases for further development of the commodity markets. However, the slower pace of development of markets production factors is seriously hindering the furthering of commodity markets. At present, Chinese production factors markets are basically in their infancy. While perfecting commodity markets, we must emphasize the reform and formation of these factors markets, including capital, labor, land, technology and information. Efforts must be made in each of the following areas:

The development and perfection of financial markets. Along with the reform of the investment system, the capital market should adopt diversified methods of financing, including bank financing as the mainstay, while actively and prudently developing financing through bonds and shares. Procedures for issuing and listing shares must be normalized and should be carried out on a larger scale based on the transformation of enterprises employing the shareholding system. As to the monetary market, a national, interbank lending industry should be created and unified, and business services for discontent and mortgage lending should be developed.

Faster formation of labor markets. The rich labor resource of

China is both an advantage and a potentially volatile source of unemployment. Up until now, the development of labor markets have achieved little leaving unchanged the traditional practice of government assuming full responsibility for furnishing employment. To promote the formation of labor markets, the government must relinquish its special roles as employer, job provider and income distributor. Thus, it will become possible for enterprises and employees to choose each other, ensuring the establishment of a rational work force, and diversified labor markets.

In order to cultivate land markets in urban areas, further reform must be carried out in city land property rights, establishing market mechanisms for the price of land-use and normalizing the forms of income from land flowing to the state.

As for price reform, prices for most commodities now have been set free. However, for some means of production, a dual-pricing system still exists. Prices for these commodities must begin to be subject to market forces. The remaining major price reform tasks are to continue to set free the prices for competitive commodities and services, speed up the formation of the market of production factors, set up and improve the reserve system for the few commodities fundamentally essential to the national economy and the people's livelihood, and stabilize market prices.

The third point is to transform governmental functions and improve macroeconomic control. At present, the Chinese economic system is in transition from a planned to a market economy while facing the task of expediting modernization. Under such circumstances, governmental economic macrocontrol must be stronger than that in countries with an established market economy. Nevertheless, government control of the economy should change from direct administrative management to indirect macrocontrol in order to create a favorable environment for economic development. Correspondingly, great efforts must be made to simplify government organizations and transform their functions. China is a vast land with a great population, so in relations between the local and central government, the advantages of localities should be given full play to form a unified domestic market with a rational division of labor, instead of macroeconomic control at all levels, which could create independent and separate local economies. Certainly local interests must be fully recognized and respected and their initiatives followed up in developing the economy.

In reform of the financial and taxation systems present emphasis should be placed on three areas: first, the local financial contract system should be replaced by the tax distribution system on the basis of a rational division of administrative power between central and local governments; second, the tax system should be reformed and improved to unify enterprise and individual income tax, and promote the turnover tax system with value-added tax as its mainstay; third, a double-entry budget system composed of the governmental public budget, the state-owned property operating budget, and the social security budget should be improved and normalized.

In reform of the monetary system, stress must be placed on rectifying financial order by strengthening macroeconomic control to provide a sound monetary environment for development. To this end, some goals and policies have been worked out for monetary reform. The major ideas are as follow: First, transform the People's Bank of China into a central bank which independently implements monetary policies and maintains currency stability under the leadership of the state. Second, set up banks to conduct policy-related business in order to separate the policy-related from the commercial-financial functions of banks and alter the banks' current roles as both policy-executors and commercial operators. Third, transform the current specialized banks into commercial banks operating as businesses. Fourth, reform the system of determining interest rates and gradually allow market forces to assume that role. As for exchange rates, the fixed rate set by the state must be replaced by a new system enabling exchange rates to fluxuate according to market forces.

These reforms concerning the establishment of a modern enterprise system, the cultivation and perfection of a market system, the transformation of governmental functions and the establishment of indirect macro economic control comprise the core for establishing the socialist market economic system. Certainly other aspects, such as labor and salary reform and the establishment of a social security system, further reform of the rural economy and opening to the outside world, as well as strengthening the legal system are all organic parts of a socialist market economic system. These reforms must be carried out with overall planning in a well-coordinated, step by step manner according to the order of priority.

The present economic situation and the changes in the world's political and economic environment urgently demand that China speed up reform. To actively promote the reform, breakthrough progress must be made in the near future in the key areas necessary for establishing a socialist market economic system, as well as in areas which will help strengthen macroeconomic control and rectify the economic structure. Now, unremitting efforts must be made to establish a modern enterprise system and new systems for finance, taxation and investment. We must try our best in the remaining years of this century to fundamentally establish a socialist market economic system, and on this basis, take another decade or two to see this new economic system gradually mature. This will ensure the full realization of the three-step strategy for the economic and social development of our country. Then, around the year 2050, the 100th anniversary of the founding of the People's Republic of China, we shall march into the ranks of moderately developed countries around the world, making new contributions to civilization and the progress of mankind.

The Challenge of Transforming from a Centrally Planned to a Market Economy

Tzong-shian Yu
President of the Chung-Hua Institution
for Economic Research of Taiwan

I. Introduction

A change in the industrial structure stems mainly from technological progress, while changes in economic systems are basically created by decision-makers. The former may cause traditional industries to decline, while the latter may bring about the end of existing economic systems. Since the late 1980s, many Eastern European countries and the former Soviet Union have taken radical measures to change their economic systems from centrally planned economies to market economies. So far they have suffered greatly from hyperinflation and serious unemployment without much positive progress.

In contrast, China began to adopt the policy of opening to the outside world and economic reform measures more than 14 years ago and has realized remarkable achievements. This, in turn, has increased the decision-makers' confidence in transforming the economic system from a centrally planned economy to a market economy. Even though the change has been gradual, it has been dramatic, and many problems have ensued. The purpose of this paper is to explore the many challenges facing China during this transformation. In order to examine these challenges we will first point out the difficulties in transforming an economic system and then analyze various challenges faced in the process of transformation and possible solutions which may be useful for decision-makers.

II. Difficulties in Transforming an Economic System

The transformation of an economic system from centrally planned to market is not an easy task. There is no historical example to follow.[1] Many Eastern European countries and the former Soviet Union have accepted the suggestion made by Western economists to adopt "shock programs," meaning to privatize state-owned enterprises with radical measures.[2] In the Russian Federation the government adopted radical economic reforms which have resulted in negative economic growth, hyperinflation, and an extremely rapid depreciation of the ruble in the last two years.[3] So far, there is no sign that the Russian economy has improved. In Eastern Europe many countries are still in trouble, some of them suffering from hyperinflation and high unemployment, some struggling with political instability or civil war. For them, the road to a market economy is obviously strewn with obstacles. Unfortunately, they don't seem to know how to clear them away.

During the last 14 years, China has adopted the policy of reform and opening to the outside world. Both have been gradual and careful, and can be described as a strategy of "crossing the river by carefully feeling stones under the water."[4] This strategy has made a great contribution to rapid economic growth and the improvement of living standards. One naturally wonders why China has had such remarkable success in economic development while the Eastern European countries and the Russian Federation have not. The answers are as follows: (1) China's political situation is comparatively stable. This allows the government to smoothly carry out its program of economic reform. (2) China has other Chinese societies such as Hong Kong, Singapore and Taiwan to observe for useful lessons. Although not all the laws and regulations of other Chinese societies can be applied in China, many of them, in revised form, can be used as blueprints. (3) The strategy itself of "crossing the river by carefully feeling stones under the water" works very well. (4) Many overseas

Chinese have made large investments in China. The Chinese are thus able to learn management techniques and other skills essential to a country in the early stages of economic development. This doesn't mean that this approach is perfect; in the process of transformation, there are still many challenges to overcome.

III. Challenges Facing the Process of Transformation

If a country has used a particular economic system for a long period of time, that economic system becomes a way of life and an integral part of the culture. If the system is suddenly and completely changed, this will produce a significant impact on the way of life and social values. There is no doubt that the transformation of the centrally planned economic system falls into this category. Once an economic system is changed, two opposing reactions usually take place: (1) Some people support the change since they suppose they may gain from it; and (2) some people resist the change since they know they will lose their vested interests. The former support the change while the latter fight against it. In the process of economic transformation, many challenges are presented. The most important are explored below.

1. The rapid growth of private enterprises has resulted in a large income discrepancy between the employees of the government and those of private enterprises.[5]

Government employees include government officials, the military, public school teachers and workers in government-run enterprises. Their wages are rather low compared to private enterprise employees. Because of this situation, it has become fashionable for a portion of the population to be engaged in private business in order to earn more. Therefore, we see professors opening factories, consulting firms and restaurants, and military servicemen running tourism and transportation businesses, for example. How should one assess this behavior? In the short run, it may be helpful in reducing the disparity of income between the public and private sectors, while in the long run, many harmful effects may result. These include: (1) the decline of administrative efficiency, since many government officials use only a portion of their office hours for their administrative work and do not concentrate on public affairs; (2) an increase in corruption because the difference in income between the public and private sectors may cause some officials to ask for extra money for their services; and (3) a serious decline in the teaching and research of professors and student behavior.

In point of fact, many countries tend to have large income differentials in the early stages of development.[6] The problem is how to reduce this inequality of income. As people become richer, the government should establish a reasonable income tax system based primarily on household income. The government can then make use of this income tax revenue to increase the salaries of government employees. To encourage people to pay income tax, the income tax rates should be simplified.

2. The decline of state-owned enterprises has gradually reduced economic centralization.

Under a centrally planned economy, the central government has the power to collect and dispose of its annual revenue, and economic centralization is the necessary result. Since 1979 when the Chinese government began adopting economic reform measures, private enterprises have rapidly increased, and state-owned enterprises have correspondingly tended to decrease. For instance, by 1992, of total industrial output value, state-owned enterprises accounted for 53 percent, and other enterprises 47 percent (of which 35 percent were collective enterprises in rural and urban areas and the remaining 12 percent private enterprises). Government-run shops accounted for 40 percent of total revenue from retail sales for the whole country, while privately run shops made up 60 percent.[7] Before 1980, the main source of central government revenue was the surplus provided by state-owned enterprises. Since 1980, however, when the principle of "self responsibility for profit and loss" for state-owned enterprises was adopted, the central government gradually has lost the main supplier of its revenue because most of these enterprises incurred losses. The central government has thus turned to the provinces for support. However, only the rich provinces experiencing rapid economic growth have been able to provide additional revenue to the central government. Over time, a strong trend toward economic decentralization began to develop.

The further move toward decentralization is obviously not what the ruling party wants. But no one can change the fact that a market economy is the goal of economic reform. What the government should do is balance centralization and decentralization through the reform of the tax system. Which taxes should be levied by the central government and which by the local governments? This must be carefully thought out. The sources of tax revenues should be assured, because the central government is still the appropriate entity to undertake many matters which cannot be given to local governments. These include national defense, foreign affairs and related concerns. It is important to keep in mind that the central government is no longer as powerful as it was in the past.

3. Unbalanced regional development may result in many socioeconomic problems.

Balance versus unbalanced development has been debated for a long time. However, evidence indicates that it is unwise for a large country to adopt a strategy of regionally balanced development. China is a huge country, of course, and its capital is insufficient for it to carry out an overall plan for developing the entire country at one time. Therefore, it was correct for the Chinese government to begin economic development in the southeastern coastal areas of Guangdong and Fujian provinces. Even within these two provinces, the central government selected only a few places as special economic zones.[8] Through rapid economic growth, the southeastern coastal areas have substantially developed, but many socioeconomic problems have ensued. The most serious problems include: (1) The cost of essential factors has increased more rapidly here than in other areas over the last 10-some years, with wages increasing five to seven fold, and (2) the areas have been characterized by highly speculative activities, raising real estate prices sharply as many attempt to get rich quick through real estate speculation. Consequently, the price of real estate has skyrocketed over the last three years.[9]

These two problems are damaging further economic growth since they harms the existing comparative advantages. Many labor-intensive industries have already moved to foreign countries such as Vietnam. To solve the first problem, and open market economy, not only for the coastal areas but also for the inland area as well, should be adopted. To solve the second problem, the leasing system must be changed.[10]

To correct this unbalanced economic growth, the time has come to open the inland area to foreign investment, and to attract foreign investment, the requirement that all products must exported should be discarded and transportation facilities enhanced. If the interior is opened to foreign as well as domestic investment, investors will relocate from the coastal areas inland, creating more job opportunities inland and improving the standard of living. Wage levels in the coastal areas will then either remain stable or increase only slightly.

4. Not all state-owned enterprises should be privatized.

In a market economy, free competition tests whether a firm survives or not. State-owned enterprises usually are weak competitors because they are subject to a myrial of regulations and official interventions. Thus, they are inflexible in coping with rapid changes in socioeconomic conditions. This is why many insist that state-owned enterprises should be privatized. Privatization is not easy to accomplish, however. In view of the experiences of Eastern Europe and the Russian Federation, we can conclude that privatization cannot be achieved overnight.

Actually, in the early stage of economic development some service industries continue to require government management. If the price of public services is not determined by market forces but rather by the national assembly or a committee, private enterprises will be unwilling to enter that sector. For instance, subway and bus fares in many countries are not set by the subway or bus companies. In other words, private companies cannot increase their fares as they see fit, since fares are closely related to the public interest. More often than not, governments charge relatively low prices for their services in order to subsidize low-income citizens.

Before some state-owned enterprises are privatized they should be made autonomous and independent of direct government intervention in order to reduce the waste of resources and increase efficiency. Their activities should be supervised by a board of directors, however.

5. Inflation is an inevitable result when a country transforms from a centrally planned to a market economy.

High inflation appears to be an inevitable consequence when a country transforms from a centrally planned to a market economy. In the last five years, Eastern European countries and the Russian Federation have suffered from hyperinflation. One reason is the drastic change in the price system. In a centrally planned economy, all prices are set by the government rather than by market forces. In order to adjust insufficient supply to meet demand, a rationing system is generally adopted. People have no choice once the price system breaks down, and it takes a long time to set up a pricing system determined by market forces. In this process of adjustment, high inflation is predictable. The second reason is the influence of transportation difficulties and the regional bottlenecks in the movement of commodities. In many areas a modern transportation system has not yet been developed. Regional regulations may also impeded the free flow of commodities. Most important, however, is that the central government has lost its power to collect and then distribute commodities to the people who need them.

In China, though inflation is not so serious as in other countries with centrally planned economies, many people are worried about inflation since it is much higher than it was 15 years ago. Recent inflation stems from three factors. First, the price of real estate has risen sharply because of highly speculative activities, which, in turn, depresses the standard of living and increases the cost of production. Second, excessive investment has occurred in many areas with insufficient resources to support production. And third, the People's Bank of China issues too much money in its effort to fuel regional development.

Recently, the People's Bank of China has adopted a tight-money policy which has been effective in reducing high inflation. However, it is not enough to use monetary policy alone. So-called "excess investment," meaning to much investment, is still being poured into some coastal areas. This must be dealt with. If investment in the interior is encouraged, and the transportation system is improved as quickly as possible, inflation can be reduced.

IV. Concluding Remarks

To sum up, the transformation from a centrally planned to a market economy is a very dramatic change. Generally, there are two types of change: One is radical, so-called "shock therapy," and the other is gradual and step by step. The former doesn't work as well as expected, while the latter has resulted in remarkable achievements in China. Even so, China still encounters many challenges which are complicated and involve institutional factors.

To deal with these challenges, the government must remain committed to the market economy. Only in a market economy can all resources be effectively employed, and efficiency strengthened accordingly. State-owned enterprises, if necessary, should gradually be privatized with sustained economic growth. Only if a country is able to maintain rapid economic growth, allowing the private sector to grow strong, can privatization be achieved. A reasonable and effective tax system must be established in order to ensure revenues flowing to both the local and central governments. To correct regionally unbalanced development, it is a wise policy to allow foreigners to invest in the interior. Once the investment environment is favorable, it will be possible to reduce the labor mobility now occurring from the north to the south and from the inland areas to the coastal areas, and to equalize wage levels generally. Inflation is inevitable, but it can be reduced to some extent if the money supply is controlled. The transportation system must be improved and intraregional bottlenecks eliminated. In these aspects, it will be necessary for the government to continue to play an active role.

Selected References

1. Kuznets, Simon, "Economic Growth and Income Inequality," *American Economic Review,* Vol. 45, No. 1 (March 1955), pp. 1-28.
2. Murphy K., A. Shleifer and R. Vishny, "The Transition to a Market Economy: Pitfalls of Partical Reform," *Quarterly Journal of Economics,* August 1992, pp. 889-906.
3. Sachs, J., "Privatization in Russia: Some Lessons from Eastern Europe," *American Economic Review,* May 1992, pp. 43-48.
4. Xu Dianqing, "Economic Reform: Speed, Cost and Strategy," *Forum of Chinese Economist Society,* Vol. 8, No. 1, pp. 1-11.
5. Center for Chinese Economic Research, etc. (ed.), *Development Towards the Market (1978-1992), China Economic Analysis 1993.*

Notes

1. There are many examples of the transformation of an economic system from a market to a planned economy. All of them used revolutionary measures to nationalize private property, regardless of public reaction.
2. Professors J. Sachs and Milton Friedman hold this opinion. In Chinese, it is also called "shock therapy."
3. According to the Plan Econ. Report (Dec. 9, 1992), in the Russian Federation, the growth rate of GNP was -13 percent in 1991 and -20 percent in 1992, and the inflation rate was 100 percent in 1991 and 2,000 percent in 1992.
4. This is an old Chinese saying popular in Chinese societies. Since one does not know how deep the river is, when crossing the river the best way is to carefully feel the stones under the water and move step by step in order to lessen the risk.
5. Including household-owned businesses, village-owned businesses and joint ventures.
6. According to Simon Kuznets' study based on international cross sections, there is an inverse U-shaped relationship between growth and equity, which means that as income increases from low levels in a developing society, the distribution of income must first worsen before it can improve.
7. Refer to Shang-chun Kao's "A Gradual Approach Towards a Market Economy" (in Chinese), International Symposium on the Theoretical and Practical

Issues of the Transition Towards the Market Economy in China, July 1-3, 1993.

8. In the early 1980s, the Chinese government first set up four special economic zones in Shenzhen, Zhuhai, and Shantou in Guangdong Province, and in Xiamen in Fujian Province. Later, Hainan Island was added, and the Pudong investment zone was created in Shanghai.

9. Since 1987, business people from Taiwan and Hong Kong have acquired a great deal of land at very low rent from local governments and then sold the leasing rights at high prices. After several turnovers, the price of land became very high. Recently, many local business people have also begun engaging in this same practice through special channels and have made big money.

10. Perhaps the Chinese government never imagined that people would make money through leasing land, but in fact they did. To eliminate speculative activities in land, private transfer of land should not be allowed. If the tenant must transfer such land, he should transfer it to the land owner at a reasonable guaranteed price.

The Marketization Process of the Chinese Economy and the Current Macroeconomic Situation

Jiang Chunze
Deputy Director of the Department
of Foreign Economic Structure of the State
Commission for Restructuring the Economic System

I

Although it was only in 1992 that China clearly put forward its reform objective to establish a socialist market economic system, in fact it had already been going through the process of marketization for 15 years. What are the changes that have occurred in the marketization process of the Chinese economy during this period?

—Increasing pluralization in the structure of property rights and management. On the principle of adhering to the dominant position of public ownership, multiple economic elements have already been coexisting and developing together. At present, in terms of industrial output value, the state-owned economy accounts for 53 percent, the collective economy 35 percent, and individual private business and foreign-invested enterprises 12 percent. Of the total retail sales volume of commodities for the entire society, the state-owned sector accounts for 40 percent, collective commerce 30 percent, and joint business, individual and private commerce 30 percent. The Chinese people not only shall break away from the traditional concepts of Marxism, nor equate a market economy with capitalism while developing a market economy in a socialist society. They also shall break away from the traditional Western concepts of economics which take privatization as the premise for marketization, and refrain from privatization while seeking a path to combine public ownership with market economic practices. This is the creation the Chinese people are bringing about with their own characteristics. Joint development of multiple economic elements and diversified management methods have brought about economic growth and prosperity and have strengthened the economic vitality of China in the 1980s.

—Hundreds of millions of peasants were the initial participants and a vital new force for China's market mechanism. A World Bank research report indicated that at the initial stage of the reform at the end of the 1970s, agriculture enjoyed a sound infrastructure, but lacked mechanisms for incentives. The implementation of the contract responsibility system with remuneration linked to output made hundreds of millions of peasants the first independent producers and managers. They started non-agricultural industries in the townships, carrying within them the seeds of rural industrialization and urbanization. For the past decade and more, the township enterprises absorbed nearly 100 million rural surplus workers, thus avoiding a drastic migration of the rural population into the large cities as experienced by many developing countries in Latin America at the initial stages of industrialization. Nevertheless, a fair amount of surplus labor from the countryside and townships still slowed into the cities, bringing about labor markets and tertiary industries in their primitive form, introducing competitive mechanisms to some extent, and constituting a shock to the originally rigid management system and its constraint on urban economic and social life. The rural population also provided a demonstration of marketization for the urban economy. Without doubt, in-depth discussions are needed on many of the new issues cropping up in practice concerning the transformation and modernization of the rural economy in the 1990s.

—Transformation and incorporation of large and medium-sized state-owned enterprises. In the 1980s when the state-owned economy did not find a way to reform property rights, diversified management methods such as the state-owned contract system, the state-owned leasing system and the shareholding system were being explored according to the principles of separating the functions of administration from the enterprises, and separating the rights of ownership from the rights of management. Now, diversified management methods such as expanding management rights, commissioned management and management on lease will be practiced on a trial basis. In addition, we will publicly auction some of the small state-owned enterprises, transfer them to collectives or individuals, or sell their equity to all the workers of the enterprises and transform them into shareholding cooperatives. These auctions or transfers will enable this part of the state-owned equity to change from a material form into a monetary form for new investment. Mechanisms for bankruptcy have already been introduced, and in 1992, 60 state-owned enterprises suffering long-term losses declared bankruptcy according to these legal procedures. In order to reduce the shock caused by the bankruptcy of these enterprises, we should do our best to combine bankruptcy with enterprise mergers. In terms of large and medium-sized state-owned enterprises, the orientation of reform is to carry out corporate transformation in stages and in batches on the basis of sorting out equity, checking capital and defining property rights. Pilot projects on the standardized share-holding system continue to be implemented. In 1992, nearly 400 new enterprises with share-holding systems were endorsed for establishment. By the end of 1992, there were 3,700 enterprises all over the country with share-holding systems, 92 of which were listed publicly. During the process of introducing the share-holding system, equity in state-owned deposits will also be marketized and socialized, while a part of the stocks could be transferred to corporations or individuals inside or outside Chinese territory on the basis of state control of these stocks.

—Marketization of the mechanism for price formation and the development of the production factors market. Price is the information language of the market. At the initial stage of the reform in China, to enhance social and political stability, the Communist Party of China conscientiously led the liberation of the mind and the initial political reform. The central leadership and the government had the authority to guide the cadres and masses to break away from traditional concepts and explore economic reform. People supported the reform, and besides, the macroeconomy at that time was not in severe crises, so China did not adopt harsh and radical measures such as "the shock therapy." The reform of China's price formation and price management system was carried out by combining readjustment with liberalization, and by steps and blocks over time. This dual system still exist today. However, prices for 85 percent of the total purchase of agricultural products, 90 percent of the total sales of industrial consumer goods, and 70 percent of total sales of production materials have already been shaped by the market. The role of price as the signal for the distribution of resources is being strengthened. The scope for the role of the mandatory plan is now very small, accounting for only 7 percent of the total industrial output value. In terms of total capital used for productive construction, the proportion relying on allocations from the state has already been reduced from over 75 percent to less than 20 percent and the proportion relying on bank loans and raised by financial markets has been increased to over 80 percent. The aggregate amount of all bonds circulated already exceeds 400 billion yuan. Market factors such as capital, real estate, human resources, and science and technology and information are rapidly expanding.

—Pluralization in the methods of income distribution. On the principle of adhering to distribution on the basis of labor, the method of distribution factors coexists with it. The labor force as one production factor should also enter the market. Therefore, the principle of to each according to his work can be better realized through market competitions as well. A new social security system is being designed, experimented with and popularized locally in combination with competitive mechanisms within the labor force.

—To dovetail with the world market. Through historical experience, China realized that it was only a Utopian idea to modernize in an isolated environment. Thus, while carrying out reform on the internal economic system, China implemented the policy of opening to the outside world. Now, a multi-level, multiform and all dimensional pattern with "special economic zones, open cities and regions, hinterland" open to the outside has already been formed. By the end of 1992, foreign-invested enterprises registered in China had reached 84,000. Tens of thousands of advanced equipment and technology were introduced. Investment through agreements reached nearly US$ 100 billion with actual investment of US$ 33 billion. China is reforming its import and export trade system in accordance with the international market practices and the regulations of GATT. In terms of the ratio of the total import and export trade to the total GNP, it was only around 10 percent in 1978, and reached over 35 percent in 1992. Opening to the outside world has expanded China's foreign economic and technological cooperation and strengthened economic links between China and the world. Meanwhile, opening to the outside world has also become a strong motive force in deepening the reform of the domestic economic system with the objectives of dovetailing the operative mechanism and working regulations and procedures of the Chinese market with that of the world market so as to enhance the international competitiveness of China.

The process of marketization of the Chinese economy has been accompanied by economic growth and the improvement of the people's livelihood. In the 26 years before the reform, the annual growth rate of the GNP was about 6 percent, while it increased to nearly 9 percent in the 14 years after reform began. The annual increase of earned income went up from 2.2 percent before reform to 6.5 percent after. This 15-year marketization process has brought China's economy onto a new stage.

II

Marked by an important speech given by Deng Xiaoping during his inspection tour to South China and the 14th National Congress of the Communist Party of China, China's economic development and structural reform have entered into a new historical stage. All regions in the country are taking hold of the opportunities to accelerate the pace of reform and opening to the outside world and modernization so that the Chinese economy can make further progress in the 1990s. Since the beginning of 1993, economic development in various regions has maintained strong momentum and rapid growth. Investment fervor in China is widespread overseas and this situation is gratifying. However, there are also some new contradictions and problems, mainly expressed in the following ways:

First, fixed assets have grown at an exceedingly high rate; and 1992 was the second peak year of investment after 1985. After the expansion of investment autonomy by the local authorities and enterprises, some of the blind investment with irrational structures grew too drastically due to imperfections in the new system and a lack of self-restrictive mechanisms. At present, the surplus production capacity for textiles is one-third, machine manufacturing, one-fourth, light industry, one-third and durable consumer goods such as electric appliances for home use, one-half.

Second, a severe shortage in the supply of major production materials, or bottleneck constraint, is intensified, and the supply of major raw materials and electricity tend to be in short supply too, with the growth rate of total industrial output value 18.8 percent higher than the total output of energy. The contradictions in the deficiency of transportation are even sharper. The growth rate of total industrial output value is 18.7 percent higher than the growth rate of the cargo turnover of the transportation departments, the saturation rate of rail freight carriages decreased from 79 percent in 1991 to 65 percent in 1993, passage carriages operate in severely overloaded conditions, and the ratio between the operating ships in port and the ships in waiting was 1:0.8 in 1991 and 1:1.25 in 1992.

Third, the over-circulation of loans and currency, and the over-expanded supply of the currency. In 1992, the increase in the amount of loans was 422.8 billion yuan, among which 354.7 billion yuan was from state banks, a 19.7 percent increase over the previous year. Sixty billion yuan in cash were planned for issuance while actually, a total of 115.8 billion yuan was issued, an increase of more than two-fold over 53.3 billion yuan over the previous year's. Such high figures in the issuance of cash projected a rise in consumer prices and the prices of tertiary industries with the consumer price index shooting up. The living expenses of the residents in 35 large and medium-sized cities had a 10.9 percent increase over the previous year and the price for service was increased by 21.3 percent. The actual interest rates for bank deposits and state bonds were already in negative value and the inflation rate was coming close to a critical level.

Fourth, production grows rapidly while the growth of financial revenue is slow and finance is weak. There was a shortfall of 63.5 billion yuan for purchasing autumn crops and cotton for 1992, so the peasants were given I.O.U. notes. The fact was that some of the local authorities diverted these billions of yuan to invest fixed assets, and even invested it in the South China to speculate in real estates and stocks. This was the phenomena of the "economic bubble" and the "southeastward flow of capital" that people were talking about at the time. Naturally, it is a law of the normal operation of capital that it tends to flow to the place offering a higher return rate. The problem lies in the lack of a standardized tax system and legal regulations to control speculations. What is worse, the banking institutions are running economic entities themselves, and this has stimulated the growth of this phenomenon through the transaction of power and money. This is non-market behavior in a market situation.

Fifth, there are no norms and standards in the development of the real estate and stock markets and they have become the source of chaotic fund-raising. Provinces and municipalities vie with each other for favorable policies and special treatment to blindly launch "development zones" which occupy 24 million *mu* (one *mu* = 1/15 hectare) of arable land and resulted in a deteriorating scientific and technological industrial structure.

Sixth, financial disorder. The phenomena of "economic bubbles" and "the southeastward flow of capital" have weakened the foundation of savings, so the interest rate as the lever of the economy is not utilized sensitively and effectively. As a result, the outflow of capital from the banks is greater than the inflow of capital into the banks, making it difficult for the financial system to control the speed of the return of capital into the banks, or effectively implement the financial policies of the government. What is worse, internal corruption in the banks is intensified and the phenomenon of commercialization of the power of banking institutions becomes severe.

Seventh, there are loopholes in the control of foreign exchange, and some of the decisions are inappropriately made. Inaddition, people worry about inflation. With the rapidly widening gap between the foreign exchange rate and the regulatory price of the market, for a time, the confidence of investors from home and abroad in the value of Renminbi was eroded.

Eighth, there is disorder in the tax system with little transparency, leading to tax evasion and unequal competition among business people.

The above-mentioned problems have made enforcement of macro-regulations more urgent than ever before. Originally, macro-regulations are internal requirements for markets with deficiencies. However, in the process of transforming the economic system, macro-control is ever more needed for the standardization of non-market behavior. The Chinese government has already adopted a series of policies and measures to govern the process of marketization from a macro point of view. This does not mean an overall tightening up, but is aimed at optimizing the structure through deepening the reform, formulating and executing the laws and regulations and maintaining order to create a better environment for investment and ensure the sustained, coordinated and effective development of the national economy.

III

Governing the macroeconomic situation in the process of marketization is a task of the governmental macro-management policy system including the management of both total demand and total supply as well as its structure, which should take care of the short-term and the long-term economic relations, between the regional economy and the unified national economy as well as among industries.

In light of the fact that China's present system is in the process of transformation and has an obvious transitional nature, it is unable to realize the objectives promptly, nor can it effectively copy the macro-policy measures of mature markets. Therefore, governing the macro-economic situation in the process of marketization also includes the task of deepening structural reform so as to make the system meet the demands of the market economy as quickly as possible. In the past, reform in China progressed by steps, by blocks, and by levels. However, it is high time to accelerate the reform by the comprehensive matching up of the accessory parts in the entire macro-control system since 15 years of reform have already accumulated rich experiences, the objectives of and thoughts on the reform are already clear, and the conditions for learning from the experiences of the world are favorable. Furthermore, the new problems brought about by the coexistence of the dual system, and some of the in-depth problems of the old system have reached the point of demanding immediate solutions. In short, reform must be accelerated, and we should not be intoxicated by the process of gradualism. As quantitative changes accumulate, this will naturally lead to qualitative changes. Of course, before the new macrocontrol system can be perfected and brought into effect, necessary administrative means are also necessary for maintaining market order and promoting the normal operations of market mechanisms.

Macrocontrol includes governmental financial, monetary, income, and industrial policies and their corresponding matching systems. I will talk about a few urgent measures in this regard.

First, rectifying financial order and strictly observing financial disciplines. In the recent past, due to the rise of the phenomena of illegal interbank lending, illegal fund-raising, unauthorized establishment of financial institutions, unauthorized rises in interest rates to launch a "war of interest rates" and financial blackmail and defraud, the financial disorder reached the point where economic development was affected. Mr. Zhu Rongji, the newly appointed Governor of the Central Bank pointed out at the National Conference on Financial Work: "The consolidation of the financial order, strict observation of the financial disciplines and the correction of the chaotic situation in finance are the keys to intensifying macrocontrol at present." He then called on the leading cadres at various levels of the financial system to take the lead in implementing the "three-point law agreed upon by all concerned." Namely, an immediate stop to and conscientious sorting out of all illegal interbank lending; capital already lent illegally shall be taken back on a deadline; no financial institutions shall raise the interest rates on savings and loans in any disguised form, nor shall they use this method to raise saving competition; nor shall they charge or accept commissions from the loan-seekers. There should be an immediate stop to the injecting of credit capital to various economic entities run by the banks themselves and the banks shall separate themselves from these economic entities completely. Those who fail to implement the "three-point law" shall be severely sought out and punished. In appearance, these measures seem to be administrative orders contradictory to the market economy, but in fact they are the legal regulations necessary to curb the internal corruption of the banks, oppose the misdeeds of money and power, safeguard market order and fair competition, and ensure the normal development of the market.

Second, accelerating reform of the financial system. It is agreed by all that reform of the financial system is lagging behind, and the problems now existing indicate that the financial field is ripe for reform. Priorities for financial reform are the following:

1. To strengthen the functions of the Central Bank. By proceeding from the realities of China and gradually moving closer to international practice, a unified and effective macrocontrol mechanism can be formed quickly. A central banking system under the leadership of the State Council which executes a unified monetary policy independently should be established as soon as possible to regulate the balance between supply and demand, and maintain the stability of the currency and provide support for economic development.

2. To establish a financial organizational system with state policy banks and state-owned commercial banks under the lead-

ership of the Central Bank as the main body coexisting with multiple financial institutions.

3. To establish an unified, efficient and orderly financial market system.

Finance is considered as the blood of society and the center of economic life, so the financial industry is considered as the vitamin for other industries. The financial system is the mechanism for raising and utilizing capital, while capital is the adhesive and the vehicle for resources. Through capital mobility, production resources are effectively distributed. Apparently, the present financial system in China is not yet suited to meeting such demands.

Third, effectively utilizing the economic lever and acquiring the skills of macrocontrol. In order to establish a market economic system, the interest rate and exchange rate should both eventually be marketized. The interest rate should reflect supply and demand as well as the credibility of the borrowers and should be adjusted through market practice. The exchange rate and the interest rate should interact to regulate imports and exports and the international balance of payments to better utilize domestic and international resources in promoting economic development. Of course, full preparation must be made in the marketization of interest rates and exchange rates. From now on, the decision makers, experts and staff members in the financial field must learn to utilize the levers of interest and exchange rates sensitively and effectively to create conditions for the normal operation of the open market and for the regulation of the economic structure through market mechanisms. In terms of technology, it is also of utmost importance to perfect the data and statistical system of the Central Bank to rapidly and accurately obtain this financial data in order to expedite macrocontrol.

Some Thoughts on Economic Reform in China

Cho Soon
Former deputy premier of
the Republic of Korea

Since China launched its policy of reform and opening to the outside world in 1978, the country has realized enormous successes. The rate of growth during this 15 year period was among the fastest in the world, and the pace at which the country is transforming itself is breathtaking. The Western world has begun speculating that China could become the largest economic power in the world around the year 2020.

But the problems facing China are also enormous. Recent success has brought the country face to face with many new challenges. These will become even more numerous and weighty in the years to come. The resourcefulness demonstrated by the government and the people in overcoming so many difficulties in the past will help surmount future difficulties, but at the same time it cannot be denied that the ascent to development is still at its initial stages. The problems facing the country are unique, and no historical precedents are available for emulation. China must find its own solutions to these problems; the country must traverse virgin ground.

The purpose of this paper is to discuss a few salient aspects of what appear to me to be the most important problems facing China. I am not an expert on the Chinese economy; I am a layman who is greatly interested in China's economic development. Since I do not know the details of recent developments in the reform process, my discussion will be limited to a few observations formed after reading various material on the Chinese economy.

I expect and hope that China will eventually emerge as an economic superpower, but before this final outcome the country may have to experience many small setbacks as well as successes. At present, the most pressing problems related to the main theme of this conference—the economy and the market appear to be: (1) The problem of inflation. That is, how to deal with the cycles of boom and bust. (2) The problem of striking a proper balance between the central government and regional and municipal governments. (3) The problem of state-run enterprises. That is, how to make them efficient enough to be profitable. Let us now explore each of these problems.

I. Inflation and Financial Reform

Since 1978, China has undergone three economic cycles. Booms occurred in 1984, 1988, and 1992. The first two booms were followed by busts; the last boom is still continuing and the government is currently coping with it.

The first boom was triggered by the growth of the GNP in the early 1980s, culminating in 1984 at about 15 percent. There was a corresponding lag between the rise of income and price levels as cost of living inflation in 1984 held at only about 4 percent. But in 1985 inflation rose to about 12.5 percent. An anti-inflationary policy was adopted dampening the growth of income and price levels in 1986 to about 8 percent and 6 percent respectively. The second boom, in 1988, was characterized by even higher inflation, over 20 percent, triggered by a high rate of income growth, 11 percent. This triggered a round of panic buying and hoarding in some cities. A forceful retrenchment policy with controls on credit and imports briefly brought the economy to a near stand-still as prices and income both plummeted. Fortunately, however, this period of slowdown was brief, and the economy soon recovered.

The third boom began in 1991. The GNP growth the next year was as high as 12.8 percent, but the cost of living index also increased by 11 percent. During the first quarter of 1993, the

GNP grew by as much as 13.9 percent, but the cost of living also rose by 17.5 percent. The authorities have adopted an anti-inflationary policy and hope this will bring about a softer landing for the economy than in 1988. There are many good reasons to expect that this indeed will occur. China has now accumulated more economic experience and is being guided by firm hands. Price deregulation during the last few years for some 600 commodities has reduced fears of shortages of basic goods. Foreign exchange reserves are now stronger, and liberalization of imports has made the economy more resilient than in the past.

It is important that a developing country be mindful of inflation, and China should be no exception. I know China is in a hurry; there are many reasons for China not to relax development efforts. The rising expectations of the people must be addressed. Jobs must be created; throngs of people are moving to urban areas and there is widespread, if disguised, unemployment. These problems can be mitigated only through a sufficiently rapid increase of national income. If the pace of reform is slowed, the inertia of subnormal performance may never be overcome. It was with such considerations in mind that the growth target during the Eighth Five-Year Plan period was upgraded from 6 percent to 8-9 percent, and the targets for production of basic industries were similarly raised.

It appears that the desire for a high level of investment by enterprises is a nearly permanent part of a centrally controlled economy which tends to respond very energetically to signals given by the center to accelerate investment. Such investment and economic management mechanisms undoubtedly exist in China, and because of this the actual performance of the economy during the last couple of years, in terms of investment and growth rate, seems to be overreaching the revised Eighth Five-Year Plan targets. Provincial and municipal governments engage in extensive investments on a competitive basis, without due regard to the profitability of the investment projects or to their impact on the national economy.

It appears that the cost of inflation at present is greater for China than for developed countries because China has yet to develop a mechanism for maintaining flexibility and resiliency with which the effect of inflation may be mitigated. The anti-inflationary measures which the government must take will directly reduce loans to enterprises, tending to result in the stoppage of construction or procurement of equipment and machinery. Under such circumstances it seems strongly desirable to avoid inflation as much as possible by eliminating the causes of inflation in its incipient stage. Slower but steadier growth is preferable to cyclical repetitions of boom and bust. The experiences of other developing countries indicate that those with chronic inflation have shown relatively poor performance in the long run, compared with those which maintain price stability. Infrastructures have to be financed, jobs have to be created, and reforms have to proceed. But these are long-term processes, which can only be effectively achieved in an environment of price stability.

Currently, China is intent on introducing the market system, but what are the functions of the market? It is out of place to dwell upon this problem here, but just to remind ourselves of the importance of price stability, let us digress a moment. A market is not solely a place where goods and services are traded. The function of the market is first to provide economic actors with information not only on goods and services, but on all matters related to economic activities, thereby enabling them to make sound decisions. Second, the market provides the economy with a system of discipline which forces the economic actors to be as efficient as possible. These market functions presuppose the existence of price stability. The virtues of the market system break down when prices are unstable. Market information is also distorted when prices are unstable, and the discipline usually provided by the market becomes lax and inconsistent. The market system fully functions, then, only when prices remain reasonably stable. And in order to maintain price stability aggregate demand and the money supply have to be held in check and the appropriate level of interest rates must be maintained. The precondition of market discipline is the monetary discipline. The Chinese people are preponderantly agricultural, and the farmers are conservative people where financial matters are concerned. It is very important to them that the value of their saving not be eroded by inflation.

One prerequisite for maintaining price stability is maintaining the stability of aggregate demand. This is not easy for the government to do so, however, in view of the strong demand for expenditures, both public and private. Furthermore, local and municipal governments vie for investments and for foreign capital. Under these circumstances, it is very important to undertake substantial financial reform in order to check excessive demands for bank loans. Financial reform must make commercial banks genuinely commercial, and while maintaining price stability, support a strong central bank whose chief responsibility is to maintain monetary stability. Of course, monetary stability alone is not enough to maintain price stability; fiscal policy is no less important, and therefore concerted efforts by the government and the central bank are necessary. But it appears true nevertheless that monetary stability remains a necessary, though not a sufficient condition for maintaining price stability.

China has established a sophisticated network of commercial, foreign exchange, industrial, and investment banks, as well as non-banking financial institutions. I think it is very important for China to establish genuine commercial banks, operating on commercial principles and led by genuine financial entrepreneurs. Currently, the so-called commercial banks seem to have created many subsidiary companies and are lavishly financing them without paying due attention to their profitability. This practice will end only when the banks operate on genuine commercial principles. The government should encourage potential entrepreneurs to establish privately owned commercial banks, and they should serve as financial mediators between savers and investors.

At the same time it is important for non-commercial bands such as the Industrial and Commercial Bank of China, the Agricultural Bank of China, the Bank of China, and the People's Construction Bank of China to commercialize their operation as much as possible. Considering that many of the state-owned enterprises they are financing are operating at a loss, it would be difficult for these banks to do business with them strictly on a commercial basis. But the banks could perhaps operate on dual principles: The commercial principle and the conformity-to-policy principle. The lending rates the banks charge on these two separate categories of loans should be differentiated, and the ratio at the initial phase may be, say, 2 to 8. The banks would then profit on the former, but lose on the latter. For the loss, the government could subsidize. But the government and the banks should strive to reverse the above ratio, that is, induce the banks to make more commercial loans and less policy loans. This may help impose more discipline on the government as well as on the banks.

I would urge that economic policy should emphasize developing the financial sector as much as the industrial sector. Most of the strategy in developing countries concentrates almost exclusively on the industrial sector. Leaving the financial sector benignly neglected. I think this is a mistake, and China should avoid this policy as much as possible. Under this policy, the firms charged with carrying out the policy-supported investments are those most likely to be subject to lax budget constraints. Many of these investments are, as is the case in China today, financed by issuing bonds which are discounted by commercial banks at very high interest rates. It is likely that many of these investments are made on questionable economic grounds. As more of such investments are made, the banks which finance them are burdened with bad assets. When the banks are in trouble, the central bank intervenes and rescues them and inflation continues unabated.

Ostensibly, the industrial sector with its newly built plants and factories seems robust, comparing favorably with the financial sector. But in reality the industrial sector is also burdened with bad investments which will eventually prove unprofitable. Furthermore, the excessive government-directed expansion of investment in the industrial sector is by no means a blessing since it will invariably bring about an imbalance in the industrial structure. The industries subsidized by the government expand far ahead of the rest of the economy, with other industries lagging behind. With such an imbalance, economic efficiency is constantly hampered.

The hallmark of the market economy is the division of function between savers and investors. In order for this division to take place, financial institutions, with commercial banks as their center, must develop strictly according to market principles. Financial institutions are not simply distributors of money or funds. The bankers must know what their business is all about; they have to be able to advise, direct, and assist the industrial sector entrepreneurs. With this in mind, the government should emphasize sound finance as much as possible, and do everything to foster financial experts and specialists. The government should make every effort to develop financial markets and assure that interest rates fluctuate according to market principles. The best way to develop the financial sector is to emphasize financial prudence and control inflation.

One might argue that the present state of development in China is such that an independent central bank is neither possible nor desirable. But I think the central bank is the most vital, if not the only institution capable of imposing effective financial discipline on enterprises and local and municipal governments, and, indeed, on the central government. As long as the central bank has the authority to control its branch offices in the provinces —and indeed it must have that authority—it is the ideal institution for establishing monetary targets and assuring these goals are met. The monetary targets, unlike the government budget, are quite unambiguous and are amenable for the central bank to control.

Many central banks in developing countries are charged with the duty of financing policy-designated enterprises as well as controlling the money supply. Thus, the central bank discounts at interest rates lower than market rates the commercial paper of exporters, medium- and small-sized enterprises and agricultural associations. As the central bank subsidizes these borrowers, it creates reserves within the commercial banks. These reserves are the source of bank loans which the central bank is then called upon to reduce. The central bank is thus engaged in mutually contradictory operations: On the one hand it creates reserves, and on the other it tries to soak up these reserves.

Admittedly, the governments of developing countries cannot completely avoid subsidizing particular sectors and industries. But when these cases arise it should be the government, not the central bank, which provides the subsidies. If the government requires funds to subsidize enterprises, it should do so with funds raised by the issuance of public bonds. If the bond market is undeveloped, as is the case in China, the government should borrow from the central bank, rather than have the central bank directly engage in providing subsidies. This would at least make the principle clear; it is the responsibility of the central bank to check the growth of the money supply, and that it is the responsibility of the central government to finance the policy-designated sector of the economy. This will make the government aware of the magnitude of the subsidy. As long as the central bank directly finances policy-directed enterprises, the government remains unaware of the extent of the subsidy.

II. Central Government and Provincial Governments

China is a vast country, and it would be most difficult for the central government to rule without the help of the provincial governments. Furthermore, for the sake of efficiency, it is better for the central government to delegate some of its economic authority to provincial and municipal governments. The Chinese government has been undertaking reforms along these lines together with reform of state-owned enterprises.

These reforms have created two problems. One is a serious reduction in the government's share of the GNP, and the other is a decrease in central government revenue relative to that of local and municipal governments.

The central government has been running a chronic deficit which has been increasing rather rapidly in recent years, while depending on the earnings of the large state-owned firms for its revenue. It is doubtful these firms are very profitable, but in any case they remain the primary source of government revenue. These firms have been unable to improve their performances lately and consequently the base of the government revenue has been shrinking as reforms emphasize liberalization and competition. According to data published by the *Statistical Yearbook*, the government deficit increased from 37 billion yuan in 1989 to 90.5 billion in 1992. The percentage of government revenue in the GNP has been steadily decreasing since the initial year of reform, falling from 31.2 percent in 1978 to 17.5 percent in 1992. The proportion of the deficit in the GNP still looks innocuous enough, only 3 percent or 4 percent, but when one takes into account the hidden cost of bank-financed subsidies to state-owned enterprises, the deficit is easily more than 10 percent of the GNP. (*The Economist*, July 10-16, 1993, pp. 64)

The fact that the proportion of central government revenue within total (central and local) government revenue has been steadily declining poses a serious problem. The financial position of the provincial governments has been greatly strengthened by the increase of out-of-budget-fund revenue. Actually, the relative deterioration of the financial power of the central government began with the agricultural reform of 1978. The government increased procurement prices for agricultural products, resulting in a sizable central government budget deficit. Thanks to this reform, rural village industries were greatly strengthened. Since 1984, the government has shifted its focus of reform from agriculture to industry, but the state-owned enterprises have not been quite as amenable to reform as the rural sector.

The decrease in government revenue, and the decline of the central government's financial ability relative to the provincial governments pose serious problems. The central government must continue to play a leading role in the socioeconomic development of the country. But the decreasing financial power of the central government will seriously limit its ability to finance such activities as infrastructure construction and environmental protection. The government should avoid running a deficit as much as possible. Furthermore, the central government must lead the nationwide reform effort and must coordinate these activities with regional development. The central government also must have leverage to finance these activities. As mentioned earlier, the out-of-budget fund for provincial governments has been increasing rapidly as those governments compete for foreign investment and other resources. This will increase the financial autonomy of the local governments, possibly thwarting coordination efforts by the central government. This would also be a source of inflationary pressure.

The central government has been taking measures to check these trends, but the revenue base must still be strengthened. First, it has to tap and enlarge the sources of tax revenue. Economic reform since 1978 has brought a rapid increase in personal income and saving, sources which may be tapped. A large number of rural people moved to urban areas, attracted by the amenities of urban life and economic opportunities, provided by the government. With a relatively light tax burden imposed on the urban population relative to rural people, the government, in effect, has been subsidizing the urban population. This population should be made to pay their own way.

In order to stem the relative decline of revenue flowing to the central government, the government has instituted the tax-sharing system, by which taxes for both the central and local governments are fixed so that an increase in tax revenue automatically increases the revenue of the central government. Revenue from some taxes, such as sales, value-added, and business taxes, are to be shared equally by the central and local governments. This system promises to help solve the central government's declining revenue problem.

III. State-Owned Enterprises

There are four types of enterprises in China: state-owned enterprises, collectively owned enterprises, privately owned enterprises, and other enterprises. In 1991 there were about 105,000 state-owned enterprises, while the total number of enterprises came to 8.1 million. The output value of the state-owned enterprises in 1991 was as much as 52.9 percent of total industrial output. The success of the Chinese economy depends to a great extent on the efficiency of these enterprises. The government has been trying hard to improve efficiency, but the industrial sector seems much slower than the agricultural sector to respond to the government call for reform.

There appear to be several major obstacles to improving the performance of state-owned enterprises. First, the lack of enterprise independence from administrative entities; second, the burden of out-of-business responsibilities borne by these enterprises; and third, distorted price structures. State-owned enterprises guarantee lifetime employment to their employees. In order to change these methods, enterprises have tried to institute a contract system of employment, restructure enterprise organization, and establish an efficiency-index for wage rates. But little progress has been made and these enterprises are still largely dependent on the government budget to cover their losses. Because state-owned enterprises remain dependent on government, government intervention continues, which in turn increases their dependence on the government.

The distorted price structure is also hindering the independence of state-owned enterprises. The distortion of prices refers to (1) the relatively lower official prices of energy, agricultural products, and transportation as compared to industrial products; (2) one commodity carrying two or more prices, e.g. the official price and market price; and (3) many prices used by enterprises are administered prices, and not market-determined ones. Because of these price distortions, the prices of goods and services do not generally reflect their availability and therefore resources are not allocated efficiently. To cite a few examples of inefficiency, state-owned enterprises producing coal, for instance, are in a disadvantageous position compared with those producing electronics products. Thus, firms producing those goods whose prices are controlled by the government are in a disadvantageous position in their restructuring effort.

Because state-owned enterprises perform many duties and functions outside of business, they are prevented from concentrating all their attention to business activities. State-owned enterprises provide their employees with medical care, housing, and educational services. They also run such facilities established within their business compounds. They are thus self-contained administrative units performing many of the duties of the municipal government. This may contribute to maintaining social stability, but it is certainly detrimental to improving efficiency.

The government has instituted some ingenious devices to deal with these difficulties and strengthen the independence of enterprise management. In 1984 the government stipulated that (1) enterprises are authorized to produce and sell in excess of planned amounts; (2) enterprises can negotiate with their buyers on the prices of these goods within 20 percent of the stipulated prices, and (3) enterprises are authorized to freely dispose of retained profits as production funds, new output development funds, and welfare funds. In April 1988 the government enacted the Law on State-Owned Enterprises, which further broadened their autonomy. This law separated the ownership from management. Management of the enterprises was relegated to business managers and enterprises were authorized to carry out production on a contract basis. And the responsibility of the manager was put above that of the Party representative. In July 1992 the Regulations of Conversion of Management Mechanism of State-Owned Enterprises was promulgated. The regulations stipulated the rights of enterprises to hold possession of and use government properties and to dispose of the products thereof. It further stipulated ways in which production plans were to be settled, prices determined, employment of personnel managed, and the social cost assigned.

Thus, China has spared no effort to achieve greater efficiency in state-owned enterprises. At the same time, however, one cannot be sure that these policies, ingenious and innovative as they are, are adequate to unleash the kind of entrepreneurial ability inherent in the Chinese people. This is so because prices, profits, sales and markets are still heavily determined administratively. Administered prices play a role in allocating resources, but they do so arbitrarily. For example, as long as prices and wages are administratively controlled, profits realized from the sale of products will not be uniquely determined, rather, they will vary depending upon the price decisions of the administrative bodies. Therefore, they do not represent genuine profits. Profits often reflect the degree of innovation effected by entrepreneurs, and sometimes they reflect minimizings cost. But as long as profits vary according to administrative decisions, efforts of the entrepreneurs will be directed less toward innovation or cost minimization, and more toward seeing that the administrative authority increases prices or volume of production. And when prices are administratively determined, profits do not reflect enterprise performance. Bankruptcy will not necessarily mean bad performance, either. As a result, as long as prices are not market-determined, it is unlikely that the autonomy granted to state-owned enterprises will lead to the right kind of managerial effort.

It would appear imperative, therefore, to establish market-determined prices and to privatize as many of these enterprises as possible. Privatization is not easy. There is no guarantee that privatized firms will always succeed, and no doubt some will fail, but the government must take this risk. Without a critical mass of privatized firms in the economy, industrial efficiency is very unlikely to improve. The process of privatization will be long and arduous, but a free market ultimately will not develop without privatizing a substantial proportion of state-owned enterprises. As privatization proceeds, the extent of the free market portion of the economy is enlarged. And as the free market is enlarged, the prices within state-owned enterprises will be set nearer to those which actually reflect their availability.

Market Reform Strategies for Dealing with Imbalances in Regional Economic Development

Shen Liren
Research Fellow of Jiangsu Provincial
Academy of Social Sciences

I. Imbalanced Regional Economic Development Is an Impediment in Promoting Market Reform

China has now, ultimately, chosen to establish a market economy. But transforming from a traditional planned economy to a market economy—a difficult and tortuous road—is frought with many difficulties, especially the reform of state-owned enterprises under the premise of public ownership remaining the mainstay even in market competition. Among a number of difficulties, imbalanced regional economic development is mixed with others. People have seen that while the gap between regional economic development is widening, imbalanced reform advances are becoming clearer, thus presenting an unavoidable circumstance—implementation strategies for carrying out market reform.

In the final analysis, imbalanced regional economic development derives from an imbalanced commodity economy or an imbalanced market economy in different regions. The history of the last century demonstrates: Some coastal regions in China have the bases to commercialize and marketize their economy while over the vast inland, a semi-natural economy has always occupied the leading position. Since the founding of the People's Republic of China, commercialization and marketization have met with one difficulty after another due to the existing practice of a planned economy or a product economy. Since the initiation of reform and opening to the outside world, the existing structures have been broken up. Consequently, the economy of the highly marketized regions has made rapid progress and the regions with well-developed economies have promoted marketization. However, the other regions have made comparatively slow progress in marketizing their economy, with the result that economic disparities between regions have grown greater and greater. In this situation, we should give careful thought to strategies for achieving market reform. We have two choices: To hope that all regions throughout the country would carry out reform under a unified plan and advance at same pace, or allow some economically developed regions to take the lead in setting-up modern market economic systems and then by that means to give impetus to other regions to also promote marketization. It is obvious that in such a large country as China with extremely imbalanced regional economies, the first option can hardly be realized. If we adopt the second strategy and at the same time pay attention to the associated effects between regions we can push reform of the entire country forward. This is orderly reform as embodied in the space program. This strategy was suggested in the past, but was ignored. Today it is necessary to mention it again, and hope that it will be considered when decisions are made.

II. Enlightenment from Several Advanced Regions

Reform and development supplement each other. All fast-developing regions depend on reform; in return, they also promote reform. The rapidly advancing regions include the Zhujiang River Delta, the South Fujian Delta, and the Yangtze River Delta, Wenzhou, South Jiangsu and others. The regions that have taken the lead in development and reform enjoy many common characteristics. First of all, they all had a good original base and a relatively advanced commodity economy as well as favorable policies containing reform factors. Many of them are experimental reform regions, with the right to make their own decisions. Also, their local cadres are fully experienced and dared to take the lead. They are also located in the forward positions for opening to the outside world, which will be discussed in the next chapter.

Another characteristic worth noting is that the regions' high-speed development and reform are attributed to their ownership. These regions are located mainly in several medium-sized and small cities, especially townships and in the countryside rather than big cities. Zhujiang's "several small tigers" (Shunde, Nanhai, Zhongshan and Dongguan counties) first gained fame and fortune by relying on township enterprises and then were grafted onto foreign-invested enterprises. In Quanzhou and Wenzhou, the market came into being first, then brought along production. The South Jiangsu Model mainly consists of township enterprises. However with only a few state-owned enterprises, these counties and rural areas have a nearly exclusive non-state-owned or non-public economy. For instance, Wenzhou was once called a capitalist warm bed. It is under these conditions that the reform of state-owned enterprises has been delayed, while the non-state economy suddenly came to the fore as a new force, putting on one important performance after another. What do they rely on? They depend on market mechanisms rather than state support; they rely on themselves to purchase raw materials, decide what items to produce, sell commodities, collect funds, and hire employees. Thanks to their break with the planned economy, they have reinforced their actual strength. Certainly they also benefited from the market-oriented reforms which have enabled the state-owned economy, with many market characteristics, to display its skills fully.

But it is necessary to point out that in the past, though we permitted a measure of market regulation, we actually relegated it to a secondary position. The non-state economy of these regions developed mainly by relying on its own vitality, and some enterprises even availed themselves of loopholes in the market rather than receive conscious support from the market. Second, up to now, some enterprises in these regions have offered a magnificent view; however in light of the demands of the market economy, they are only displaying their talents for the first time in a primitive market environment. These models, born in the market, have accelerated the growth of the market economy. Meanwhile, the market provides opportunities for them, enabling them to grow up with the market economy. It is just like the relationship between the chicken and the egg. In a word, they should continue to go forward toward a full market economy.

In sharp contrast, the advance and reform of the large cities in these regions, including Guangzhou, Fuzhou, Hangzhou, and Nanjing, have been definitely inferior. The total industrial output value of even some star cities, such as Wuxi, Suzhou, and Changzhou, have been less or will be less than their suburban counties. For instance, last year the industrial output value of Wuxi County was more than that of Wuxi City. The main reason for this is that state-owned enterprises in the cities are still playing the leading role. It has not been fundamentally changed in the tide of reform. No one can deny the fact that one third of these state-owned enterprises suffer losses in the open, and one third of them do so secretly. By an extension of this logic, some provinces and municipalities, including Liaoning and Shanghai, suffer from "big city disease," and "old industrial base disease," that is, "planned economic disease," and "state-owned enterprise disease." The inland economy has had difficulty stepping forward, which may possibly be attributed to those having the same illness sympathizing with one another. This means there is only one way out—while actively accelerating the reform of state-owned enterprises, these regions must make efforts to develop the non-state economy, that is, the people-run economy. Through the people-run economy, they should cultivate markets, develop the market economy, and closely catch up with those advanced regions which have already walked a few steps further toward the market economy.

III. Deepening the Reform by Opening Wider to the Outside World

Imbalanced regional economic development was described as a ladder-shaped state in the past, East China going fastest, central

China ranking second, and West China moving slowest. Practice during the past few years has shown more clearly that the economy of the special economic zones has developed at the highest speed, followed by the coastal open cities and open regions, and then the interior. Since the practice of all-directional opening to the outside world, the interior areas have been divided into border and riverine areas and provincial capitals, plus the areas along the Lianyungang-Lanzhou and Lanzhou-Xinjiang railways. This indicates that carrying out reform and opening to the outside world region by region happens to coincide with the practice of a market economy.

Reform and opening to the outside world also supplement each other. Without experience to refer to, these two new elements require a gradual extension from points, to lines, to aspects. The only difference is that reform experiments were not carried out region by region, but opening to the outside world was obviously practiced region by region. Consequently, to people's great surprise, reform closely follows opening to the outside world; and the market economy keeps pace with regional opening up.

The special economic zones are the advance guards of opening to the outside world as well as the testing grounds for reform. The special economic zones in China have achieved success in both reform and opening to the outside world. Among them Shenzhen, which took lead in opening up and reform, first put forward "taking market regulation as the mainstay," which is different from "taking planned economy as the mainstay." Shenzhen was then followed by the interior. Many new reform measures, from an enterprise's administration of state-owned capital to the shareholding system, from the pool of human talent, to the real estate and stock markets and foreign exchange regulation market, from the tendering and bidding of construction projects to the structural wage system and the social security system, were all born in Shenzhen, a tiny area, and then were immediately introduced into the interior. Another example is Hainan Island, a region with a weak base and a rigid system. Soon after the founding of Hainan Special Economic Province, emphasis was first put on "the socialist market economy," resulting in quick advances in all aspects. The slogan "a small government and a big society" especially pointed out the orientation for reforming the administrative system and changing governmental functions. The achievements of the special economic zones are there for all to see, and cannot be separated from opening up the market economy.

Why does opening to the outside world require reform and how can it stimulate reform? There are at least two reasons. First, the special economic zones and the open areas need to import foreign capital for joint ventures, cooperative enterprises, and enterprises exclusively owned by foreign capital, all of which operate in accordance with the laws and regulations of the market economy. With the proportion of foreign-invested enterprises increasing daily, the old system is unable to meet their demands without timely reform. Second, these enterprises brought along with them a complete set of market mechanisms, greatly stirring the localities. Comparing the new with the old, we must surely adopt the new system. It would be unthinkable for the fast-growing special economic zones to only introduce foreign capital but not quicken reforms and gradually replace the planned economy with a market economy. Actually, for the interior, Shenzhen's reform is a pioneering undertaking; but for the local people, Shenzhen only "learned mostly from Hong Kong."

Along with further opening to the outside world, a new method for all-around opening was formed, stretching from the special economic zones and open cities and regions to frontier and riverine areas and inland provincial capitals, greatly accelerating market reform. The most prominent example is Shanghai. For a long time Shanghai relied on state planning. As a result, it became more and more stagnant and poor. However since Pudong opened, Shanghai has become full of vitality. Pudong requires brand new mechanisms, and consequently Shanghai seems to put on a new look every year. So do other opened areas. Of course, due to different conditions and different levels of foreign investment, there are differences in the width of the openings to the outside world, and in the strength and depth of market reform. But when we are marching toward the same market economy objective, opening up is, after all, an indispensable and powerful component.

IV. Government Guidance Should Be Based on the New Trails Blazed by Localities

Proceeding from facts, we have discussed the relationships between development and reform and between opening up and reform to indicate that each of these relationships is carried out region by region in China. This requires that when formulating an overall program for the market economic system, we must guided, region by region, according to varying local conditions; and treating all regions in the same way must be strictly forbidden. It also means that no harm will come to the country as a whole if unified reform strategies are worked out; but they should be used for guidance rather than as rigid rules. In a sense, programs and plans should be worked out on the basis of the new achievements in all localities, including absorbing the successful experiences of all places. At any rate, no locality's initiatives should be stifled.

Practice has demonstrated that since the reform initiatives all correct policies have basically derived from the creation of grass-roots units. At the same time, many mistakes were mainly the result of subjective judgments by government leaders. As everyone knows, the fixing of output quotas based on individual households which appeared during rural reform was created by the masses rather than by officials. The leaders should confirm and popularize the people's creations in order to continuously give full play to these creations. Guangdong's progress depends on "flexibility" and "trying to skirt round red lights," which could not be completely denied since this method broke through the traditional system and empancipated productivity. Wenzhou's market and township enterprises in south Jiangsu Province have all grown up among curses, but finally proved that they accord with the demands of the development of the market economy. All these reminiscences contain experiences and lessons, experiences which refer to the grass-roots units actively bringing forth new ideas and pressing forward in the face of difficulties and setbacks. They believe they will be finally confirmed by the government leaders and that these leaders will not arbitrarily require actions which may hinder the people's innovations.

Carrying out strategies region by region means that those regions with imbalanced progress will institute market reforms at varying speeds. After the reform objectives of the socialist market economy are decided, a national unified plan and a concrete implementation program should be drawn up. These rough assumptions, however, should be general rather than specific. It is more important to respect the creations of localities and grant them more rights to make decisions by themselves, never tying their hands. So long as we combine foreign experiences and lessons with actual conditions in our country or in a province rather than insist on a fixed model, the foreign experiences and lessons can serve a vital function. The planned economy is highly concentrated and has only one form, while the market economy may assume many and various forms.

V. The Regional Market and the Unified Market

The question of regional and unified markets was discussed long before the confirmation of the socialist market economy. Judged by the current situation, this question is related to imbalanced economic and market development. In general, China still lacks the full conditions necessary for truly unifying the market. Especially within the planned economy, cutting the links among departments and regions is becoming more serious daily in spite of the emphasis on unification. At present, with the abandonment of the traditional system and the acceleration of market reforms, the market's congenital deficiencies are still obstacles restricting the birth of a unified market. The founding of a unified market must be based on well-developed markets everywhere. Because market development varies from place to place and some places are rather primitive, seeking a unified market is unrealistic. The vast area of our country and poor transport facilities are only two restrictions. Fundamentally, the main problem at present is that the market is both immature and imbalanced.

The author holds that China's current market reform means following a course from the regional market to a unified market. This viewpoint is not without foundation. In regions with a well-developed market economy, such as the coastal areas, their goods have broken through administrative divisions and gone out all over the country and the world. The "Northern Expedition of Guangdong Goods" is a vivid description. But the regions with an underdeveloped market economy still have difficulties trading with other regions. Their difficulties are more obvious in the key production element market than in the commodities market. This is also true for the financial market which serves as a pivot in the market system. Even though our financial market is not yet standardized, it has developed at a comparatively higher speed in the coastal areas, with the interior lagging behind. it is also true for the technology, labor, information and real estate markets. All of these have clear regional characteristics. The "remote areas" are rich in technology, but they can hardly be commercialized or marketized. On the one hand they are short of talented people, and on the other hand many people of ability are allowed to remain idle. This is similar to the circulation of capital. As credit funds are granted by administrative divisions, some places are short of credit while other places have surpluses. It is very difficult to regulate these credit funds. Even the stock exchange markets in Shenzhen and Shanghai exist independently and don't interact with each other, remaining characteristically regional. In the future when we review these phenomena we will think them naive and ridiculous. However in today's awkward situation, they are, in a sense, reasonable and necessary.

VI. The Function and Role of Government Departments

When a planned economy is changed into a market economy, the function and role of government departments should be fundamentally changed, since they are the keys to changing the economic mechanism. Why do enterprises now have so many difficulties in changing their operating mechanism? This is because governmental functions remain intact, so that government cannot be separated from enterprises and enterprises cannot be enlivened. In a word, direct control should be changed into indirect control. And the government must not be concerned with matters better left to market regulation.

Can this principle be used to work out strategies for market reform? In other words, while market reform is being carried out, it is unnecessary for the government to attend to everything, and indirect control is sufficient. The market economy has its own basic principles. First and foremost, the central government's responsibility is to formulate unified laws and standards and supervise their implementation. Some matters, such as the founding of national enterprise groups and stock exchange markets, should be organized in a unified way. In concrete implementation, developed regions should be handled differently from less developed and underdeveloped regions. Different regions should expand their markets in accordance with their various conditions. Hopefully, under a unified plan, imbalanced conditions among regions will be taken care of. Trying to grasp the eyebrows and the beard all at once is foolish. Some people maintain that only the central government's unified control is needed, and that regulation and control by local governments at different levels is unnecessary. They seem to believe that in China with its population of 1.1 billion, headquarters can handle everything well and that the initiative of localities needn't to be brought into full play. Isn't this a fairy tale? Another suggestion has it that the central government may specify that certain things are "forbidden," and allow the localities to deal with the other matters.

On the Speed of Transition in Central Europe

*Philippe Aghion** and *Olivier Jean Blanchard***

Abstract

Transition in Central Europe involves the closing and restructuring of state firms, as well as the emergence of a new private sector. The speed of closing and restructuring and the rate of private job creation determine the dynamics of unemployment. And unemployment in turn affects both the decision to restructure and to create new private jobs. Our paper presents a model which captures these interactions. It characterizes the positive and normative properties of the equilibrium speed of transition and unemployment rate, and the role of policy.

Introduction

In all Central European countries, the legacy of the previous economic system is a large and ailing state sector. Labor productivity is low. Many firms, or parts of firms, must close, while others need drastic restructuring and labor reduction before they can be made to prosper. But so far the pace of restructuring has been extremely slow.

The evolution of the state sector accounts, however, for only one side of the transition process. The other is the growth of a new private sector. This growth has been impressive so far, but it has not taken place across the board. And it is facing many obstacles, from poor financial markets to insufficient human capital and expertise.

*Nuffield College, Oxford and the European Bank for Reconstruction and Development.
**Massachusetts Institute of Technology.

This transition process raises many important issues. What is determining the speed of transition? How and why might it derail? What are the risks of going too fast or too slow? Should the government try to affect the speed, and if so through which instruments?

These are the issues we examine in this paper. We think of the economy as having two sectors, the state sector and the private sector. Workers are either employed in one of the two sectors, or are unemployed. We think of the pre-transition economy as one in which all workers work in the state sector. We then formalize the concept of transition as the result of two interacting processes, the restructuring of state firms on the one hand, and the growth of new private firms on the other. The rate of restructuring determines the flow into unemployment; the rate of private job creation determines the flow out of unemployment. Together they determine the evolution of unemployment and the speed of transition.[1]

We think our contribution lies as much in offering a simple and flexible conceptual structure as in the results we obtain. But those can be stated simply. Most—but not all—of our results point to an unacceptably slow speed of transition, and thus toward a role for governmental acceleration of the process. They also point to a clear risk that too great a speed can lead to derailment and an ultimately unsuccessful transition.

Our paper is organized as follows:

Section 1 offers a benchmark model. We consider state firms as low productivity enterprises which are closed at some constant rate, leading to a flow into unemployment. The flow out of unemployment comes from private-sector job creation, which is a function of both wage and non-wage costs. Wages in turn are a decreasing function of unemployment, while non-wage costs are an increasing function of unemployment. By assuming that state firms simply close at a constant rate, the model does justice neither to the possibility of restructuring nor to the decisions of state firms regarding restructuring. But it does shed light on the joint dynamics of unemployment and private-sector job creation. Those dynamics are characterised in sections 2 and 3. The main lesson is that too high a rate of closing can, through its effect on unemployment, kill private-sector growth and derail the transition.

Sections 4 and 5 refine the treatment of the state sector. Section 4 allows for restructuring rather than closing. Restructuring is formalized as a process where firms become private, productivity is increased, and a proportion of the workers are laid off. Section 5 focuses on the decision to restructure. We argues that in effect, workers can block restructuring, so that restructuring only happens if workers approve it, and we derive the implications of this assumption. Clearly, since restructuring implies that some workers will lose their job and that wages will be set as in private firms, restructuring is less appealing the higher state-firm wages are compared to those in private firms, resulting in higher unemployment.

Sections 6 to 8 put the pieces together. Section 6 characterizes the equilibrium rate of unemployment and speed of transition. Section 7 looks at their normative properties, and the case for government intervention. Section 8 presents rough calibrations.

Section 9 indicates what we see as some of the limitations of our analysis. Let us mention one at the start. We make our analysis under the assumption of hard budget constraints, wherein firms cannot act in such a way as to obtain larger subsidies from the government. We see this as having been mostly true so far in the major central European countries (but not in Russia; hence the title of our paper). But the constraint is likely to be tested again and again, and may well not apply the future. Our only excuse for not modeling it is that this would have taken us too far into that unforseeable future.

I. A Benchmark Model

The economy is composed of two sectors, the state sector with employment E, and the private sector with employment N. The labor force is normalized to one, so that $E + N + U = 1$, where U is unemployment. We assume that before the transition, all workers work in the state sector, so that $E = 1$ and $N = U = 0$.

We describe the behavior of employment and wages, first in the state and then in the private sector.

1. The State Sector

Both price liberalization and the demise of the Council for Mutual Economic Assistance had the effect of making many jobs unproductive from the start of the transition process. We capture this by assuming that, as transition starts, employment in the state sector drops to $E_0 \leqslant 1$.[2]

We assume that the remaining workers, E_0, have a constant marginal product, x. The low productivity of state firms is captured by assuming that x is less than y, the marginal product of workers in the private sector, described below.

Three years into the transition, most state firms have remained nominally state owned. But, in the absence of state supervision and control, firms have acted largely in the interest of their workers, with a fairly short horizon. Thus, in many firms workers have gained increased wages so as to appropriate quasi rents.

We capture this by assuming that the wage in state firms is equal to:

$$w_E = ax - z \qquad (1.1)$$

where a is greater than one, reflecting the appropriation of quasi rents by workers, and z are taxes per worker. Once the workers have appropriated all rents, the incidence of taxes levied on the firm must fall entirely on wages.

Finally, we assume that the speed of closing in the state sector is given by s:

$$dE/dt = -s \qquad (1.2)$$

We shall begin by thinking of s as an exogenous parameter, say under the control of the government. Starting with the assumption of an exogenous s is useful in showing the basic dynamics of the model most starkly. But later we shall relax this assumption in two ways. First, we shall allow for the fact that some firms, or parts of firms, can be saved and restructured, albeit at the cost of reductions in employment. Second, and more importantly, we shall endogenize s by looking at the choice of state firms and workers regarding whether to restructure or not.

2. The Private Sector

The private sector has grown rapidly, but clearly cannot replace the state sector overnight. We assume private job creation given by:

$$dN/dt = a \, (y - z - w) \qquad (1.3)$$

where is the constant marginal product of labor in the private sector, w is the wage in the private sector, and z are again taxes per worker, which are assumed to be the same for private and state firms.

Private job creation is thus characterized by a relation between the change in employment and the profit per worker. This relation can be seen as coming from the constraint that investment in new capacity not exceed retained earnings.[3] The evidence is indeed that new private firms do not use outside financing. Or we can think of it as coming from adjustment costs, some physical and conventional, and some from such experiences as learning by doing, accumulation of information, development of reputation in goods and financial markets and so on.[4] If the relation comes from adjustment costs, it is likely, however, to be forward looking: before creating jobs, firms will worry about both current and future expected profits. We ignore this aspect for the time being, but take it up in Section 3 below.

Evidence relating to private sector wage determination is still sketchy, but the notion that private sector wages depend on labormarket conditions appears reasonable. We take private sector wages to be determined by:

$$w = b + c \, (r + H/U) \qquad (1.4)$$

where b is unemployment benefits, r is the interest rate, and H/U the ratio of hires to unemployment is the exit rate from unemployment, and c is a constant. This equation is easily derived from efficiency wage considerations. It is useful for future consideration to derive it explicitly:

Let V_u and V_n be the values of being unemployed and

employed in the private sector respectively. Assume further that there is no turnover in the private sector, so that hires, H are equal to dN/dt, and that all hires are from the unemployed.[5] Under those assumptions, the probability of being hired when unemployed is equal to H/U.

The two values thus follow "arbitrage" equations:

$$rV_u = b + (H/U)(V_n - V_u) + dV_u/dt \quad (1.5)$$
$$rV_n = w + dV_n/dt \quad (1.6)$$

When unemployed, a worker receives unemployment benefits b, and has probability H/U of being employed. When employed, a worker faces, by assumption, no risk of becoming unemployed again, and thus receives the private sector wage forever after.

Many efficiency wage considerations can be summarized by the condition that firms choose a wage such that the value of being employed exceeds the value of being unemployed by some amount, thus such that $V_n - V_u = c, c \geq 0$. Under that assumption, which obviously implies that $dV_n/dt - dV_u/dt = 0$ as well, taking the difference between the two equations above gives the wage equation (1.4). Note that, in that equation, higher unemployment benefits increase the wage one for one. Note also that the wage is an increasing function not of the unemployment rate itself, but of the exit rate out of unemployment. It is clearly the probability of getting a job, not the unemployment rate *per se*, which is of concern to workers, and thus, which affects the wage.

3. Taxes and Unemployment Benefits

The remaining assumption relates to taxes, unemployment and unemployment benefits. We assume that taxes are levied equally on employment, state and private, to finance unemployment benefits. This implies:

$$U_b = (1 - U)z \quad (1.7)$$

This relation has a straightforward implication. Higher unemployment, given unemployment benefits, leads to higher taxes per worker; thus, ceteris paribus, higher unemployment decreases private job creation.

There is obviously more to the relation between the process of transition and fiscal balance than this simple relation. We see this normalization as a metaphor for the different channels through which a depressed economy adversely affects profitability, and thus the growth of the new private sector. These may be other, but related, fiscal channels. For example, in Poland there has been an unusually large number of retirements, clearly an alternative to unemployment for older workers; those higher retirement benefits also need to be financed. These also may be through aggregate demand: higher unemployment may mean lower aggregate demand, and lower demand for the output of private firms. One can think of yet others: Higher unemployment decreases support for reform and thus the likelihood that the reform process will continue; this in turn leads to lower profitability, higher uncertainty, and in turn lower private job creation.

There is a strong assumption implicit in (1.7). It is that the tax burden on private firms depends on unemployment alone, and does not depend on the mix of employment between the private and state sectors. One may easily think of channels through which the burden may depend on this mix, for example if state firms receive subsidies and private firms do not, or if state firms and private firms are taxed differently. Allowing for such distribution effects would complicate the analysis below; but we do not think it would significantly change the substance of our results.[6]

4. Taking Care of Corners

In stating our assumptions, it might have been more natural to specify the equations for state and private employment in terms of rates of change rather than changes, i.e. in terms of $(dE/dt) E$ and $(dN/dt) N$, rather than in terms of dE/dt and dN/dt. We have chosen this specification because it simplifies later analysis, leaving only one state variable, unemployment, rather than two, employment in one sector and unemployment. As a result of these assumptions, however, the economy can hit corners, and we have to account for what happens when those are reached. Those conditions only play a role at the end of the transition, or when the economy goes very wrong, but they must be specified nevertheless.

First, state employment can only decline if it is positive in the first place, so that the condition (1.2) only holds for $E > 0$: for $E = 0$, $dE/dt = 0$. Second, a similar condition must hold for private employment. Here it is convenient and innocuous to make a slightly different assumption, that for $(y - z - w) < 0$, $N = 0$. Namely, private firms can close if they are losing money. We shall ignore these conditions in the text, (but not in the derivations and graphs which underlie the text), only mentioning them when directly relevant.

II. Unemployment and the Speed of Transition

In our benchmark model, the speed of closing determines the inflow into unemployment. Unemployment in turn determines private job creation, the out-flow from unemployment. Together, these two relations thus determine unemployment dynamics.

Working backwards, we first derive the relation between unemployment and private job creation. Solving for the wage, using equations (1.4), (1.3) and (1.7) yields:

$$(w - b) = [ca/(U + ca)] [y + (r/a) U - (1/ (1/U - U)) b]$$
(2.1)

Replacing W by its value from (2.1), and Z by its value from (1.7) yields private job creation as a function of unemployment:

$$dN/dt = a [U/(U + ca)] [y - rc - (1/(1 - U)) b] = f(U)$$
(2.2)

Unemployment affects private job creation through two channels. The direct channel is captured in the first term: The higher is unemployment, the lower is the wage, and thus the higher is private-sector job creation. The second term captures the effect of unemployment through contributions, implicitly taking into account the incidence on the private-sector wage, which partly offsets the effect. The higher the unemployment, the higher are unemployment contributions, thus the lower the private sector job creation.

How these two relations determine unemployment is shown

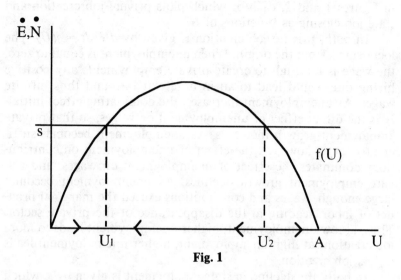

Fig. 1

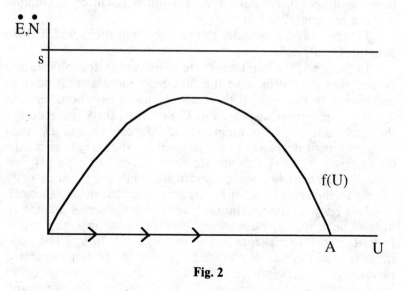

Fig. 2

in figures 1 and 2, each of which plots private-job creation and state job closing as functions of U.

In both, private job creation is given by $dN/dt = f(U)$. The locus starts from the origin. When unemployment is equal to zero, the wage is too high to create private employment; any positive hiring rate would lead to an infinite exit rate and thus infinite wages. As unemployment increases, the dominating effect initially is the direct effect of unemployment on wages, so that private employment growth increases. As unemployment becomes sufficiently large, however, the effect of unemployment on contributions dominates the effect of unemployment on wages, and private employment growth declines. As unemployment becomes large enough, wages and contributions exceed the marginal product of labor, leading to the disappearance of the private sector. Thus, at low unemployment, higher unemployment leads to more job creation; at high unemployment, higher unemployment leads to less job creation.

In both, the decline in state employment is given by s, which is, by assumption, constant and thus independent of unemployment, a horizontal line at s.

Figures 1 and 2 consider the two configurations which these equations can yield:

In Figure 1, the maximum rate of private sector job creation is such that it exceeds s, so that unemployment at that point is decreasing. In that case, if the economy starts anywhere between 0 and U_1, unemployment goes to U_1 and then stays there during the transition. If the economy starts between U_1 and U_2, then unemployment decreases to U_1. Beyond U_2, the weight of contributions is too large, the private sector does not take off fast enough and unemployment grows until the private sector actually closes. To the right of point A, the private sector never takes off.

In Figure 2, the maximum rate of private sector change is, instead, such that unemployment is still increasing at that point. In that case, starting from low unemployment, things look good initially, and the rate of change of private sector employment is increasing. But, before private employment growth can offset state employment decline, the fiscal effects become dominant, and private employment starts slowing down. Unemployment relentlessly increases until everybody is unemployed.[7]

There is one simple lesson to be drawn from this model: There is a maximum speed at which the state sector can be closed. It is that value of s such that the two loci are exactly tangent. If the speed is higher, the rise in unemployment never allows the private sector to grow fast enough to replace the jobs lost in the state sector.

III. A Forward Looking Private Sector

As we pointed out earlier, private sector job creation is likely to be forward looking, at least in part. Many private firms, and especially foreign direct investors, will not invest if they expect conditions to deteriorate and profits to shrink in the future. But in turn, profits in the future may be low if private job creation is insufficient to avoid rising unemployment.

To explore this interaction, we modify our description of private employment creation, equation (1.3), to read:

$$dN/dt = arV \qquad (3.1)$$
$$rV = (y - z - w) + dV/dt \qquad (3.2)$$

where V is the value of a new private job. Job creation now depends on the value of a new job. The value of a new job follows an arbitrage equation, which implies that it is the present value of the difference between y and direct and indirect costs, $z + w$. Such a relation is easily derived from quadratic losts of adjustment.

Under these assumptions, the economy can be reduced to two equations, in U and V:

$$dU/dt = s - arV \qquad (3.3)$$
$$rV = f(U) + [U/(U + ca)] dV/dt \qquad (3.4)$$

where, as before, $f(U) = [U/(U + ca)] [y - (1/(1 - U)) b]$.

The locus $(dU/dt = 0)$ is a horizontal line in the $V - U$ space, at $(V = s/ar)$, such that private employment creation is equal to state employment destruction. The locus $(dV/dt = 0)$ is given by

$V = f(U)/r$ and thus has the same properties as the $f(U)$ locus characterized earlier. It goes through the origin as, if U is zero, wages extract all the rents and thus V is zero. It is upward sloping initially as unemployment decreases wages more than it increases unemployment contributions. Eventually, it is downward sloping, and V becomes equal to zero at $U = 1 - b/y$.

There are again two cases, depending on whether the two loci intersect or not. We concentrate on the case where they intersect; the conditions for this are the same as before.

The dynamics are characterized in Figure 3. There are always two equilibrium paths. The first path is given by A'B' (under myopic expectations, it would be given by OB' instead). The private sector is optimistic, and quickly creates enough jobs to maintain an unemployment constant and the transition is a smooth one. The second path goes to the wrong place. Firms are less optimistic, create less jobs, employment creation is never enough, and their worst fears are realized. The economy goes from A to B and asymptotes to C as above.[8]

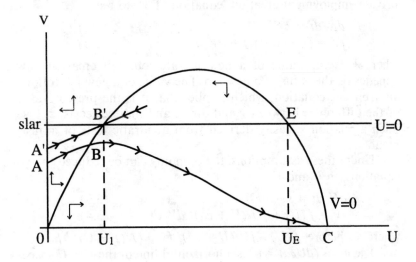

Fig. 3

Thus, even if the speed is below the maximum speed derived in the previous section, expectations are essential. If s is constant, there are always two self-fulfilling paths, one where transition succeeds, and one where it is expected to fail and indeed does fail.

What are the policy lessons from this exercise? Suppose that the government can control s. There is no obvious sense—at least that we can see—in which a lower speed makes a good outcome more likely. But the government can, however, announce a policy which eliminates the bad outcome. Any policy which announces that the speed of closing will be equal to zero for an unemployment rate higher than, say U_l, achieves this result. Under such an announcement, the only perfect foresight path will be the good path. One can think of other announcements which achieve the same result. For example, the announcement that unemployment benefits will be eliminated if unemployment exceeds U_l formally serves the same purpose. But one senses that there is a substantive difference between the two announcements. Even without an explicit treatment of the government's objectives, it is clear that the announcement of lower unemployment benefits is more likely to suffer from problems of credibility.

Thus, within our model the lesson is that in order to avoid self-fulfilling forecasts of the failure of transition, for example, by foreign investors, the government may want to announce a flexible policy that, conditional on high unemployment, it will slow down the process of closing state firms. In doing so, the government will avoid the emergence of high unemployment, and therefore will not have to actually decrease s.

How robust is this result? It goes against the often expressed view that it is as risky to go slow as it is to go fast. One possible rationale for that view is that overtime state firms may increasingly ask for and obtain subsidies, more so than private firms. Our model strongly relies on the assumption that state firms operate under hard budget constraints. While this assumption is clearly incorrect in Russia, it has been largely the case in the major central European countries so far.

IV. Restructuring Instead of Closing

The approach so far has been to assume that all activity must eventually come from the new private sector. The evidence, however, suggests that this view is wrong, and that a number of state firms are likely to be profitable, although not without ending some activities, and not without considerable staff reduction.

This possibility for transformation can be introduced easily —perhaps too easily—in the following way. Reinterpret the initial assumptions about state firms as follows. Initially, there are E_0 state firms, each producing x units of output, and employing one worker each (a convenient normalization). Over time, those firms are transformed. Transformation is such that:

1) Each firm now employs only λ workers, $\lambda < 1$, and each worker produces $y, y > x$ units of output, so that each firm now produces λy units of output, which can be greater or less than x. Closing, the case we have considered so far, is clearly just a special case of this more general formulation, with $\lambda = 0$.

2) The new firm operates from then on like a private firm, so that wages are now set as in the rest of the private sector, at level w.

Thus, we think of transformation as restructuring plus privatization. The private sector will now include both transformed state firms and new private firms; when convenient, we shall refer to the second source as "new" private job creation.

We shall assume for the moment an exogenous speed s, where s is now the speed of restructuring rather than of closing. We shall endogenize it in the next section.

When restructuring takes place at rate s, $(1 - \lambda)s$ workers become unemployed. The equation for the behavior of unemployment becomes:

$$dU/dt = s(1 - \lambda) - f(U) \qquad (4.1)$$

The dynamics of unemployment and transition are thus the same as in figures 1 and 2, with the flow into unemployment given by the horizontal line at $(1 - \lambda)s$ rather at s. The conclusions we derived earlier above still hold, in slightly modified form:

There is a maximum speed of restructuring—which is simply equal to the maximum speed of closing we derived earlier, multiplied by $1/(1 - \lambda)$—consistent with a successful transformation. For speeds beyond this maximum, even if restructuring directly increases output, that is even if λy › x, unemployment increases too much. This eventually kills private sector job creation. Eventually, both the new and the transformed private sector become unprofitable and close.

For speeds lower than the maximum, and as long as U_0 ‹ U_2, the economy eventually converges to U_1, the lower of the two unemployment rates at which $dU/dt = 0$, and stays there during the transition. When unemployment is equal to U_1, restructuring is contributing both directly (λs) and indirectly ($f(U)$) to the increase in the private sector. The indirect effect is through the increased unemployment, which, given that $f'(U_1)$ › 0, leads to faster job creation in the new private sector as well.

When forward-looking behavior is introduced in the new private sector, as considered in the previous section, then constant announced speeds of restructuring are associated with two paths, one successful and one unsuccessful. And, again, announcing that restructuring will be halted if unemployment is too high can help sustain the virtuous circle equilibrium.

V. Restructuring as a Choice

We have so far viewed the speed of restructuring as a given parameter, under the control of the government. We now view it instead as a choice by state firms. Many of them indeed have the choice, at least for a while, between continuing to operate at low levels of productivity, or restructuring, getting rid of redundant operations, eliminating labor hoarding, and increasing productivity. When will they take the decision to restructure? If firms' decisions mostly represent, as we have argued, the interests of their workers, the answer must be that firms will be restructured only when the workers agree to it.

What it means for "workers to agree" is ambiguous, and this raises a very relevant issue. To see this, let V_E represent the value for a worker of employment in the untransformed state sector. Let, as before, V_U be the value of being unemployed. And let V_N be the value of being employed in the transformed firm, which, under our assumptions, is the same as working in the new private sector so that we can use the same symbol. Recall that restructuring implies that a proportion λ of the workers will remain employed after restructuring, and a proportion $1 - \lambda$ will become unemployed.

If all workers perceive an equal probability of keeping their job after restructuring then, under the assumption of risk neutrality, an assumption we have made implicitly until now in defining the various value functions as linear in wages and benefits, the condition for restructuring is:

$$\lambda V_n + (1 - \lambda) V_U \geq V_E \qquad (5.1)$$

For restructuring to take place, the expected value after restructuring must be greater than or equal to the value without restructuring.

But, in most firms, the assumption that workers choose under a veil of ignorance is clearly wrong. In most cases it is easy to identify those parts of the firm which will surely have to close. What happens then depends on the decision process within the firm. Even if decisions to restructure require, as they do de facto in Poland, quasi unanimity of the workers, the condition above may still hold if those workers who know they will lose their job can be fully compensated, through severance pay for example, by those who are likely to keep theirs. But the evidence is that in many cases workers who were likely to lose their job as a result of restructuring have blocked attempts at restructuring. Under the extreme assumption of unanimity and no-transfers, the condition for restructuring must be:

$$V_U \geq V_E \qquad (5.2)$$

This condition, that restructuring will take place only if those who lose their jobs as a result are as well-off as if they remained employed in the untransformed firm, is probably too strong, and reality is somewhere between the two conditions, (5.1) and (5.2). We shall work in what follows with condition (5.1), and indicate how things are modified when working with (5.2) instead.

VI. Endogenous Restructuring, Unemployment and the Speed of Transition

We now put both parts of the model together, and start by giving a general description of the transition, with details and qualifications to follow:

Starting from an unemployment rate U_0, the economy converges to an equilibrium unemployment rate, U^*, such that the condition (5.1) holds with equality. From then on, the economy stays at this unemployment rate, until the end of the transition.

At $U = U^*$, job creation in the new private sector is equal to $f(U^*)$. The speed of restructuring is thus given implicitly by the condition that inflows into unemployment equal outflows, or $(1 - \lambda)s^* = f(U^*)$. Thus, at $U = U^*$, total private sector job creation, from transformation of state firms and from new private sector creation is equal to:

$$s\lambda + f(U^*) = f(U^*)/(1 - \lambda)$$

Along the transition path, the value of being employed in the private sector is given by $V_N = w/r$. As the wage is a decreasing function of unemployment, V_N is a decreasing function of unemployment. And from the conditions $V_N = V_U + c$ and $V_E = \lambda V_N + (1 - \lambda)V_U$, the three values are all decreasing functions of unemployment. And from the same conditions, those employed in the private sector are better off than those employed in the state sector, who are in turn better off than the unemployed:

$$V_N > V_E = V_N - (1 - \lambda)c > V_U = V_N - c \quad (6.1)$$

1. Characterizing U^*

We now characterize U^* formally. The value of being employed in a state firm without restructuring is characterized by:

$$rV_E = ax - z + dV_E/dt \quad (6.2)$$

Along the transition path, when U is equal to U^*, unemployment benefits and thus taxes per worker, z are constant. Thus, $dV_E/dt = 0$, and V_E is given by $(ax - z)/r$.

The values of being unemployed and of being employed in the private sector respectively are given by equations (1.5) and (1.6). If U is constant, then w, $f(U)/U$ are also constant, and $dV_N/dt = dV_U/dt = 0$. Thus, V_N and V_U are given by:

$$rV_N = w = b + c(r + f(U^*)/U^*) \qquad (6.3)$$
$$rV_U = b + (f(U^*)/U^*)(V_N - V_U) \qquad (6.4)$$

Replacing in equation (5.1) and noting that $V_N = V_U + c$ gives:

$$ax - z = b + cf(U^*)/U^* + \lambda cr \qquad (6.5)$$

Equilibrium unemployment, U^* must be such as to make the wage in the state sector, the left hand side of (6.5), equal to the sum of three terms. The first two are unemployment benefits, and the exit rate out of unemployment times c, the difference in value between being employed in the private sector and being unemployed. The third is the annuity value of being employed in the private sector over the value of being unemployed, times the probability of being employed in the restructured firm. If we had used condition (5.2) instead of (5.1), that is if restructuring had to be approved by those who knew they were going to lose their jobs, this third term would be absent.

How does the economy get to U^*? If at the start of the transition the unemployment from the initial shock, U_0, is less than U^*, there is a discrete amount of restructuring, and a discrete increase in unemployment until $U = U^*$. If instead, U_0 exceeds U^*, there is no restructuring until private sector growth has reduced unemployment to U^*.

To characterize U^* further, rewrite (6.5) using the expression for $f(U)$ and the balanced budget condition that $z = bU/(1 - U)$. This gives:

$$ax - \lambda cr = A(U)$$
$$\equiv \frac{ac}{(U + ca)}(y - cr) + \frac{U}{(U = ca)}(b/(1 - U)) \qquad (6.6)$$

Figure 4 plots both sides of the equation. The left hand side is an horizontal line at $ax = \lambda cr$. The right-hand side, $A(U)$ is equal to $y - cr$ for $U = 0$. If $y - cr - b \rangle 0$, the condition that the marginal product of the private sector exceeds the lowest wage the private sector may pay, $A(U)$ is initially downward sloping. Eventually however, it increases and tends to ∞ as U tends to one. Figure 4 shows that, depending on parameters, three configurations are possible:

$$A(U) \equiv \frac{ca}{(U + ca)}(y - cr) + \frac{u}{(U = ca)} \frac{b}{(1 - U)}$$

In the first, state workers just do not want to restructure, and prefer to keep their state wages, which in part capture quasi rents, to the risks of restructuring and associated unemployment. This will be the case when $A(0)$ is below the horizontal locus, or equivalently if $ax - c\lambda r \rangle y - cr$. In that case, if U_0 is initially equal to zero, the process of transition will never start. No restructuring will take place, and zero unemployment will lead to high private wages, inhibiting the growth of the new private

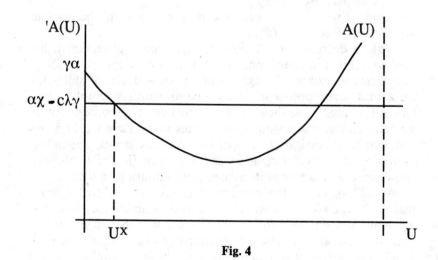

Fig. 4

sector as well. If unemployment is initially positive, private sector job creation will also be initially positive, but as unemployment decreases, job creation will stop altogether. In that case, the transition will fail by being too slow.

In the second, state workers want to restructure no matter what the unemployment rate. This will be the case when the horizontal locus is so low as not to intercept the $A(U)$ locus. The outcome will be instantaneous restructuring. If $f(U_0 + (1 - \lambda) E_0)$ ⟩ 0, then all state firms will be restructured, and from then on the new private sector will expand until unemployment has returned to zero. If instead $f(U_0 + (1 - \lambda) E_0)$ ⟨ 0, then restructuring will take place up to the point where the unemployment it generates is such that $f(U) = 0$. At that point, the new transformed sector will break even, and the private sector will never start. Thus, the transition will also fail, this time by being too fast.

In the third case, the case we shall focus on, $A(U)$ and the horizontal locus cross twice. This is the case actually drawn in Figure 4. In that case, only the lower unemployment rate is stable, and we shall concentrate on it as we turn to comparative statics.

2. Comparative Statics

Using Figure 4, we can ask how changes in the various parameters affect both U^* and s^*.

Take a decrease in a, a goal that the Polish government has tried to achieve through punitive taxation of wage increases in state firms in excess of wage norms. Such a decrease shifts the horizontal locus down, increasing equilibrium unemployment. This is because, while they have no direct effect on production in the state sector, lower state sector wages make state workers less reluctant to embark on restructuring. As they do so, unemployment increases. As $f(U)/U$ is a decreasing function of U, the exit rate from unemployment decreases until equation (6.6).

What happens to the speed of restructuring and to the speed of new private sector creation is, however, ambiguous. Note first that what happens to both is linked by the fact that if unemployment is constant, the flow into unemployment, which is proportional to the speed of restructuring, must be equal to the flow out of unemployment, which is equal to new private sector employment creation. What happens to both is thus determined by the value of $f'(U^*)$, the effect of unemployment on hires at U^*. As we saw in Figure 1, $f'(.)$ is initially positive, and becomes negative for high unemployment. And $f'(U^*)$ cannot in general be signed. If $f'(U^*) > 0$, if the effects of unemployment through wages dominate the effects through taxes, then higher unemployment increases both the speed of restructuring and of private sector employment creation. But, if $f'(U^*) < 0$, then higher unemployment leads to slower restructuring and private sector employment creation. Our numerical simulations below suggest that the first case is the more relevant, but this is ultimately an empirical matter.

Consider now an increase in λ, a higher proportion of jobs saved in restructuring. It shifts the horizontal locus down, increasing equilibrium unemployment. This is because a higher λ decreases the probability of unemployment after restructuring. The exit rate from unemployment must thus decrease for equilibrium to be maintained, and the unemployment rate must therefore increase. Note, however, that this effect goes away if we assume condition (5.2) instead of (5.1), if those workers who know they will lose their job are in favor of restructuring. The same ambiguity is at work for the effects on the speeds of restructuring and new private employment creation. If $f'(U^*) > 0$, then both increase.

Finally, consider an increase in unemployment benefits, b. This shifts the $A(U)$ locus up, leading to more unemployment. This is both because higher unemployment benefits make unemployment more attractive to state sector workers, and because higher taxes decrease the wage in the state sector. The effect this increase has on the speed of transition is again ambiguous, this time for two reasons. The first is the sign of $f'(U^*)$. But even if $f'(U^*) > 0$, the effect may still be negative because b affects z which enters $f(U)$: Given unemployment, higher unemployment benefits lead to higher unemployment contributions, which reduce hires at any given unemployment rate.

These results raise the next obvious question. If a decrease in a raises unemployment, and, say, raises the speed of transition, should the government try to decrease a? More generally, is the speed of transition too high or too low, and should the government try to affect it? We now turn to this issue.

VII. Optimal Unemployment and Speed of Transition

To answer whether the transition is too fast or too slow, we have first to answer two questions. Compared to what? And assuming which tools are at the government's disposal?

We shall take as the objective function of the government the present discounted value of output. Thus, we focus on efficiency, and give no weight to income or unemployment distribution.

This leaves the issue of what the government takes as given in solving its optimization problem. There is a sense in which the government can affect most of the parameters we have defined so far. For example, the strength of the effect of profitability on private sector job creation, the parameter a, must depend in part on the organization of credit markets, which the government can improve. But allowing the government to choose a freely clearly makes the optimization problem both trivial and unrealistic. Thus, we shall assume that the government takes the unemployment benefits and their financing, the wage determination process, and the equation for private job creation, as given. This implies that the government takes the function $dN/dt = f(U)$ as given, and chooses the rate of restructuring. It can do this in our model, through changes in a, or by imposing top-down privatization and restructuring, or by modifying decision rules within firms. We shall not specify how at this point, but will just take the speed of restructuring as the control variable.

1. Optimal Unemployment and Speed

Let E_N denote employment in the transformed state sector. The optimization problem of the government is thus:

$$max \int_0^\infty (Ex + Eny + Ny)e^{-rt}dt \qquad (7.1)$$

subject to:

$$1 = E + E_N + N + U; \quad E_N = \lambda(1 - E_0);$$
$$dN/dt = f(U)$$

The first equation is simply the condition in which people are either employed or unemployed. The second states the relation between employment in the transformed state sector and employment in the untransformed state sector. The third is the relation between private job creation and unemployment that the government takes as given.

Using the first two equations to eliminate both E and E_N gives:

$$max(1 - \lambda) \int_0^\infty [x - U(x - \lambda y) + N(y - x)e^{-rt}dt \qquad (7.2)$$

subject to:

$$dN/dt = f(U)$$

The solution is characterized by an optimal unemployment rate, U^0, and an associated speed of private sector job creation, $f(U^0)$. This in turn implicitly defines the optimal speed of restructuring, which must be such that the inflow into unemployment is equal to private sector job creation, and is thus given by $s^0 = f(U^0)/(1 - \lambda)$.

If initially, $U_0 < U^0$, then a discrete amount of restructuring takes place up to the point where $U = U^0$. If instead, $U_0 > U^0$, no restructuring takes place until private sector job creation has reduced unemployment to U^0. From then on, the transition takes place at constant unemployment, U^0.

U^0 is implicitly defined by:

$$x - \lambda y = f'(U^0)((y - x)/r) \qquad (7.3)$$

The intuition is as follows: From the objective function (7.2), a marginal increase in U given N is associated with a change in output $-(1 - \lambda)(x - \lambda y)$. If the gains in productivity from restructuring are large enough, if $\lambda y > x$, an increase in unemployment can be associated with an increase in output. In addition, a marginal increase in U affects private sector job creation by

$f'(U^0)$. From (7.2), the present value of a marginal increase in N given U is given by $(1 - \lambda)(y - x)/r$. The optimal unemployment rate must be such that the net gain of a marginal increase in unemployment is equal to zero. Dividing both sides by $(1 - \lambda)$ gives (7.3).

U^0 is characterized graphically in Figure 5, which, once again draws the locus $dN/dt = f(U)$. The optimality condition is that the slope of the tangent be equal to $r(x - \lambda y)/(y - x)$. Note that if $\lambda y \rangle x$, then the optimal speed of restructuring is such as to push unemployment beyond the point which maximizes new private sector growth, somewhere to the right of A.

2. Comparing U* and U⁰

To compare actual and optimal U's and associated speeds of transition, it is convenient to rewrite the equilibrium condition for U^* in terms not of the underlying parameters, but in terms of w_E and w, the wages in the state and the private sector. Using (6.4), (6.3), (6.2) and the equilibrium condition (5.1) yields:

$$w_E - b = \lambda(w - b) + [f(U^*)/U^*](w - w_E)/r \qquad (7.4)$$

The equation has the same structure as that for U^0, but this time with the private benefits and costs as perceived by workers. Note in particular that from the point of view of the workers, what matters is not $f'(.)$, the marginal effect of unemployment on private job creation, but rather the exit rate from unemployment $f(U)/U$.

Can we sign $U^* - U^0$? In general, we cannot. Comparing (7.3) and (7.4) shows two opposite sets of effects at work.

To the extent that the difference in wages between the private sector and the state sector $w - w_E$ is small than the difference in productivity $y - x$, a condition which is likely to hold, the incentive to start restructuring will be weaker than is optimal, leading to too low unemployment. A second similar effect is that, if the decision to restructure is such that even those who will lose their jobs do not oppose it, so that the relevant condition is $V_E = V_U$, then the first term on the right hand side of (7.4) disappears. This leads workers to be more reluctant to restructure and thus leads to a lower unemployment rate.

But two other effects work in the opposite direction: Unemployment benefits make unemployment less painful, leading to higher equilibrium unemployment. And, while the marginal effect of unemployment on private job creation, $f'(U)$ is the relevant factor for optimal unemployment, what matters to workers is the average effect $f(U)/U$. By concavity of $f(.)$, the marginal effect is always smaller than the average effect; this factor leads again to too high unemployment.[9]

Assuming we can sign $U^* U^0$, can we then sign $s^* - s^0$? Here again, the answer is ambiguous, and depends on the sign of $f'(U^*)$ and $f'(U^0)$. If they are both positive, which will be the case as long as the two unemployment rates are less than A in Figure 5, too low an unemployment rate will also imply too low a speed of transition.

These ambiguities capture the complexity of effects at work. In light of these ambiguities, statements that transition is obviously too fast or too slow appear to us to be too bold. But we do not want to end on this note. We think that, for plausible parameter values, many of the ambiguities can be removed, and that equilibrium speed is indeed likely to be too low. This is what we consider the next section.

VIII. Cautious Calibrations

Choosing numbers for the various parameters of the model is not easy. While much empirical work is currently going on, our knowledge is not at the point where we can confidently choose parameters.[10] With this caveat, we define benchmark parameters as follows:

1. Choosing Parameters

We normalize the marginal product in the state sector, x to be equal to 1. Assuming that workers appropriate the returns to capital in the state sector, we take $a = 1.3$. We take the marginal product in the private sector, y to be equal to 1.8. We take unemployment benefits, b to be equal to 0.5, or about a third of the wage in the state sector. We take the interest rate, which here is an index of effective horizons, to be relatively high, 0.1 per year.

This leaves three parameters where even more guess work is involved. We take λ as the proportion of state employment which can be saved by restructuring to be equal to 0.4. This is lower than the numbers observed so far, but restructuring of the worst firms is still to come. This implies that the direct effect of restructuring on the output of a state firm is to reduce it from 1.0 to $1.8 \times 0.4 = 0.72$. We take c to be 2, leading to a difference between the value of being employed in the private sector and the value of being unemployed of $0.1 \times 2 = 20$ percent on annual basis. Finally, and without shame, we choose a, the effect of profit on private job creation, in such a way as to generate roughly the speed of new private sector creation in Poland, or about 4 percent of the labor force per year. This yields a value of a of 0.1.

2. Optimal and Equilibrium Unemployment and Speed

The results of these assumptions are given in Table 1. Table 1 gives three unemployment rates, U^*, the equilibrium unemployment rate obtained assuming the condition $V_E = \lambda V_N + (1 - \lambda) VU$, U^{**}, the rate obtained assuming instead $V_E = V_U$, and U^0, the optimal rate. For each of the three, it also gives the speed of new private job creation, $f(U)$, and the marginal effect of unemployment on that speed, $f'(U)$.

Table 1   Unemployment and Speed of Transition

	U^*	$f(U^*)$	U^{**}	$f(U^{**})$	U^0	$f(U^0)$
Benchmark	12	3.9	8	3.0	20	4.8
$b = .6$	15	3.8	10	3.1	18	4.1
$b = .4$	10	3.8	7	3.0	23	5.7
$b = .3$	9	3.6	7	3.0	26	6.7
$a = 1.4$	8	3.0	5	2.1	20	4.8
$a = 1.2$	20	4.8	13	4.0	20	4.8
$a = 1.1$	-	-	22	5.0	20	4.8

All numbers are percentages of the labor force. Benchmark values for the parameters are: $x = 1$, $y = 1.8$, $a = 1.3$, $b = 0.5$, $\lambda = 0.4$, $c = 2$, $r = 0.1$

The first line gives the implications of the benchmark parameters. Equilibrium unemployment U^* is equal to 12 percent, and the rate of private sector creation is 3.9 percent of the labor force per year. This implies a total increase in private employment, from both restructuring and new private sector job creation, of 6.5 percent per year. When restructuring decisions have to be such that those who lose their job are not worse off, equilibrium unemployment U^{**} is equal to 8 percent, and private sector job creation to 3 percent. Both unemployment rates are lower than the optimal rate of 20 percent, which is associated with a speed of 4.8 percent. And all three are much lower than the unemployment rate at which $f'(.)$ becomes negative, which is equal to 31 percent.

The next three lines give the effects of changing unemployment benefits. Increasing unemployment benefits lead to higher equilibrium unemployment. Interestingly, higher benefits and higher unemployment both imply higher taxes, and from equation (6.2) and (6.1), lower values of being employed in either sector, and of being unemployed. But this has almost no effect on the speed of transition. The effects of higher unemployment on wages are offset by the effects of increased benefits on equilibrium wages and of higher unemployment contributions. At the same time, higher unemployment benefits lead to lower optimal unemployment: higher benefits decrease the marginal effect of a given level of unemployment on job creation.[11]

The last three lines show how the effects of changing a, one of the potential instruments at the government's disposal, affect the equilibrium speed of transition. Decreasing a from 1.3 in the benchmark to 1.2 leads to more unemployment, and an equilibrium unemployment rate and speed nearly equal to the optimal ones. Interestingly, further decreasing a to 1.1 leads to the second configuration studied in Figure 4 earlier. Staying in state jobs becomes so unattractive that all state firms are instantaneously restructured, leading to high unemployment. At this high level of unemployment, $f(.)$ is still positive however, so that positive private sector job creation eventually reduces unemployment to zero.

IX. Conclusion

We have presented a model of transition where unemployment affects both the rate of private job creation and the speed of restructuring of the state sector, and where both in turn affect unemployment over time.

We have characterized the equilibrium rate of unemployment and speed of transition. We have concluded that, while ambiguous on theoretical grounds, the equilibrium speed of transition is likely to be too slow, justifying measures by the government to accelerate the transition. These measures may include restraints on wages in the state sector, and top-down privatization and restructuring, imposed on firms rather than chosen by them. But we have also pointed to the dangers of going too fast, and of sticking to inflexible policies, which do not reduce the speed of restructuring in the face of high unemployment. Going too fast may lead to too high unemployment and derail the transition. Inflexible policies open the scope for self-fulfilling expectations of an unsuccessful transition.

We have at various points discussed formalization choices, and potential extensions. In conclusion, we have compiled this list:

1) We have assumed throughout that state firms we subject to hard budget constraints. With the exception of firms in very bad shape, this has been true so far in the major central European countries. But this should not be taken as an assumption. It is better thought of instead as the outcome of a game, a game which will be played for many years to come.

2) We have assumed, in parallel, that the government operated on a balanced budget. Transition has been associated with large revenue losses, and the temptation to have recourse to inflation finance exists. So far, this temptation has been mostly avoided. But the same caveat applies.

3) We have assumed simple interactions between the tax burden and the process of transition, namely that the tax burden depended only on the level of unemployment. But in fact, the composition of employment and the financial position of firms

also matter. Profit taxes from state firms have largely vanished.[12] Collecting taxes on private firms has proven difficult. New, across the board taxes, such as VAT's, are not yet in place.[13]

4) We have only skirted the issue of decision-making within firms. The specific roles of ministries, workers, unions, and managers are crucial to the outcome and vary across countries.[14] We have also skirted a number of issues by associating restructuring and privatization. Some firms have been able to partly restructure without privatization, and some privatized firms, in particular those privatized through buy-outs, have not restructured.[15]

5) We have assumed that, except for a number of firms affected by the initial shock, state firms were identical and could survive, albeit at a low level of productivity. This is not true. There is a distribution of marginal revenue products across state firms. And the degree to which state firms can really wait and see, while maintaining employment, is unclear.

6) We have taken a black box approach to private job creation. Looking within the black box, by exploring in particular the role of credit markets, could potentially modify some of our conclusions. We also have not distinguished between two types of private job creation, the initial burst of job creation in trade and services, which aim at filling holes left by the previous economic regime, and private sector growth aimed at competing with and replacing state firms. The process so far has been dominated by the first; much of the success of the transition, however, will depend on the second.

Notes

1. Our paper is short on facts, which have been documented elsewhere. The reader is referred in particular to the papers presented at the NBER Conference on Transition in Eastern Europe. Our analysis is very much based on the interpretation of what has happened in Poland over the last three years, presented in Blanchard and Dabrowski (1993), and by the evidence on the evolution of labor markets summarized in Blanchard et al (1993). Other more specific references are given along the way.
2. In Poland, the first shock was felt in early 1990, the second in early 1991. In

those countries which started reform in early 1991, such as Czechoslovakia, the two were roughly coincident. In most countries also, while the decline in output was sudden, the effect on employment was much slower. These additional dynamics are ignored here.

3. This is, however, only an interpretation, as a retained earnings constraint leads to a slightly different formulation: If all finance is internal, if $(y\text{-}w\text{-}z)$ is the net cash flow from employing one worker, earnings will be equal to $N(y\text{-}w\text{-}z)$. Thus, if a proportion of earnings are reinvested, and if job creation is proportional to investment, job creation will be given by $(dN/dt)N = a(y\text{-}w\text{-}z)$, a rate of change rather than a change relation, as in the text. As discussed below, our specification turns out to be more tractable.

4. Chadha et al (1992) develop a model, which is a cousin of ours, but where the growth of the private sector is based explicitly on learning by doing.

5. The evidence shows that things are more complex. First, there is substantial turnover in the private sector. Second, a substantial fraction of hires from the private sector is directly from the state sector. See Blanchard et al (1993). Both aspects can be integrated, but usually at the cost of analytical simplicity. One extension which can be straightforwardly incorporated is that the pool of potential hires includes not only the unemployed but also a proportion of those employed, in either the private or the state sector.

6. Another interesting extension would be to consider the possibility of deficit finance and its interaction with the dynamics we analyze below.

7. The details of the end process depend on the corner conditions. Under our assumptions, when unemployment reaches A, the private sector closes, so that unemployment increases discretely at that point. Thereafter the private sector remains closed, and unemployment increases until everybody is unemployed.

8. While B' is a saddle point, point E can be either a sink or a node. If initial unemployment is small than U_l, then, even if E is a sink, the economy can only be on one of the two paths we describe.

9. This effect also plays an important role in Gavin (1993).

10. Many of these countries have long collected and are still collecting detailed data on wages, flows and stocks. Results from country studies using those data are reported in Blanchard et al (1993).

11. A clear warning is needed at this point. As in the Harris-Todaro model, unemployment benefits appear to be unambiguously bad in our model. But this comes from our Harris-Todaro-like assumption that, even if the unemployed are ex-post worse off, unemployment is the result of the voluntary decision to restructure. In a more realistic model, some of the unemployed would be involuntary unemployed, and the case for unemployment benefits reappears.

12. A warning that this might indeed happen was sounded by McKinnon (1991).

13. See for example Lipton (1992) on the effects of transition and the government budget.

14. These issues are closely related to how to buy off stockholders in top-down

privatization plans. See Shleifer and Vishny (1992).
15. See for example Pinto et al. (1993) for recent survey evidence on Polish state firms.

References

Aghion, P., 1993, "Economic Reform in Eastern Europe: Can Theory Help?" *European Economic Review*, April.

Blanchard, O., Commander, S., and Coricelli, F., 1993, "Labor Markets in Eastern Europe," mimeo, World Bank.

Blanchard, O. and Dabrowski, M., 1993, "Restructuring in Central Europe; the Case of Poland," mimeo, MIT, forthcoming in *Reform in Eastern Europe; Pain and Progress,* MIT Press.

Chadha, B., Coricelli, F., and Kranjak, C., 1992, "Economic Restructuring, Unemployment and Growth in a Transition Economy," mimeo, IMF.

Gavin, M., 1993, "Unemployment and the Economics of Gradualist Policy Reform," mimeo, Columbia University, January.

Lipton, D. and de Combrugghe, A., 1992, "The Government Budget and the Economic Transformation of Poland," mimeo, November.

McKinnon, R., 1991, "The Order of Economic Liberalization," Johns Hopkins, Baltimore.

Pinto, B., Belka, M., and Krajewski, S., 1993, "Transforming State Enterprises in Poland: Microeconomic Evidence on Adjustment," mimeo, World Bank.

Shleifer, A., and Vishny, R., 1992, "Privatization in Russia: First Steps," mimeo.

Reflections on the Open Policies After the Opium War of 1840 and Since the Reform and Opening in 1978

Li Yiyuan
Institute of Economics and Management,
Qinghua University

Both the Opium War of 1840 and the reform and opening to the outside world since 1978 are crucial turning points in Chinese history. In the last century, the Western big powers broke through the door to China via the Opium War by force, compelling the Qing Government, which had enforced a tightly closed policy, to open China. This action turned China, the oldest, largest, and most civilized feudal state in the world, into a semi-feudal and semi-colonial society. Thus began the darkest period in Chinese history. In modern times, new China, through its active reform and open policy, has opened itself to the outside world. As a result, within a decade or so China has achieved more in that short time than in the previous 100 years. Now China has come into the greatest period of development in its entire history. This article will analyze the two periods of opening to the rest of the world, one in the 19th century and one going on right now.

I. Opening to the Outside World and the Commodity Economy

Before the Opium War of 1840 China was a feudal society in which the natural economy was predominant. In that society small farming combined with small handicraft, the male farming and the female weaving. Weaving complimented farming, but simple commodity production was developing increasingly with each passing day and workshops for smelting iron, weaving, and mining salt and coal appeared. This shows that China's commodity economy lagged behind that of the advanced capitalist countries, which had completed their industrial revolution at least 200 years before. However, the Qing Dynasty (1644-1911) was ignorant of what was happening in the world and out of parochial arrogance believed that "foreign countries, with territory only as small as a mud ball, were actually exclaves of China, and their waters, as small as a spoonful, were just like dew in the imperial palace,"[1] and that "the empire, rich in products of all kinds and not relying on foreign goods, it was not necessary to exchange goods with them."[2] Therefore, the Qing Government treated the foreign envoys who came to China for trade as those who came to China to pay tribute, forcing them to greet the ruler with the three-kneeing-nine-bowing salute, or driving them out of China if dissatisfied with them. In 1757 the Qing Government allowed Britain, France and other countries to trade in the summer and autumn only at Guangzhou and only with the "state-owned trades" appointed by the government. Foreign merchants were allowed to live in buildings only for foreigners and could not go out without permission or ride a sedan chair. Foreign women were not allowed to enter the city of Guangzhou. Affected by this long period of a tightly close policy, the gross import and export trade volume between China and Britain was less than 20 million Customs taels by the 1830s, and more than half of the imported goods was opium. In fact, the commercial proportion of farm products at that time was very low, 10.5 percent for grain, 26.3 percent for cotton and 92.2 percent for silk.

Through the Opium War, and especially through the Sino-Japanese War of 1884-1885, the Western big powers used gunboats to break China's door open and replaced feudal inequality with imperialist inequality. Through a series of unjust treaties they first made China open five ports for trade, and as a result foreign goods, such as cigarettes, matches, candles, gasoline, flour, cotton, yarn, cloth, iron sheets, nails and cement, filled urban and rural markets. "Shanxi Province is known for the thrifty and simple life of its people, but none of them in a family of eight, in an area of 10 households, could be found wearing clothes not made of foreign-processed cotton or silk or not in possession of foreign goods."[3] Opium flowed into China on a large scale, and the volume increased by five times during the 16 years between the two Opium Wars. Opium smokers could be seen everywhere. Even the British said that the slave trade was benevolent compared with the opium trade. Later, foreign capital was invested in China to set up joint ventures: The total invested volume in 1902 was 1.509 billion US dollars; that of 1914, 2.256 billion US dollars; of 1930, 3.488 billion US dollars; of 1936, 4.285 billion US dollars; and of 1941, 9.152 billion US dollars. This foreign capital controlled much of China's main economic lifeline.

Karl Marx pointed out in 1853: "Complete isolation was the prime condition of the preservation of old China. That isolation having come to a violent end by the medium of England, dissolution must follow as surely as that of any mummy carefully preserved in a hermetically sealed coffin, whenever it is brought into contact with the open air."[4] The aggression of the Western big powers brought China into "contact" with "the open air" of modern large-scale production, thus advancing China's commodity economy while dragging the Chinese people into disaster. In 1840, China had little industrial capital; even by 1895 industrial capital was less than 100 million yuan. In 1913 it reached 1.541 billion yuan, in 1920 2.368 billion yuan, and in 1936 8.21 billion yuan. By then there were 2,441 registered factories, modern industrial output accounted for 58.8 percent of gross industrial output value and 10.8 percent of the total industrial and agricultural output value. Income from modern transportation systems accounted for 51 percent of all transport revenue. The commercial portion of farm products greatly increased with the commercial portion of grain in 1941 3.26 times, cotton 4.06 times, and silk 2.70 times what it had been in 1940.

Along with the development of a commodity economy, China's foreign trade was also continually enhanced. Before 1840, China's total export volume was 10 million Customs' taels at most, that of 1861, 52 million taels, that of 1881, 71.45 million taels, that of 1901, 169.65 million taels, that of 1921, 601.25 million taels, that of 1931, 909.48 million taels. In less than 100 years, China's export trade volume increased by 81 fold.

After the founding of the People's Republic of China, China had trading contacts mainly with the former Soviet Union and the Eastern European countries due to the Western countries' strict implementation of embargoes. On the other hand, China, long oppressed and bullied by the imperialists, longed for the establishment of its own independent and complete industrial system and treated foreign trade as mutually beneficial. China, in fact, once more became a closed state to some extent. As a result, before the initiation reform and opening to the outside world in 1978 foreign trade volume remained at the level of 15 billion US dollars, far behind that of Japan and the Republic of Korea, whose per capita GNP was below China's.

Since 1978, China has made it clear that peace and development are the two major challenges facing the contemporary world, and has emphasized that the practice of opening to the outside world is a basic national policy essential for reform and construction. At the same time, China should absorb and make use of all advanced and civilized achievements of countries all over the world, including those of the developed capitalist countries. At first, China established the special economic zones, followed by the opening of coastal cities and economic development regions, and then opened border areas and the areas along the Yangtze River to gradually form the opening setup in a multi-level, multi-channel and overall direction. From 1979 to 1992 China utilized 98.83 billion US dollars of foreign capital, of which 34.355 billion US dollars were direct foreign investment. During this period China's GNP increased from 213.1 billion US dollars to 418 billion US dollars due to reform and opening to the outside world. The peasant consumption of self-supplied products decreased from 58.64 percent to 34.53 percent, while the commercial rate of grain increased from 20.3 percent to 34.6 percent and that of cotton rose to 96.7 percent. Correspondingly, foreign trade volume went up to 165.5 billion US dollars in 1992 from 20.64 billion US dollars in 1978, with an opening rise of 39.6 percent, which is rarely found among large countries.

China's Foreign Trade Before and After the Opium War
(million Customs' taels)

Year		Total import and export volume	Net export volume
Before Opium War	1790-94	9.8	0.8
	1800-04	13.6	-0.1
	1820-24	14.7	3.0
	1824-33	15.6	2.4
After Opium War	1843	43.9	7.1
	1851	68.4	-3.8
	1861	111.0	-7.0
	1871	140.0	-3.3
	1881	163.4	-20.2
	1891	235.0	-33.1
	1901	438.0	-98.6
	1911	848.0	-94.2
	1921	1,507.0	-304.9
	1931	2,343.0	-524.0

Sources: The data before the Opium War, quoted from *Selected Statistic Data of Chinese Modern Economic History* by Yan Zhongping, are the annual average figures of Sino-British trade, accounting for about 80 percent of China's foreign trade. (111 taels of silver = 100 Customs' taels). The data after the Opium War are quoted from *Outline of Chinese History of Foreign Trade* by Li Kanghua, Xia Xiurui and Gu Ruozeng.

China's Foreign Trade After the Reform and Opening Up
(US$ 100 million)

Year		Total import and export volume	Net export volume
Before reform and	1950	1,130	-300
opening up	1957	3,100	100
	1962	1,330	320
	1965	4,250	210
	1970	4,590	-70
	1975	14,750	-230
After reform and	1978	20,640	-1,140
opening up	1980	38,136	-1,898
	1982	44,106	3,036
	1984	53,549	-1,271
	1968	73,846	-11,962
	1988	102,791	-7,759
	1990	115,437	8,746
	1992	165,610	390

Sources: The data before and after the reform and opening up are quoted from *The Chinese Statistic Yearbook (1992)* and *China's Complete Economic Statistics of Foreign Trade* respectively, except the data for 1992, which are quoted from the report given by Vice-Premier Zou Jiahua at the First Session of the Eighth National People's Congress.

Comparisons of the two opening periods clearly show that the former opening was the product of colonial policy, that is, imposed by the Western big powers on the Chinese people by force, while the latter opening is the product of a peaceful foreign policy, actively carried out to realize the modernization of New China. The two openings to the outside world also tell us that opening is closely connected with the commodity economy just like "twins." But whatever the opening, it promotes the market economy to some extent. Under the tendency of

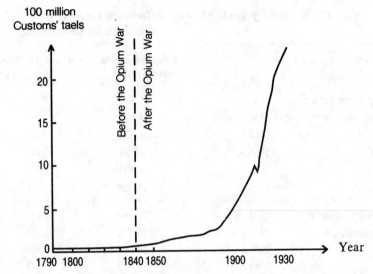

Comparison of China's Foreign Trade Before and After the Opium War

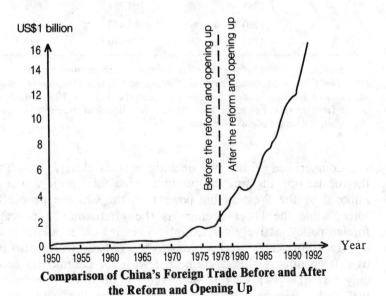

**Comparison of China's Foreign Trade Before and After
the Reform and Opening Up**

integration of the world's economies, each country should not and cannot close its door. Closing up will lead to backwardness, and only opening can promote development. This is the experience of the Chinese people learned over 200 years, and we should never forget it.

II. Opening to the Outside World and Protecting Sovereignty

Those who have a deep impression of the aggression by the Western big powers after the Opium War may naturally compare the two openings and misunderstand the present opening policy:

In the past, beginning with trade at the five trading ports, more than 30 concessions, leased territories, subzones, commercial port districts, commercial belts, dwelling districts, and summer resorts were opened from Macao to Dalian, from Shanghai to Chongqing, and from Dandong to Ili. Now, starting with the opening of 14 coastal cities and followed by the opening of the coastal and border areas and the areas along the Yangtze River, the establishment of economic zones, the opening of inland cities, and the building of apartments, restaurants and holiday villas for foreigners, the number of open areas is much greater than in the past.

Formerly, the autonomy tariff was changed to an agreement tariff, causing the tariff rate to decline from 35-40 percent to below 5 percent. Under the pretext of all countries "sharing benefits equally" foreign commodities were transported to every part of China, causing bankruptcy for domestic goods dealers. Now foreign funded enterprises enjoy either reduction of or exemption from taxes, and reduced tariffs. As a result, imported products, either assembled in the original producing countries or in other countries, now appear everywhere in China. Are there any difference between what is happening at present and what occurred in the past?

In the past, the Western big powers exported capital until China accumulated several billion US dollars in debt. Now,

China is trying every possible means to import capital, and in 10 years or so it has imported tens of billions in US dollars. But what is the difference between capital import and capital export? In the past, the Western big powers rented parts of China's territory with 99-year leases. Now China is inviting foreign investors in and the rental period is as long as 70 years. The difference seems just like the distance from 50 steps to 100 steps.

...... Indeed, the ways and methods of opening to the outside world at present are actually similar to those in the past. Of course, the opening up has to adopt these ways and methods. But the key point is whether independence and self-determination can be preserved and sovereignty can be protected! The following should be made clearly: What are the common practice and principles that should be followed in international fair competition, and what is the plunder allowed by the privileges provided for in the treaties of inequality? What are the decisions made independently according to national interests, and what are the shackles put on by the Western big powers through force?

As you see, around time of the Opium War the Qing Government surrendered the country's sovereign rights under humiliating terms, ceding 1.5 million square kilometers of its territory, but since the initiation of reform and opening to the outside world in 1978 China has not lost a single inch of its territory, and Hong Kong and Macao will return to their motherland successively in the near future.

In the past, the Qing Government could do nothing but agree when the Western big powers wanted territory to lease for trading. Moreover, it had to give up consular jurisdiction and administrative rights. Actually, the concession was "a state within a state," independent from the Chinese administrative and legal system. Now which places should be opened and when and how they should be opened will be decided by the Chinese Government, and foreign investors must act in accordance with the relevant policies; otherwise, they will be handled according to Chinese law. Someone once asked whether it was possible to contract for the entire province of Hainan, including the provincial government. This is absolutely impossible.

Opening ports, leasing territory, borrowing money, investing capital and according most-favored-nation treatment are important forms of international cooperation if they are handled according to the principles of equality, self-determination and mutual benefit. Some developed countries, as everybody knows, invest large amounts of capital, rent land, and accord most-favored-nation treatment among themselves. China has also invested capital in developed countries, issued negotiable securities and leased or bought land there. But the current problem is: Why doesn't capital flow from rich to poor countries?[5] Why are consortiums not actively investing capital in the opened areas? Why do we have to spend so much energy talking about most-favored-nation treatment every year? Obviously, the old practice of "foreign debts" through robbery, that is, first resorting to force to get reparations and then turning them into loans to carry out economic aggression, will not do. While the tariff in every country is as high as 40-50 percent, they try to make China take "five from each hundred" of foreign products for tariff and take 2.5 percent once for all for their inland tax. This is quite different from domestic products, which should pay tax at every outpost of the tax offices. This kind of preference is one-sided, and we are resolutely opposed to those who use their own domestic laws to damage the sovereignty of other countries trying to revive their sweet dreams. Of course, all forms of international cooperation based on the five principles of peaceful co-existence are acceptable.

III. Opening Up and Structural Reform

The two openings to the outside world caused fundamental changes in the economic system involving the industrial, ownership, policy-making, and distribution structures, as well as in the administrative systems of finance, banking and foreign trade. After the Opium War, the Qing Dynasty turned from an independent, centralized feudal monarchy into a semi-feudal and semi-colonial country, while after the reform and opening up of 1978 New China changed from a socialist planned economic system with high centralization to a socialist market economic system based on market forces. To compare the economic systems of these two periods thoroughly requires special analysis, but the following aspects may be mentioned here.

1. The Foreign Economic System

After the Opium War, China's door was opened wide and the foreign trade was changed from an overall monopoly economy controlled by the "public trades" set up by the government, to a free and uncontrolled economy. After the Sino-Japanese War of 1894-95 in particular, the Western big powers, having obtained the privilege to directly invest in China, shifted the center of gravity of exports from commodities to capital, and first seized the autonomy over tariffs and the right to build railways, mine, and navigate China's seas and inland rivers, thereby controlling China's economic lifelines. By 1913, on the eve of the First World War, of China's total industrial capital, foreign capital made up 80 percent occupying an absolute ruling position. Foreign capital in coal and iron mines, spindles, looms, electricity, railways, navigation, and banks was 79.6 percent, 99.2 percent, 42.6 percent, 49.7 percent, 77.1 percent, 90.7 percent, 83.8 percent, and 90 percent respectively, while Customs and foreign trade were also under the control of foreign capital.

Since the initiation of reform and opening to the outside world, China's foreign economic structure has been improved step by step from a unified operation conducted by China Import and Export Corporation to the opening structure of multi-layers, multi-channels and overall directions, in which thousands of enterprises enjoy the rights to do foreign trade on their own. Foreign capital has accounted for about 6 percent of the investment in social fixed assets, about the same amount invested from the state budget. The main problem at present is not doing too much, but rather not doing enough in opening to the outside world. So there is much to do to raise the level of the domestic market to international standards. Therefore, the following should be done: To expand the open area; to widen the scope of utilizing foreign capital; to adopt more flexible forms of international cooperation; and to establish a new system to handle foreign trade and its correspondent policies and laws and regulations to conform with international commercial standards. However, judging from the experience and lessons learned from opening to the outside world after the Opium War of 1840, the following point is worth noting: Guiding the investment of foreign capital actively according to industrial policy and closely controlling on an appropriate scale, the foreign capital investment in industry is essential. Granting preferential treatment to foreign capital and guaranteeing an environment of fair competition for domestic enterprises and joint ventures by bringing them to the same starting point is also essential, as is protecting the growth of the newly developing industries by making use of preferential terms for the developing countries prescribed in GATT to avoid their being killed in the cradle. Financial auditing must protect against the outflow of funds caused by unclear capital, false losses, exchange-rate games, and false joint ventures. We must keep macro-adjustment and control, avoiding unnecessary repeated imports and internal strife.

2. The Comprador

Along with the import of foreign capital, middlemen and agents soon made their appearance. In old colonial China they were called compradors, who "relied on foreigners to make a fortune." Actually, the compradors can be divided into two groups. One group was servile, making a fetish of foreigners and foreign goods and these were looked down upon by the Chinese people as "Second Foreigners" who "did not care about anything except profit and enjoyment." They enjoyed the privilege of foreign businesspeople usually by buying shares, under false pretences, of foreign firms. The other group learned from foreigners the workings of the market economy and used their knowledge to set up modern industrial enterprises, fighting commercial battles against foreign capital. This group was the main source of China's early national capital.

The import of foreign capital and its utilization naturally caused a number of people to serve foreign interests. In fact, foreign merchants dealing with import and export trades, foreign agents and their offices and commission agents are now more numerous than ever and can be found in every part of China. In old China, which lost part of its sovereignty, compradors opened the door to dangerous foes, became their dependents, and acted as criminals toward the people. Now the people have taken their destiny into their own hands. These new-type "compradors" have made great contributions to the utilization of foreign capital in China and have become heroes rendering outstanding service in reform and opening to the outside world. They cannot be separated from the further improvement of the investment environment. The enthusiasm for seeking a job "involving foreign affairs" is certainly a good phenomenon, suitable to the present situation, and should be encouraged. At the same time, these seekers should be educated to serve the Chinese people. If they are employees in foreign-funded enterprises they should serve the interests of foreign capital, but at the same time, they should abide by discipline and laws and safeguard the rights and interests of the Chinese nation. As for their comparatively high income, this is historically inevitable and perfectly normal and can be redistributed through their tax income.

3. The Relationship Between Enterprises and the Government

Feudal forces, rooted deep in Chinese society, which is twice as old as Western society, form a power structure like a pyramid even in modern enterprises. From 1860, the enterprises run by the Qing Government were gradually transformed into enterprises run by merchants and supervised by the government or jointly run by merchants and the government. Among these the enterprises of the officially run munitions industry were called by the names of official organs, such as manufacture bureau, machine bureau or ship administration bureau, and not closely connected with the market: Their expenses were paid by the state treasury, their operation relied on administrative power, and their products were handled by the government. The civil enterprises run by the government and those jointly run by the government and merchants belonged to the commodity-production type, but served the military to a large extent and were strongly in feudal character. These enterprises, called merchants bureau, mining affairs bureau, and textile bureau, were controlled by the officials appointed by the government, though their capital was invested by merchants. These feudal bureaucrats allocated funds between enterprises at their own will. Under these circumstances expenditures not in the regular accounts occurred and funds were used for their own expenses or went into their own pockets. Moreover, these enterprises had to pay "tribute" to the government. To take the Mohe gold mine for example, it handed in 30 percent of its net profit for "soldiers' pay and provisions" and on the occasion of the birthday of Empress Dowager Ci Xi, had to "donate" tens of thousands of silver taels. As a result, the enormous capital of businesspeople flowed away like water down a river, and they turned pale at the mere mention of official management. These civil enterprises had the features of a monopoly and enjoyed various privileges. The feudal bureaucrats often used their power to monopolize operations. The Shanghai Textile Bureau stipulated: "Chinese businesspeople are not allowed to set up bureaus within 10 years but buy shares." The Kaiping Mine Administration also stipulated: "Setting up other coal companies is not allowed," and "the coal mined is not allowed to be sold to other merchants, but only to the commercial bureau at the market price." In fact, 56 percent of the earliest national capitalists were feudal landlords, and most of them had official titles or had been granted certain titles, so the essence of the matter was just big fish swallowing small fish. These national capitalists, small in scale and with little capital, had to struggle in the gap between foreign and domestic bureaucratic capital. Even if a few enterprises developed to some extent, their primitive accumulation of funds was eaten up by the government through taxes, donations, and charities. This is one important reason why the Chinese national capitalists remained weak.

Since the founding of the People's Republic of China in 1949, Chinese political power has changed completely. Under the planned economy enterprises were still attached to the governments at various levels. Since 1978 the government has regarded the separation of enterprises management from government administration as the central task in reforming the economic system, and has tried to transform enterprises into economic bodies with self management and operation and responsibility for its own profits and losses. Up to now, fundamental changes have not taken place in the operation mechanism of the state-owned large and medium-sized enterprises, the functions of the government and those of enterprises have not been separated, and the confusion of property right and the gaining of private benefit through seized power can be found here and there. This does not fit the conditions necessary for a market economy and free trade, set for the return of Chinese membership in GATT. If China fails to make substantive progress in this field, reform will be stalled, the socialist market economy system cannot be established, and China's economic system will not be compatible with the world economic system.

4. The Balance Among Regions

According to the experience of other countries, it is normal for imbalances to occur during the development of a market economy before a new balance is achieved. One important change which occurred in the first stages of opening to the outside world was that an already imbalanced economy became still more imbalanced. Modern enterprises were concentrated in cities along the coast. According to statistics, the capital and output value of Shanghai, Tianjin and Guangzhou alone accounted for nearly 60 percent of the nation's total. "After the middle of Emperor Guang Xu's reign, the market developed, a large number of factories were erected, and men and women went to work in these factories ... jobs increased with each passing day and less people were engaged in farming and weaving."[6] In the vast area of China's interior, a self-supporting economy reigned, and in some areas the slave system still existed. As a result, the wide gap between the rich and the poor became larger with each passing day, and the differences between workers and peasants, urban and rural areas, and mental and manual labor grew sharply. In Shanghai, a worker who worked for 11 to 18 hours a day got only half the wages paid to a worker in a Western country. The foreigners at the end of the 19th Century said: "With such small wages an

American worker cannot support himself. This happened in Shanghai, but the wages in other places were even less. Thanks to the high wages in Shanghai, the number of men and women who left their home for Shanghai to look for a job increased daily."[7] Similar records can also be found in other parts of China: "Women 'go to Shanghai batch after batch' 'scrambling for jobs,' some of them even leave their home with determination and their parents and husbands cannot stop them."[8] According to statistics, an ordinary worker at that time, earning an annual wage of less than 100 yuan in most cases, could not support himself, and a peasant with an annual income of just over 10 yuan was in even worse shape. As modern industry in the cities was limited in scale, there were less than 100,000 industrial workers before the Sino-Japanese War of 1894-95, and 300,000 workers before the First World War. As a result, a large number of peasants who had come to the cities had to return to their rural areas again, or else went abroad to look for work. Because of these sharp social contradictions the Taiping Heavenly Kingdom uprising and the Yihetuan Movement (Boxer Rebellion) occurred.

Since the adoption of the policy of reform and opening to the outside world in 1978, the Chinese government has paid much attention to balanced development, allowing some areas and groups of people to become rich first, while at the same time striving for common wealth gradually. The township enterprises absorbed millions of surplus rural laborers. This is a great undertaking of the Chinese people: Transformation from an agricultural to an industrial country. Because of the sharp contrasts between localities their economies developed to vastly different extents. Now many regions have grown to a level of comparative well-being, but about 100 million people do not have enough to eat and to wear. And differences between the coastal areas and interior regions and urban and rural areas are becoming greater. Therefore, with China's pending return to GATT membership, the policies made especially for the special economic zones should extend to the poorer areas in order to alleviate these contradictions.

IV. Opening to the Outside World and Ideological Emancipation

Opening to the outside world must rid itself of the closed policies, and this will certainly cause conflict with various traditional concepts. Facts prove that the degree of ideological emancipation is decided by the width, depth and speed of opening to the outside world.

The representatives of the open policy after the Opium War of 1840 were those who initiated the Westernization Movement (1860s-1890s). The two Opium Wars made some feudal bureaucrats see the Westerner's "solidly built vessels and powerful guns" and caused them to believe that "if China had guns and ships, the Westerners would pull in their horns." They advocated "learning the merits of the Western countries to subdue them." Their guiding principle was "Chinese ethics is the main body while Western science and technology play the role of serving it." At first, they believed "the Chinese official and military system is much better than the Western one except for the guns, which the Chinese weapons cannot compare with." Therefore, besides buying guns and building ships, 19 munitions factories were set up. Later, they found that "a rich and powerful man with great a fortune can beat a powerful army of one million soldiers," and that "practicing military operations is inferior to practicing commercial competition." So by this thinking they set up more than 40 modern industrial enterprises. These events caused "knowledge hunger." To cope with the situation, some 30 schools were established to translate books from Western foreign languages into Chinese and send Chinese students to study abroad. The Westernization Movement was thus launched aimed at "turning China into a rich country by increasing its strength." However, progress was small and limited to a few fields, like "a small quantity of goods bought from retail shops, but not like large quantities bought wholesale." As a result, the Beiyang naval forces were destroyed in the Sino-Japanese War of 1894-95, and the Westernization Movement was defeated by Japan's 1868 Meiji Restoration.

The Westernization Movement, by not taking radical steps, but only stopgap measures, was attacked fiercely by the conservative feudal bureaucrats. They held aloft the banner of nationalism and patriotism to support the learning of Chinese ethics but opposed the utilization of Western science and technology. They said the guiding principle of "Chinese ethics is the main body while Western knowledge serves it," advocated by the Westernization Movement, was not the approach to "restrain the foreign powers through the utilization of foreign knowledge," but rather that this would "change China." They taught that Western knowledge would threaten Chinese ethics. "The suggestion to take advantage of foreign knowledge began with technology and continued to politics and then to education, while the moral obligations of king and minister, father and son, husband and wife collapsed!" "People across the land will call propriety, righteousness, honesty and the sense of shame useless, and think that Western knowledge will not work either; therefore, the morality will collapses."[9] They emphasized that "the way to build the country should rely on propriety and righteousness, not on expediency. The essence of the matter is morality, not techniques."[10] With these thoughts in mind, Yi Xin, the sixth prince and leader of the Westernization Movement was nicknamed "Devil VI" by the conservatives, and someone even presented a petition to the emperor calling for the mutilation of the body of Guo Songtao, the first Chinese ambassador, after his death, as an apology for what he had done.

Criticism of the Westernization Movement also came from the reformists with bourgeois tendencies. They agreed with the utilization of Western knowledge but were opposed to the Chinese ethical system. Their attitude toward the munitions industry run by the government can be seen from the following passage: "The refusal to learn their ways while only imitating the things they do, such as engaging in Westernized coastal defence, without efforts to gather the intelligence and financial resources of the nation, cannot result in prosperity. The nation's financial resources now only make officials rich. This behavior of considering the incidental without touching the fundamental can only bring loss instead of benefits."[11] As for their attitude toward civil industry, it can be found in the following comments: "Westerners never join with officials in the management of money matters, but Chinese officials and merchants now join hands. As officials have authoritative rights while merchants have not, merchants cannot amass capital, and profits constantly will go to officials,"[12] and "This kind of management by the government under heaven cannot last very long."[13] As for those who were educated in Western knowledge and advocated Constitutional Reform and Modernization (1896), they went further and aimed their attack at the Chinese ethical system: "To purchase boats and machinery means the change of equipment, but does not equal to a fundamental change; and to set up post offices and exploit mines are great changes, but will not result in a change in politics."[14] "In short, the essence of reform is the education of talented people; a large number of talented people can be brought out after setting up schools; and the establishment of schools relies on changing the imperial examination system—all this can be done only when the administrative system has been changed."[15] "All successful reforms without exception make equal efforts to eliminate the old and create the new. The creation of the new without eliminating the old will inevitably bring the demerits of the old political system into the new and this will do harm to the new."[16] Finally, they said, "Either Europe or Asia needed 300 years for systematic transformation. Japan spent 30 years in its transformation by following the example of Europe and the United States. If China, with vast land and a huge population, adopts the Japanese approach, three years are enough for forming the overall scale, five years for straightening things out, eight years for securing effectiveness, and 10 years for obtaining the strength to seek hegemony."[17]

The dispute over the open policy ran through not only the Westernization Movement but also the 100-day Constitutional Reform and Modernization, the Revolution of 1911 and the May Fourth Movement. As for the contemporary reform and opening to the outside world, the whole Party and nation have a common understanding, though some different viewpoints exist. According to the theory of building China into a socialist country with Chinese characteristics, put forward by Comrade Deng Xiaoping, the Central Committee of the Communist Party of China (CPC) sticks to taking economic construction as the center, adheres to the four cardinal principles (adherence to the socialist road, adherence to the people's democratic dictatorship, adherence to the leadership of the CPC, and adherence to Marxism-Leninism and Mao Zedong Thought) and the reform and open policy, and announced that this firm stand will remain unchanged for 100 years. However, some people follow the beaten path; actually, they want to take the class struggle as the key link and advocate: "preferring socialist weeds to capitalist sprouts." They are worried about the open policy, believing that foreign ventures will be a hotbed for peaceful evolution and the special economic zones a road to capitalist restoration. Some people improperly belittle themselves, advocating and practicing privatizing all enterprises. There are fears that China will be transformed into a feudal, bureaucratic and comprador capitalist country, but not a modern capitalist country if China does as they had advocated. Some people even think that if China became a colony after the Opium War, it would have become a developed country long ago. In fact, India had become a colony before China became semi-colonial; however, India remains a developing country even now. If the imperialists had not ruled over them for so long, India and China would have both developed faster.

The 5,000 years of Chinese history, especially the years during the two openings, are filled with struggle. *The Book of Changes* says: "When all means are exhausted, changes have been necessary; once changes have been made, a solution emerges; when solution works, it lasts long." This is the naive dialectical viewpoint. Dong Zhongshu says, "The way of nature, as large as the heaven, originates from the heaven. The heaven is unchanging, so is the way of nature." This is the metaphysical viewpoint. Chinese feudal society lasted an extremely long time, largely because Confucianism was respected as a guide for living. "There has been no debate for two thousand years, which is true. Whatever confucius said is the conclusion, so there is no debate. There has been no debate on right and wrong, which is true. The criterion for right and wrong is set forth by Confucius, so there is no debate on right and wrong."[18] At present, we should be on guard against both the rightist and the "left" especially the "left." Liang Qichao was right when he said, "Change is absolute whenever we are willing or not. Changing when we are willing, the initiative of change is in our hands, which can protect our country, our race and our ethics. Changing when we are reluctant, the initiative of change falls into the hands of others, which will fasten or spur the change. Then what will happen? Alas, I dare not say."[19] The opening to the outside world after the Opium War was passive, it belongs to reluctant change, which resulted in change to a semi-colony. The opening to the outside world since 1978 is active change, belonging to willing change, which is turning China into a socialist, modernized and Pacific Century country.

Notes

1. Xia Jiajun's *The Historical Narrative of the Qing Dynasty*, p. 165.
2. *Qing Emperor Gao Zong's Instructions*, Vol. 276, p. 13.
3. *Materials of Modern History of Chinese Agriculture*, Vol. 1, p. 492.
4. Revolution in China and in Europe, *Karl Marx and Frederick Engels Collected Works* (English edition published by Progress Publishers, Moscow, 1979, Vol. 12, p. 95.
5. Robert E. Lucas, Jr., Why Doesn't Capital Flow from Rich to Poor Countries? The "New" Growth Theory, Vol. 80, No. 2.
6. Custom, *Fahua Township Annals*, Vol. 2.
7. *Materials of Modern History of Chinese Agriculture,* Vol. 1, p. 921.
8. Quoted in *The Supersession of the Old by the New in Chinese Modern History* written by Chen Xulu, p. 217.
9. *Letters to Friends* by Zeng Lian.
10. Quoted in *The Supersession of the Old by the New in Chinese Modern History*, p. 121.
11. Song Yuren's *On Current Affairs*, block-print edition in the reign of Emperor Guang Xu of the Qing Dynasty, p. 1.
12. Tang Zhen's *Words for Alarm*, Vol. 2, block-print edition, the 16th year of Emperor Guang Xu's reign in the Qing Dynasty, p. 16.
13. Preserved manuscripts in the Qiuyi Studio, *Materials of the Westernization Movement*, Vol. 1, p. 365.
14. Kang Yuwei's *Textual Research in Japanese Political Transformation*.

15. "On Harm Caused by Not Knowing the Essence and Origin of Reform," *Materials of the Reform Movement of 1898*, Vol. 3, p. 21.
16, 17. Liang Qichao's "Record of the Reform Movement of 1898," *Materials of the Reform Movement of 1898*, Vol. 1, pp. 273-274.
18. Chen Xulu's *The Supersession of the Old by the New in Chinese Modern Society*, p. 19.
19. "On Three Harms Caused by Not Changing," *Materials of the Reform Movement of 1898*, Vol. 3, p. 18.

Clearing Up Some Doubts About China's Change to a Market Economy
—Also on the Compatibility Between a Market Economy and Socialism

Xia Zhenkun
President of Hubei Provincial Academy
of Social Sciences

Without a doubt, for a big, socialist country like China to embrace the market economy, in contrast to the restrictive commodity economy of the past, is a revolutionary and epoch-making achievement. For a long period of time, due to ideological shackles and insufficient experience, the adjustment of relations between the planned and market sectors of the economy has undergone a tortuous and difficult development. Thanks to our great efforts, we have overcome great difficulties and started to go forward. During the 10-year period from the initial introduction of the market mechanism in the early 1980s to the promotion of a socialist market economy in the 1990s, China's economy has made tremendous progress, a fact well known to all. However, there are still some people, especially in the West, who harbor doubts about whether a market system can be established in a socialist country. Their essential questions are: Whether adherence to a basic socialist system can be compatible with the practice of a market economy, or if so to what extent? What in fact is a "socialist market economy?"

This article tries to make a preliminary study of these issues.

I. Theory: Socialism with Chinese Characteristics

Socialism is a way to understand the evolution of societies. During the last 100 years, great changes have taken place in the understanding socialism and its implications, changes which range from the original concepts of "scientific socialism" put forward by Marx, to today's socialism. Classical Marxism was born in Western Europe in the 19th century, but the practice of socialism actually took place in the East during the 20th century. Such delays in time and shifts of location have given rise to new questions and areas of academic inquiry in the minds of Oriental socialists. These questions are mainly represented by the following contradictions:

—*The Contradiction Between Safeguarding Equality and Social Justice and the Problem of Insufficient Material Wealth*

The ultimate aim of socialism is to eliminate various unfair phenomena existing in capitalist societies, and to realize real social justice and equality. From the viewpoint of classical Marxism, the realization of this objective can be made possible only by a "miraculous" emancipation of productivity on the part of the capitalist class. Indeed, this is one of the basic differences between "scientific" and "utopian" socialism. Marx once said: "Power can never be disconnected with the economic structure of a society and the cultural development as constrained by such structure."[1] He assumed that in the first stage of a communist society, the rights of laborers are proportional to the labor they provide; as a result, equality should be measured by the same indicator—labor. This is what we have come to understand as the principle of "income distribution according to work."

However, due to feudal shackles and imperialist invasion, the capitalist class in China was unable to accomplish its historical mission of industrialization, and the emancipation of productivity. When the Communist Party of China began the country's socialist construction, it encountered severe material shortages in all sectors of the economy. With such a poor basis on which to start, the principle of "distribution according to work" was obviously far beyond the limits that contemporary social and economic structures could endure. As a result, a form of overall equality, or "equalitarianism," throughout the whole society, and this brought economic development to a standstill and led to deterioration in the country's economic framework.

—The Contradiction Existing Between Public Ownership of the Means of Production and the Low Level of Production in the Command Economy

All social inequity originates from private ownership of property. This viewpoint is shared by all socialists, including the utopian socialists. The difference between Marxism and utopian socialism lies in that the former believes that the elimination of private ownership depends upon certain conditions rather than a simple return to a primitive communist society, a path exemplified in the "counter-industrialism" suggested by Foulier. The most basic pre-condition is that of realizing large-scale socialized production on the basis of industrialization.

Within the socialist countries of Asia, however, production often remains limited and small in scale, and the task of industrialization is far from being completed. Establishing public ownership on the basis of such a small scale of production would undoubtedly lead to the exploitation of peasants. Following the example of the former Soviet Union, almost all socialist countries proceeded to implement policies of overall public ownership, or even nationalization, in order to advance the course of their economic development. It is well known to all that the unfortunate consequence of these policies was to suppress the development of a commodity economy, and to severely smother the incentive mechanism for economic development.

—The Contradiction Between Planned Allocation of Resources and Disorganized Small-Scale Production

Planning, in order to be successful, is understood by Marxists to require the preconditions of large-scale socialized production, as well as the modern operational and managerial techniques concomitant on such a scale of production. So long as China and other Oriental countries had failed to themselves of the "medieval yoke" of loose, small-scale production—with its incomplete information, weak statistics and supervision systems—the implementation of a comprehensive planning system could only be deemed a utopian proposal.

Experience has shown that highly centralized planning and the adoption of public ownership in a blanket manner led to a unitary main body of development, and to the weakening of motive forces for development, not to mention the bureaucratic-style of operation in socialist countries, in which "giving arbitrary and impractical directions" becomes the order of the day. This resulted in the misuse and waste of resources and to a weak economic framework.

All of the above contradictions may be encapsulated as being a contradiction between an over-radical model of socialism and the reality of backward and lagging social productivity.

Having summed up the positive and negative experiences of China's economic construction to date, the Chinese socialists as represented by Deng Xiaoping have gradually realized: It is impossible for a large developing country like China to establish socialism in just one step. We must be flexible about determining different policy objectives and structures, appropriate for different stages of development. Today's China remains in the primary stage of socialism, and during this stage we should not seek to pursue absolute social equality regardless of the actual level of productivity. Differences between those who get rich earlier and those who get rich later, between the rich and the less rich, should be allowed. The ultimate aim of common prosperity will be realized through the incentive mechanism, a mechanism strengthened by the fact of "differences" within society. The policy of public ownership should not be practised in an all-round way; instead different types of ownership should be allowed to coexist, with public ownership as the mainstay. Likewise, highly centralized planning should be avoided; the role of the market should be cultivated and brought into full play so as to establish a market economic system with regulation and control. In summary, we should, under the guidance of the Chinese Communist Party, aim to make the best use of all elements, forces and methods to greatly expand social productivity, and to achieve the goals of national industrialization and social modernization.

The reform process of the past 10 years or so has demonstrated that a market-style economy has advantages over the former highly centralized economy when it comes to the task of enhancing productivity. The advantages can be summarized as follows:

(1) The existence of more agents for development, and faster formation of capital;

(2) Stronger motivational forces for development and more vigorous incentive mechanisms;

(3) A decentralization of the risks of development and more initiatives owned by the government; and

(4) Higher economic returns and more advanced technologies resulting from the policy of survival of the fittest.

II. Reality: Necessary Conditions

The market economy is a product of production socialization, under which the resources of social production are obtained through market mechanisms. According to the *Dictionary of Modern Economics* published in the United States, the market-directed economy is an economic organizational form under which what to produce, how to produce and for whom to produce are all determined by supply and demand.[2]

The concept of a market economy has its own strict implications and indications. Can socialism satisfy these indications and conditions? In other words, can the basic principles of the market economy be realized without basically changing the socialist system? Our reply is: Yes. A trial analysis follows:

—*First, Many Forms of Ownership Is the Basis of the Market Economy.*

In general, forms of ownership refers to independent economic entities entitled to ultimate ownership or control of assets, which are directly related to the increase or decrease of these assets and includes legal responsibility. Under the Western market economy, many forms of ownership are realized by privatization, in addition to some state-owned enterprises. The government does not take part in the direct operation of state-owned enterprises. Rather, they are operated through entrusting assets to agents or to the shareholding system. For instance, in Germany state-owned enterprises strictly adopt the policy of separating government administration from enterprise management, and they enjoy the same treatment afforded to private enterprises in their operation and administration. As a result, state-owned enterprises may efficiently take part in market competition. This is also true in Japan, France, Italy and other countries.

Under the premise of firmly taking public ownership as the mainstay, enterprises in China may fully absorb foreign experiences by establishing many forms of ownership. A general assumption is that it is best to carry out these reforms step by step: (1) Readjusting the overall structure of ownership by developing the private economy, in addition to the public economy, and accelerating market development by employing private ownership. China has adopted these measures over the past 10-odd years and has achieved great success, especially in the coastal areas. (2) Making efforts to develop the collective and cooperative economy within the public economy and gradually turning the public economy into the mainstay in terms of quantity. Vast areas in south Jiangsu Province have shown that these measures can work. Practice also indicates that this structure is full of vitality. Enterprises can easily adopt the shareholding system or the stock cooperative system, both favorable for the realization of multiform ownership. (3) Dividing the state-owned economy into three different categories to realize multiform ownership. First, the assets of a small number of trades and enterprises that have great influence on the national economy and people's livelihood may be wholly owned by the state; and by completely separating capital administration from capital operation, they may adopt authorized (or contracted) operations, abolish all privileges and burdens incompatible with market principles, and turn themselves into independent incorporated enterprises. A standardized subsidy system may be worked out for those enterprises engaged in public services or undertaking tasks concerning state policies. Secondly, ordinary large and medium-sized state-owned enterprises can gradually adopt the shareholding system and become enterprises with the state as one of the shareholders. Many other forms may also be adopted such as Chinese-foreign joint ventures and domestically financed state-private cooperative enterprises. In accordance with the demands and financial capacity of the state, the state may choose to be a holder of golden-shares or ordinary shares. These enterprises may be managed in light of Western market economic principles. Public ownership (or final ownership) as mentioned above may be separately held by the central government, province (including city or county), the departments or non-governmental organizations, such as the Party, trade unions, etc. Thirdly, small-scale enterprises without state participation may be transferred to collectives or individuals through auctions or leasing to speed up the circulation of state-owned assets.

—*Second, the Free Movement of Essential Elements of Production (Commercialization and Marketization) Is the Lifeblood of a Market Economy.*

Allocating production resources through the readjustment of the relations between supply and demand in the market requires that key resources be exchangeable and their ownership freely transferred. This means that commodities may flow freely between sectors, enterprises, regions and countries. Otherwise, a market economy is out of the question.

The reform of the past 10-odd years has greatly improved the commercialization of the overwhelming majority of essential production elements; however, the commercialization of ownership and the labor force still lags behind.

The commercialization of ownership is directly related to the circulation of assets. Under a market economy, if demand exceeds supply investments must be increased and the imbalance readjusted. The free movement of assets among sectors and enterprises can enable equilibrium to be achieved quickly. Due to the restrictions of a planned economy in the past, ownership was not considered a commodity, so state-owned enterprises and sectors had no right to transfer ownership on their own. Therefore, when demand exceeded supply, the economy relied on increased investments. Undoubtedly this mechanism brought forth three different results: The first was the inability to solve the structural imbalance among sectors; the second was the low rate of capital turnover, leading to the long-standing problem of "hunger for investment." The third was inflation as triggered by the first two results. Therefore, when China's reform set the goal of achieving a socialist market economy, the reform of ownership became imperative. Practice will demonstrate that under socialist conditions the problems of ownership commercialization and free movement can be solved through the transformation of the shareholding system and reform of the administrative system of state-owned assets.

The commercialization of the labor force by eliminating the phenomenon of labor being "owned by sectors" is a difficulty for China's march toward a market economy. However, China has made breakthroughs in practice. Along with the successful completion of reforms in the employment and personnel systems, this difficulty will be readily overcome. Theoretically, there are some questions. Can the labor force be a commodity under socialism? Doesn't this contradict the theory of the supremacy of the working people? How will Marx's theory of surplus value be interpreted? My view is that these questions can be answered in the following way. At the macro-level, we should recall a famous sentence from Marx: Proletarians cannot finally liberate themselves if they cannot liberate mankind. The working class' status as master cannot be established, especially economically, when a large number of small producers have not been liberated from backwardness and ignorance, industrialization and modernization have not been realized, and excessive social wealth has not emerged. At the micro-level, the commercialization of the labor force does not absolutely conflict with labor's primary status. At the socialist stage, the masters should be those who can consciously lead society to focus on the development of productivity, for which they are willing to make necessary sacrifices. "Masters of society" should not simply be equated with those who control servants; and the "commercialization of the labor force" should be connected with the people's "right to freely choose a job." How can he or she be a master without the right to choose his or her occupation and work place? In this way, we can see no contradiction. The theory of surplus value is a complete theory created by Marx to expose the exploitation of labor by capital. I maintain that under socialist conditions surplus value still exists, in a form once called "surplus products." As materialists, we should not try to avoid such words as taboo. How can a socialist society accumulate capital and expand reproduction without surplus value? The crux of the matter is the question of who will finally possess the surplus value.

—*Third, Free Entry into Production and Operations Is an Important Requirement of the Market Economy.*

Without free entry, there can be no market allocation of resources, no real competition, and consequently no real market economy. In the past, the government monopolized many sectors including energy, communications, and finance. The drawbacks produced by the government monopoly, such as the waste of resources and a worsening structure, have gradually been recognized by the people. Now restrictions on investment in energy and communications have been relaxed and non-government enterprises, such as privately owned and foreign-invested enterprises, are allowed to be created. in the future, restrictions on other aspects will also be relaxed. The difficulty in this regard is the contradiction between "free entry" and "the leading position of the public economy." Regarding this question we need, first of all, a change of concepts. Under a market economy, except for a small number of special enterprises, the "leading role" or "main body" should not mean those enterprises owned by the whole people or collectively owned enterprises, but should be represented by the shares held by state-owned and collectively owned enterprises. As for this, the "state participation system" as practiced in Italy provides a good example. Free entry may be represented as an operation with single ownership, but it is largely practiced by free shareholding. As a matter of fact, such enterprises adopt different kinds of ownership. Secondly, a small number of enterprises or trades which have specific significance to the national economy and people's livelihoods, such as the central banks and most advanced military industries, should still be subject to state monopoly. But in operations, these enterprises or trades should

adopt a system of entrusting agents, strictly separating government administration from enterprise management. They should
also conduct independent financial management, which will be
beneficial to the healthy operation of the market economy.

—*Fourth, the Opening (or Flexibility) of Market Signals Is
a Hallmark of the Market Economy.*

In light of social costs and the relations between supply and
demand, market signals, including prices, wages, interest rates
and exchange rates, fluctuate freely and accelerate the readjustment of allocations of resources and products. This is none other
than the soul of a market economy.

This requirement, as well as market legislation, which is not
discussed in this article, does not conflict in principle with the
basic system of socialism. With the deepening of reform, these
requirements will assume their places step by step.

In a word, though the market economy was born during the
evolution of capitalism, it is, by nature, the outcome of large-scale
socialized production. Socialism, also based on large-scale socialized production, may very well be compatible with the market
economy.

III. Operation: Guarding Against Some Errors

Transformation from a highly centralized planned economy
to a socialist market economy cannot be accomplished in one step.
People need time to gradually alter their concepts; and economic
and social structures require time to reform and develop step by
step. During this transition period, errors and mistakes can hardly
be avoided. At present, we should pay particular attention to the
following aspects:

—*First, Preventing a Situation Where Everybody Is Engaged
in Commercial Activities, and Adhering to the Division of Labor.*

Highly advanced division of labor gave birth to the market
economy. In return, the market economy has promoted division
of labor. Socialization and specialization of production constitutes two sides of the same phenomenon. The more highly developed the division of labor, the higher the socialization of produc-

tion. "The level of productivity of a nation is most obviously represented by the degree of division of labor in that nation."

In the transitional period from a planned economy to a market economy, it is normal that some people's jobs will be readjusted or changed; and some people will find themselves holding second jobs. However "everyone, of all trades and professions engaged in commercial activities," is by no means the focus of the reform. On the contrary, this would be a step backward for the social division of labor. A phenomenon worth special attention is the tendency for speculation by economic regulation and control departments. Such retrogression and confusion will lead to three major harmful results. The first is causing harm to the long-term interests of the nation, such as a serious "education crisis"—loss of teachers and the new "idea of the uselessness of study." The second is the loss of state-owned capital. Some state-owned enterprises will be turned into collectively owned ones, and then into private enterprises. And the third is that income disparity between individuals and regions will be dramatically widened. These harmful results will endanger the stability of our society! In the course of utilizing the market economy, we must not allow unrestrained freedom—"defying the laws of man and the divine." We are now carrying out reform of the socialist market economy in 20th-century China, not in 19th-century Europe.

The market economy is a historical outcome of production socialization; however, production socialization is a result of the division of labor in society. "All people in a country engaged in commercial activities" is actually the isostructuralization of the division of labor. Therefore we hold that the planned economy in China should be transferred into a market economy in an orderly fashion. We must work out market laws and readjust the policies on the distribution of income among people of every occupation and status. Only in this way can we enable the development of the market economy to benefit the growth of social productivity and social stability as well as the long-term interests of our nation.

—Second, Preventing a "Laissez-Faire Attitude" and Adhering to "Changing Government's Functions".

Some people hold that establishing a socialist market economy requires neither planning nor administrative organs. They believe the government may say to an enterprise: "I won't interfere," and that an enterprise may say to the government: "Don't interfere!" In fact, these people are confusing a modern market economy with a classical market economy.

A market economy with unrestrained freedom was the market economy of free capitalist stage in the distant past when Adam Smith's "unseen hand" was thought to dominate everything. But after the capitalist world experienced one economic crisis after another, especially after the Great Depression at the end of the 1920s shook the entire capitalist system, even the capitalist countries realized that a pure market economy could not effectively guarantee balanced development. And, moreover, a completely unrestrained economy could cause tremendous damage to capital resources and social stability. The emergence of Keynesian economics after the depression was an objective requirement for a major capitalist reform. In the contemporary era, the economies of all capitalist countries are regulated to some degree by their governments. Even in the United States, a country known for its objections to a planned economy, government regulation of agriculture is by no means weaker than in other capitalist countries practising planned regulation and control. This has become characteristics of the market economy.

The reform objective of China's socialist market economic system is a modern market economy, regulated by both an "unseen hand" and a "seen hand," with the former as the basis and the latter as guidance. The "seen hand" shall be used to guide the market's regulations and information, regulating and controlling the "unseen hand"; and the "unseen hand" will be used to regulate enterprise activities and the operations of the entire economy. This may also be called a government-guiding market economy.

In the capitalist world, the economic models of the Republic of Korea and Japan are good examples. Both of them have basically adopted a government-guiding market economy, the former being a market economy regulated and controlled by the government, and the latter a market economy guided by government economic planning and industrial policies.

—*Third, Preventing "Not Seeing the Wood for the Trees" and "Adhering to Other Necessary Reforms."*

A market economy is not just a question of the "market." There is currently an oversimplified explanation that equates the market economy with the "market." In practice, many people are interested in market construction, but pay little attention to the requirements of a market economy. Moreover, their understanding of the market is restricted to a narrow definition as a place for the exchange of commodities. They maintain that setting up markets, such as exchanges, wholesale, and specialized and comprehensive markets everywhere, means the expansion of the market economy. Of course, the founding of these markets is indispensable to a market economy, but does not comprehend its full scope.

Though a market economy is mainly characterized by market regulation of economic operations and the allocation of economic resources, its implications are far beyond the market itself. Market regulation of economic operations and the allocation of resources requires not only the market, but also many other conditions, including the establishment of market order, market competitiveness, a supply-and-demand mechanism, and the perfection of price forming mechanisms. Without these conditions, a market economy cannot really be established, no matter how many visible markets there are. Along with the development of a market economy, a great increase in the number of locations for commodity exchange is no doubt necessary. However, it is the relations between supply and demand and between exchanges, and the allocation of resources, rather than locations themselves that regulate the market economy. Therefore if we want to establish a socialist market economy, we must stress restructuring economic operational mechanisms, and we can accomplish this through the reform of economic structures. For example, the formation of the market's main body involves reform of the entire ownership and ownership system structure of enterprises, including rectifying relations between enterprises and governments.

Therefore, if we want to develop the socialist market economy we must make efforts to deepen economic structural reform.

Up to now, the tide of the Chinese reform has mainly addressed the economic system. Since the idea of a socialist market economy was first conceived, people have mainly paid attention to economic activities and the economic system, and little attention to other aspects. However, delayed reform of other aspects will inevitably hinder advances toward a socialist market economy.

Marx once said that with the change of economic foundations, the superstructure would evolve quickly or slowly, which is a universal rule known to everybody. Doubtless the existing superstructure is basically compatible with the traditional planned economy. Now as we develop the socialist market economy, the changes in the economic foundations will inevitably call for corresponding reforms in law and politics, and the rethinking of ideological concepts.

As previously stated, the establishment of enterprises as the main bodies of the market means a change in the relations between enterprises and the government. To realize this change, the setting up of government organizations, the division of functions, the personnel system, and economic behavior will all undergo profound revolutions. Even after the separation of the functions of the government from those of the enterprises, the government must retain the right to control, coordinate and supervise economic life. If there are no restrictive measures, and if we cannot halt the commercialization of power by which government officials now profit, it is impossible to guarantee and orderly socialist market economy. Therefore the development of a market economy requires speeding up economic legislation and political democratization. The transition from a traditional planned economy to a socialist market economy will inevitably lead to a redistribution of the people's interests, which may bring about political conflicts. In order to guarantee an equitable interest distribution required for the development of the socialist economy, we must readjust the relations between people with the aid of the law. Therefore we must speed up the reform of legislation. A change in man's social being requires the reform of his thinking. What are the moral principles and behavioral norms required by a socialist market economy? These are questions worthy of further study.

In brief, establishing the socialist market economy is a very complicated social project. We must be prepared for a "persistent ideological war"; and many reforms and development measures are needed. We are certain that with the efforts of several generations, an utterly new socialist economic system will surely be established in China.

Notes

1. Critique of the Gotha Program from *Selected Works by K. Marx and F. Engels* Vol. 3.
2. From *Dictionary of Modern Economics*, p. 275, the Chinese translation edition.

Strengthening Macrocontrol in the Transition to a Market Economy

Li Jingwen
Director of a Research Institute of
the Chinese Academy of Social Sciences

I. Why Does China Emphasize Strengthening Macrocontrol?

After hitting a low in 1989-1990 and rising again in 1991, the Chinese economy entered a period of high-speed growth in 1992. The economic growth rate that year reached 12.8 percent, and quotas for both the economic and social development sectors were completely fulfilled, thus grabbing the attention of the entire world. Economic growth was even more vigorous in the first half of 1993, with the GNP 14.1 percent greater than in the same period the previous year. Based on our estimates and qualitative analysis of the macroeconomic model, the economic growth rate in the latter half of this year will slow, but still will be around 12.5 percent for the entire year, and around 10 percent in 1994. A bumper summer harvest also has been reaped and the rural economy continues to grow, while the total industrial output value was 25.1 percent greater than in the same period last year. Total losses suffered by state-owned enterprises dropped by 16.5 percent, while total retail sales were 21.6 percent greater than for the same period last year. After allowing for price rises the actual increase was over 10 percent. According to market research of 582 industrial consumer items in the first half of 1993, the supply was greater than the demand for 96 percent of the items, while supply lagged behind demand for only 4 percent. The income of the people continued to rise, and total workers' wages were 21.6

percent higher than in the same period last year, or rose by over 10 percent after allowing for price rises. Wage disbursement rose by 35 percent as compared with the same period last year. This shows that the growth of real income of workers and staff members was faster than wage growth.

Along with the rapid growth of the economy come problems that merits serious attention, such as excessive investment in fixed assets and too many new projects. In the first half of this year, the total investment in fixed assets for the entire country was 61 percent greater than in the corresponding period of 1992, and the number of new projects nearly doubled. The structure of investment was irrational and the problem of investment in the "three heats" (real estate, stock and development areas) was even more serious. For example, in the first eight months of 1993, the total investment in real estate was close to 90 billion yuan, more than one fifth of the investment in fixed assets. The financial situation was grim and currency was overissued. Financial and banking institutions were engaged in interbank loans in violation of regulations, and a number of non-financial institutions lent money and raised funds illegally, and also raised interest rates in disguised forms, some as high as 30 percent. As a result, a large amount of money was invested in real estate, stock speculation and the opening of development areas in a blind way, while urgently needed funds for major construction projects under the state plan could not be carried through as scheduled. Fifty billion yuan more in currency was put into circulation in the first half of this year than in the same period last year. According to the usual practice in China, the money put into circulation at the beginning of the year should have been withdrawn from circulation by the end of June, but this was not done this year. On top of all this, the transportation bottleneck became more acute, inflationary pressure increased, and the cost of living index rose sharply. Between January and July, the retail price index of social commodities rose by 10.8 percent while the cost of living index for urban residents rose by 16.6 percent.

Confronted with this situation, the state perhaps has several choices. First, taking a laissez-faire attitude, and leave it to the automatic regulation of the market. According to the market theory of classical Western economics, the market automatically reaches its best state of effective allocation of resources through and "invisible hand" and full competition, thus achieving high-speed economic growth in good order. However, the historical experience of many countries in developing a market economy has long demonstrated that full competition in its strictest sense has never appeared. Because monopoly and new protectionism always obtain, the possibility of achieving smooth economic growth through automatic regulation by the market is not possible. If the Chinese government does not take macrocontrol measures to solve the problems now emerging, the economy will continue to grow blindly and contradictions will become more acute, finally leading to overall economic disorder, acute inflation and a serious undermining of the economy. This is often seen in Western economies, and China has had similar experiences. So this choice is both unrealistic and undesirable.

Second, adopting the administrative control measures which have been used in the planned economy, such as cutting investment, reducing the number of construction projects, readjusting mandatory planned quotas, decreasing the allocations of state funds and materials, and lowering wages and employment. If these are done, the economy may gradually improve, but vitality will be sapped and production will decline sharply. It often takes one to several years to restore production to its original level through readjustment, thus greatly delaying progress in developing the macroeconomy. This practice has played a role in China historically, but it cannot and should not be reconsidered at present, or in the future.

The third choice is the only choice possible at present. That is, promoting and strengthening macrocontrol under market economic conditions. The purpose of macrocontrol is to restrict the negative effects of the market, make up for market deficiencies, promote the process of regulation through the market, and adjust and alleviate the contradictions and problems related to high-speed economic growth. The purpose of China's efforts to strengthen macrocontrol, starting in June 1993, has been to improve the economic structure by consolidating financial order and improving the economic environment so that the industrial structure will be optimized and the economy will grow still better and faster.

It must be made clear that China's present stress on strengthening macrocontrol is not only a temporary measure to cope with present problems, but an objective requirement for changing the economic system. At present, the Chinese economy is in transition from a planned economy to a modern market economy. In order to reduce the friction in this shift from an old to a new system, it is necessary to strengthen macrocontrol to some degree in order to facilitate a smooth and quick transition.

As I understand it, the modern market economy is based on highly developed social productive forces, a high degree of socialization of the economy, and closer economic ties among enterprises, industries, regions and countries in the gradual formation of a world market system. The formation, development and maturity of the modern market economic system has been a long process, and was gradually established between the 1920s and the 1930s. This economy is an outstanding achievement of human civilization. It has the general features of the market economy, namely, the role of the market covering social life and occupying the key position in the allocation of resources. At the same time, as a result of the high development of socialized mass production, it is a market economy under macro guidance. This is because in modern society with rapidly developing science and technology, and high social productive forces, the economic and technical ties among enterprises, departments, regions and countries are becoming closer, though they remain independent bodies with their own interests and goals. Contradictions and friction among them are unavoidable, especially when economic development is not normal. Whether the economy is in recession or overheated, these contradictions and frictions become obviously acute and may even undermine the entire chain of economic ties, leading to an economic collapse when they become serious enough. Therefore, it is an inherent requirement of economic development to adjust and change economic imbalances through regulation and macrocontrol by the government. The systematic economic theories of

John Maynard Keynes in Western economics on interference and macrocontrol by the government were developed and acknowledged in the capitalist world economic crisis of 1929-1933, and at the same time provided the theoretical basis for the New Deal of American President Franklin Roosevelt.

The socialist market economy is also a modern market economy established on the basis of socialized mass production. it must not only give full play to the basic role of the market in the allocation of resources, but must also strengthen division of labor and coordination among enterprises, departments and localities through macrocontrol. Moreover, as socialism stresses state and collective interests, it is even more vital to establish an effective macrocontrol system. After the Chinese government adopted the macrocontrol measures of July 1993, the initial results became apparent in only one month. Interbank loans in violation of regulations were partly retrieved, the illegal raising of funds basically checked, the drop in bank savings during the second quarter of the year began to rise in July and August, the exchange rate between Renminbi yuan and the U.S. dollar has become stable, and the prices of consumer goods leveled off. All this demonstrates that the Chinese economy began to grow in a healthy direction once macrocontrol measures were adopted. Of course, strengthening macrocontrol is not the same as returning to the old road of using administrative measures. Rather, it is an appropriate means of adjusting the main sectors of the economy, alleviating the contradictions among them, and enabling the development of the macroeconomy to better embody the goals of socialist production. Although in the course of strengthening macrocontrol some building projects (mostly in overheated industries such as real estate, development areas, and some processing industries already over-producing) will be curtailed, delayed or even halted, some products will be unmarketable or their prices will fall. And many enterprises are short of circulating capital and affected by a triangle of debt. Macrocontrol measures are not necessarily applied to all industries, enterprises or departments, but mostly to those industries with overproduction, while bottleneck industries and important infrastructure projects are being strengthened. Moreover, along with the normalization and standardization of the economic order, the people and all industries and trades in the country will benefit from such measures. It is expected that the Chinese economy will continue to grow in a still better economic and social environment in the fourth quarter of 1993 and 1994.

II. Strengthening the Role of Macrocontrol in Establishing the Socialist Market Economy

Chinese and foreign scholars have published many brilliant accounts of China's intension to establish a socialist market economy. Here, I would like to give a brief summary of the views expressed by some scholars at the Chinese Academy of Social Sciences when the strategy was worked out for the establishment of the special economic zone on Hainan Island in the spring of 1988.

In September 1987, the Central Committed of the Communist Party of China and the State Council decided to make Hainan Island a province and turn it into the largest special economic zone in China. Preparations began in October that same year, and the first task was to formulate strategy for the economic development of Hainan Island. The Preparatory Group for the Founding of Hainan Province invited the Chinese Academy of Social Sciences to undertake this assignment. The academy sent an exploratory group, headed by Professor Liu Guoguang, to Hainan Island. Within two months the group proposed a strategy for the economic development of the island. Their report was completed and submitted on January 10, 1988 and published by the Economic Management Publishing House in June 1988. A large portion of this report was devoted to the problems of reform. For the first time, Chinese economists systematically discussed the necessity and importance of introducing the socialist market economic system in one province and formulated the basic framework. The strategy pointed out: "Reform is the key to making Hainan prosperous.... We propose the introduction of the socialist market economic system under the leadership of the Communist Party on Hainan Island. This market economy is guided...." It also explicitly described the framework for the socialist market economy, saying, "1. establishment of a multi-ownership structure; 2. formation of a perfect open market system; and 3. introduction of macroregulation." It also explicitly pointed out that "in introducing the socialist market economy, the government must not give up and weaken its administration and regulation of the economy, but strengthen and improve administration and regulation. However, the mode of administration and regulation is different...." Although there has been much progress in the study of the questions raised by this report in recent years, there has not been much change in the basic auguments. It is clear that we already regard the necessity of macrocontrol as one of the basic features of the socialist market economy.

In the socialist market economy, macrocontrol is necessary and important chiefly because the market is not all-powerful.

Under the market economy, the market is the chief allocator of resources in various spheres of social production, distribution, circulation and consumption. Through the competition of the market these resources flow to the enterprises, departments and localities with the best economic performances. Therefore, in establishing the socialist market economy in China, the most important factor is to establish economic operation mechanisms and modes of resource allocation on the basis of the market. While this system is being built, the relationship between the state and the market must be carefully handled. On the one hand, the state should leave all economic problems which can be solved by the market to the market, including the supply and demand of commodities, fluctuating prices, and the circulation of commodities. They should be regulated through the market, as this alone can provide conditions which allow the market to operate properly. On the other hand, since the market is not all-powerful, its shortcomings and deficiencies should be rectified through proper government regulation. The government's role and purposes ought to be:

1. Establishing market regulations. Market activities require rules and order. Apart from those laid down for market activities, the state or localities must formulate unified methods and regulations so that these activities are also standardized.

2. Stopping monopolies from undermining market functions. Monopolies tend to undermine fair competition, and lead to a breakdown or distortion of the regulatory functions of the market. This calls for the formulation of anti-monopoly laws and regulations, and supervision over their implementation to ensure fair competition.

3. Solving external problems. External problems refer to those economic activities which result in benefits or losses for people outside these activities. When they are not included in the cost and price of the product, the problems arising therefrom can only be solved through government regulation. For example, if an enterprise does not pay attention to environmental concerns, or make vigorous efforts to solve these problems in their desire to increase profits, this can only be handled through laws and regulations formulated by the government.

4. Solving the problem of blind economic growth. The plurality of economic interests in the market will lead to redundantcy in production, investment, marketing, purchasing and transportation among different enterprises and regions, resulting in unbalanced supply and demand. This calls for governmental guidance, through macroeconomic and industrial policies in particular.

5. Correcting the unfair distribution of income. Under the market economy, the distribution of wealth among enterprises and individuals is inequitable. Unfair distribution and greater differences between the rich and the poor are now a common sight. This problem becomes even more acute when monopolies are allowed to form. Therefore, the government must take action and implement correct policies on income and tax to ensure a fair and relatively equal distribution of income.

6. Reducing the losses arising from these subsequent regulations. Market regulation is a subsequent regulation. Great damages and losses appear during the process of the formation of

prices, information feedback, the input of human, material and financial resources, the output of products and labor services and consumption. Therefore, the government must organize the parties concerned to analyze future economic development trends and put forward plans to coordinate the relationship between immediate interests and long-term interests in guiding the effective development of enterprises.

7. Coordinating the material interests of the state, collectives, enterprises and individuals so that attention is given to both local and overall interests without harming these interests.

Therefore, in the course of structuring the market economic system, we must not only emphasize the role of the market in allocating resources, but also stress by the government's macrocontrol over economic activities.

The situation in China at present shows that the state's role in strengthening macrocontrol has become more evident because the degree of market development is still relatively low. As a whole, it is in the elementary stage of development. Although the commodity market has taken an initial shape, that market is still in disarray, and operations remain disordered. The market of production factors is still in the budding stage, the labor market has developed very slowly because no answer has been found to the theoretical question of whether labor is a commodity, and also because of the residence system. Also, the capital market has not yet been fully developed because the commodity nature of capital has not been completely determined. There is still disagreement over some points, financial reform has not been completely carried out, and land and technical markets remain abnormal. Under such circumstances, it is difficult to give the market full play. This situation requires that the government continue to play a role in economic operations and participate in and promote market development.

III. The Objectives of Macrocontrol

The general objective of macrocontrol should be to make the economy stable and able to grow at a relatively high speed.

All countries with a market economy take the primary goal of macrocontrol as the ensuring of stable growth. Therefore, when the market is sluggish and the economy slows down, it is necessary to adopt an expansive policy to stimulate economic revival. When the economy over-expands or "overheats," a tightening policy should then be adopted. This policy was once effective in Western countries. However, since the 1970s the economy has grown slowly in the West, and these policies have not worked. The smooth development of a socialist market economy in China also calls for stable economic growth and fewer fluctuations in economic development. Sharp rises and declines should be avoided, for this is the foundation of continued healthy economic development. Therefore, the goal of macrocontrol should be first of all to maintain a virtual balance between total social demand and total social supply. Of course, opinions are still divided on the definition of "basic balance." At present, it is generally believed that it would be the best if the total supply is slightly larger than the total demand (around 5 percent), and this would be beneficial to economic stability. Moreover, because China has a weak economic foundation, a low starting point, but great potential, in order to narrow the gap with developed countries, increase overall national power, and improve the life of the Chinese people, all localities and departments have shown a strong desire to hasten economic development. Therefore, for a considerably long period of time into the future, the goal of macrocontrol should be not only to maintain stable economic growth, but also to achieve highly effective and high-speed growth of the economy while retaining the basic balance between social demand and social supply.

These goals are directly related to the optimization of the financial structure. Only when a total balance is achieved on the basis of a rational structure is it possible to achieve good economic results and ensure that stable, highly effective and high-speed economic development will continue, at least with fewer fluctuations. At present, economic development in China is in the stage of large-scale industrialization and transition to the "well-off" level with a per capita GDP of around 1,000 US dollars (based on the 1980 exchange rates). The role of technological progress is steadily growing, the demand for infrastructure and foundation industries is growing, large numbers of agricultural producers are shifting to nonagricultural industries, and the people's consumption is gradually shifting from quantitative growth to qualitative improvement. All this has made the demand for the adjustment and optimization of the industrial structure more urgent than ever. Moreover, the international economy and technology are developing rapidly, the tendency of internationalization and regionalization of the economy has become more obvious, the process of adjusting and upgrading the international industrial structure is being advanced, and the demand to bring the Chinese economy into line with the world economy is pressing. All this has created new and higher demands for the optimization of China's industrial structure. Therefore, the optimization of the industrial structure must be regarded as an important goal of macrocontrol.

It has been argued that in order to balance the Chinese economy the government should adopt the policy of "increasing the supply and checking the demand." This is reasonable in one sense. Because resources are always limited, the problem has always been in short supply. However, under the market economy, supply and demand should be regulated chiefly by the market. Moreover, they influence and condition each other. If there is no demand, or if demand is weak, supply will lose its own role. The increase of supply should also be guided and decided by market demand. Therefore, the government can only give some guidance and control on the basis of the action of the market. According to the theory of control, control does not mean restriction, but is meant to keep the system sound through the functions of automatic regulation, coordination and manipulation of the feedback system. Of course, the process of regulation also includes checks to some degree, but chiefly it is not restriction, but dredging, so that the economy operates in a coordinated way. Therefore, in controlling the macroeconomy in China, I am in favor of the policy of "increasing the supply and dredging the demand" to urge the supply to constantly increase according to market demands and adjust the demand from time to time according to market signals about the supply of the resources so that they coordinate and promote each other to create the basis for the coordinated operation of the macroeconomy.

Prevention of an excessively high inflation rate is another important goal of macrocontrol. Although slight inflation is unavoidable in any country, excessively high or galloping inflation can have an extremely bad influence on the economy, and there are many such examples. Some Latin American countries developed their economies by heavy borrowing and high inflation. In the 1980s, these countries suffered galloping inflation, as high as three- and four-digit in some cases. As a result, their economies became stagnant, the growth of production could not meet the new demands of population growth, and in some countries there was negative economic decline. In China, as bank credit became too large and too much money was put into circulation, serious consequences ensued. For example, more money has been put into circulation each year than the previous year since 1985: 19.5 billion yuan in 1985, 23 billion yuan in 1986, 23.7 billion yuan in 1987, and 67.96 billion yuan in 1988, or an increase of 24.7 percent, 23.4 percent, 19.4 percent and 46.7 percent over the previous year respectively. In 1978, the money in circulation amounted to only 21.2 billion yuan, but this rose to 145.4 billion yuan by 1987. This was partly because the economic scale expanded year after year, and the degree of economic activity rose continuously, but the increases in the amount of money issued and circulated were greatly higher than the economic growth rates. For example, between 1978 and 1987, the total output value of industry and agriculture rose by 130 percent and the total retail sales of social commodities by 230 percent, but the money in circulation rose by 690 percent. As a result, both investment and consumption were inflated in 1988, and the retail price index also rose from 8.8 percent in 1985, 6 percent in 1986 and 7.3 percent in 1987 to 18.5 percent in 1988. This was followed by period of overall tightening of the economy in the subsequent years, thus dealing a heavy blow to the development of the national economy. These lessons must be kept in mind. Therefore, we think it is undesirable to use high inflation to promote high-speed economic growth. In accordance with the economic strength of the country and the ability of the people to withstand higher inflation rates, one of the goals of macrocontrol in China is to keep the inflation rate within 10 percent. Once it surpasses this warning line, macrocontrol should be a strengthened to halt any further rise. For this reason, it is essential to control the growth rate of the money supply. Factors affecting this include the economic growth rate, the price growth rate, the speed of money circulation and the quantity of money needed to meet marketing needs. There must be an overall analysis of these factors to determine a reasonable money supply, the amount of credit, and interest rates. These are all important factors influencing the macroeconomy.

Moreover, maintaining a balance of international revenue and expenditure is another important goal of macrocontrol. For China, which is opening wider to the outside world, it is most necessary to keep a slightly favorable balance of international revenue and expenditure, and have a requisite foreign exchange reserve. This involves further reform of the foreign trade system and the implementation of a reasonable foreign capital import policy. It is necessary to establish an open economic system throughout the country, and build export-oriented economies with export trade as the mainstay in certain areas. At the same time we must push forward an import replacement policy to promote domestic industries. Since 1992, foreign investment has risen by a large margin, but at the same time a considerable amount of domestic funds has gone out of the country. In import and export trade, export growth was slow while import growth was high, and an unfavorable balance of trade was registered in the first half of the year. All these problems must be solved through macrocontrol.

IV. Macrocontrol Methods

Macrocontrol in the socialist market economic system should use the economic lever as the chief means of indirect control. This is different in essence from administrative measures and direct control employed under the planned economy.

One of the major defects of China's old system was the direct administration and control of enterprises by the government, which regarded enterprises as appendages of the government, exercising "control, check and pressure" over them and depriving them of the right to make independent business decisions. As a result, enterprises were unable to assume sole responsibility for their own profits and losses or seek their own development, but relied on the government for everything. Facts have proved that this system is a failure. Under the new system, macrocontrol is no longer exercised directly over the enterprises, but rather indirectly. Its core is to truly give the independent commodity producers and sellers the power, place the market law of value at the center of regulations, and keep the government's macrocontrol at the service of and in the interest of the development of the market system for the optimum allocation of resources, and in the interest of giving play to the enthusiasm and creativity of both enterprises and individuals.

The chief means of exercising macrocontrol is to use the economic lever and handle affairs according to market rules. The economic levers include financial credit, taxes, income distribution and prices. They link all aspects and the economic interests of the main bodies of the interests in the form of value, and are the chief economic means used by the government to regulate economic activities. These economic levers have the following functions: One, the function of regulation, including regulation of the relationships among the different links of social reproduction (production, distribution, exchange and consumption) and among different industries, and the regulation of the interest relationships among the state, enterprises, collective units and individuals; two, the function of control, namely the use of the economic levers of tax rates, interest rates and prices to guide the economic activities closer to the general goal of the state (or society or locality); three, the function of business accounting, namely the use of the economic levers of prices, taxes, wages and profits; and four, the function of supervision, namely the use of bookkeeping, auditing, and bank supervision to supervise the economic activities of enterprises and individuals and their relations with government, staff members and workers and concerned enterprises in accordance with the laws and regulations.

Of all economic levers, the most important are financial and revenue policies and plans.

1. Financial policies are of special importance in the course of structuring the socialist market economy. Finance means the borrowing and lending of funds among banks, or is the general term for the circulation of those funds. It is composed of two parts, namely money circulation and credit. Therefore, financial policies have two focal points: The money policy, namely the policy of the central bank controlling the money supply; and the credit policy, namely the bank policy of granting credits. Credit is the general term for borrowing and lending activities with repayment as the condition. Its special function is employ idle funds by lending them to economic entities (enterprises and individuals) which are in need of them without changing their ownership. In China, the organization and regulation of the circulation of money, and the mobilization and distribution of credit funds are facilitated chiefly through the banks. With the establishment and development of the market economy in China, finance and banks are becoming more and more important in the stabilization and development of the economy, and the demands on them become greater and greater. First, as the source of the funds for investment changes from state allocations to bank credits, banks are urged to raise more funds and give better play to the advantages of lending and borrowing money among the banks indirectly; second, banks are urged to lay more emphasis on exercising control and supervision over enterprises and create conditions for invigorating the economy; and third, banks are urged to quickly set up the financial control system through the simultaneous use of credit plans, banking policies, interest rates, exchange rates and deposit reserves to strengthen the role of macrocontrol.

With the deepening of economic reform and the acceleration of economic growth, financial reform has become the center of economic reform in China. At present, the Chinese government is preparing to carry out the overall reform of the financial system. We think that the goal of this reform should be to gradually achieve a plurality of financial institutions and a diversity of financial instruments, allowing the market to determine interest rates and thereby exercising indirect macrocontrol. The following measures should be implemented: 1. transforming the present People's Bank of China into a central bank responsible for issuing money, formulating financial policy and supervising its implementation; 2. reforming the present financial organizational setup and establishing a financial organizational system which separates policy-related banking from commercial banking, with state-owned banks as the mainstay and the existence of other banking institutions, separating commercial business from policy-related business and short-term loans from long-term investment, transforming the existing specialized banks into commercial banks, establishing policy-related banks or long-term development credit banks, positively developing trust, leasing and stock institutions, continuing to develop the urban credit societies, and taking the formation of urban cooperative banks into consideration. To meet the needs of opening wider to the outside world and learn from the financial experience of other countries, some foreign banks should be allowed to operate in China; 3. establishing a unified and open financial market with competition and strict management. Proportional control should be exercised over the classified assets and liabilities of all kinds of financial institutions. The adoption of these measures will vigorously allow the market to determine interest rates along with the introduction of a deposit reserve system and open market business, finally leading to the gradual formation of an indirect control system for the money supply and giving further play to the important role of financial credit in the macrocontrol system.

2. Revenues and taxes. Revenues are an important tool with which state power is used to concentrate and distribute part of the national income to meet state expenditures and push forward economic construction. It reflects the interest relations among the state, collectives, enterprises and individuals, and between the

central government and the local governments. Chinese revenues and taxes also have the mission of stabilizing the economy, and also play an important role in promoting the optimization of the industrial structure, the improvement of the economic performances and the smooth development of the economy through fair taxation and competition.

In the course of establishing the socialist market economy, Chinese revenues have the following functions:

1) Exercising total control and promoting total balance. Through taxation and the state budget, the government directly influences total consumption and total investment, and regulates economic growth speed and the change of the structure so as to maintain a basic balance between total social demand and total social supply, and bring about the healthy growth of the economy.

2) Embodying the state's policies on industries and local development through different tax rates to strengthen the pillar and bottleneck industries and check the industries with overproduction, speed up economic development in the special economic zones and certain localities, and support economic development in the old revolutionary base areas, areas inhabited by ethnic minorities, frontier areas and poor areas.

3) Giving play to the function of revenues in the redistribution of the national wealth and adjusting the relationships between the central government and the local authorities, and among the state, enterprises, collectives and individuals so that they are beneficial to the integral and long-term interests of the state. Therefore, the importance of state revenues and taxation must be fully recognized. It is true that the previous practice of "big part for revenues and small part for banking" is not correct, but the present talk of "small part for revenues and big part for banking" is also incorrect. The correct way should be the equal importance of the use of revenues and banking, their mutual support, and interaction with each other.

The effect financial policies have on economic operations is mainly one of stimulating or reducing the scale of economic operations through the increase and decrease of state revenues and expenditures. When the market is slack and demand is low, the government can increase its expenditures on the building of new projects to extend the scale of construction, or reduce tax rates to increase the effective demand. When the economy is overheated and purchasing power is too strong, the government can cut down its purchase of labor services as commodities to lower social purchasing power, or increase taxes to reduce the purchasing power of public money.

In order to give full play to the function of the important economic lever of revenues and taxes, it is necessary to speed up reform of financial and tax policies. First of all, replacing the "revenue quota system" with the "tax division system." Before the start of economic reform, China adopted a highly centralized system of state monopoly on revenues and expenditures, which seriously restricted the initiative of local governments and enterprises. In the early 1980s, China began the practice of "taking meals in different canteens," and gradually formed the system of dividing revenues and expenditures between the central government and the local governments with fixed proportions for sharing the extra revenues (or subsidies) which remained unchanged for five years instead of changing the proportions every year. This was a big step forward in the reform of China's financial system. In 1985, the government proposed a new reform program of "dividing the tax categories, checking and fixing the revenues and expenditures, and setting quotas for the governments at different levels," and introduced the new practice of dividing total revenues between the central and local governments, specifically, different forms of quotas for progressive increases in revenues, fixed quotas for revenues to be turned over to the central government, and fixed quotas for the subsidies given by the central government to local governments. This system played a positive role in mobilizing the initiative of the local governments and ensuring increases in revenues. However, it also encouraged blockades among various localities and redundant construction, gradually diminishing the percentage of revenues for the central government (especially in the years of high inflation, the revenues turned over to the central government from the local governments did not increase progressively, but in fact decreased progressively), resulting in a serious shortage of funds at the disposal of the central government and greatly weakening its ability to exercise macrocontrol.

Therefore, the primary reform in the revenue and tax system should be to replace the system of setting revenue quotas for the local governments with a system dividing the scope of taxation at different governmental levels, and raising the percentage of revenues for the central government out of total revenues. First of all, classifying the sources of the basic revenues for the central and local governments according to tax categories, and classifying all taxes into central taxes, local taxes and taxes collected jointly by the central and local governments. For this purpose, two different lines of taxation should be set up, one for the central and one for local governments, with the central taxation bureaus collecting central taxes and joint taxes, while the local taxation bureaus collect local taxes. Secondly, dividing the scopes of expenditures according to their functions for the central and local governments, and on this basis granting to the local governments the power to handle their own expenditures. Third, establishing a system which shifts part of the central revenues into localities to help the local governments with financial shortages.

Moreover, it is necessary to solve the problem of a relatively low percentage of taxes going to the national income, the irrational structure of the taxation system, incomplete taxation laws and the scattered power to collect taxes. Possible solutions are to enlarge the tax base, lower the tax rates, perfect the tax laws and simplify the procedure of tax collection and control so that taxation is truly fair (the same treatment for all), neutral (creation of a tax environment to ensure fair competition in the market), simple (a tax system and methods of collection which the taxpayers will find easy to understand and observe), and internationally compatible. The concrete ideas are: (1) perfecting the indirect tax setup and establishing the circulating tax system with the added value tax as its main body; (2) establishing and perfecting the income tax system, and introducing a unified income tax rate for all enterprises with domestic investment and, correspondingly, abolishing the regulating tax for state-owned enterprises; and (3) perfecting the tax structure, gradually enlarging the scope of taxation, and introducing new tax categories such as social insurance tax, negotiable securities tax, capital gains tax, inheritance tax and gift tax.

3. Economic plans and industrial policy. To establish a market economy it is essential to abolish mandatory plans, but it is still necessary to have plans for guidance in directing and coordinating macroeconomic activities. Most of the quotas in this type of plan are not compulsory. It is a plan for making informed calculations and analysis for guidance. In this respect, Japan, France and other developed countries have a wealth of experience for reference. For example, Japan not only creates medium- and long-term plans, but also draws plans for implementing the budget. Its Economic Planning Agency is a very powerful planning instrument and the plans it proposes play an important role in Japan's economic growth. However, these countries implement only guidance plans, and chiefly rely on economic policies and economic levers to encourage enterprises to carry out these plans. After we establish a socialist market economy, we should also introduce similar guidance or policy plans. By establishing such a planning system, we can shift the focal point from the individual balance to the total balance, from control over total supply to control over total demand and its structure, and from setting planned quotas to making policies, thus combining planning with market flexibly.

Of all guidance policies, industrial policy has a place of special importance. The function of industrial policy is to remedy or make up for deficiencies in the market, support the industries which are to be developed, and restrict the industries which have to be restricted or eliminated so as to achieve the coordinated development of the entire national economy. If we rely on the market for regulation, the upgrading of industry is a slow process. Moreover, under the conditions of sharp international competition, in order to protect young industries at home and strengthen the superior industries, industrial policies and regional industrious policies are needed. Correct formulation and implementation of these policies is absolutely essential to the sustained and stable high-speed development of the national economy and the improvement of economic efficiency, and should become the core of the guidance plan. The Chinese government promulgated its first industrial policy outline in 1988, and is now organizing forces to formulate the state industrial policy outline for the 1990s.

In addition, income policy is also a concern for macroeconomic control. It is a means of government action to control wages and prices to check the speed of rising prices. Its purpose is to achieve full employment without inflation, or with low inflation. However, income policy alone does not work well, it must be used together with other control measures or it will arouse discontent among staff members and workers, affect their working enthusiasm and cause social instability.

The aforementioned macrocontrol measures, including the financial, revenue and tax, income and industrial structure policies and the guidance plan are all essential for making up market deficiencies, economic stability and coordinated and high-speed economic growth. They cannot be replaced one by the other, but are influenced and conditioned by each other. In different periods and under different conditions, they have different effects, but they play their role together in macroeconomic control in any given country. Therefore, they produce good results only when they cooperate with each other and are used in an overall way. The method of overall use and how much effort should be made to use them depends on the needs of economic development at the time. Both immediate and long-run efficacy should be taken into consideration. For example, when the economy is overheated, it is necessary to implement an economic tightening policy to force down the temperature of economic development, but it must be made sure that the economy will not decline too fast or the negative effect will possibly have negative effects on the long-term development of the entire economy. This is one of the difficult points, but one of the most important points in building a socialist market economy.

Emergence of the Market Economy and Income Distribution in China: A Comparison with the Japanese Experience

Ryoshin Minami
Professor of the Hitotsubashi University of Japan

I. Introduction

In this essay I would like to consider the widening income disparity in China and its possible effects on society with reference to the Japanese historical experience, including the prewar period. The emergence of the market economy in China has caused several serious problems. One of them is over-heating of the economy. Over-heating was due basically to the fact that the government lost power to control the economy, while indirect control does not yet work in this underdeveloped economic and financial system. The second problem is worsening income distribution reflected in a widening income differential between agriculture and industry. This widening income differential is due to the rapid growth of industry and the stagnation of agriculture.

It seems to me that neither government officials nor economists in China have paid a due attention to the second problem. Many economists, depending on the Kuznets hypothesis that income distribution tends to regress in the early stage of economic development, and in the later stage progress, claim that income distribution in China will improve in the future.[1] To me this claim seems too optimistic. The Kuznets hypothesis itself is controversial. Almost all studies of the various countries have been pursued with short-term perspectives, and historical studies, including the prewar period, are very limited. My recent scrutiny of Japanese history has revealed an applicability of the first part of the Kuznets hypothesis (income distribution tends to regress in the early stage of industrialization), and has revealed a limited applicability of the second part of the hypoothesis (income distribution tends to progress in the later stage).[2] Furthermore, my study suggests a possible relationship between worsening income distribution in the 1920s and 1930s and the social and political instability and the emergence of fascism and imperialism in the same period. China must become more aware of the problem of income distribution.

In Part II, changes in income distribution will be examined both in China and Japan, and in Part III, changes in the income differential between agriculture and industry are studied as a major factor affecting income distribution. In Part IV, I will summarize the conclusions in the previous sections and refer to the social implications of these conclusions.

II. Changes in Income Distribution

Because of a paucity of data, a study of income distribution comparable to one possible for developed countries is very limited. Table 1 shows Gini coefficients of China estimated by T. Mizoguchi and Y. Matsuda based on a family income and expenditure survey. Gini is decisively low compared to other developing economies, and rather comparable to developed countries (0.31-0.32 in 1985 and 1987 in Column A). However, this seems heavily underestimated.

This underestimation comes from a difficulty in the income data for urban households. Most urban employees work in state-run enterprises where wages are regulated by the government and bonuses vary little. However, if the Party and government officials, employees of enterprises with large welfare expenditures (for example free medical service) and other privileged groups are considered, the income distribution in urban areas is less equal than it might at first appear. One study shows that a high-ranking official with an annual reported salary of 3,000 yuan might actually earn more than 6,000 yuan when all the extra benefits are taken into account, including a car for personal use, spacious accommodations, high-quality medical care, servants paid for by the government and so forth.[3] Because it is almost impossible to ascertain the exact amount of these subsidies, Mizoguchi and Matsuda estimated Gini under alternative assumptions of subsidiary funds. The first assumption is that all urban households receive subsidiaries proportional to their income; the second assumption is that all households receive the same amount of subsidiary funds. Estimates of Gini under these assumptions are shown in columns B and C respectively. These adjusted estimates of Gini are larger than the original estimates in Column A.

Table 1　Gini Coefficient of Income Distribution in China

Assumptions on the distribution of subsidies	1985	1987
A. No subsidies	0.313	0.317
B. Proportional distribution	0.405	0.407
C. Equal distribution	0.377	0.367

Notes: Subsidies are assumed to be 80 percent of non-farming household income.

Sources: Estimates by Toshiyuki Mizoguchi and Yoshiro Matsuda. "A Comparative Study on Income Distribution in the People's Republic of China and India," in Mizoguchi (ed.), *Making Economies More Efficient and Equitable: Factors Determining Income Distribution*, Tokyo and London: Kinokuniya and Oxford University Press, 1991, p. 260.

This adjustment, however, is not enough because income for self-employed workers seems to be considerably under-enumerated. This group of people has emerged very rapidly, and has generary received high incomes, which tend to be under-reported in income surveys. Thus, we can say that income distribution is worse than that shown by the estimates in Table 1.

Table 2   Coefficient of Variation of Per Capita Consumption Among Provinces in China and the Ratio of Guizhou Province to Shanghai in Per Capita Consumption

	Coefficient of variation of per capita consumption	Ratio of Guizhou to Shanghai in per capita consumption
1984	0.327	0.35
1985	0.354	0.30
1986	0.366	0.29
1987	0.360	0.29
1988	0.384	0.25
1989	0.385	0.22
1990	0.380	0.23

Sources: Statistical Yearbook of China 1986-1992.

Because of a lack of estimates of Gini for recent years comparable to those in Table 1, we are proposing another kind of study. Table 2 gives the coefficient variation of per capita consumption for 30 administrative divisions (autonomous regions, provinces, and centrally administered municipalities). It shows a clear increase trend from 0.327 in 1984 to 0.380 in 1990. (A decrease from 1989 to 1990 may have been a result of the recession after the over-heating of 1989.) The ratio of Guizhou to Shanghai in per capita consumption, an index for the income differential between the poor and the rich districts, demonstrates a decrease for the same period, which supports the above conclusion of a widening income differential. In conclusion, there is no doubt that income distribution worsened during these recent years.[4]

Japan

It is well known that income distribution is more equal in contemporary Japan than in other countries, either developing and developed. Gini is from 0.34 to 0.36 since the 1960s until the 1980s (Table 3). However, this was not the case in prewar

Japan. There have been almost no substantial studies of income distribution in this period because of a lack of reliable income data. In this respect the *kosuwari-zei* (household-rated tax—a kind of local tax) data which is available in some villages, towns and cities from about 1922 until 1939, is worth attention because it provides us with income figures for individual tax payers, almost all households. I have collected this data from 150 villages, towns and cities and attempted to estimate income distribution in Japan as a whole for the three bench mark years, 1923, 1930 and 1937.

Table 3   Gini Coefficient of Income Distribution in Japan

(1)	1923	0.504
	1930	0.518
	1937	0.550
(2)	1956	0.313
	1962	0.382
(3)	1963	0.361
	1968	0.354
	1973	0.350
	1979	0.336
	1986	0.356

Sources: (1) Minami, Kim and yazawa, "Long-term Changes in Income Distribution," Table 4.

(2) Richard Wada, "Impact of Economic Growth on the Size Distribution of Income: The Postwar Experience of Japan," *Income Distribution, Employment and Economic Development in Southeast and East Asia,* Vol. 2, Tokyo and Manila: Japan Economic Research Center and Council for Asian Manpower Studies, 1975, p. 541.

(3) Yasuhiro Terasaki's estimates. Cited from Minami, *The Economic Development of Japan,* Table 11-7.

Strictly speaking, the income distribution of Japan has been estimated by combining two sets of income distribution, that for high-income classes and that for low- and medium-income classes. Income distribution for high-income classes was obtained from the *kojin shotoku-zei* (personal income tax—a kind of national tax) data; that is, income distribution for the families with an annual income of 1,500 yen or more who paid income tax. These families are about 5 percent of all households in the bench mark years. On the other hand, income distribution for low- and medium-income classes was estimated from the household-rated tax data in the 150 administration districts, under the assumption that their income distribution reflected the income distribution for low- and medium-income classes of all Japan.

From this estimation important conclusions can be obtained. First, Gini had an increasing tendency from 0.50 to 0.55 between 1923 and 1937 (Table 3). For the years until 1921 the availability and reliability of household-rated tax data was very limited. For this period, Gini was estimated only in 15 villages and towns. It was 0.475 for 1891-1900, 0.505 for 1901-1910 and 0.555 for 1911-1921.[5] Therefore we may conclude that the tendency of worsening income distribution continued from the end of the last century. This trend in entire prewar period seems to be explained by considering two aspects. 1) With the existence of surplus labor in agriculture and the low-productivity sector of non-agriculture, wages could not increase in parallel with labor productivity, and as a consequence, labor's share of income decreased. The decrease in the labor share of income tended to increase the inequality of income distribution, because income distribution was less equal in non-wage incomes than in wage incomes. 2) The difference in per capita income between agriculture and non-agriculture expanded in this period (this aspect will be argued in the next section).

Second, income distribution in prewar Japan was surprisingly unequal; Gini was not lower than 0.5. This is comparable to some contemporary developing countries in Latin America, and considerably unequal compared to postwar Japan. The large gap between the prewar and postwar periods in the degree of unequal income distribution was due to institutional changes immediately after the war. These may be classified into two groups: Factors which decreased the income of the rich, and those which increased the income of the poor. The first group includes: 1) destruction of physical assets of the rich in large cities (especially Tokyo) due to bombing during the war; 2) resolution of *zai batsu* in 1946-47; 3) devaluation of monetary assets due to hyperinflation in 1948-51, and 4) decrease of assets of the rich due to new taxes on assets (the *zaisan-zei*—asset tax for 1946-51 and the *fuyu-zei*—wealth tax for 1950-52). The second group includes: 1) land reform in 1946-47, and 2) the substantial growth of trade unions. Examining these factors we concluded that the impact of the new tax system on assets was the most important.[6]

In the postwar period, according to studies by others, Gini showed an increase in the 1950s and no steady increase afterwards (Table 3). That is, income distribution turned from regressive to stable and equalized around 1960.

Based on these findings we are able to consider the applicability of the Kuznets hypothesis to Japanese history. The prewar experience demonstrates the applicability of the first part of the hypothesis: Income distribution tends to regress in the early stage of economic development. However the applicability of the second part of the hypothesis, that income distribution turns progressive at a certain point during economic development, looks dubious. The end of worsening income distribution around 1960 can be explored by referring to my thesis that the Lewisian turning point (the point in time when surplus labor disappears) was passed in that year.[7] By passing the turning point, labor's share of income changed from decline to stability. However, the change in income distribution in this period was moderate compared to the gap between the prewar and postwar periods. That is the greater equality of income distribution in contemporary Japan was not a result of economic development, but rather a result of institutional changes.

III. Income and Productivity Differentials Between Agriculture and Industry

China

As suggested in the previous section, income differentials between agriculture and non-agriculture should be one of the major factors affecting income distribution. Here we are studying changes over time in the income differential, and changes in the labor-productivity differential between the two sectors as the basic factor. However, considering the paucity of data for the service sector in China, we will study the labor-productivity differential between agriculture and industry.

In Figure 1, one may find that real income increased steadily for the entire period 1978-92 for non-farm households, while in farm households real income rapidly increased during 1978-84 and became constant for 1984-92. It is clear that agricultural reform beginning in 1978 improved farmers' economic condition to a great extent, but the urban industrial reform starting in 1984 did not provide a similar result. Because of these changes, as shown in Figure 2, the farm to non-farm income differential decreased for the years 1978-83, and expanded for the period 1985-92. The expansion of income differential in recent years has been responsible for the recent inequality of income distribution.

Figure 3 demonstrates a ratio of labor productivity, both at current and constant prices, of agriculture to industry. In the long-run perspective the ratio at current pieces showed a decrease in 1952-63, a constancy in 1963-77, an increase in 1977-84, and a decrease again in 1984-92. It is obvious that the changes in income differential during 1978-92 were the result of the changes in labor productivity, productivity at constant prices showed lager changes than that at current prices. In this case, the widening productivity differential since 1985 was more obvious.

Japan

For the prewar period, as depicted in Figure 4, farm household income was decidedly smaller than non-farm household income. Furthermore, the income series at constant prices demonstrated a different pattern of changes between farm and non-farm

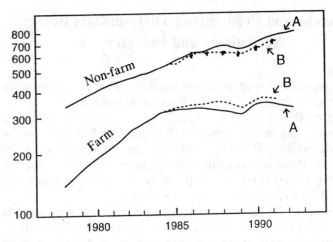

Notes:

A: deflated by the national retail price index (1978 = 1).

B: deflated by the rural and urban retail price indexes (1978 = 1).

Sources:

Statistical Yearbook of China 1981-1992.

A Statistical Survey of China 1993.

Fig. 1 Per Capita Income of Farm and Non-farm Households at 1978 Prices in China

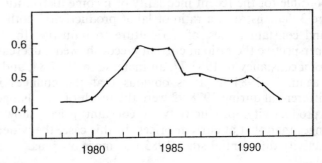

Note:

Ratio of per capita income for farm households to that of urban households.

Sources:

Same as Figure 1.

Fig. 2 Farm to Non-farm Household Income Differential in China

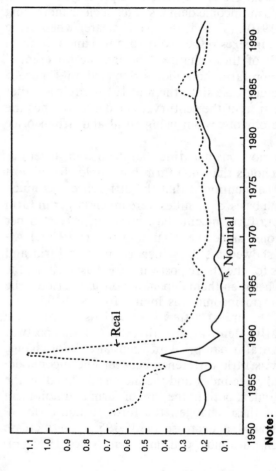

Note:

Labor productivity is a ratio of national income to social labor force.

Real value is expressed in 1985 prices.

Real income is estimated by multiplying nominal income in 1985 by the annual series of real income index (*Statistical Yearbook of China 1992*, p. 33).

Sources:

Nominal income and labor force are from *Statistical Yearbook of China 1992*, pp. 32, 101, and *A Statistical Survey of China 1993*, pp. 8, 16.

Fig. 3 Labor Productivity for Agriculture and Industry in China

households. Farm-household income decreased remarkably in the 1920s and early 1930s after an increase in the 1910s, and therefore did not show a clear trend for the entire prewar period. On the other hand, non-farm income demonstrated a clear increasing trend since the mid-1910s. (This difference is clearer when using rural and urban price indexes respectively for farm and non-farm incomes.) As a result of these changes, the income differential between farm and non-farm households depicted in Figure 5 demonstrated a large decrease since the mid-1910s, after a rather constant trend at the turn of the century. (The decrease since the mid-1910s was more obvious when using rural and urban price indexes.)

In the postwar period, one may find that the income level was higher in farm households than non-farm households for almost all years. (It should be mentioned that the difference was much smaller on a per capita basis, as families were much larger in farm households. Per capita farm income has, however, exceeded per capita non-farm income since the beginning of the 1970s.) Although real income showed a steady increase in both farm and non-farm households for the entire postwar period as a whole, the growth rate differed between them depending on sub-periods; the growth rate of non-farm income was higher for 1949-1959 and lower for 1959-1976 (Figure 4). After these periods both income series showed a nearly identical growth rate. (In the postwar period, because the rural-urban price differential did not change significantly, there was little difference between the income deflated by the national price index and the income deflated by the rural or urban price index, both in the case of farm and non-farm incomes.) Because of these changes, the farm to non-farm income differential showed a decrease (1949-1959), an increase (1959-1976) and then an almost constant trend since 1976 (Figure 5).

Combining these findings with the conclusions on income distribution in Part II, we can state the following. First, the widening income differential between farm and non-farm households from the end of the 1910s to the beginning of the 1930s was partly responsible for the increase in Gini for Japan during the

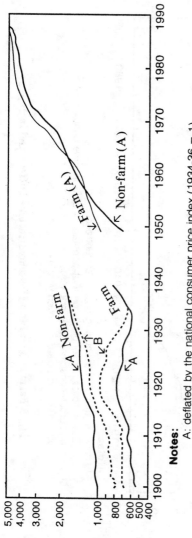

Notes:

A: deflated by the national consumer price index (1934-36 = 1).
B: deflated by the rural and urban consumer price indexes (1934-36 = 1).
All figures are based on seven year moving averages.

Sources:

Farm and non-farm household income in the prewar period is from Toshiyuki Otsuki and Nobukiyo Takamatsu, "On the Measurement and Trend of Income Inequality in Prewar Japan," *Papers and Proceedings of the Conference on Japan's Historical Development Experience and the Contemporary Developing Countries,* Tokyo: International Development Center of Japan, p. vii-15.

Farm and non-farm household income in the postwar period is from Somucho Tokeikyoku (Management and Coordination Agency, Statistics Bureau), *Nippon Choki Tokei Soran (Historical Statistics of Japan),* Vol. 1, 1987, pp. 486, 490, 548, and 550.

For the consumer price index, see Minami, *The Economic Development of Japan: A Quantitative Study,* London: Macmillan Press, 1993, Figure 9-4.

Fig. 4 Farm and Non-farm Household Income at Constant Prices in Japan

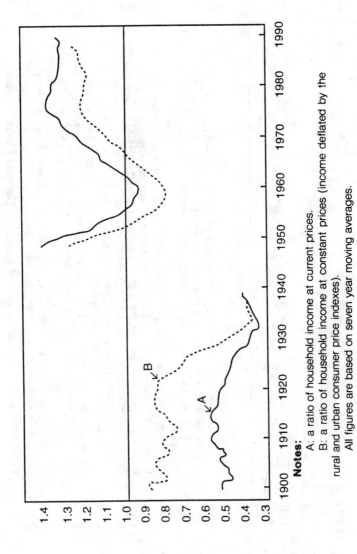

Notes:
  A: a ratio of household income at current prices.
  B: a ratio of household income at constant prices (income deflated by the rural and urban consumer price indexes).
  All figures are based on seven year moving averages.

Fig. 5 Farm to Non-farm Household Income Differential in Japan

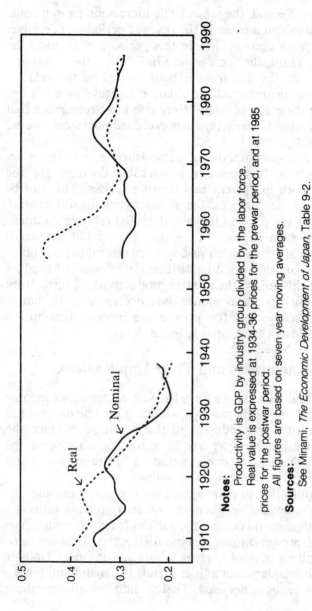

Notes:
Productivity is GDP by industry group divided by the labor force.
Real value is expressed at 1934-36 prices for the prewar period, and at 1985
prices for the postwar period.
All figures are based on seven year moving averages.

Sources:
See Minami, *The Economic Development of Japan*, Table 9-2.

Fig. 6 Productivity Differential Between Agriculture and Industry

1920s and 1930s. Second, the remarkable increase in farm income compared to non-farm income in the postwar period was decisively responsible for a smaller Gini in this period compared to the prewar period. Third, the increase in Gini during the 1950s and the decrease since the 1960s were both related to the relative decrease in farm income and the relative increase in non-farm income during these sub-periods. (Here one must remember that on a per capita basis farm income has exceeded non-farm income since the 1970s.)

Relative labor productivity of agriculture to industry is depicted in Figure 6. It showed a remarkable decrease for the prewar period both in current and constant prices. This can be considered one of the causes for the widening income differential. In the early postwar period (1950s and 1960s) relative productivity did not change in case of current prices, but decreased considerably in case of constant prices. Agricultural price support policy cancelled out the widening differential of nominal productivity. Without this policy, the relative productivity of agriculture to industry at current prices should have decreased more than it actually did decrease and the progressive income distribution after 1960 should not have been realized.

IV. Conclusions and Their Implications

In Part II and Part III, we have found a worsening of income distribution, and one of its causes a widening income differential between agriculture and industry in the recent years since the mid-1980s in China. Now we are in a position to discuss the implications of this phenomenon, including future prospects and their possible impact on society and politics.

First, I would like to emphasize that regressive income distribution is an unavoidable phenomenon in a growing economy with surplus labor. In this economy, such as found in contemporary China and prewar Japan, income differential between agriculture (typically a pool of surplus labor) and industry (mostly characterized by modern technology) tends to expand and labor's share of income tends to decrease. These conditions all contribute to regressive income distribution throughout the economy.

Second, as a consequence of the first point, income distribution in China is likely to regress still more in the future. This is based on the first part of the Kuznets hypothesis stating that income distribution tends to regress in the early phase of industrialization. One may say that income distribution in China will improve with further development of the economy, based on the second part of the Kuznets hypothesis stating that income distribution tends to improve in fully industrialized countries. I think this view is too optimistic.

1. Japanese experience in the postwar period demonstrates that an increase in the equality of income distribution was very small (Gini decreased from 0.36 to 0.34 between 1963 and 1979 —Table 3), and that more equal distribution in contemporary Japan was, rather, a result of institutional changes immediately after the war. Without drastic institutional changes comparable to those in postwar Japan, more equal distribution cannot be realized in China.

2. Contemporary China is in a less favorable situation than prewar Japan. a) The geographically large size of China makes matters more difficult. The variations in soil fertility and climate from region to region contributes to unequal income distribution. b) Population movement from rural to urban areas is limited in China due to policy and an underdeveloped transportation network. This is one of the major factors sustaining income differentials among regions. c) In spite of this limited population movement, rural people are aware of urban life through mass communications, especially TV, and this may stimulate frustration among them. d) There are no efficient means of controlling the economic over-heating which sometimes occurs. (A system of macroeconomic control has not yet been developed and the central government is losing control over the local governments.) Income differentials tend to easily expand in these situations. e) There is a difference in the degree of economic development between contemporary China and prewar Japan in the 1920s and 1930s, the period being compared in this paper. In China, the market economy is in the process of emerging, while in Japan it

had already been established by that period. It seems to me that income differentials tend to increase rapidly during the emergence of a market economy.

Third, the impact of more regressive income distribution on Chinese society and politics in the future must be considered. Here again the Japanese experience can be instructive. We have learned that during the prewar period farmers became much poorer relative to urban dwellers. This caused anti-urban and anti-industry sentiments among the farmers. This sentiment was easily combined with movements directed by young military officers who came from farm families, protesting against the capitalistic industrial regime controlled by *zaibatsu,* and the democratic political regime of Taisho democracy. Their goal was to establish a nationalistic regime centered on the Emperor, whose final form of growing nationalism and imperialism was the birth of the fascist regime and the imperialistic expansion which caused World War II. This bitter experience of Japan demonstrates that we may not be too optimistic about a change in income distribution.

In this respect we must state that contemporary China is in a more difficult position than prewar Japan. In China there are many ethnic minorities (8.0 percent of the total population in 1990), who live in remote areas with low incomes.[8] Therefore the income distribution problem can easily be turned into a racial problem. If this is the case in the future, the economic reforms which began in 1978 and seem to be successful will be interrupted. So the government must carry out efficient policies to mitigate income differentials among regions, industry groups and occupations. Basically, it should be acknowledged that slower economic growth is best for equalizing income distribution.

Notes

1. Simon Kuznets, "Economic Growth and Income Inequality," *American Economic Review,* March 1955.
2. Ryoshin Minami, Kwan S. Kim and Hirotaka Yazawa, "Shotoku Bunpu no Choke Hendo: Suikei to Bunseke (Long-term Changes in Income Distribution: Estimation and Analysis)," *Keizai Kenkyu (Economic Review),* October

1993.

3. For details, see Minami, *The Economic Development of China: A Comparison with Japanese Experience*, London: Macmillan Press, 1993, p. 222. Also its Chinese translation published from Jingji Guanli Chubanshe in 1991, pp. 267-268.

4. Recent trends in income distribution seem to be a controversial issue among Chinese scholars: Zhang Ping ("Zhongguo Nongcun Quyu Jian Jumin de Shouru Fenpei," *Jingji Yanjiu*, 1992) claims a worsening distribution, while Yang Wei Min ("Diqu Jian Shouru Shuju Biandong de Shizheng Fenxi," *Jingji Yanjiu*, 1992) claims an improved distribution. We need deeper discussions.

5. Minami, Kim and Yazawa, "Long-term Changes in Income Distribution," Table 7.

6. Hirotaka Yazawa and Ryoshin Minami, "Dai-2-ji Taisen Chokugo no mokeru Shotokubunpu no Byodoka Yoin (Factors Affecting the Equalization of Income Distribution Immediately After World War II)," *Keizai Kenkyu* (*Economic Review*), October, 1993.

7. Ryoshin Minami, *The Economic Development of Japan*, Section 2 of Chapter 9. For more detailed discussion see Minami, *The Turning Point in Economic Development: Japan's Experience*, Tokyo: Kinokuniya, 1973.

8. Average per capita consumption in 1990 was only 606 yuan in seven provinces (Ningxia, Yunnan, Guizhou, Guangxi, Qinghai, Xinjiang and Tibet) in which the percentage of ethnic minorities in the total population exceeds 30 percent, compared to 1,630 yuan in the richest three cities (Beijing, Tianjin and Shanghai). for per capita consumption see Table 2. Population figures are from *China Population Statistics Yearbook 1990*, pp. 78-79.

Financial Reform Is Key to Economic Transition

Wang Jue
Professor of the Central
Party School and chairman of the China
Market Economy Research Association

China's current economic reform is changing the highly concentrated planned economic system into a market economic system; and is changing from an economy in kind to a money economy in terms of economic type. As for progress in economic reform, consumer goods, means of production and labor markets have all developed to a considerable extent, and there is more and more competition. Reform of the commodity price system is nearing completion, and the extent of the commodity economy has been raised greatly. So far as these areas are concerned, economic reform in China has made great strides forward. However, in light of the final goal of establishing the socialist market economic system, the extent of the money economy in China is still very low. An outstanding manifestation of this is the seriously delayed reform and development of the financial system, which in turn has become a bottleneck affecting reform of the economic system and development of the national economy as a whole.

1. The reform in other areas is restricted by the delayed reform of the financial system.

Economic reform has now shifted from breakthroughs in single areas to an all-embracing systematic reform in every field. The change of the operation mechanism in large and medium-sized state-owned enterprises, the cultivation and development of the market system, and the change of governmental functions are interlocked and mutually influential. From an overall viewpoint, the major factor restricting these reforms is the financial system. Delayed reform of the financial system has become a serious restriction on the deepening of other reforms.

In the course of giving enterprises autonomy and reforming the property-right system, and essential question is how to ensure that enterprises can effectively raise and use funds. The management of an enterprise is the management of its funds. If an enterprise is to develop, the problems of accumulation, liabilities and investment must be solved. If an enterprise is subject to market regulation and adjusts its production and operations, there arises the problem of the transfer and reallocation of funds. An enterprise under modern market conditions is not only a commodity producer but, more importantly, a manager and user of money, and the financial factor is decisive in these activities. Therefore, changing the operation mechanism of enterprises demands support and guarantees from a strong financial system. The multi-level money lending market and the investment credit mechanism enable enterprises to switch from reliance on the government to reliance on the market. This will bring about a fundamental change in operating mechanism of enterprises and help them become free from relying solely on the government.

The foundation for developing a market economy is a developed market system, and the financial market is the core. First of all, resources must flow freely in competitive use, and this will inevitably promote investment by the people, thus necessitating the formation of an effective shift from savings to investment. In this way people's savings resulting from their increased income can be effectively accumulated to increase savings deposits. The financial system plays an irreplaceable role in forming the savings-investment mechanism. If the financial system make an adjustment in this respect, it will be difficult to form a reasonable mechanism for investment by the people. Moreover, the development and perfection of the financial market system are fundamental prerequisite for multi-level market regulation. Under modern market economic conditions, the allocation of social resources is manifested in the concentrated way of the flow and allocation of money throughout society. Once capital is mobilized, the resources are mobilized. If there is no reasonable and effective financial market regulation, it is impossible to form a true and overall market regulation mechanism. Karl Marx said long ago that the final formation of the market economic regulation mechanism is presupposed and marked by the establishment of the modern credit system with the banks at its core.

Changing the government function from direct administration of the economy to indirect macrocontrol calls for certain necessary conditions and policy measures. A fundamental breakthrough in this respect would be to free the financial system from its position as the tool of government planning and turn it into the means of market regulation. Under the modern market economy, interest rates as the price of money have direct and delicate influence on the sum total of structure, flow and distribution of money. Only when there is a developed financial system is it possible for the government to enforce an effective money policy and accomplish its intentions through indirect control. If there is no financial market link, it will be difficult for government macrocontrol to be practiced effectively.

All this clearly shows that reform of the financial system has become the most important factor restricting overall reform.

2. The national economy is restricted by the delayed reform of the financial system.

The Chinese economy has entered a period of high-speed growth with unprecedented investment activities. In order to powerfully support the high-speed growth of the economy, it is necessary to effectively mobilize social funds and make full use of them. This function should be performed by the financial system. However, in the present situation, this is done to a large extent through reliance on the government at all levels. This demonstrates that development of the financial system has lagged behind economic growth and development.

The financial system in China as a whole has not yet shed the traditional pattern of a large government treasury under a planned economic system, and in some localities the lack of market regulations has led to disorder in some financial institutions. As a result, the financial system, which should have played an effective role in supporting and regulating high-speed economic growth, not only has failed to do this, but also has become a target for reconsolidation. This cannot but be a grave secret worry for the fast growing Chinese economy.

Therefore, for the financial system in China, more urgent than the question of reform is the question of growth and development. The form of financial institutions, business scope, and methods and regulations of organizations and operations all must be greatly developed. For example, the level of consumption of the Chinese people is in a period of transition. For urban residents, durable consumer goods such as color TV sets, refrigerators and video-tape recorders that cost from 1,000 to 10,000 yuan have become commonplace in ordinary families, but the peak of consumption for such goods is already over. The new hot spots in consumption to support economic growth should be consumer goods like housing and cars that cost more than 100,000 or several 100,000 yuan. However, so far as most city dwellers are concerned, they now have a slight surplus income, but not enough to pay for such expensive items. Even in developed countries, the purchase of a house is beyond the reach of most people. Is it possible to introduce personal consumption credit universally under the condition that rules have been perfected in this regard, and support the consumption level to rise to new heights through credit extended by the financial institutions? This will mean killing three birds with one stone. First of all, it will help the real estate development industry to form a rational construction structure and change the present situation in which there are too many expensive apartment buildings and villas while housing for ordinary families is in very short supply. Second, it will stabilize the surplus income of the majority of people and effectively stops disorder in raising funds and over-speculation in the market. Third, it will use marketing means to promote the reform of the housing system and avoid overburdening the government and the loss of the state housing assets. All this presupposes that the financial system can effectively develop personal consumption credit.

This is only one example. In short, under modern market economic conditions, stabilization and effective functioning of the economy are dependent on whether or not the financial system is in good order and can be used reasonably and effectively.

3. Speeding up reform of the financial system to promote progress toward establishing a money economy.

Delayed financial reform shows that China is still in the process of shifting its economy into a money economy, and that finance is crucial for this transition.

To push the reform of the financial system forward, it is necessary to take a firm hold of the banks, the center of the modern credit system, and really separate the administrative function of the government from the control function of the banks, and promote efforts toward making banking institutions fully rectified enterprises. Banking and operations of the commercial banks are an organic component part of market economic activities and at the same time a component link in the market's regulatory mechanism. The deepening of the money economy will enable the tentacles of the financial system to penetrate into every corner, thus providing a necessary organizational channel for effective market regulation and objective control by the government.

The reform of the enterprise shareholding system, and the emergence and development of the futures market and other economic activities and organizational forms show that the real estate business is becoming more brisk and important, and will take the leading position in the economic activities of the entire society. For this reason, the financial system should be reformed and developed together with the other reforms related to it to effectively adjust real estate activities.

Reform in China has entered the stage of establishing the socialist market economic system in an all-round way. During this stage, the establishment of a new financial system is the key to overall reform and development. To achieve these changes, that key must be grasped.

Price and Commodity Control in Japan's Postwar Inflationary Period*

Masahiro Kuroda
Professor of the Keio University of Japan

I. Introduction

Japan began efforts to restore its economy, totally destroyed by World War II, immediately after accepting an unconditional surrender in 1945. These efforts would take time to bear fruit. Per capital real GDP in 1946 was less than 55 percent of the prewar peak level in the 1934-1936 period. The manufacturing production index in 1946 recorded only one fifth of its peak level in 1944. Moreover, the rice harvest was the worst since 1887 and people were forced to live at a subsistence minimum. Economic woes were compounded by galloping inflation. The wholesale prince index recorded a nearly 300 percent increase in 1946 and continued to rise more than 100 percent for the next several years.[1] The consumer price index also recorded more than a 200 percent increase in 1946.[2]

This hyperinflation was in part due to the imbalance between supply and demand. The supply of goods was severely curtailed and shortages of raw materials damaged production capacity, while the demand for goods increased with the rapid expansion of the domestic population.[3] Increases in the money supply also contributed to inflation; these rises accompanied growing government expenditure to settle war-time accounts. In order to deal

* I would like to express my appreciation to valuable comments and advice provided by Juro Teranishi of the Hitotsubashi University, James E. Vestal and Sumi Tani of the Keio University. Of course the usual caveat applies: Any remaining faults are solely my own.

with inflation, the Economic Stabilization Board (ESB) was set up in August 1946, initially addressing the inflation problem through price controls and the rationing of commodities. Soon, however, the ESB began to implement the "Priority Production System (Keisya Seisan Hoshike)," allocating and concentrating limited resources to specific basic industries such as coal mining and iron and steel. Specifically, the ESB first allocated resources to the coal industry, and increased coal output was then allocated to the iron and steel industry. Finally, increased iron and steel output was allocated back to coal mining in order to further increase output in that industry. By utilizing Japan's limited resources to create these virtuous production circle, the ESB hoped to ease inflation as well as promote Japanese economic independence.

In spite of price controls and the priority production system, inflation continued at somewhat lower but still very high rates until 1949 when it was dramatically halted by Joseph Dodge's deflationary policies, the so-called Dodge Line. Dodge, a subscriber to classical economic beliefs, cited as causes for Japan's economic problems her over-dependency on foreign aid from the United States and the over-protection of private sectors by government subsidies. By slashing subsidies, increasing government revenues, and cutting expenditures, Dodge's disinflationary policies rapidly halted inflation.

Figure 1 denotes four different types of price indices for consumer goods during the 1945-1952 period: (A) the free market price index of consumer goods constructed by the Bank of Japan (BOJ); (B) the effective market price index of consumer goods constructed by the Prime Minister's Office, which represents a weighted average of free market prices and official retail prices; (C) the official retail price index constructed by BOJ; and (D) the estimated official retail price index constructed by the Ministry of Finance (MOF). These indices are comparable both with each other at any given moment and also across time.[4] Figure 2 represents four types of price indices for producer goods; (E) the free market price index of producer goods constructed by BOJ; (F) the effective market price index of producer goods construct-

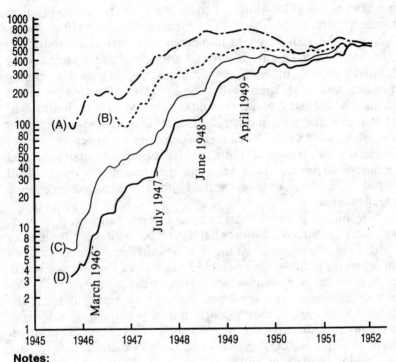

Notes:

(A) Black market price index of consumer goods constructed by BOJ.

(B) Effective market price index of consumer goods constructed by Ministry of Prime Minister.

(C) Official retail price index constructed by BOJ.

(D) Estimated official retail price index constructed by Ministry of Finance.

**Fig. 1 Four Types of Price Indices of Consumer Goods
During the Period 1945-1952**

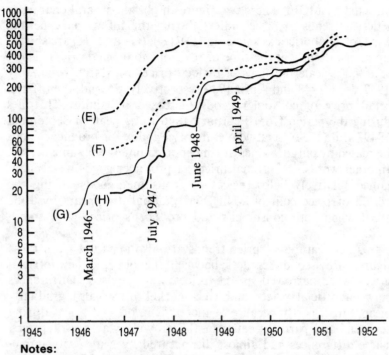

Notes:
(E) Black market price index of producer goods constructed by BOJ.
(F) Effective market price index of producer goods constructed by BOJ.
(G) Official wholesale price index constructed by BOJ.
(H) Estimated official wholesale price index constructed by MOF.

**Fig. 2 Four Types of Price Indices of Producer
Goods During the Period 1945-1952**

ed by BOJ; (G) the official wholesale price index constructed by BOJ; and (H) the estimated official wholesale price index constructed by MOF.[5] These two figures highlight several characteristics of trends in price indices during the inflationary period. First, official prices as shown in (D), (E), (G) and (H) are shifted up intermittently at the time of revisions to official prices. There were large-scale revisions of official prices in March 1946, July 1947, June 1948 and April 1949 respectively. Second, the official retail price of consumer goods increased by almost 21 times during the period from February 1946 to its peak in September 1949, while the official wholesale price index for producer goods increased by only 19 times during approximately the same period. In other words, the official prices of producer goods were maintained relatively below prices for consumer goods during the period of price controls. This bias gradual disappears by June 1951, when both consumer's and producer's prices were stabilized.

Other features of price trends are also apparent from these figures. Revised differences between the old and new official prices were narrowed as the prices were revised. Differences between official prices and free market prices also gradually disappeared, partly because of increases in official prices during revisions and partly because of the growing stability of prices. These differences had almost disappeared by May 1950, immediately before the outbreak of the Korean War. Free market prices of consumer goods and producer goods had largely stabilized by June 1948; consumer goods prices trended to decrease after April 1949 and producer goods prices tended to fall after February 1949. Interestingly, measures for free-market prices show stability prior to the introduction of the Dodge Line and the fourth large upward revision of official prices. Finally, we can observe that trends in the market prices for producer goods are more closely correlated with changes in corresponding official prices than are market prices for consumer goods correlated with official consumer goods prices. This indicates that the government was more effective at controlling producer rather than consumer prices.

As we can see in the above figures, the struggle with inflation continued for almost five years. It was a major long-term effort, and adopted policies were not necessarily uniform or consistent, especially since policies were the combined effort of the Japanese government and the staff of the Supreme Commander for the Allied Powers (SCAP) and the two sometimes disagreed. This paper analyzes the contour of this five-year struggle with inflation from the viewpoint of the adopted policies, evaluating policy's role in resource allocation in the Japanese economy. In the next section, we analyze trends of observed inflation and adopted stabilization policies during the period 1945-1952, which provide some understanding of the efficacy of implemented policy. In Section 3, we try to evaluate the implications of adopted policies from the viewpoint of the economic theory, taking into account the immediate post-war conditions of the Japanese economy.

II. Chronological Contour of Policy to Stabilization

As we can see from figures 1 and 2, the Japanese economy took almost five years to achieve price stability. During these five years, the implementation of policy often changed as did Japan's general economic circumstances. These changes serve to divide the period from 1945 to 1952, the time from just after Japan's unconditional surrender to the closing of the ESB, into seven sub-periods which are summarized below.[6]

1. Initial Condition: August 1945-February 1946

On August 21, 1945, just after the end of the war, MOF began to reconsider its recent experience with economic controls. During the war, prices and wages had been anchored at the level of September 18, 1939 by the Price Control Law (*Kakakutou Touseirei*) and the Emergency Measure for Wages (*Chingin Rinji Sochirei*). Also, production and consumption were controlled under the rationing systems set up by the Goods Control Ordinance. Even during the war, however, these regulations had not necessarily succeeded. This lack of success was particularly noticeable just before the end of war, when huge differences between controlled and market prices, together with a complex regulatory system, dramatically undermined the government's ability to regulate prices and ration goods.

Because of this failure, MOF originally intended to decontrol almost all goods and services in postwar Japan, excepting necessities, favoring liberalization by market forces. On the other hand, SCAP insisted that it was highly important to control prices and ration commodities as emergency measures because of severe supply shortages.[7] In November 1945, the Price Division (*Bukkabu*) was established as an administrative office in MOF and at the same time the Committee for Emergency Measures for Prices (*Sengo Bukka Taisaku Iinkai*) was established as an advisory committee. The Price Division in MOF tried to forge a framework for anti-inflationary policy in collaboration with this advisory committee. Groping for concrete policy measures while narrowing the perception gap between SCAP and the Japanese government about price controls, the government finally wrote "An Outline of Policy Measures on Prices in the Postwar Period" (*Sengo Bukka Taisaku Kihon Yoko*) in February 1946. This outline focused on the construction of policy measures dealing with (1) excess purchasing power, (2) price controls, (3) food shortage, (4) expansion of production capacity, (5) rationing and (6) employment. However, measures were not implemented until after February 1946.

During the initial period characterized by policy indecision, wholesale prices jumped sharply, increasing almost 17 percent monthly from August through December, 1945. Inflation was partly due to the rapid increase in the money supply related to the postwar expansion of government expenditure,[8] and partly due to a sharp fall in production caused by the destruction of production capacity and the shortage of raw materials.[9]

2. Deposit Freezing and the 3.3 Official Price Setting: March to July 1946

The government issued the Emergency Ordinance for the Economy (*Keizai Kiki Kinkyu Taisaku*) in February 1946. This represented the first systematic and concrete government response to the problems facing the postwar economy. Central to this emergency ordinance were (1) the freezing of bank deposits, (2) the redenomination of the yen,[10] (3) the imposition of a new property tax and (4) a new system of official prices. Under this ordinance, the yen was redenominated on March 3, 1946 subject to the following: (a) an individual could change only 100 yen of the old currency into the new currency, (b) all deposits were frozen, (c) the withdrawal of deposits was forbidden excepting certain amounts for living and production activities, and (d) the government recommended that wages in new yen be limited to 500 yen per month, a wage level that was consistent with the new system of official prices. The new system of official prices was enforced beginning March 3, 1946, the same day that the Price Level Control Law (*Bukka Tōsei Rei*) was implemented to replace the wartime Price Control. Under this 3.3 system, so named because of the date it was implemented, all of the official prices were decided according to linkages with the basic prices of rice, wages and coal products. The basic price of rice was set at 300 yen per 150 kg for producers, the price at which the government purchased rice. The rice price for consumers (the government's selling price) was set lower at 250 yen per 150 kg,[11] and the government-calculated monthly living costs per household was set at 526.2 yen, consistent with wages and maximum allowable withdrawals from deposits.

The government set the basic price of coal at 250 yen per ton for producers and 150 yen per ton for users, also consistent with the rice prices and wages. Although other related official prices were decided by their linkages with these three basic components —rice prices, coal prices, and wages—the government intended to set the average level of official prices eight times higher than the regulated wartime price levels. The gaps between producer prices and user prices in this official price system were subsidies, paid out of the government budget. In 1946, these price subsidies totaled 9 billion yen, 7.8 percent of total government outlays under the central government budget. These price subsidies, officially named the System of Subsidies for the Price Adjustment (SSPA; *Kakaku Chōsei Hokyūkin*), were originally intended to halt the spiral between prices of materials and finished products. However, the subsidies themselves led to increases in government spending and growth in the money supply in the postwar economy.[12]

In spite of the lower levels for purchase prices, considerable differences between official prices and free market prices remained.[13] The 3.3 official price system really reflected expectations about economic recovery, growth, prices, and income: the government expected that real national income would recover to 1937 levels in 1949, that prices in 1949 would be eight times the level of 1937, and that the foreign exchange rate would be 20 yen per dollar. These expectations were unrealistic, undermining the efficacy of pricing policy. The government found it difficult to continue its financial reform program, including the freezing of deposits, under rapidly increasing prices, and so suspended the deposit freeze in July 1947. However, while operative, the deposit freeze did help to absorb the excess supply of money, decreasing potential demand pull in the short-run thus working in an orthodox fashion to control inflation. As we can see in [figures 1 and 2], the free market price of consumer goods was stable for much of 1946, increasing again only at year end. Prices for producer goods picked up earlier.

Although these postwar emergency measures did not succeed in stabilizing the economy instantaneously, they at least reveal the government's attitude toward economic controls. Moreover, Japan's initial experience with policy also indicates that orthodox policy measures such as financial reform[14] are not necessarily effective when people are existing at a minimum subsistence level and when there are enormous supply shortages in the market.

3. Start of the Economic Stabilization Board and Price Bureau; August 1946-May 1947

The Economic Stabilization Board (ESB; *Keizai Antei Honbu*) and the Price Bureau (PB; *BukkaChō*) were established in August 1946 as a planning agency and an administrative office for price policy respectively, in order to unify government policy.[15] Although the government felt that it urgently needed to reduce potential purchasing power through emergency financial reform in order to stop hyperinflation, the government also felt it needed to plan the next step of restoring production capacity to reduce the gaps between demand and supply. The ESB began formulating a complete plan of emergency economic measures, focusing on the following three basic problems: (1) increasing the level of production of basic producer commodities; (2) reducing excess purchasing power through fiscal and financial policy; and (3) strengthening the rationing system for commodities. Tanzan Ishibashi, minister of Finance (May 1946 through May 1947) insisted that it was more important to restore production, even if this necessitated reduced control over prices. He stated: "The inflation resulted from economic destruction at that time. In order to overcome this type of inflation, the revival of economic activities was more important than a deflationary policy. To this end, fiscal deficits as well as an increase in currency circulation could be allowed."[16] Ishibashi did not advocate expanding effective demand due to the fiscal deficits, but he did argue for support for certain basic industries in order to restore production capacity. However, his ideas were totally opposed by SCAP, who insisted on strong regulation of quantity and price.[17] It should be noted that SCAP policy at that time was based on ideas of regulation and planning, reflecting in part the influence of the New Dealers in the Occupation. SCAP policy was not based upon orthodox fiscal and monetary stabilization measures, and differed radically from the market-oriented emphasis of Dodge's policy. Given SCAP's faith in rationing and planning, they strongly pushed for laws to regulate commodities and thereby control prices. Hence, the government established the Emergency Law of Demand and Supply Adjustment for Commodities (*Rinji Jukyu Chosei Ho*) in October 1946. Under this law, 34 producer goods and 52 consumer goods were designated as rationed commodities and were rationed uniformly according to the planning of the ESB.

The ESB used this law not only to try to stabilize prices but also to actively promote the recovery of production in certain industries. The ESB designated basic industries such as coal mining, the chemical fertilizer industry, and the iron and steel industry as targets for development, and specifically rationed materials to these industries. This was the Priority Production

System (PPS, *Keisha Seisan Hōshiki*), under which the government offered not only financial support to select industries but also rationed commodities in such a way as to stimulate the recovery. In order to enforce smoothly the rationing system, the ESP proposed to establish eight public corporations (*Kōdan*) to carry out the necessary administration. Three public corporations were set up for reconstruction of industry, price adjustment and maritime credit, and four were set up to handle public trade.

4. Emergency Economic Measures and the Revision of Official Prices, June 1947-June 1948

After the stabilization program of February 1946 failed, prices began to increase again in the fall of 1946, despite efforts by the ESB to break the inflationary trend. Free market consumer prices increased by almost 80 percent from September 1946 through march 1947. This forced the government to revise official prices for both producer and consumer goods; these revisions amounted on average to 65 and 85 percent from March through September in 1946 and 20 and 40 percent from September 1946 through March 1947 respectively. On the other hand, the level of production also stagnated further due to the shortage of material goods in the fall of 1946, where the production index (= 100.0 in 1935) fell to 38.0 in November 1946 and 34.5 in February 1947.

After the general election for the Lower House of the Diet, Tetsu Katayama, the leader of Socialist Party, was elected prime minister. The Katayama Cabinet concentrated on countermeasures to halt inflation, and the ESB in June 1947 announced policy changes emphasizing the establishment of order over resource allocation and a revision of official prices. To that end, the rationing system was strengthened and a major revision of official prices, the second largest in the postwar period, was implemented in July 1947. In revising prices, the ESB introduced Price Stabilizing Zones (PSZs; *Kakaku Antei Tai*), where maximum price levels were fixed. Initially, the levels were set about 65 times higher than 1934-1936 prices. Goods subject to this system were called Price Stabilized Commodities (PSC; *Antei tai Busshi*). PSZs were established in order to adjust imbalances in production costs arising for differences in utilization rates and to stabilize relative purchaser's prices. For example, if the producer price had been increased by more than the PSZ, producers were subsidies provided by SSPA. The number of Price Stabilized Commodities was expanded from already-regulated basic commodities (rice, coal and basic foods) to other important commodities including coal, iron, nonferrous metal, chemical fertilizer, and caustic soda. Subsidies in 1947 amounted to 22.5 billion yen, which was 10.7 percent of the general government budget.

In addition to establishing PSZs, the ESB determined appropriate levels for producer prices for basic manufacturing commodities based principally on the cost of production, where the cost of production included not only variable and fixed costs, but also normal profit margins. Prices for agricultural products were generally decided by the parity method, where price increases for agricultural products paralleled those of material goods used in agricultural production.[18] The new ESB measures also did not attempt to control wages directly, although there were certain guidelines for wage levels by industry and by occupation. These guidelines were consistent with the cost of living based upon the new system of official consumer prices.

Table 1 presents the system of official prices in this revision. The new official producer prices differed widely compared to 1934-1936 averages. For example, prices for coal, pig iron, ammonium sulfate, caustic soda, transportation fees and electricity were increased by 127, 136, 80, 67, 23 and 10 times respectively. Prices for commodities which were selectively subsidized under the Priority Production System such as coal, pig iron and fertilizer were increased much more than average, while prices of consumer goods including agricultural products and services such as transportation fees showed increases small than the average. Despite this wide variation in producer prices, the introduction of PSZs was intended to stabilize the price system and offset imbalances by setting the purchase price for commodities at levels 65 times those in 1934-36. For example, the producer price of pig iron was set at 6,370 yen per ton, which was 135.9 times the price of 1934-36, while the purchaser price was set at 3,050 yen per ton, which was almost 65 times the price in 1934-36. Differences between the producer and purchaser prices were subsidized by SSPA.

Table 1   Price of Important Commodities Constructed by Price System in July 1947

		New official price (A)	Average price (1934-1936) (B)	Competition (A)/(B)
Coal (ton)	producer price	956.08	7.50	127.5
	public consumer price	1,208.58	12.43	97.2
	specific consumer price	600.00	12.39	48.4
Oil (Kl)	crude oil price	3,461.00	70.00	49.4
	consumer price	6,539.64	116.18	56.3
Coke (ton)	producer price	2,240.38	46.00	48.6
	consumer price	2,710.25	46.00	58.9
Pig iron (ton)	producer price	6,370.00	46.87	135.9
	consumer price	3,050.00	46.98	64.9
Steel thin: 1.6 mm (ton)	producer price	14,220.00	108.10	131.6
	consumer price	8,690.00	133.70	65.0
Lead (ton)	producer price	33,000.00	253.00	130.4
	consumer price	23,000.00	253.00	90.9
Sodium ash (ton)	producer price	10,000.00	—	—
	dealer sales price	6,562.00	100.00	65.6
Sodium hydroxide (ton)	producer price	8,600.00	127.93	67.2
	dealer sales price	11,051.00	170.00	65.0
Ammonium sulfate	producer price	8,000.00	100.00	80.0
	consumer price	6,500.00	101.11	64.4

Cement (ton)	wholesale price	1,649.25	19.00	86.8
	retail price	1,714.25	20.00	85.7
National rail-way fare	passenger (km b)	0.35	0.015	23.3
	transportation (t/km)	0.25	0.015	16.7
Gas (m³)	standard rate	3.50	0.084	41.7
Electricity	electric light (c)	8.00	0.67	11.9
	power rate (kilowatt/month d)	40.00	4.21	9.5
Barber charge		20.00	0.50	40.0
Rice	producer price (1 rock)	1,700.00	27.16	62.6
	consumer price (10 kg)	99.00	2.47	40.0
Potato (10)	producer price	87.00	1.58	55.1
	consumer price	85.00	2.36	35.9
Bread (45)	consumer price	1.91	0.08	31.8
Sake 1st class (1.81)	retail price	132.00	1.70	77.7
Beer (standard bottle)	retail price	23.00	0.33	69.7

Revisions of official prices may not have accelerated inflationary trends. In fact, by reducing excess purchasing power, they helped alleviate inflation. The rate of increase in the issuance of BOJ notes was fairly stable from the beginning of 1947, and manufacturing production had recovered to two-thirds the pre-war peak level by June 1948. Hence, free market prices for consumer and producer goods became more stable from the beginning of 1948, and these prices actually decreased in September 1948 compared to the levels of the previous year. As a result, differences between official prices and free market prices gradually shrank. The gap for consumer goods, which was 30-40 times just after the war, fell to 23.7 times in March 1946, 10.4 times in

July 1947, and 7.6 times in June 1948, while that for producer goods was reduced from 9.2 times in July 1947 to 5.9 times in June 1948. However, increases in wages continued unabated: in the year following the revision of official prices, wages rose from 1,800 yen per month to 4,300 yen. As a consequence, official prices again lost consistency, necessitating another revision.

As hyperinflation abated, the government focused increasingly on ways to promote a full scale economic recovery. Two plans were presented to the Katayama Cabinet almost simultaneously, the Economic Reconstruction Plan (ERP; *Keizai Fukkō Keikaku*) and the Intermediate Stabilization Plan (ISP; *Chūkan Antei Keikaku*). Although neither of these was adopted, they helped promote the concept of economic planning as a policy tool. The ERP was a five-year economic plan, under which production was expected to recover to prewar peak levels, a balance of payments equilibrium was to be attained at the same time, and inflation was gradually to fall through 1949-50. After initial discussion, the ERP was revised and filled in, finally reaching completion in May 1949 under the second Yoshida Cabinet. The economy at this time was suffering from the initial impact of the Dodge deflation, one consequence of which was that the ERP was generally ignored.

Discussions of the ISP began in early 1948. The ISP did not support orthodox stabilization measures such as tight monetary and fiscal policy to stabilize the economy; rather, it advocated measures such as increased foreign aid to temporarily ease inflation, and the recovery of production thereafter to permanently break the wage-price spiral. On the other hand, SCAP insisted that wages be controlled directly under the May 1948 Wage Stabilization Program (*Chingin Antei Keikaku*) in order to stabilize the economy. However, the Ashida Cabinet which followed Katayama was reluctant to implement wage controls, worried that guidance of nominal wages would cause turmoil in labor markets because of real wage instability. In place of direct controls, the Japanese government attempted to introduce indirect control measures, at the same time requesting increased US aid to stabilize the economy.

During this period of policy debate, there was an interesting discussion between advocates of the Immediate Stabilization Policy (*Ikkyo Antei Ron*) and those of the Intermediate Stabilization Policy (*Chūkan Antei Ron*). The Immediate Stabilization Policy essentially consisted of monetary tightening according to institutional monetary theory; it was proposed by an economist with Marxist training. In contrast, the Intermediate Stabilization Theory, which had the support of economists at MOF and BOJ, emphasized the recovery in production as a prerequisite for stabilization. The Immediate Stabilization Policy stressed monetary reform based on the gold bullion standard, while the Intermediate Stabilization Policy opposed rapid reform of the monetary system for fear of a stabilization crisis. While advocates of the Intermediate Stabilization Policy did believe that the increasing money supply stemmed from the government deficit and its over-lending as a financial intermediary, they believed that restoring production was the first priority in alleviating inflation. Although elements of both of these policies can be found in the Dodge Line (i.e., emphasis on the uniformed exchange rate or the belief that government deficits lay behind the rising money supply), this policy debate did not really shape the adoption of Dodge's deflationary policies.

Table 2   Average Annual Increasing Rate of Issuance of BOJ

(%)

| Month | Year | | |
	1946	1947	1948
1	4.1	11.4	6.0
2	-19.1	7.5	-0.1
3	-22.3	7.0	0.4
4	-17.0	7.0	1.2
5	22.1	5.6	1.8
6	20.1	5.5	3.1
7	16.5	5.1	4.4
8	14.4	4.7	4.3

9	12.1	5.3	5.0
10	9.0	5.8	5.1
11	13.8	12.5	11.1
12	12.3	8.9	6.7

Notes: Comparison of movement average for three months to last month.

Table 3   Nationwide Average Wages of Industries
(in yen)

| Month | Year | |
	1947	1948
1	964	2,951
2	1,022	2,981
3	1,083	3,219
4	1,233	3,670
5	1,425	3,761
6	1,689	4,395
7	1,835	4,872
8	2,031	5,459
9	2,181	5,975
10	2,309	6,574
11	2,536	6,921
12	3,517	9,038

5. Third Revision of Official Prices and Wage Stabilization Program: June 1948-March 1949

During this period of policy debate, nominal wages rose rapidly as shown in Table 3. The average wage in June 1948 was 4,395 yen, almost 2.5 times higher than that of the previous year. This implied some inconsistencies in the July 1947 revision of official prices, necessitating further revisions which were implemented in June 1948. This third large-scale revision in official prices since 1945 can be summarized as follows. (1) Transportation fees for passengers and freight on the National Railway were raised by 3.5 times while telecommunication fees were increased by 4.0 times. (2) The average monthly wage was set at 3,700 yen, estimated sufficient to keep living standards constant under the new price system. (3) The purchaser price of Price Stabilized Commodities (PSC; *Antei Tai Busshi*) was set at 110 times the level of 1934-36. (4) The purchaser prices for basic producer goods and consumer goods were fixed at 1.7 times and 1.8 times the maximum levels respectively. (5) Differences between purchaser prices and producer prices were subsidized by SSPA. (6) The producer prices of mining and manufacturing commodities were mainly estimated on the basis of production costs, while prices for agricultural commodities were estimated by the parity method (the parity index of rice was anchored at 1.32 times the level of 1934-36). (7) The average exchange rate (yen/dollar) was assumed to be 300 yen. At this exchange rate, official prices were compared with U.S. domestic prices. Gaps were adjusted by setting the separate exchange rates for certain commodities. This marked the first time that the level of the exchange rate and the comparison with international market prices were considered when official prices were determined.

After this third revision of official prices, nominal wages continued to increase. As can be seen from Table 3, nominal wages rose almost 46 percent between May and September 1948. However, real wages also increased, gaining 24 percent, because consumer prices rose only 22 percent during this time. Moreover, real wages after taxes increased more than 30 percent because of a reduced income tax rate on labor. Despite these encouraging developments, price subsidies and special subsidies soared further: Subsidies on SSPA amounted to 62.5 billion, 13.2 percent of the general government budget. These figures included not only subsidies for price adjustment, but also special subsidies such as compensation for deficits of firms and wage payments.[19] Special wage subsidies proved particularly damaging to anti-inflation efforts. Subsidies to compensate for increases in nominal wages when real wages were rising tended to promote over-compensation for workers, generating demand-pull inflation. These subsidies also undermined economic efficiency since they supported loss-making firms. Inflation was also fueled by the rise in Bank of Japan notes caused by the government deficit associated with price subsidies; the surge in credits through the Reconstruction Financing Corporation (RFC) also increased note issuance since BOJ discounted RFC bonds.

SCAP suggested three principles for breaking the spiral between subsidies, lending to the deficit firms, and increases in official prices. The Three Principles for Wages (*Chingin 3 Gensoku*) proposed in November 1948 advocated the following. (1) Subsidies to compensate for increased wages would be permitted only as long as new government funds were found. (2) Loans to firms would not be permitted if they aimed to compensate for deficits generated by the payment of increased wages. (3) Wage increases which might generate a rise in the general price level were not permitted. These three principles were designed to break the tendency of firms to depend upon the government, and they acted as a sort of indirect wage control, differing from SCAP's earlier demand for direct wage controls.

In addition, the Occupation also considered the introduction of a uniform exchange rate to halt inflation and stabilize the economy. The Young Report stressed the need for such a uniform exchange rate to replace the multi-tiered exchange rate structure in place at the time.[20] Exchange rates were set differently for each export and import; the average rate for exports was 330 yen per dollar and that for imports was 130 yen per dollar. Hence, even though the dollar-denominate trade balance was in deficit, yen-denominated exports actually exceeded yen-denominated imports. These "hidden subsidies" to exporters were financed through the government's special accounts, with funding provided by the Bank of Japan. Consequently, the multiple exchange rate structure contributed to the increase of both Japan's money supply and inflation.[21] In an attempt to respond to these SCAP suggestions the Japanese government tries to reorganize its stabilization policies, proposing the Outline of New Economic Policies (*Shin Keizai Seisaku Taikō An*) in November 1948. In the Outline, the government showed a willingness to adopt a new system of prices, one based on internationally accepted standards, once a uniform exchange rate was set. Firms were not to be dependent on the government, although government protection would be used to guarantee economic stability. This outline marked Japan's first step toward an open economy.

During this period of efforts to stabilize the economy, inflation did abate somewhat. The ratio of the free market price of consumer goods to the official price fell from 7.5 fold in June 1948 to 2.8 fold in March 1949, while that ratio for producer goods declined from 5.9 fold to 2.8 fold. The rate of increase in free market prices for consumer goods had fallen to an annual rate of 20 percent and prices for producer goods were rising only by 5 percent. It was during this time of a declining rate of inflation that the Dodge Line was implemented.

6. Dodge's Stabilization Policy and the Fourth Revision of Official Prices: April 1949-December 1949

The desirability of a uniform exchange rate was again asserted in a directive to SCAP from the US government in December 1948.[22] The uniform rate was expected to be set at about 300 yen per dollar. As such, the exchange rate for exports would appreciate (from an average of 330) while that for imports would depreciated (from an average of 130). The subsequent increase in prices for imported goods would have an inflationary impact on the economy, but the reduction of hidden subsidies would have a disinflationary impact. The Japanese government expected that any trade deficit caused by the uniform exchange rate could be covered by US foreign aid which would also be used to help subsidize prices for imported goods. Joseph M. Dodge reached basically these same conclusions in his stabilization policy for the Japanese economy.

J. M. Dodge was a director of the financial division in the US Occupation Government in Germany in 1946 and he later served as president of the Detroit Bank. President Truman requested that he lead US efforts to reform the Japanese economy. Dodge, a believer in classical economics, focused on two weaknesses in the Japanese economy, its over-dependence on aid from the US and its over-protection of the private sector by government subsidies. Dodge, intending to restore the market mechanism, constructed a balanced government budget, slashing subsidies. In fact, the government budget in 1949 was not only balanced but it showed a surplus of 15.76 billion yen. Dodge addressed inflation not only through this surplus budget but also through tight control of the money supply. He also set a uniform yen-dollar exchange rate at 360.

Although this collection of policies, commonly called the Dodge Line, is generally evaluated as orthodox, Dodge did recognize that it was also highly important to restore production, not through subsidies but through management efforts by firms. As such, Dodge refused to allow the Japanese government to use subsidies funded by BOJ notes to compensate for import price hikes which accompanied the yen depreciation. Instead, special accounts for collateral funds, the so-called US Aid Counterpart Fund (*Mikaeri Shikin Tokubetsu Kaikei*) were established. These funds did not necessarily generate a rise in the money supply, since fund sources were revenue from the sale of government purchases of foreign aid commodities to the public, as well as other funds from general government accounts. Subsidies for exports were prohibited.[23] Dodge also decided to gradually abolished subsidies for Price Stabilized Commodities (PSC), in place since 1947. Direct wage controls were not used, and special wage subsidies such as those for deficit forms were also abolished.

Corresponding to the policy reform of the Dodge Line, official prices were again revised on a large scale. Although revisions were divided into several stages according to commodity group, changes were intended to abolish controls and restore the free market. Official producer prices were partly decreased and official purchaser prices were partly increased in order to reduce the differences between them. Higher import prices also had a certain impact on general price increases. However, after the revisions official price rises were smaller than those expected, with official prices increasing only 10-20 percent during the period from April 1949 to January 1950. Free market prices actually declined, with drops seen for the free market price of consumer goods, the price of non-rationed consumer goods and the free market price of producer goods. These declines were partially caused by the suppression of demand caused by the Dodge Line as well as a gradual recovery in production. Gaps between free market prices and official prices also fell: Whereas free market prices for both consumer and producer goods were 2.3 times official prices in March 1949, these ratios had fallen to 1.2-1.3 times by June 1950.

7. Deregulation of Prices and Commodities Following the Dodge Line: April 1949-July 1952

Commodities had been rationed under the Emergency Law of Demand and Supply Adjustment for Commodities (*Rinji Jukyū Chōsei Hō*) since October 1946, while prices were regulated under the Price Control Law (*Bukka Tōsei Rei*) since March 1946. To handle the rationing of commodities, the government established 15 public corporations (*Kōdan*) in 1946. Under the deregulation policy of the Dodge Line, eight of these were abolished in March 1949 and all of them were abolished by March 1951. The number of rationed commodities also fell, from 252 producer goods and 64 consumer goods at the peak, to 48 and 15 respectively by April 1950. The outbreak of the Korean War in June 1950 stimulated the Japanese economy tremendously, and the Dodge deflation gave way to a boom driven by special procurements of the US government. This stronger demand put pressure on Japanese prices again, as did tightness in international markets for commodities which increased import prices. The government, however, did not change its basic policy of deregulating the economy. Deregulation, such as the abolition of the System of Price Adjustment Subsidies, reduced differences between prices in the domestic and international markets, effectively linking the two.

In June 1951, the government released a statement concerning its economic policy in which it reconfirmed that prices would be controlled only as long as necessary to stabilize the economy. This marked the end of focusing on price and commodity regulation to quell inflation. After this, inflation policy centered on indirect measures rather than direct controls, using fiscal and monetary policy to halt price increases. The Price Bureau and the Economic Stabilization Board, both of which filled important roles in the period of direct controls, were closed in March and

July 1952, respectively.

III. Planning and Control

The discussion of inflation policies in Part II reveals that measures adopted to combat price rises were not the orthodox ones of tight monetary and fiscal policies. Rather, adopted measures included direct plans and controls mixed with certain orthodox stabilization measures. Plans and controls were used as micro-policy instruments. Within a legal framework, prices of selected goods were officially controlled and these commodities were rationed by designated organizations. However, the impact of these measures was not limited to the micro-level but also influenced the macroeconomy. Hence, to assess these measures, it is necessary to look at their effect on both individual behavior (the micro-level) as well as the money supply and the government budget (the macro-level). In other words, it is necessary to determine whether plans and controls, through their impact on consumers and producers, accomplished their goal of restoring the balance between supply and demand. Moreover, the possible benefits of these prices and controls must be evaluated against the inflationary pressures they generated through their adverse impact on the money supply and the government budget.

The series of monetary reforms enforced in February 1946 through the Emergency Ordinance for the Economy were a type of orthodox stabilization policy. One objective was to reduce the purchasing power of the public. The public was prohibited from withdrawing money from bank deposits excepting a certain amount for living and production activities. The monthly wage per person of 500 yen, established as the maximum wage level permitted in the new currency, was low in relation to actual living costs. According to statistics of the Price Division of MOF, the level of 500 yen was consistent with standard living expenses for the average-sized household, assuming an eight fold increase in prices from those in 1934-36. (See first two columns of Table 4). However, price increases were in fact much greater. Table 4 also shows observed monthly expenditure totals and breakdowns for

1946 and 1937. According to data in this table, the standard living cost in the 3.3 system of official prices was assumed to be about 70 percent of the observed living cost in 1946 (0.712 = 526.02 yen / 72.75 yen). Yet the consumer price index shown in the last column of Table 4 reveals that the average rise in consumer prices between 1935 and 1945 was almost 50 fold. Price increases for food and clothing were particularly great, rising 78 and 82 fold respectively. Hence, if households intended to maintain their 1935 living standards at 1946 prices, they would need at least 3,540 yen per month, almost seven times the designed standard living cost under the 3.3 system of official prices. Figures for living expenses in 1946, shown in Column Three of Table 4, also imply that the observed living standards in 1946 were only 20 percent of those in 1935; for food alone, 1946 was 30 percent the level of 1935 at most. Hence, the observed living standards in 1946 represent almost a minimum subsistence level of expenditures. This analysis suggests that households could not exist upon only the maximum monthly payment of 500 yen but needed to withdraw funds from their bank deposits. Furthermore, households found it necessary to supplement rationed foods with purchases on the black market. Since black market transactions were only conducted in the new currency, the new yen appreciated against the old compared to the official exchange rate between the two. This actual appreciation increased the purchasing power of the new currency. Consequently, controlling deposit withdrawals and wages under the Emergency Ordinance did not much reduce the purchasing power of households nor did these measures suppress inflation. Monetary policy, as expected, failed to suppress consumption below minimum subsistence levels, and the appreciation of the new currency generated effective excess demand in the black market.

In the chaotic situation immediately following the war, fiscal and monetary policies alone did not suffice to halt inflationary trends in the economy. Inflation arose not only for monetary reasons, but also because of supply shortages caused by the destruction of production capacity and the interruption of raw material imports. Price and wage controls attempted to address these supply side issues, in contrast to demand management of monetary and fiscal policy. The government intended to increase incentives to produce when it fixed prices and subsidized the differences between producer and purchaser prices. Government rationing of commodities attempted to allocate raw materials to selected industries in order to raise output. Under the subsidy system, producers were guaranteed at least full recovery of their production costs. Should they reduce these costs below government estimates used to set the official producer prices, then their profits rose.

At the time of the 1947 price revision, the System of Subsidies for Price Adjustment (SSPA) was expanded both in size and in scope. Price subsidies focused increasingly on three important industries, coal, iron and steel, and fertilizer. These industries, which were designated under the Priority Production System (PPS), also received priority in obtaining raw materials and benefited from other financial support provided by the Reconstruction Finance Corporation (RFC). Table 5 shows the importance of these three industries: They accounted for the majority of government subsidies after 1946, and government subsidies rose almost 12 fold between 1946 and 1949. Especially, subsidies were focused on three important industries; coal, steel and fertilizer. The sharp rise in output for these industries during this time favors a positive assessment for price subsidies.[24] Together with other measures, such as rationing raw materials for selective industries[25] under the PPS, price subsidies, by offering incentives to producers, helped promote a recovery in production, thus acting to restore the balance between supply and demand. Price subsidies also need to be differentiated from other special subsidies such as those for wage payments, for deficit firms, and for imported goods. These other special subsidies, which also rose after 1947, did not act as a direct incentive to raise output. They may actually have somewhat discouraged production by over-protecting industries.

Unfortunately, the macroeconomic impact of the SSPA was not as favorable as its impact on the production levels of individual industries. As shown in Table 5, subsidies totaled more than 10 percent of general government expenditure. Subsidies increased claims on the government and led to an increase in the issue of BOJ notes. Table 6 designates the trends of sources the issuance of BOJ notes. After the financial reform in the Economic Emergency Ordinance in the spring of 1946, new issuance of BOJ notes again started to increase and this trend continued until the Dodge policy of 1949. BOJ note issues increased by 125.7 billion yen in 1947 and by 136.1 billion yen in 1948, largely because of these greater claims on the government. Although in 1949 new issuance of BOJ notes had been reduced rapidly by the Dodge reform, it should be noted that instead of increases in the claims on government, BOJ credit due to the lending of commercial banks in the private sector and purchasing government bond, increased and maintained the increases of the money supply in the market. This sharp rise in the money supply caused inflation to accelerate, creating the need to raise wages. However, these higher wages created excess demand, generating further inflationary pressures. Moreover, since wage increases were subsidized by the government, they also generated higher money supply growth which again fueled inflation. This vicious spiral between subsidies, the money supply, inflation and prices, apparent since 1947, might have been broken by direct wage controls which were, in fact, recommended by SCAP. Controls could have ensured that wage increases did not outstrip productivity gains, and the continued use of price subsidies could have acted to promote productivity increases. However, the Japanese government was reluctant to introduce direct wage controls, choosing instead to regard and expansion of foreign aid as the means to break the inflationary spiral. However, greater foreign aid did not accomplish this goal: The government used this aid to increase subsidies for imported goods, thus raising "hidden subsidies" to almost 100 billion in 1948. This increase in subsidies then raised the money supply and exaggerated inflation.

We tried to show trends in production, employment and real monthly wage rates during the period 1944-1950 in selective industries. According to the production index as shown in

Table 7, it can be seen that almost all industries were enormously damaged: The production of food, textiles, chemicals, stone, steel and machinery in 1947 were decreased by 31, 21, 21, 23, 14 and 28 percent of that in 1940, respectively. During the period 1947-1950, some selected industries such as chemicals and steel were rapidly restored. On the other hand, the employment index shows that employment in these industries was not necessarily decreased by the shock of the end of the war. This implies that almost all industries had to employ an excess labor force and their utilization was obliged to be lowered with over-employment because of the shortage of raw materials and energy. Hence, their productivity was lowered, as shown in Table 7. Although the industries shown are limited by the lack of data, we can see the trends of efficiency wages during these period. An increasing trend more than unity in Figure 3.1 and Figure 3.2 implies that the real wage rate increased more than the increase in productivity. In all industries we can see that the efficiency wage had increased rapidly during the period 1944-1947 and decreased gradually during the next three years. In other words, the increasing rate of real wage was higher than that of productivity before 1947, which was the higher inflationary period, and growth of the real wage rate was not correspondingly parallel to the growth of productivity. Although the efficiency wage after 1947 decreased gradually in almost all industries, it was still more than the unity. Trends of the efficiency wage more than unity implies that real wage increases more than productivity improvement had a possibility to induce the demand pull effect in the market due to the increase of the effective demand, and the cost push effect due to the rise of production costs as the causes for inflation.

Dodge's stabilization strategy in 1949 was largely orthodox, consisting primarily of tighter monetary and fiscal policies. This was the second attempt in the postwar period to introduce orthodox stabilization measures, but the economic situation in 1949 differed greatly from that of 1946. Most importantly, inflation was abating not accelerating. From autumn 1948, free market prices for producer and consumer goods had become fairly stable, implying that excess demand had eased. Another difference was that growth in the money supply prior to the implementation of the Dodge line was largely the result of government subsidies. It was against this backdrop that Dodge balanced the government budget, introduced a uniform exchange rate and slashed subsidies. Although the outbreak of the Korean War makes difficult a complete evaluation of Dodge's policies, they were more successful at stabilizing the economy than 1946 policies. What success the Dodge Line enjoyed arose from the more favorable economic situation at the time his policies were implemented, and this more favorable economic environment was at least partially created by government planning and control policies from 1946-1949. Although price controls did not succeed in eliminating inflation by themselves, they did lay the foundation for successful stabilization.

**Table 4   Monthly Standard of Living Cost
Per Household in 1946**

(yen)

	Designed standard of living in 3.3 system		Observed standard of living in 1946		Observed standard of living in 1937		Consumer price index in 1946
	(yen)	(%)	(yen)	(%)	(yen)	(%)	(p1935 = 1.0)
Foods	260.47	49.5	543.12	73.6	29.02	39.9	78.0
Housing	52.65	10.0	31.50	4.3	11.97	16.5	23.1
Clothing	35.00	6.6	37.00	5.0	7.22	9.9	81.7
Light & fuel	31.58	6.0	35.00	4.7	3.94	5.4	18.7
Miscellaneous	146.32	27.9	91.26	12.4	20.60	28.3	16.5
Total	526.02	100.0	737.88	100.0	72.75	100.0	48.7

Source: Showa Fiscal History, cp. cit. vol. 10, p. 260 and vol. 19, Pp. 52-53.

Table 5   Subsidies for Price and Wages

(100 million yen)

Price subsidies	Year 1941	1942	1943	1944	1945
Food	144	201	440	545	413
Coal	95	207	428	1,021	1,919
Iron	-	-	134	261	545
Nonferrous metal	2	3	21	117	1,145
Electricity	20	7	32	71	86
Petroleum	3	4	18	7	9
Others	3	-	-	87	219
Total (A)	267	422	1,073	2,109	4,330
General government expenditure (B)	8,134	8,276	12,552	19,872	21,496
A/B (%)	3.3	5.1	8,5	10,6	20,1
Increase in claims on government (C)	7,769	9,634	10,742	16,243	28,986
A/C	3.4	4.4	10.0	13.0	14.9

(*Continued*)

Price subsidies	Year			
	1946	1947	1948	1949
Food	6,480	5,542	-	-
Coal	2,531	9,957	18,119	21,675
Iron	-	3,873	21,372	46,375
Nonferrous metal	-	808	2,392	1,803
Chemical fertilizer	-	1,815	10,470	25,625
Caustic soda	-	159	1,433	2,450
Electricity	-	-	-	-
Petroleum	25	-	-	-
Textile	-	-	-	-
Others	-	-	-	-
Total (C)	9,036	22,154	53,786	97,928
Other special subsidies (D)	0	356	8,713	72,286
Total (C) + (D)	9,036	22,510	62,499	170,214
General government expenditure (E)	115,207	206,523	462,956	699,598
(C + D)/E (%)	7.8	10.9	13.5	24.3
Increase in claims on government (F)	16,910	107,800	171,000	-120,000
(C + D)/F	53.4	20.9	36.5	-

Table 6 Sources of Issuance of BOJ Notes

(billion yen)

Quarterly	Total issuance of BOJ notes	Increase in claims on govern.	Other claim	Increase in claims on public	Increase in deposit on public	Increase BOJ credit	Lending to comm. bank	Govern. bond	Govern. T.B.	Purchase RFC bonds
1945.1	2.8	2.9	-0.1	0.0	-0.5	0.5	5.5	-5.2	0.2	0.0
4	5.7	5.2	0.8	-0.3	-1.3	0.9	6.5	-5.6	0.0	0.0
7	15.2	11.8	8.0	-4.5	-0.1	-4.4	2.6	-7.0	-0.1	0.0
10	14.0	9.2	-1.7	6.5	-0.3	6.9	14.2	-7.5	0.1	0.0
1946.1	-32.1	-14.3	0.4	-18.3	-3.9	-14.4	-9.2	-5.4	0.2	0.0
4	19.4	14.1	-0.2	5.5	-0.6	6.1	3.4	1.5	1.2	
7	21.7	6.6	6.9	8.2	-1.9	10.1	10	0.1	0	
10	29	10.5	3.5	15	-0.3	15.3	8.4	1.1	5.8	
1947.1	22.3	10.1	-0.6	12.8	-0.4	13.2	1.5	2.2	7	2.5
4	20.6	10	-0.2	10.8	-0.2	11	-4.9	0.3	8.2	7.4
7	20.1	22.1	2.1	-4.1	-5.1	1	-10.3	0.6	-2.7	13.4
10	62.7	65.6	6.3	-9.2	-4.4	-4.8	-4.4	1.3	-10.7	9
1948.1	-0.4	-24.7	-5.9	30.2	2.7	27.5	25.7	0.6	-8.9	10.1
4	11.8	20.8	-1.8	-7.2	2.5	-9.7	-5.8	0	-12.9	9
7	31.6	37.4	2.5	-8.3	-6.5	-1.8	10.9	1.5	-14.5	0.3
10	93.1	137.5	6.6	-51	-0.4	-50.6	-11.2	1.2	-20.9	-19.7

1949.1	-42.7	-108.4	45.3	20.4	-0.4	20.8	16	4.8	
4	-11.9	-21.6	-3.9	13.6	1.7	11.9	1.8	8.9	1.2
7	-2.4	-39.6	2.8	34.4	1.7	32.7	20.8	7	4.9
10	57.1	49.6	4.2	3.3	-2.5	5.8	-1.9	7.7	
1950.1	-44	-73.2	-4.4	33.6	3.8	30.1	21.3	8.8	
4	-0.2	-36	1.9	33.9	3.8	30.1	21.3	8.8	
7	17.6	-25.5	4.1	39	-1.2	40.2	25.9	14.3	
10	93.3	138.9	6.3	-51.9	-6.8	-45.1	-41.5	-3.6	
Yearly									
1945	37.695	28.986	7.029	1.68	-2.247	3.927	28.895	-25.234	0.266
1946	37.957	16.91	10.622	10.425	-6.71	17.135	12.592	-2.632	7.175
1947	125.7	107.8	7.6	10.3	-10.1	20.4	-18.1	4.4	1.8	32.3
1948	136.1	171	1.4	-36.3	-1.7	-34.6	19.6	3.3	-57.2	-0.3
1949	0.1	-120	48.4	71.7	0.5	71.2	36.7	28.4	6.1
1950	66.7	4.2	7.9	54.6	-2.9	57.5	25.9	31.6	

Source: The 100 Year History of BOJ (Nihonginko Hyakunenshi).

225

Table 7 Production and Productivity

Industry	1944	1947	1950
Real Wage Index			
Mining	1.0285581	1.0527048	0.9500812
Food	1.2274325	1.4079718	1.4419695
Textiles	1.3132307	1.0535384	1.5169230
Wood Mfg.	1.2926023	0.9088507	0.8672391
Chemicals	1.2790621	1.1260175	1.4705307
Stone	1.2581860	1.1370617	1.1286583
Steel	1.2008753	-	1.4402211
Machinery	1.2805369	1.0265771	1.0928859
Employment Index			
Mining	1.3010033	1.1153846	0.9882943
Food	0.7915742	1.0221729	1.7184035
Textiles	0.6265822	0.8306962	0.8750000
Wood Mfg.	0.7995283	1.6910377	1.1533018
Chemicals	0.9526627	1.7721893	1.1597633
Stone	0.7920792	0.7623762	0.9174917
Steel	1.1729428	0.9609483	0.8270571
Machinery	1.1597883	1.1851851	0.3714285
Production Index			
Mining	0.9705676	0.4751226	0.7112824
Food	0.5313283	0.3132832	0.6207184
Textiles	0.2453488	0.2116279	0.5186046
Wood Mfg.	0.8277425	0.7262012	0.8848594
Chemicals	0.5501930	0.2168597	0.6447876
Stone	0.3976744	0.2360465	0.5848837
Steel	1.2951205	0.1434450	0.7142857
Machinery	2.2199329	0.2850982	0.5874460
Productivity Index			
Mining	0.7460147	0.4259720	0.7197070
Food	0.6712298	0.3064874	0.3612180

Textiles	0.3915668	0.2547569	0.5926910
Wood Mfg.	1.0352885	0.4294411	0.7672401
Chemicals	0.5775318	0.1223682	0.5559648
Stone	0.5020639	0.3096194	0.6374811
Steel	1.1041633	0.1492744	0.8636473
Machinery	1.9140844	0.2405516	1.5815856

Note: Base year (1940) in index = 1.0.
Source: Syowa Fiscal History (Syowa Zaiseishi vol. 19).

References

1. Arisawa, Hiromi (1948), *Inflation and Socialization (in Japanese: Infuresyon to Syakaika),* Nihon Hyouron Sya.
2. Bank of Japan eds. (1985), *History of Bank of Japan (in Japanese: Nihon Ginko 100 Nen shi).*
3. Bronfenbrenner, M. (1975), *Inflation Theories of the SCAP Period,* History of Political Economy, No. 2.
4. Economic Planning Agency eds. (1973), *Survey: Economic White Paper Since 1947, (in Japanese: Shiryo: Keizai Hakusyo 25 Nen),* Nihon Keizai Shinbun Sya.
5. Economic Planning Agency (EPA) (1976), *History of Economic Planning Agency During 30 Years (in Japanese: Gendai Nihon no Tenkai-keizai Kikak-ucyo 30 Nen shi).*
6. Economic Stabilization Board (1974), *Report on Economic Situation (in Japanese: Keizai Jisso Hokokusyo).*
7. Ida, Tsuneo and Others eds. (1976), *Economic History of Postwar Japan, (in Japanese: Gendai Nihon Keizai Shi),* Chikuma Syobo.
8. Kosai, Yutaka (1981), *Age of High Economic Growth, (in Japanese: Koudo Seicyou no Jidai-Gendai Nihon Keizai Shi Note),* Nihon Hyouron Sya.
9. Kosai, Yutaka and Yoshitaro Ogino (1980), *Prospectives of the Japanese Economy (in Japanese: Nihon Keizai Tembou),* Nihon Hyouron Sya.
10. Kuroda, Mashiro (1985), "Economic Growth and Productivity" (in Japanese: Keizai Seicyou to Zenyouso Seisansei no Suii), *Mita Syogaku Kenkyuu,* vol. 282, No. 2.
11. Ministry of Finance eds. (1980), *Fiscal History in Syowa (in Japanese: Syowa zaisei shi),* Toyou Keizai Shinpou Sya.
12. Ministry of International Trade and Industry eds. (1985), *History of International Trade and Industry (in Japanese: Tsusyo Sangyo shi).*
13. Nakamura, Takafusa (1978), *Japanese Economy—Its Growth and Structure (in Japanese: Nihon Keizai—sono Seicyou to Kouzou),* Tokyo Daigaku Syppan Kai.

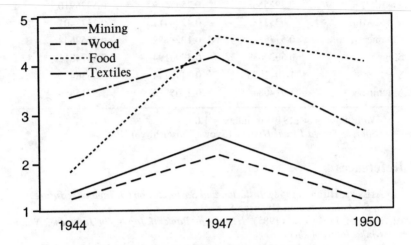

Figure 3.1 Trend of Efficiency Wage

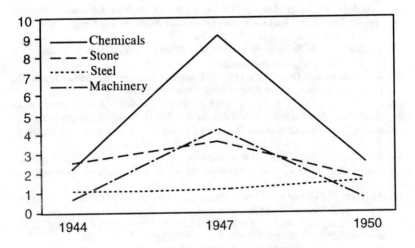

Figure 3.2 Trend of Efficiency Wage

14. Nakamura, Takafusa and Kounosuke Odaka eds. (1989), *Dual Structure (in Japanese: Nijyuu Kouzou)*, vol. 6, *Japanese Economic History (in Japanese: Nihon Keizai Shi)*, Umemura, M. and Others eds., Iwanami Syoten.
15. Nakamura, Takafusa (1968), *Postwar Japanese Economic Growth and Cycle (in Japanese: Sengo Nihon Keizai—Seicho to Junkan)*, Chikuma-syobo (1970), *Fixing of the Economic Growth (in Japanese: Keizai Seicho no Teichaku)*, Tokyo Univ. Press (Tokyo Daigaku Syuppan Kai) (1981), *The Postwar Japanese Economy*.
16. Nakamura, Takafusa ed. (1989), *Planning and Democratization (in Japanese: Keikakuka to Minsyuka)*, vol. 7, *Japanese Economic History (in Japanese: Nihon Keizai shi)*, Umemura, M. and Others eds. Iwanami Syoten.
17. Okawa, Kazushi and Henry Rosovsky (1973), *Japanese Economic Growth —Trend Acceleration in the 20th Century*, Stanford University Press, Stanford, California (1972), *(in Japanese: Nihon no Keizai Seicyou—20 Seiki niokeru Syyusei Kasoku)*, Touyou Keizai Shinpou Sya.
18. Okawa, Kazushi and Ryoshin Minami eds. (1975), *Economic Development in Modern Japan (in Japanese: Kindai Nihon no Keizai Hatten)*, Toyo Keizai Shinpou Sya.
19. Okawa, Kazushi, Shinohara, Miyohei and Umemura, Mataji eds., *Long-term Economic Statistics (in Japanese: Cyoki Keizai Toukei)*, Toyo Keizai Shinpou Sya.
20. Suzuki, Takeo (1952), *Fisical History in Japan (in Japanese: Gendai Nihon Zaiseishi)* Tokyo Univ. Press (Tokyo Daigaku Syuppan Kai).
21. Teranishi Juro (1991), *Inflation Stabilization with Growth—Experience of Japan During 1945-1950*, Conference Paper on the Role of Government in Economic Development.
22. Uchino, Tatsurou (1978), *Economic History in Postwar Japan (in Japanese: Sengo Nihon Keizai Shi)*, Koudansya Gakujyutsu Bunko.
23. Yasuba, Yasukichi and Takenori Inoki eds. (1989), *High Economic Growth (in Japanese: Koudo Seicyou)*, vol. 8 *Japanese Economic History (in Japanese: Nihon Keizai Shi)*, Umemura, M. and Others eds., Iwanami Syoten.

Notes

1. Refer to wholesale price index by the Bank of Japan in Showa Fiscal History (*Showa Zaisei Shi, Shūsen Kara Kōwa Made*), vol. 19, pp. 38-39.
2. Refer to consumer price index by the Prime Minister's Office in Showa Fiscal History, *op. cit.* pp. 47-48.
3. The labor force increased rapidly by the demobilization of the soldiers and the repatriates from abroad. Population increased by 5 million during 1944-1947, including a 1.5 million increase of the labor force. More than 4 million of the labor force were absorbed by the primary sector due to the deterioration of manufacturing activities.
4. Price indices (A), (B) and (C) are estimated figures which are based upon

officially published price indices in each organization. Originally, they were not comparable because of differences in the commodities or regions covered. However, MOF has adjusted for these differences. Refer to Showa Fiscal History, *op. cit.* vol. 10, pp. 585-586.

5. Price indices (E), (F) and (G) are also adjusted figures which are based on officially published price indices. MOF has made these adjustments to make the different series comparable.

6. T. Nakamura suggested dividing the period into three sub-periods; August 1945-February 1946, March 1946-August 1946, and September 1946-April 1949 in Showa Fiscal History, *op. cit.* vol. 12, p. 149. Here, we tried to divide his third period into four more sub-periods in order to clarify the policy correspondence chronologically.

7. Refer to "Directive No. 3" by Office of the Supreme Commander, September 22, 1945.

8. The new issuance of Bank of Japan notes in 1945 amounted to 37.7 billion yen. This was almost 14 times the average annual issue of 1940-1944.

9. The manufacturing production index in 1946 was only one-fifth of the peak level in 1944. The rice crop was the worst since 1987. Imports of coal and iron ore were decreased to 12 and 2 percent of the 1935 level in 1945.

10. Speaking exactly, it should be called "the issuance of new yen currency," since it was not intended to revalue the yen by the denomination policy.

11. 15 kg is equal to 1 koku in the Japanese measure.

12. SSPA was originally enforced in 1940 as subsidies for coal. During consideration of price control measures just after the end of war, the Japanese government originally intended to suspend SSPA. In the Price Level Control Law, the government also wanted to reduce its own burden by setting up special accounts, in which subsidies for price adjustment were combined with the disposition of marginal profits arising from the setting of official prices. These ideas were not realized.

13. For example, the purchase price of rice on the free market was 6,500 yen per 150 kg, which was almost 26 times the official price.

14. It might be questionable to classify the Emergency Ordinance of February 1946 as an orthodox measure. In the sense that it was intended to suppress the excess demand by the reforms of the financial and fiscal ordinances originally, we tried to evaluate it as a kind of orthodox measures.

15. ESB and PB correspond to the US Office of Economic Stabilization and the US Office of Price Administration.

16. Refer to Adams, T. F. M. and I. Hoshii (1972), *A Financial History of the New Japan* and Bronfenbrenner, M. (1975), "Inflation Theories of the SCAP Period," *History of Political Economy* No. 2.

17. Refer to Essentials of the ESS Economic Stabilization Program (*Keizai Antei Keikaku no Gaiyō*), Economic and Scientific Section (ESS), SCAP, May 1947.

18. For rice, price increases of 71 goods used in rice production were estimated

at about 62.55 times the level of 1934-36. Thus, the producer price of rice was calculated as 62.55 times the rice price in 1934-36 of 27.16 yen per 150 kg, or 1,700 yen per 150 kg.

19. Special subsidies included compensation for deficits of firms such as private railway companies, passenger traffic companies and coal mining companies and compensation for wage payments in coal mining and electric companies. (*Shitetsu Sonshitsu Hosyo Hokyukin, Ryokakusen Sonshitsu Hosyo Hokyukin, Sekitan Seisan Sonshitsu Hosyokin, Denki Jigyo Jyugyouin Chingin Hokyukin, Tankou Jyuugyouin Chingin Hokyukin* etc.).

20. "Report of the Special Mission on Yen Foreign Exchange Policy," June 1948.

21. This point was emphasized by Young who used the phrase "hidden subsidies" (*Miezaru Hojokin*).

22. "Nine Objectives for the Stabilization of Economy," (*Keizai Antei 9 Gensoku*).

23. According to the estimates of MOF, hidden subsidies amounted to more than 100 billion yen in 1948. Adding these to the usual measures of subsidies, the total amount was almost 30 percent of government expenditure and 6 percent of GNP. Subsidies were largely funded by BOJ lending.

24. For example, by 1948 the output of crude steel had more than doubled from the 1946 level of 0.56 million tons.

25. Although the production of coal mining products in 1946 dramatically decreased by almost 37 percent of the peak level during the war period, and rationed coal products were reduced from 60.522 million tons in 1943 to 22.389 million tons in 1946, rationing of coal products had been continued for selective industries such as steel, chemicals and gas and electric since the middle of 1947.

The Market Economy and Macro Regulation and Control

Wu Wei
Professor of the People's University of China

China has made the establishment of a socialist market economy the objective of economic reform. In the early days of the transition from a planned economy to a market economy which has now lasted for over a decade the Chinese government put forward the idea that while strengthening the enterprise vitality and perfecting the market system, we should reinforce macro regulation and control, and regard it as one of the key tasks of the reform. Later, the government emphasized time and again that macro regulation and control, enlivening enterprises, and invigorating the market are an integral whole, and no single one of them can be dispensed with. In 1991, China further confirmed that establishing and perfecting the system of macroeconomic regulation and control was a major objective of the reform, and this objective was included in the Ten-Year Program. However, judging by experience so far, these measures have obviously lagged behind. But this situation has shown signs recently of improving. In spite of this, however, some theoretical questions are still unclear and need further study.

I. Macro Regulation and Control Negates the Argument That the Market Allocates Resources in the Best Way

Since the reform assumption of allocating resources through the market was put forward in China, an opinion is prevalent that the market may reasonably allocate limited economic resources in the best and most effective way. Since China's economy is "in a precontemporary state, the classic economics of the 19th century may be applicable." It seems that as soon as China adopted the market economy, it began to run along the expressway of economic growth. Unfortunately, this viewpoint is not supported by facts. If China follows the market economic road taken by most European countries—developing from free competition to monopoly and then to government interference, the realization of China's modernization will be much delayed and the social costs will be huge. International experience proves that if a country that lags behind wants to reach an advanced level within a short time period, it must walk on two legs, and needs both the market and government forces to bring their combined advantages into full play.

The market is like a wild horse that needs an excellent rider. This is none other than the government. When the horse runs to a side road, or runs too fast or too slow, the rider should tight its reins or give it the whip. This is macro regulation and control. Therefore, macro regulation and control is the negation of the theory—"The market allocates limited economic resources in the best way."

The present market economy is, in fact, under macro regulation and control. Different countries adopt different regulation and control methods at various stages of development.

China's socialist market economy means that the market under socialist macro regulation and control will play a basic role in allocating resources to accelerate the further development of productive forces and modernization of the national economy. The market economy practiced by other countries shares the following characteristics with China's social market economy: a. Market regulation refers to the basic regulation of resource allocation. b. Macro regulation and control is an important component part of the market economic system. c. The state is the mainstay of macro regulation and control. d. The original meaning of macro regulation and control is indirect control over enterprises, i.e., micro-decisions will be influenced by readjusting policies and structures to realize the expected macro-objectives. Therefore, macro regulation and control is a universal form for utilizing government economic control in a market economy, rather than a characteristic of only a socialist market economy.

China established a market economy under special conditions and this economic system must be brought into line with its basic socialist system. At present, China's economic and technical levels are fairly low as we spare no effort to achieve the steady transition from a planned to a market economy. At the same time, the income difference between urban and rural people and between various regions is growing and international competition is becoming more fierce. Therefore, the system should have unique objectives and macro regulation and control modes should inevitably have their own characteristics. For instance, on the one hand we should unceasingly take public ownership as the mainstay so that macro regulation and control may fully rely on and bring into play the large state-owned enterprises' role as the main body. On the other hand, we should make the management and operational mechanisms of state-owned enterprises meet the demands of the market economy. With regard to individual income, within the public economy, distribution according to work should be practiced, which coexists with distribution according to production within the non-public economy. We should admit that there is a rational gap, while preventing the gap between the richest and the poorest to become too great. The transformation of the production structure, the readjustment of the economic layout, the coordination of the development between regions, the perfection of the market system, and so on, are difficult problems that should be solved with macro regulation and control in accord with the principles of socialism. During this transformation of the economic system it is even more urgent to solve these sensitive problems. In sum, the system's objectives are important and the process through which these objectives are realized must not be ignored. Though an ideal macro regulation and control mode may be feasible in a mature market economy, it is hard to say if it will be effective during this transition period.

Since the market economies of all countries have common

characteristics, we must study their theories and practice, of which the unique characteristics of the market economic system, including different macro regulation and control modes and the history of their formation and evolution, are especially important for us in establishing and perfecting a socialist market economy step by step.

II. Four Major Pillars of Macroeconomic Regulation and Control

The experience of countries with market economies indicates that their governments generally exercise macro regulation and control through four means—policy, planning, legislation and administration, known as the four major pillars of macro economic regulation and control. Each of them has its own special nature and functions, but they comprehensively play their roles in macro regulation and control.

Doubtless, economic policies and legislation are the main methods of macroeconomic regulation and control. However, it is wrong to think that when the market economy has replaced the planned economy, macro regulation and control of the market economy will do away with mandatory plans and administrative control.

The countries adopting a market economy plan long- or short-term regulations and control to varying degrees. Some countries have comparatively complete state plans, grant greater power to the planning bodies, and take into account the objectives of the plan when regulating and controlling the economy. Other countries neither make state plans nor set up planning organs, but they have economic policies and state budgets which reflect the state goals and expectations on the basis of a conscious understanding of the objective trends of economic development. In terms of macrocontrol, these countries mainly take the economic growth rate, employment rate, inflation rate, international revenue and expenditure, and other short-term targets as standards. This means that policies, budgets and planning embody the subjective will that controls the objective tendency of economic operations as well as the tools for macro-regulation and control.

China is a developing socialist country with clear-cut strategic objectives and fundamental policies. Only through planning can these objectives and policies be put into practice. The state plan approved or revised by the highest organ of state power should be the main basis for macro regulation and control. Under these conditions, the state's plan is realized mainly by economic means rather than by mandatory targets for enterprises.

Administrative means, including administrative organs, legislation and techniques, have always been the government's managing tools. In macroeconomic regulation and control, administrative means play the roles as the standards, guidance, coordination, supervision, service and guaranty to other means and their implementation.

If we admit that the government serves as "general housekeeper" in the market economy, we cannot deny the necessity for administrative macroeconomic regulation and control. Some administrative errors, such as neglecting supervisory duties, malfeasance, being out of control and not working properly, must be corrected by administrative means. It must be stressed that the adoption of administrative means should be for economic development and accord with economic laws. Any bureaucratism and blind guidance that exaggerate the role of administrative means can only damage the macroeconomy the same as blindly opposing all administrative means.

III. Establishing an Efficient Macro Regulation and Control System

The state is the main body implementing macro regulation and control, and different government departments are in charge of the means for accomplishing this. The governments at all levels also have some responsibilities for implementation. How to establish this system efficiently is one of the problems that urgently need to be solved in perfecting a market economy.

The main economic means that macro regulation and control rely on are fiscal and monetary policies and planning. International practice shows that a country adopting a market economy will use certain methods to regulate and control its economy in accordance with its own circumstance. Some countries take fiscal policies as the mainstay, some rely mainly on monetary policies, while others stress planning. Each country finds its own system by establishing institutions which adopt one means for regulating and controlling its economy while using other means as supplements. The work of these institutions must be coordinated, each with its own duties and responsibilities. Under the guidance of macro-decisions made by the central government, they should regulate and control the economy in a way which will promote and increase efficiency.

The current problems in China's macro regulation and control include weak planning, lack of financial strength, a disordered monetary system and an incoherent organizational system so that the roles played by macro regulation and control are very limited. Macro regulation and control also depends on local governments to organize implementation. As there are inevitably great imbalances among regions in a country as large as China, each local government must be responsible for solving its own special problems. Therefore how to treat well the relationship between the central and local authorities remains to be solved.

In summary, the state (or central government) is the main implementor of macro regulation and control. This does not mean all functional organs and local governments at all levels are main implementors. The economy is centrally regulated and controlled by the central government, rather than by other organs or governments at other levels. The function of all macro-regulation-and-control departments of the central government and local governments is to implement the macroeconomic policies formulated by the central authorities. In order to guarantee the smooth performance, efforts should be made to make clear the relations among them to avoid conflicts and independent operations. In addition, the state should appoint certain departments as functional organs to implement comprehensive regulation and control and concrete coordination, following the principle of "unified regulation and control, and management level by level" between the central and local governments, and adopt special policies on concrete matters to avoid submitting all matters, large and small, to the State Council or state affairs meetings for resolution.

IV. The Effectiveness of Macro Regulation and Control

Adopting a market economy will further strengthen the economic vitality of our country, quicken economic development with a new starting point, and create the conditions necessary for China to participate in international competition. At the same time, generally acknowledged shortcomings of the market economy will become apparent. The new economic system will unavoidably produce social and economic contradictions and conflicts, and periodic fluctuations will become an inevitable phenomenon. On the basis of public ownership and socialist policies, the government will carry out macrocontrol, trying to achieve good results.

However, we must make appropriate estimations of the effectiveness of these policies. First, the prerequisite for successful regulations and control is sound judgement of the present state and tendencies of social and economic conditions. Only with correct evaluation can correct regulation and control decisions be made; however, some mistakes are unavoidable.

Macro regulation and control is not omnipotent. We should admit that as far as they are concerned, there is still much to learn. We should not regard theoretical models as unchangeable dogmas. Only by constantly searching for new ways to meet the demands of the developing productive forces in our economic reform can we ultimately realize our objectives.

Monetary Transformation and Macroeconomic Management in China*

On Kit Tam
Professor of the Department of Economics
and Management of the University of
New South Wales, Australia

Abstract

The notion of unification has always been considered desirable by the Chinese government in its many political and economic endeavors. In China's gradual process of economic reform, however, there are a number of important areas in which unification is clearly needed before the benefits of reforms can be fully realized and sustained. One area where unification is now urgently needed, but is generally ignored is the institution of artificial separation of cash and non-cash money flows.

The Chinese monetary management framework, national financial planning, and banking system all continue to operate under the traditional centrally planned model which restricts the use of cash to the household sector for consumption. With increasing marketization and internationalization of the economy, this segmentation becomes painfully incompatible with the new

* This is a paper presented at the International Conference on Market Economy and China, Beijing, 17-21 September 1993. Parts of this paper is based on Chapter 1 of On Kit Tam (ed), *Financial and Banking Reform in China* (Routledge, forthcoming). The author is grateful to Carl Riskin, Heinz Arndt, Hsu Chenmin, Yang Peixin, Wu Jinglian, Xu Naijiong, Du Rensheng, Lu Baifu, Zo Mu, Kong Deyong, Wang Guangqian, Wang Dayong for their comments on an earlier draft.

economic institutions.

This paper argues that monetary management is central to achieving macroeconomic stability and sustained growth in China, and that the present ineffectual centralized system of money and credit controls must be discontinued. The key to achieving this goal is to unify the formally separated cash and non-cash money categories. A complete monetary transformation is therefore necessary.

The paper concludes that the present banking system can and should be drastically changed. The Chinese economy, having embarked on the road back to a market economy, cannot be expected to operate efficiently without a market-based financial and banking system that allows risk-taking and is subject to the exercise of prudential monetary controls. Immediate policy options include: Allowing the four state-owned specialized banks to break up, merge and reorganize to improve their performance, facilitate enterprise reform, and end their public finance burden; abolishing the segmented monetary flow system for cash and enterprise money; allowing individuals to open checking accounts, and enterprises or organizations to hold and use cash; establishing a modern bank-clearing national network; and subject to some asset and performance requirements, removing entrance barriers for new domestic and foreign banks and financial institutions.

Unification has always been considered desirable by the Chinese government in its many political and economic endeavors. In China's gradual process of economic reform, however, there are a number of important areas in which unification is clearly needed before the benefits of reforms can be fully realized and sustained. One vital area is monetary unification.

Because of mobility obstacles and entry barriers, many products have yet to gain national markets, although progress in this area has been evident in recent years. Dual or multiple prices for some key commodities and resources including foreign exchange still exist. However, one area where unification is now urgently needed, but generally ignored, is the artificial separation of cash and non-cash money. The Chinese monetary management framework, national financial planning, and banking system continue to operate under the traditional centrally planned model which restricts the use of cash to the household sector for consumption, and the use of non-cash money ("transfer money" or "enterprise money") to the non-household sector for production, investment and most government activities.[1] With the rapidly expanding role of the market in all activities, this monetary segmentation is undermining the fundamental basis through which market-based economic calculations and transactions are made. The developing linkages between saving and investment, and among the households, enterprises and the government are thereby distorted and impaired. Without monetary unification, it is not possible to achieve a sound basis for financial reform and management of the macroeconomy in the new era.

While there are now many suggestions on how China's financial system should be reformed and developed, a blueprint for monetary transformation based on an analysis of the fundamental processes of money supply and demand has yet to emerge. This paper will address this important but neglected issue by presenting an analysis and explanation of why the Chinese government cannot exercise effective monetary control unless monetary unification is achieved and the present financial and banking system is fundamentally transformed. It rejects the suggestion by Mc-Kinnon (1991, 1992) that reform of the banking system is separated from, and can therefore await the successful completion of, reform of the tax system and the "liberalization" of state enterprises. This paper shows that McKinnon's argument is not consistent with the realities of China's financial system, monetary planning and supply processes, although there is no disagreement over McKinnon's and others' emphasis on establishing a wider and more viable tax base and achieving macroeconomic stability.

It is now widely accepted among the more informed observers of reforming centrally planned economies that simply transposing from mature market economies some facets of their organizations and institutions is neither sufficient nor appropriate for what is, in effect, the transformation of an entire economic, political and social system. This paper argues that a fundamental transformation of China's monetary and banking system cannot be delayed if growth and stability are to be attained. The formal unification of the two segmented monies, with all their associated institutions and complementary measures, is overdue and should be implemented immediately.

China's economic reform process has made fundamental changes to the basic structures of its economic system. The Chinese economy today has a very high degree of openness by historical and international standards. The role of the market is being restored to an increasing range of economic activities. Money, credit and banking are entering a new phase of importance in determining production, consumption, investment and exchanges. The perennial public concerns about the overheating of the economy, the threat of uncontrollable inflation, the shortage of funds and the rising budget deficits are but a few of a growing list of indications that Chinese monetary management under a partially reformed economic system is assuming much greater significance and faces uncharted challenges.

How well the Chinese government can tackle the management of the rapidly developing monetary system will have a major impact on the success of reform and development in other areas. This paper will present an analytical framework to examine China's monetary management under the facade of a reformed financial system. It will raise a number of issues in highlighting the urgent need in formulating a more effective approach and strategy for monetary management. Options for immediate and radical changes to the outdated mode of monetary management inherited from the days of centralized planning are also examined.

This paper argues that monetary management is central to achieving macroeconomic stability and sustained growth in China, and that the present ineffectual centralized system of money and credit controls must be discontinued as it is no longer compatible with the new economic institutions. The key to achieving this goal is to unify the formally segmented cash and non-cash money categories. A complete monetary transformation is necessary.

The paper concludes that the present banking system can and should be drastically changed. The Chinese economy, having embarked on the road back to a market economy, cannot be expected to operate efficiently without a market-based financial and banking system that allows risk-taking and is subject to prudential monetary controls. Immediate policy options include: Allowing the four state-owned specialized banks to break up, merge and reorganize to improve their performance, facilitate enterprise reform, and end their public finance burden; abolishing the segmented monetary flow system for cash and enterprise money; allowing individuals to open checking accounts, and enterprises or organizations to hold and use cash; establishing a modern bank-clearing national network; and subject to some asset and performance requirements, removing entrance barriers for new domestic and foreign banks and financial institutions.

Part I outlines an analytical model of China's financial and monetary planning. It also discusses the concept and definition of money appropriate to China's institutional and organizational structures. Part II discusses recent changes in money demand and the money supply process. Part III investigates the role of the Chinese banking system, including the central bank, in facilitating effective monetary management and enterprise reforms. Part IV discusses a number of policy options that could be implemented to transform the financial and banking system, and provides some conclusions.

I. Chinese Model of Monetary Management

Before economic reform, China's monetary system was based on two strictly separated channels of monetary flow: Cash for household income and consumption expenditures, and bank account transfers (or transfer money) for all non-household transactions. These two channels of monetary flow were basic parts of China's central planning system for resource mobilization and allocation. A mono-banking system was created to act as an agent and cashier to implement the monetary side of the physical plan. Monetary management was accordingly dichotomized into controlling cash in circulation and bank credit allocation. The objective of monetary management in respect of cash (in the form of a cash plan) was to maintain stability in some notional numerical relation between currency in circulation and various measures of retail sales. In conceptual terms, this was implicitly based on the quantity theory of money. In the sphere of transfer money (in the form of a credit plan), the primary policy concern was to ensure that bank credits, mainly for working capital loans to state enterprises and collectives, and for state procurement of agricultural output, were supplied and used according to the central plan. However, China's monetary management before reform focused on controlling the narrow definition of the money supply through its cash plan.

Rapid development in financial innovation and deregulation in industrialized market economies during the last two decades has led to a reexamination of the concept and definition of money as debates over the relationship between income, prices and money continue. It is argued that significant institutional changes can result from a revision of our concept of money.[2]

With the market-oriented reform of its economy and financial system, the Chinese government has advocated the exercise of more effective macroeconomic management through indirect levers such as monetary and fiscal policies. At the same time, China has seen significant institutional changes in its financial system in recent years. A better understanding of this neglected issue of money will therefore be important if such policies are to be effective.

Giving empirical content to the concept and definition of money is obviously the first step in the estimation of money demand in conventional studies. There have been a number of recent works that attempt to establish a functional relationship between some measures of money (usually currency) and prices in the Chinese economy.[3] Most are concerned with household money demand, consumer goods market imbalance, and the methodology of constructing a price index for testing the relationship between prices, cash supply and household income. On the basis of these recent works, it is clear that there is a need to incorporate considerations of the actual process and institutions through which the money supply and prices are changed.

The empirical definition of money must in turn be based on an appropriate theoretical concept of money. However, even in the well-established literature on money demand in industrialized market economies, choices of an explicit measure of money are not always clear-cut. Indeed, problems with the definition of monetary aggregates are a continual concern.[4] Uniform measures of money are not common, and the choice is often dictated by data availability. In any analysis of money in a centrally planned economy, the issue of the theoretical concept and empirical definition of monetary aggregate is a particularly important one, though often neglected. The reason for paying special attention to this issue here is that the governments of such economies have historically reshaped money and their monetary system to serve the requirements of the central planning mechanism so that the concept and functions of money are distorted and changed.

Ultimately, a workable empirical definition of money depends on its conceptual functions. Traditionally the major functions that money performs in a market economy include its role as a unit of exchange, transaction (medium of exchange) and as an asset (store of value). For market economies, it has been argued that money demand theories based on a transaction approach provide the best guidance and lead to a narrow definition of money that includes currency and negotiable deposit (M_1). However, if we move away from a transaction view of the world, then the appropriate empirical definition of money may become less clear.[5]

In the case of the Chinese monetary system, there were two segmented and separate circuits of money flow: Currency and transfer money used by the non-household sectors to settle their transactions through a designated single check account[6] in the state-owned mono-bank (the People's Bank of China before economic reform). Currency is used primarily for household consumption, whereas transfer money is the medium for investment and production activities.

In essence, planning and the use of transfer money replaced

the use of narrow money (currency) in the non-household sectors (which are only allowed to hold a minimum amount of cash). Under the unified financial planning system during the pre-reform years, there were two major sources of transfer money for production enterprises and collectives and they consisted mainly of budget grant allocations and bank credits.[7] Under China's financial planning system, it is clear that the supply of transfer money was determined by the demand of the physical and credit plans. As for the currency circuit, it is also commonly accepted that the supply was not external.[8]

The two types of money are not substitutive. If we adopt the conventional definition of monetary aggregates in market economies such as M_1 (currency plus checking account i.e. currency and transfer money), or M_2 (M_1 + savings deposits), the vital distinction between these segmented moneys will be lost and any explanation of their demand or velocity behavior will be conceptually difficult to construct and reconcile.[9]

It should be noted that since economic reform the segmentation of the two money circuits is breaking down, although in an asymmetrical way. Unfortunately, the formal regulations, financial planning mechanisms and institutions associated with the segmented money circuits remain. Since 1978, currency's functions as a medium of exchange (i.e. purchasing power) and store of value are extending rapidly from the realm of consumption to investment and to production as state controls over the economy are relaxed and as the size of the non-state sector grows. At the same time, official restrictions over the use of transfer money are basically intact so that its money functions do not go through a significant transformation similar to the one for currency. However, with increasing operational and financial autonomy given to state enterprises and sub-national governments, there is a growing number of ways by which transfer money can be leaked into the currency circuit to take advantage of the latter's newly acquired monetary functions.[10] On the basis of the analysis of the econometric results in another study by this author,[11] this partial breaking down of the dichotomy of money flow in China has significant implications for the explanation of money demand behavior since reform. Recognizing and understanding such behavioral changes in a new institutional setting will be a necessary condition for more effective monetary control.

It is now well-established in economic theory that economic development benefits greatly from a process of financial development. A well-functioning and efficient financial system is the key factor in a country's financial development. Economic reform, China's gradual transition to a more market-oriented and open economic system, although incomplete, has given rise to a new and significantly expanded role for money and finance in all spheres of economic activity.[12] Whereas traditional financial development theories such as McKinnon-Shaw emphases liberalization and deregulation of interest rates, China's financial reform will require appropriate institution-building as well as a reduction in government's direct intervention in the flow of financial resource.

However, the reform of China's financial system has so far been carried out primarily as a vehicle for achieving other broader reform objectives. In its static role, financial reform will need to become more effective and efficient in mobilizing and allocating financial resources for both the traditional state-owned industries and the increasingly more important and vibrant non-state sector. At the same time, reform of the financial system should also have a dynamic and developmental role in the economy by inducing positive changes and reforms in other areas. A major function in this context is the provision of appropriate mechanisms and environment consistent with the demands of economic reform and through which macroeconomic and monetary management can be carried out effectively.

At the microeconomic level, reforming the financial system can help enhance factor and product mobility, market development, and price and ownership reform. Because the Chinese economic system before reform severely restricted the role of finance and retarded the development of a financial system, and since the Chinese government does not intend to withdraw all regulations and interventions, financial reform will need to create the right kind of institutions to improve both the fledging market

247

and the public sector, and not just reduce the role of government.

To examine the impact of the financial reform process, three basic elements of the mechanism of China's monetary management are identified: The cash plan, the credit plan and the state budget. This paper presents a simple model that depicts their interrelationship under the overall financial planning framework[13] (hereafter referred to as OFP). While the cash plan and to some extent the credit plan has quite justifiably received most of the attention in studies of China's monetary system, their relationship to the overall monetary management scheme is not often well understood or made clear.[14] One of the problems is that the Chinese government has never published its OFP. On the basis of publicly available Chinese material and this author's estimates, an analytical framework incorporating the relationship between the state budget (B,E), the credit plan (L), and the cash plan (C) is expressed in the equations below.

(1) $\quad B + L = E$

(2) $\quad L = f(C)$

It is important to recognize that under the central planning and mono-banking system bank credits were treated as a predetermined source of funds to finance public sector expenditures including the underwriting of the operating costs of state industrial and commercial enterprises. Therefore, the credit plan and the state budget were the two main sources of funds for the OFP, as foreign loans were non-existent before economic reform. In the absence of official published data on the OFP, this author estimates that the share of bank credits in the OFP's source of funds before the reform years was less than 10 percent.[15]

Chinese policymakers and economists have always placed their monetary policy focus on currency in circulation since most have defined cash as money supply. As the narrowly defined money supply (cash) in China was demand-determined, it played an accommodating role in the rise of prices and real output.[16] Under the centralized system of resource allocation and comprehensively regulated prices, before economic reform, the aim of the cash plan was primarily to maintain some tolerable balance between monetary purchasing power and supply in the consumption of market goods. In the general scheme of the OFP, dependence was placed on the state budget funds, while bank credits played only a relatively minor supporting role during those years.

The economic and financial reform of the 1980s has transformed many fundamental structures and institutions of China's economic system. However, the OFP framework remains very much the cornerstone of the Chinese government's macroeconomic and monetary management despite the changes brought about by reform.

China's financial reform, apart from establishing the facade of new financial institutions and assets commonly found in market economies, has also produced changes that can, in effect, undermine the capacity of the monetary authority to carry out its monetary management function under the existing OFP framework.

First, with fiscal and enterprise reform, the importance of bank credits as a source of fund in the OFP (equation—(1)) has risen rapidly. The unexpected fiscal decline over the reform years has also helped to raise the relative share of bank credit. Given the continuing existence of the OFP framework, improving the effectiveness of controls over bank credits and currency flow should have been given greater emphasis in monetary management during the reform. This is particularly important as there will be an increasing leakage between the two previously separate circuits of cash and transfer money flow (although data is unavailable to estimate the trend and magnitude of leakage). Unfortunately, the current outdated monetary management framework is not capable of facilitating effective controls. On the one hand, transfer money is no longer limited to the production sectors but has been out of control for nearly the entire reform period (as evidenced by the consistent and significant overshooting of annual lending targets). On the other hand, the use of lending quotas as a last resort has further severed the link between deposits and loans so that the token bank reserve system cannot be made to operate to restrain bank lending.

Second, the rapid process of monetization and marketization

of the economy means that the implementation of cash planning has become even more difficult. Thus, continuing with the attempt to maintain a desired level of growth in currency in circulation through manipulating the injection and withdrawal of cash has lost any remaining applicability since the key variables have shifted even further beyond the influence and control of the authorities and the government. In addition, an increasing share of the currency in circulation is now divorced from the state banks in what Chinese economists called "outside circulation." The rapid development of informal finance and non-bank financial institutions creates a situation in which exercising control over currency flow through the state banks cannot be effective. The traditional approach to monetary management and financial planning through the OFP framework must therefore be changed to meet the demands of the new economic environment. Western observers such as McKinnon (1992) have already pointed out the need to maintain price stability and create a more sustainable and broader tax base. However, without a clear understanding of how the function and behavior of money have changed, and how the banking system is interwined with government and enterprise finance, a new and more effective approach to monetary management cannot be formulated.

II. Money Demand in the Reform Period

Since economic reform, various processes of decentralization, deregulation and market mechanism have been gradually introduced into the planned economy. The original economic and monetary structures have been changed. This section discusses the influences of reform on money demand during the period from 1978 to 1990.

The major structural changes relevant to our investigation are outlines as below:

(a) The institutional segmentation of money flow into cash and non-cash (enterprise money or transfer money) circuits is breaking down in actuality, if not yet in name. Cash is fast extending into the previously prohibited realms of production and investment. Cash is no longer just the money used by households for consumption. At the same time there is emerging expanding opportunities for transfer money to leak (be converted) into cash, partly to avoid monitoring and supervision of enterprise money use by the banking system under the unchanged framework of monetary controls.

(b) The capacity to raise household cash income is now no longer limited to the state budgetary process. Enterprises, state-owned and collectively-owned, have sufficient autonomy to effect discretionary power for raising household income in significant ways. This has resulted in a rapid increase in both household income and cash supply. For instance, the average annual growth rate of household income from 1952 to 1990 was 10.15 percent. In the pre-reform period, the average annual growth rate was just 6.59 percent but the rate rose to 17 percent during the reform period from 1978 to 1990. Since 1985, household income has been effectively out of the control of the central government.

(c) The authorities have loosened their control on prices at the market of consumer goods and means of production. Prices are now more responsive to market supply and demand.

(d) The process of decentralization has made enterprises relatively more independent. They can to an increasing degree decide what and how much to produce and at what prices, as well. A notable development is the corporatization of an increasing number of state enterprises, many of which have set up separate corporate entities that operate autonomously in the competitive markets, and a few are now listed on China's (and more recently Hong Kong's stock exchanges).[17]

To survive, the fast growing rural industrial enterprises must operate profitably in a highly competitive environment.[18] Even many state-owned enterprises, despite the institutional constraints imposed on them, are behaving competitively to maximize profit.[19] This means that the market, rather than planning, is becoming the more important allocative mechanism.

(e) In rural areas, reform has resulted in *de facto* privatisation of most areas of economic activities. Farmers can now sell their products directly to households in cities. More significantly, the new market exchange relationship between the urban and rural sector is now driven strongly by the growth of rural township and village factories. Huge populations have moved into the non-agricultural sector. This development certainly promotes monetization and the breaking down of the artificial separation of the two monetary circuits.

(f) Households in the cities are now allowed to operate private enterprise businesses and so are now participants in the investment process and in the market of means of production.

(g) Accompanying the changes in the economic sectors, a new and independent circuit of currency flow appears. This portion of cash flow circulates directly among sellers and buyers. So the informal financial sector now plays an important intermediary role. Cash no longer passes only through the state banks. Hence this new circuit is called "circulation outside the body." This implies that cash has moved from the consumer goods market to the market of means of production. Currency is therefore now linked directly to both household and enterprise income and expenditures. Meanwhile, however, the banking system in China has yet to give up its function as an administrative organ for government intervention in the economy.[20] This prevents development.

Increase in household income, the growth of rural industries and decollectivization, the emergence of private businesses, and the expansion of markets, have all raised money demand, particularly the demand for cash. In addition, the continuing inability of households and private businesses to hold checking accounts, and the fact that the entire fund transfer and settlement mechanism among financial institutions and economic agents remains outdated, inefficient and open to abuse, have combined to exert tremendous pressure on the country's payments system.

Saving deposits have risen sharply since the start of reform. With an increasing supply of consumer goods, the saving deposits increase may be attributed to the rise in household income. In addition, there are extensive reports that state enterprises are also channeling their funds into the currency circuit by putting them in savings deposit accounts. This is done either by setting up bogus personal accounts or through their cooperative or collective enterprise offshoots. The net effect is a continuing rise in the volume of saving deposits and the amount of currency in the hands of households and enterprises. A major cause is that households and individual businesses cannot hold checking accounts and must make their transactions in cash. At the same time, enterprises are still bound by highly restrictive regulations over the use of their transfer money. Therefore, as banks still play their role as governmental administrative organs, the increase in money demand is concentrated primarily on cash. This causes the currency-money ratio to move upward. As a result, the monetization process in China is reflected more in the increase in cash use than by the conventional notion of monetization in which barter exchanges are replaced by the use of money and spread of commercial banks.

Because of the differences in the structure and institutions of the economic and monetary systems between China and market economies, conventional standard money demand theories and models are not applicable in explaining the trend of money demand in China. In a separate paper[21] the author presents an alternative approach to explaining Chinese money demand by developing an analytical model that attempts to capture the characteristics of China's macroeconomic adjustment mechanism and their inherent links with specific processes of money supply and demand.

Our alternative approach generates results that suggest a trade-off between changes in price level and money velocity in the pre-reform period. It explains the mechanism through which investment demand impacts on the trend of money velocity in China's quantity-adjustment economic system. The empirical test results also support these explanations. We have also been able to explain the behavior of money velocity during the period of China's economic reform.

Since 1978, China's economy has been brought closer to the market system although the banking system is still repressed and financial markets undeveloped. The partial breaking down of the previously segregated monetary circuits has promoted a rapid process of switching to the use of currency. Economic development after 1978 was proceeding under conditions of a partially transformed economic system and continuing financial repression. The repressed and underdeveloped financial sector has impeded economic development and raised money demand artificially. There is no doubt that the Chinese monetary authorities will have to increasingly employ market-based policy instruments in order to attain their macroeconomic and monetary goals as the economy continues its transition, dismantles centralized allocation of resources, and restores the functions of the market in the economy. A better understanding of the money behavior pattern during this process of transformation is therefore essential.

III. The Role of the Banking System and Direction of Reform

For most low-income developing economies, the financial system consists predominantly of banks of various types. In centrally planned economies where the role of money and finance is limited by institutional arrangements, a mono-bank system was installed to ensure the supply of financial resources for the implementation of the economic plans. China's financial reform began with institution building as the mono-bank system was replaced. Thus, China's banking reform is a key determinant of the effectiveness of monetary management.

Before economic reform, the People's Bank of China (PBC) was responsible for the execution of the credit plan and the cash plan. To facilitate the process of fiscal reform and associated changes in enterprise finances, a two-tier banking system was established in 1984 to replace the Soviet-type mono-banking system. A banking system with a central bank (the PBC) and four specialized state banks was established. However, because the Chinese government was not prepared to give up all centralized controls over the economy (particularly the state-owned industrial sector), the new banking and financial system had to operate under the existing OFP framework and develop under continuing government intervention and restrictions.

Descriptions of the various major Chinese banking institutions and their organizational arrangements under reform are well-documented. This section focuses on analyzing performance determinants of both the central bank and the specialized banks. After more than nine years, the two-tier banking system has certainly facilitated some reform policies, but has also been made to develop and operate in ways that are often contrary to the objectives of a well-functioning banking system, and are not in the interest of economic reform and macroeconomic management. The explanations for this can be found in the banking sector's operational mechanism and policy environment mandated by the Chinese government's pursuit of various economic and political goals. Although the PBC now nominally functions as a central bank, the specialized banks and the PBC are, in fact, integral parts of a complex and often contradictory contraption of banking relations which passively serve the government's needs through the increasingly ineffectual OFP mechanism.

1. The Performance of the Central Bank

The performance of the PBC can be understood in terms of several basic factors: The general economic environment created by the partial economic reform, the independence and management of the central bank, the autonomy of the specialized banks, the conflicts of policy goals and the monetary policy instruments available to the central bank, and the demands and constraints placed by the Chinese government's growth-oriented policy. Many economists both inside and outside the government regard the inadequate number of monetary policy instruments as one main reason for the PBC's ineffectual monetary and credit controls. However, the lack of central bank independence, the growth and social policy mandates imposed by the government, and the internal organizational problems of the PBC itself were no less important in determining the actual outcome of its monetary management.

As far as the PBC is concerned, there seems to be ample evidence to suggest that serving the Chinese government's economic growth policy has priority over maintaining monetary stability. This growth-oriented policy essentially means that the Chinese government will not tolerate economic and financial adjustments that require prolonged static growth and might threaten to bring about large-scale retrenchment and open unemployment. In practical terms, the banking system is required to ensure funding to maintain the survival of state enterprises and to provide loans to designated projects or enterprises under the government's industrial policy.

More importantly, the PBC has in practice allowed and facilitated the banking sector's overall continuing credit expansion in support of the unprofitable and inefficient state-owned enterprise system, and deficit spending at all levels of government. This soft approach to managing bank credit expansion, quite apart from problems of credit controls, is the result of the PBC having a subordinate position in the Chinese government. Suggestions (for example by McKinnon 1992) that the enterprise budget constraint be made "hard" at the firm level without transforming the banking system and severing the link between the banks and the financial planning framework are therefore unlikely to work in the long run.

When the PBC was established as the central bank of a new two-tier banking system in 1984, it was envisaged that the new central bank would, in concert with the gradual transition to a more market-oriented economy, develop indirect monetary policy instruments based on market forces rather than direct command and centralized allocation. However, the conventional market-based policy instruments have so far failed to become a viable means for effective monetary and credit control. As explained elsewhere, the reasons for this are many and complex.

Hence, the PBC has relied mainly on predetermined quantitative controls as monetary policy instruments. In this context, the PBC is really continuing its traditional functions in a vastly different economic and financial environment. The PBC's major regulatory tools are still the credit and cash plans despite their apparent increasing inadequacy. While some Chinese economists and some Western observers may believe that such quantitative controls are necessary and effective given current circumstances, the reality is that even such centralized means of monetary control did not work well. The continuing and frequent upward revisions in recent years of the largely ineffectual annual bank lending targets and quotas attest to this fact. Many of the difficulties stem from the institutions and behavioral responses derived from the continuing formal segmentation of cash and non-cash moneys.

One conclusion that can be drawn is that, under the OFP framework and economic mandates from the Chinese government, the central bank is not in a position to pursue active and effective policies to ensure monetary stability. Its present role is not significantly different in essence from the past and appears to be still passive and subordinate. It has so far not been able to employ conventional market-based policy instruments to influence and adjust monetary conditions. The administrative controls available to the PBC, the credit and cash plans, are not enforceable for long in the face of demands for growth and survival of the massive and inefficient state-owned enterprise sector.

2. The Performance of the Specialized Banks

With over 80 percent of the assets of the financial system, the four specialized banks are China's dominant financial institutions. These banks were originally set up to effect the transition from a centralized public enterprise and financial system to a more decentralized and market-oriented one. Each bank is to serve a designated sector or type of transaction, although the demarcation has become blurred as specialized banks actively compete for business.

Apart from the usual problems associated with credit rationing, the Chinese banks are handicapped because they are also given quotas and targets under the current credit plan for most types of lending. Therefore, the ability of the banking system to perform efficiently in the mobilization and allocation of financial resources is seriously impeded when both the quantity and price of finance, as well as liabilities (reserve requirement) and assets (credit quotas), are subject to quantitative controls. In addition, there is also the well recognized problem of localization and fragmentation of financial flow in the Chinese banking system.[22]

Local branches of the specialized banks readily succumb to political pressure from the local administration to extend bank credits. They have also restricted the mobility of funds across administrative jurisdictions or even between different banks within the same region. This has certainly not contributed to the best utilization and allocation of financial resources in an increasingly marketized economy. Recent attempts to set up inter-bank money markets aim at improving this situation. However, such institution-building efforts cannot be expected to produce the desired result without tackling the cause of the problem: The system of segmented money flows and its impact on the autonomy of the banking system. Indeed, the inter-bank market had not succeeded precisely because operational bank branches simply took a territorial approach to their borrowing and lending.

The autonomy of the specialized bank is compromised on three fronts. The political pressure from local government and the quantitative restrictions placed by the PBC are the two obvious constraints on bank autonomy. The third factor is the increasing tendency of the Chinese government, at all levels, to insist that banks fund designated priority areas or projects. Directed credits, or "policy loans," coupled with all the other regulatory constraints, make it difficult for banks to even play a limited role as arbiter in the imperfect process of credit rationing. It has been estimated that over 90 percent of the annual increase in bank credit for working capital in recent years resulted directly from government directions and intervention.[23]

Improving the performance of the specialized banks to meet the demands of China's economic reform also requires changes in the central bank's monetary management approach and, ultimately, a genuine rethinking of how to finance the public sector and state-owned enterprises. In other words, the OFP framework with its associated institutions has to be abandoned.

For now, apart from strengthening the financial and accounting discipline of the banks themselves, specialized bank performance can be improved by reducing or eliminating all lending activities that are really a disguised form of monetizing state budget imbalance. This means all directed credit should be discontinued. If the targeted projects or enterprises are considered socially or politically desirable, the Chinese government will have to either subsidize them directly or set up separate institutions (such as development banks) to supply them with specially funded capital. The development of securities markets will also be required. Furthermore, instead of being preoccupied with regulatory quantitative controls over credit quota allocation and interest rates, the central bank should devote more effort to creating a competitive and secure environment for the development of commercial banks and non-bank financial institutions, and a system of monitoring, evaluation and prudential supervision over both the quantity and quality of assets and liabilities of financial institutions.

It is important to note that despite all the regulatory restrictions the state-owned banks (including the PBC), with its sheer business volume, have become a *major source of budget revenue* during a period when state enterprises are declining as a revenue contributor. This author has found that the banking system contributed about one quarter of the tax and profit revenue for the state (consolidated) budget in 1989 (Tam (1992)). Therefore, it is expected there will be vested interests at the Ministry of Finance and other government departments that depend on state budget funds to make sure this revenue source is not endangered. The implication is that increasing profit from continuing bank credit expansion may not be inconsistent with the short-term interest of many powerful ministries. In the absence of relevant information, it is not possible to determine whether the bank profits are genuine and represent a real contribution to the budget. Nevertheless, as state industrial enterprises could show accounting profit under a distorted price system and contribute revenue to the budget, it is conceivable that banks can do the same.

Reform Options and Conclusion

The question now is what can be done to improve the performance of the banking system so that economic growth can be sustained and the market-oriented reform can proceed without undue instability. It is clear that China will need to unify its money by ending the segmentation of cash and transfer money, and abandon the traditional framework of financial planning and management.

Appropriate institution-building and development are an important component of this reform process, and must be implemented on the basis of a clear understanding of the realities and characteristics of the economic system.

There has certainly been no lack of suggestions from both Chinese and Western observers for reforming the Chinese banking system. For instance, McKinnon (1992) recently suggested restricting bank credits to traditional state enterprises and excluding "liberalized enterprises" from bank credit eligibility at the first stage of transition. McKinnon's aim was to harden the budget constraint on enterprises. However, notwithstanding the problems arising from the fungibility of finance, the suggested scheme is unlikely to work in the present phase of Chinese economic reform because the distinction between traditional enterprises and "liberalized enterprises" is no longer clear. More importantly, as noted earlier, if the banking system were not fundamentally changed and its role in monetising the state budget imbalance (whether in open or disguised forms) were not discontinued, the hardening of state enterprise budget would be impossible and insignificant in its effect.

Bearing in mind the need for a new model of public finance including a wider and more viable tax base and revenue sharing arrangements, a number of specific reform options for the monetary system can be considered and are outlined below:

First, the segmentation of the cash and non-cash money circuit must be ended. Individuals and enterprise should all be allowed to use cash for transactions and all should be allowed to use checking accounts. The traditional financial planning model should be abandoned and the banking system's link to state finance severed. Disguised monetization of the state's income and expenditure imbalance through direct and indirect bank borrowings should cease.

Second, the banking system must improve its performance as a financial system and at the same time assist public finance and enterprise reform. It is paramount that the commercial banks be allowed to pursue their own market objectives within a suitably reconstituted prudential framework of bank regulations. In this context, there are merits in allowing each of the four major specialized banks to break up and merge with one another on an voluntary and commercial basis. For instance, the provincial branches of the ICBC and ABC in a particular province or region may decide on merger to form a new regional bank. Such reorganizations are consistent with the reality of market development and social and political interests.

Furthermore, such new regional banks will be able to perform the functions of a main bank in the Japanese mode so that genuine enterprise reform can be facilitated and implemented more extensively and effectively. It can be expected that positive competition among banks and banking practices that enhances competition in other sectors will themselves be enhanced.

These new banks will bring an important element of stability to China's fledgling stock markets as cross shareholding spreads. The passive accommodating nature of the Chinese banking system can thus be corrected.

As for the entry of private banks and foreign banks, there is a case for their full operation particularly in the economically more advanced regions. There are an increasing range of services and market niches that such banks are able to provide such as quality products and the introduction of new technology and management expertise. On the basis of recent experience in Australia, for instance, most foreign banks are unlikely to be competitive in the retail banking area provided that the domestic banks are permitted to operate in all areas. Thus concerns about the threat to the survival of domestic banks may be unjustified.

As China's economic reform proceeds, prices are becoming less regulated and rigid, and market competition is being reintroduced in many spheres of economic activity. Monetary management, however, still remains tied to central planning and held hostage to the government's financial needs. The traditional pre-reform financial planning mechanism, as represented in the OFP model in this study, has not been abandoned, even in the face of significant changes in the economic and financial systems. The supply-oriented and plan-quota based monetary stand, as expressed in the cash and credit plans, has become increasingly untenable within the process of monetization and financial reform.

The ultimate cause of many problems in China's monetary management can be traced back to the maintenance of its OFP framework supported by a passive banking system at a time when marketization and monetization have changed the premises of such a mechanism. Financial reform in China, despite the introduction of some new institutions and instruments, has not yet created the conditions necessary for more effective monetary management based on market demand and supply.

The reform of the financial system has reached a stage where rethinking how best to continue the process becomes vital to success. While both bank and non-bank financial sectors have experienced rapid changes and growth in recent years, there remain major problems and conflicts that need to be resolved before the financial system can perform its basic functions efficiently. This will involve a fundamental reappraisal of the government's economic and political goals. For instance, the role of the government at various levels, the financing of the public sector in the economy, and the form and extent of the ownership of state enterprises are basic questions which must be urgently addressed to ensure that the reform process can be sustained without incurring the high costs associated with recent disruptions and instability.

There are also issues directly linked to the functioning of the financial system which can generally be tackled from within the system. These relate to how efficiently the financial system can mobilize financial resource allocation and provide an effective mechanism and environment for monetary management.

It is clear that both the central and specialized banks will need to attain a much higher degree of independence and autonomy, with corresponding financial responsibility and discipline, before China's financial system can perform all its macroeconomic functions efficiently. Such a move will inevitably require adjustments in fiscal and enterprise finance. However, there still remains a vast scope for initiatives by the Chinese central and specialized banks to improve their operations and management of the country's money and credit flow without all the prerequisites of systemic changes in other areas. The interest rate structure, the mechanism for credit volume control, deposit reserve requirements and central bank lending to the specialized banks all can be improved quickly to produce positive results. There is no scarcity of proposals and studies, both in and outside China, on how various measures can be implemented. With the unification of the segmented moneys and the transformation of the banking system, what is needed is a well-coordinated program of policy actions to increase efficiency and market discipline on the basis of a more transparent and stable regulatory framework.

The growth of the non-state sector and decentralization at the regional and enterprise level make new demands and exert pressure on further reform. The banking system has passively responded to this new challenge, whereas the non-bank financial sector has actively supported, and indeed thrived on, this fast-developing product of the reform process. The issues of intra- and inter-sector competition and prudential supervision must be addressed by the monetary authorities. The recent experiments with market-based trading of some government bonds and the establishment of stock markets demonstrate the possibilities and benefits that can be attained when new and well-conceived reform measures are introduced.

Although the Chinese government has retained a complex system of foreign exchange controls that have isolated the domestic financial system from the internationalization of financial markets, the rising openness of the Chinese economy means that such controls will become increasingly inconsistent and incompatible with the economic development process. Therefore the reform of the financial system will also have to make necessary adjustments in its external financial relations in view of such trends. Despite the constant disruptions, problems and uncertainties, the broad direction of economic reform has been maintained. The reform has made discernible progress and produced new opportunities and benefits. The financial system can and should be further transformed so that it can assist the economic reform and development process and reduce the likelihood and magnitude of economic instability.

Notes

1. For more detailed discussions of the analytical implications of this dual but segmented money system in China, see, on Kit Tam (1992), *Model of Chinese Monetary Management,* (Department of Economics and Management Working Paper No. 1, 1992, University of New South Wales); On Kit Tam (ed) (forthcoming), *Financial and Banking Reform in China*; Benjamin Xu Huang, *An Analysis of Money Control in China* (unpublished Ph. D. dissertation, 1993, the University of New South Wales, Canberra, Australia).

2. Goldfeld and Sichel (1990), pp. 300-301, who also argue that money demand relationships are still in "a state of flux."

3. See Gregory Chow, "Money and Price Level Determination in China," *Journal of Comparative Economics,* 11, 1987; Andrew Feltenstein and Z. Farhadian, "Fiscal Policy, Monetary Targets and the Price Level in a Centrally Planned Economy: an Application to the Case of China," *Journal of Money, Credit and Banking,* 19, 1987, pp. 137-156; Andrew Feltenstein, D. Lebor and S. van Wijnbergen, "Savings, Commodity Market Rationing, and the Real Rate of Interest in China's *Journal of Money, Credit and Banking,* Vol. 22, No. 2, May 1990, pp. 255-252.

4. See, for Example, William A. Barnett, "The Optimal Level of Monetary Aggregation," *Journal of Money, Credit and Banking,* November 1982, Part 2, pp. 687-710; and James L. Swofford and Gerald Whitney, "The Composition and Construction of Monetary Aggregates," *Economic Inquiry,* Vol. XXIX, October 1991, pp. 752-761.

5. Goldfeld and Sichel (1990), pp. 313.

6. It should be noted that only an insignificant amount of enterprise deposits in such an account could in fact be drawn through the use of checking accounts. Most deposit and withdrawal transactions were effected through book entries carried out and monitored by the bank.

7. Transfer money would have fitted comfortably with Wicksell's "pure credit economy" in which all exchange was mediated by the transfer of bank deposits (Laidler 1991, p. 296). In such a case, the quantity theory is not relevant.

8. Researchers who have come to this conclusion from various approaches include, for example, Feltenstein and Farhadian (1987), Portes and Santorum (1987), Anita Santorum, "The Control of Money Supply in Developing

Countries: China, 1949-1988," *ODI Working Paper 29,* 1989; Huang Xu, "Huobi gongqiu fenxi" (An Analysis of the Supply and Demand for Money), Chapter 6, in Zhang Fengbo (ed) (1988); and on Kit Tam, *Monetary Management and China's Financial Reform,* paper for the 21st Australian Conference of Economists, University of Melbourne, July 1992.

9. The author has in fact performed econometric tests of China's money velocity behavior on the basis of the conventional definition of M_1 and M_2, using the two approaches below: (1) a standard benchmark equation; and (2) Bordo and Jonung's institutional approach. Tests using these approaches on Chinese data for the period 1950-1990 are performed and the results are available from the authors. Neither approach was found to produce satisfactory results.

10. For instance, it is widely acknowledged that many state enterprises avoid the constraints associated with the use of transfer money by dealing with one another in cash or through the establishment of bogus cooperative or collective enterprises.

11. On Kit Tam and Benjamin Xu Huang, *Money Velocity Behavior in China,* (1993).

12. World Bank (1988); On Kit Tam (1991), "Capital Market Development in China," *World Development,* May.

13. Full details of the model is present in On Kit Tam (1992).

14. For instance, Hsiao has provided very detailed description of the plans but made no attempt to relate them to the overall financial scheme. See K. Hsiao (1971), *Money and Monetary Policy in Communist China* (New York: Columbia University Press).

15. Tam (1992).

16. Tam and Huang (1993).

17. On Kit Tam, *Corporate Governance and China's Enterprise Reform,* a paper presented at the 34th International Congress of Asian and North African Studies, August 1993, University of Hong Kong.

18. For discussion of the growth of the rural industrial sector, see for example, William A. Byrd and Lin Qingsong (eds), *China's Rural Industry: Structures, Development and Reform,* (Oxford University Press, 1990).

19. Jefferson and Rawski argued that such behavior can now be detected among state enterprises as their profitability converges with non-state sectors. Gary H. Jefferson and Thomas G. Rawski, *A Theory of Economic Reform* (Memeo: University of Pittsburg, 1992).

20. See On Kit Tam (1986), "Reform of China's Banking System," *The World Economy,* December; Paul Bowle and G. White, "Contradictions in China's Financial Reforms: The Relationship Between Banks and Enterprises," *Cambridge Journal of Economics,* Vol. 13, No. 4, 1989.

21. Tam and Huang (1993).

22. On Kit Tam (1987), "The Development of China's Financial System," *Australian Journal of Chinese Affairs,* No. 17, January; Y. C. Jao, "The Financial System of China and Hong Kong," *Pacific Economic Papers,* 1990.

23. Ma Hong and Sun Shangqing (eds), *Economic Situation and Prospect of China 1989-1990* (in Chinese) (Beijing: China Development Press), 1990.

Focal Points and the Difficulties of Changing China's Double-Track Economic System into a Market Economy

Gu Shutang and *Liu Xin*
The College of Economics, Nankai University

Thanks to the effort in the past 10-some years, the former highly centralized planned economy has become a coexisting planned and market economy. We must take the characteristics of this present double-track system and its operations as the basis for studying existing problems and the transition toward a market economy. First of all, this article will analyze the operation of the present double-track economic system. On this basis, we shall discuss the focal points and difficulties in changing into a market economic system.

I. The Operation of the Double-Track Economic System

1. Two Types of Enterprises

In the early 1980s, with the enlargement of the enterprises' autonomy, the double-track economic system was gradually formed. The enlargement of autonomy in state enterprises resulted in an expansion of regulation by the market. And, with the deepening of reform, a large numbers of new and developing enterprises were set up and began to grow. That is to say, the setting up and expansion of these new enterprises were an important reason for formation of the double-track economic system. These new and developing enterprises include:

(1) Township enterprises. Since 1984, the output value of

township enterprises has experienced a very high growth rate. In the past 10-some years, the average annual growth rate has reached over 20 percent, much higher than that of state-owned enterprises. At present, their industrial output value has reached almost 40 percent of the gross national product (GNP). It is estimated that within three to five years, their total industrial output value will surpass that of state-owned enterprises.

(2) Foreign-invested enterprises (or Chinese-foreign joint ventures, Chinese-foreign cooperative enterprises and enterprises wholly owned by foreign capital). The policy of opening to the outside world has promoted the development of foreign-invested enterprises. The scale and output value of foreign-invested enterprises have coincided with that of township enterprises. But most of the foreign-invested enterprises are included in city enterprises, such as enterprises with investment from individual foreigners, joint ventures and cooperative enterprises established jointly by state-owned enterprises and foreigners, and the like.

(3) Some state-owned enterprises have been reorganized into new forms, such as stockholding enterprises. This includes Chinese-foreign joint ventures and Chinese-foreign cooperative enterprises. The organizational form of these enterprises differs greatly from that of most state-owned enterprises. Basically, they have independent operational autonomy, such as some state-owned enterprises in Shenzhen and in the southern provinces, including Guangdong.

(4) Private enterprises. In recent years, private enterprises have made great progress, though at present they only occupy a small proportion of the national economy. Their development, and the state's policy of encouraging them, have greatly influenced the formation of the emerging market mechanism.

The above-mentioned four types of enterprises coincide at many points, though there are also differences in their property rights relations and managerial forms. But they do have some things in common, that is, they are all new and developing enterprises set up and growing in a market economy environment. They are all market oriented, and have basically broken connections with the old planned economy. They will not be bound by direct state planning, but will only be influenced by the state's macroeconomic policies. It is estimated that the industrial output value of these enterprises now accounts for more than 50 percent of the national economy. The establishment and growth of these new and developing enterprises is the most important factor in China's economic structural reform and the operation of China's present economy.*

Therefore, we may sum up an important feature of the present double-track economic system. There are two types of enterprises. One is the enterprises that are regulated by market mechanisms. Their production will be guided by the needs of market. The capital of these enterprises comes from bank loans and individual investments. The others are the enterprises that are controlled by the state, mainly the large and medium-sized state enterprises. According to statistics, the output value of these enterprises occupies approximately 40 to 50 percent of the GNP.

For the purposes of analysis, the large and medium-sized state-owned enterprises are divided into two categories according to industry. One is the basic industries such as energy resources, raw materials, transportation, and post and telecommunications. The other is the processing industries, which include consumer goods production enterprises and commerce. According to estimates, the proportion of output value of the industries in these two categories is about 50 percent each. The reason we divided large and medium-sized state-owned enterprises into two groups is that at present China's basic industries are mostly controlled by the state, while the processing industries are mostly regulated by the market. This means that in the production and processing industries there are enterprises with two kinds of ownership and regulating forms.

2. Market

Enterprises with different ownership and managerial forms

---

* At present, research into the Chinese economy often begins with the reform of state-owned large and medium-sized enterprises. We think that the success of China's reform depends to a large extent on the new and developing enterprises. The development of these enterprises has promoted the reform of state-owned enterprises and the elementary formation of market mechanisms.

and controlled by different regulating mechanism are often competing at the same market. This is an important reason why market mechanisms cannot play a definitive role at present. After years of reform, though the large and medium-sized state-owned enterprises began to face the market, and have certain decision-making power in their operations, their standards and regulations are still fundamentally different from these of township enterprises and foreign-invested enterprises. Can these differences be suited to the operation of market mechanisms?

First, besides the original fixed assets, the main sources of capital for these large and medium-sized state enterprises are from state investment and bank loans granted according to the state plan. The difference between the new and developing enterprises and the large and medium-sized state enterprises is that the value of the asset of these state-owned enterprises cannot be completely appraised according to prices decided by the market and economic results. This, results in a serious blurring of property rights. So managerial achievements cannot be evaluated entirely according to their results. For example, in order to divide the power, responsibility and benefits of an enterprise, we must first know the value of an enterprise's assets. Can the value of the assets be calculated according to the amount of original investment? This is obviously impossible because the value of the original investment is different from the market value. Can we calculate the original value of an enterprise's assets according to current market value? This is also impossible because at present this kind of calculation is used to subsidize current asset values according to the profits of an enterprise. According to this type of calculation, managerial achievements are included. This shows that the value of the assets cannot be separated from managerial results. The above problem is a contradiction between state enterprises and market mechanisms that is difficult to solve. When the enterprises obtain gradual increasing investment and bank loans with low interest from the state and report to a higher body, how can they divide ownership and managerial rights? In recent years, the main focus of enterprise reform has been trying to find a way to separate these two rights, and efforts have been made to establish managerial responsibility, contract and stock systems. What have been the results? Most of the enterprises still depend on the state, "only eating the rice cooked in one big pot." They don't have motivation of vitality. Officially, they earn profits and never suffer losses. Some enterprises turn public property into private property, thus becoming new and developing enterprises. But these types of enterprises are different from the publicly owned enterprises controlled by state planning.

The differences between the results and the original intention of reform have proved that it is impossible to reform state-owned enterprises by separating ownership and managerial rights. It was the idea of separating these two rights that has resulted in the present indistinctness of property rights in state-owned enterprises. The property rights of township enterprises are even more indistinct. Compared with state-owned enterprises, the obvious characteristics of township enterprises are that their managers have boundless power to control their enterprises, and basically have this power for life. So to some extent this has remedied the indistinctness of property rights. (The new and developing enterprises mentioned before also have the same characteristics, in varying degree.) But anyhow, this indistinctness of property rights remains the greatest obstacle to further reform.

Second, the two kinds of enterprises have resulted in differing regulations, making it difficult to form a market environment with fair competition. At the beginning of reform, large and medium-size state enterprises could occupy only a tiny space in the market because they possessed a huge amount of fixed capital, an economy of scale, and raw materials and bank loans provided by the state at low cost. But with the development of new enterprises, and a further opening of the market, the low efficiency of the state enterprises was completely revealed, and it was obvious that they were unable to compete with new and developing enterprises. It also became apparent that one important reason for this was that state-owned enterprises were bound to the original planned economy. Many people maintained that "pushing the enterprises into the market" could be accomplished by further expanding their decision-making power. This proposition, and the supporting reform measures designed for it, seemed correct, but its implementation brought a negative result as the enterprises received more and more administrative protection. The greatest protection was the state's continued subsidies for losing enterprises and increased loan investments. By doing so, the state tried hard to save the losing state enterprises. How did the idea of "pushing the enterprises into the market" become protection of large and medium-sized state enterprises? The original intention was for the state to try and allow large and medium-sized state enterprises to maintain a position in market. So, what kind of policy could be adopted to maintain this when the enterprises were not allowed to go bankrupt or be eliminated through competition? In fact, many present policies are just the result of bargaining and negotiations between managers of state-owned enterprises and the government. Many policies seem designed to enhance adaption of market rules, but by their nature also belong to traditional planned regulations which are contrary to market forces. Therefore, the more progress these policies have made, the more difficulties state-owned enterprises have had to face. Thus, state-owned enterprises will demand more protection in order to stay in existence.

Third, the existence of the two kinds of enterprises mentioned above seriously obstructs the setting up and perfecting of financial markets and the labor force market. The extent of perfection of these markets is one way to measure whether or not market mechanisms are able to perform their normal functions. It is also an important objective of reform. But until now, a labor force market has not been established. And the financial market has always been like this: If it is managed, it will be rigid; if it is set free, it will be in a state of chaos. Since 1984 it has been in serious chaos several times because there have been different regulations for the two kinds of enterprises, and government protection for state enterprises. Let's analyze the problem from the viewpoint of state-owned enterprises' present deficits.

As a commodity producer, an enterprise aims at winning profits from direct production. Profits come from the difference between input price and output price. When the output price is less than the input price, the enterprises will be operating at a deficit. Under normal market conditions, it is impossible for enterprises to remain in deficit indefinitely. First of all, the enterprises buy raw materials at low prices, and sell their products at high price. Before making an investment and paying for labor force, enterprises must try to make output price higher than input price, otherwise their decision is wrong. When an enterprise is in deficit, it has to adopt such measures as reducing the number of employees or closing, ceasing, merging and changing the lines of production to prevent from further losses. Secondly, under uncertainly conditions, it is unavoidable for an enterprise to make some wrong decisions, which will result in losses. But under normal conditions, it is impossible for the enterprise to be in deficit for a long time. Because once an enterprise is in deficit, it will lose capital, and its employees cannot get due payment or might be out of work. Consequently the losing enterprise will not get capital from the financial and labor markets. The capital and laborers will shift from the losing enterprise to a profit-making enterprise, thus restricting the losing enterprise. So it is unimaginable for an enterprise to be in deficit for a long time.

However some state-owned enterprises have been in serious deficit for quite a long time now. Statistical data show that about one-third of all state-owned enterprises are operating at a deficit, excluding potential deficit enterprises. It is estimated that including these potential losing enterprises, about two-thirds of the state-owned enterprises are in deficit, and this condition has persisted for a long time. How can so many losing enterprises remain in existence? One reason can be deduced from the financial and labor markets. The government has adopted a series of policies to maintain the existence of the losing enterprises by using planned credits to meet the capital demand of these enterprises. It also subsidizes losing state-owned enterprises to maintain high wages for their workers and staff.* This has resulted in difficulties for the financial market in their attempt to realize unified interest rates.

---

* High wage expenditures are calculated into costs in disguised form.

In China's present financial market a large part of normal capital is used as planned credit funds to supply state-owned enterprises with low interest loans. But the new and developing enterprises that badly need capital can only get these loans at high interest. High interest rates on deposits can increase the supply of unscheduled capital, but this increase in the capital supply results in inflation, a decline of the actual interest rate, and a further stimulation of capital demand. All this has sent the wrong price signals, and interest rate regulation and capital demand have been reduced. The differential interest rates have caused difficulty for the central bank in regulating the money supply because this supply is decided by interest rates and the profit rates of enterprises (indigenous money supply). When the government divides credit funds into two parts and adopts different interest rates, the increase in the unscheduled money demand is unavoidable because the government cannot control the total amount of the money supply. All this results in the possibility that if the money supply is set free it will lead to a state of chaos; if it is managed, it will be rigid.

The development of the labor force market is much more difficult. The "big-pot" system of state-owned enterprises has seriously obstructed the development of the labor force market. Now the wage rate of township enterprises and foreign-invested enterprises is higher than that of state-owned enterprises, but the workers and staff in state-owned enterprises get many more benefits than those in non-state enterprises. Such benefits are better welfare, social security and a sense of security. Furthermore, the work intensity in state-owned enterprises is much lighter than in non-state enterprises. We can say that wage rates in state-owned enterprises is much higher than their efficiency rate as compared with that of non-state enterprises. This has resulted in difficulty for labor mobilization. This also results in wrong price signals. In order to attract skilled workers away from state-owned enterprises, township enterprises and foreign-invested enterprises must have very high wage rates. If an enterprise is not free to hire or fire workers, it is impossible to organize efficient production. For a losing enterprise, an important and imperative measure is to fire workers in order to reduce its deficit. But at present this cannot be implemented, making it impossible for market mechanisms to fully play their role.

Fourth, the existence of two kinds of enterprises with two sets of regulation rules have seriously obstructed the formation and development of entrepreneurs. Entrepreneurs are the prime entities in a market economy. They are different from factory directors and managers in traditional state-owned enterprises. Entrepreneurs are indispensable to the market economy. Without entrepreneurs, the market economy could not effectively play its role.

Under the current economic system, when someone finds an opportunity, such as new technology or managerial methods, can he set up an enterprise and put the new knowledge to work? At present, in state-owned enterprises even the factory directors and managers are restricted on all sides in their activities. How about the managerial staff at medium and lower administrative levels? No need to say. On the other hand, many managerial staff in state-owned enterprises cannot put their new ideas into practice, but are subject to orders and must go step by step to higher managerial levels. More importantly they lack strong material incentives and enduring mental capacity. Under the traditional economic system, they are used to avoiding risks. This is all reflected in reform at present. Only a few managerial staff who have worked in state-owned enterprises for a long time have become entrepreneurs, but most of them are at a loss when they face the new realities of the market.

In recent years, a large number of entrepreneurs have emerged, especially in non-state enterprises. But under the double-track system, their behavior is not standardized. At present, because the financial and labor markets are not perfected, these entrepreneurs cannot obtain capital to set up enterprises. Can an entrepreneur practice when he finds a new opportunity? For the time being, this is impossible. The present market situation has produced a large number of government merchants and speculators. They are the main entrepreneurs at present. Only through them can new technology and new knowledge and information be put into practice. The combination of privileges and access to commodities has resulted in the reaping of huge profits by non-economic means, and serious abuses of power for personal gain. All this seriously obstructs the creation of the market economy and the formation of a real entrepreneurial class. The traditional system has also produced a large number of managerial staff who strive for safety first, and avoid all risk. Meanwhile, the present system has also created a large number of speculators. Now, some intellectuals give up teaching and literature to go into business. And a large number of scientists are engaged in commerce. Most of them want to seize the chance to make money. This kind of consciousness destroyed one generation of intellectuals after the "cultural revolution." It will be much more difficult in the development of a new entrepreneurial class. Will there be a failure before an entrepreneurial class can be formed?

3. Economic Fluctuation and Macrocontrol

The double-track economic system with the coexistence of two types of enterprises has resulted in serious economic fluctuations. Furthermore, it will make the state's macrocontrol ineffective and seriously obstruct the process of changing to a market economy.

Since the formation of the double-track economic system in 1984, China's economy has gone through two serious fluctuation, the inflation and economic recessions of 1985-86 and of 1988-91. One conspicuous feature of these two fluctuations was the structural proportion dislocation. This means that inflation appeared at those times because of a shortage of energy resources, communications facilities and raw materials, and an economic recession occurred because of the government's retrenching policies. So in order to analyze this problem, we must first clarify the reasons for this structural dislocation. Let's analyze it using a simple model.

We can divide all enterprises into two groups. In one are the enterprises under the state's direct control. We can assume that this group represents the basic industrial sector such as energy resources, communications and raw and finished materials. The other group consists of enterprises not controlled by state planning. These are the non-basic industrial sector such as the processing industry and consumer goods production. We assume that the development of the basic industrial group must rely on state funding and investment. The state funds mainly come from the profits of the non-basic industrial group. The development of the non-basic industrial sector relies on bank loans and private investment. Its scale of development is decided by its profits after taxes.

According to these assumptions, we can analyze the reasons for structural dislocation. The reason for the structural dislocation of the two sectors was that profit rates after taxes for the non-basic industrial sector was too high, which brings up the fact that the speed of development for the non-basic industrial sector surpassed that of the basic industrial sector. The two reasons for the non-basic industrial sector's high profits were the speed of the development of technology and the state's inadequate taxation of these industries. These two aspects are interrelated. In short, because the state did not anticipate the speedy development of technology, the tax stipulation was low. This resulted in structural dislocation. So structural dislocation can be solved by raising the tax rate. On the one hand, the increased tax revenue can be directly used for investment in basic industries; on the other hand, the actual profit margin of the non-basic industrial sector can be reduced in order to restrict expansion. Of course, if state monetary policy is employed, expansion of the non-basic industrial sector can be restricted by raising interest rates.

Reform began by expanding the enterprise's autonomy, thus making some state-owned enterprises face market conditions. But as mentioned above, since 1984 the conspicuous feature of reform has been the development of new and developing enterprises. Their efficiency and rapid development are much greater than that of state-owned enterprises. These enterprises also introduced new technology and created employment for the rural surplus labor force. All these factors have promoted the great increase of the consumer goods industry. No doubt the state adopted several policies for reducing taxation in order to stimulate the development of these enterprises. Under the double-track economic system, state-owned enterprises can obtain energy resources, capital, raw materials and other things at low price from the state, while new and developing enterprises are restricted by market conditions. As compared with state-owned enterprises. These new and developing enterprises are thus in inferior position and they cannot develop unless the tax rate is kept low. This circumstance has brought about a serious problem. That is, their speed of technology development is fairly high, and the state's tax on them is too low. This results in the development speed of non-basic industries remaining excessively high while profit remains comparatively high. At the same time, the basic industrial sector receives insufficient investment from the state because the state's financial revenue has been gradually reduced. All of these factors have touched off serious structural proportion dislocation.

Inflation is the direct result of structural proportion dislocation. When the pace of development in the non-basic industrial sector is higher than that of basic industries, the shortage of energy resources and raw materials will cause their prices to rise. It is quite evident that production costs in the non-basic industrial sector will also rise, and this will cause consumer prices to go up. When people's income remains the same, rising prices reduces the demand for consumer goods, and the prices do not go up. If the state is able to increase revenue from the rising prices of energy resources and raw materials in order to increase its investment in basic industries, it may be able to restrain inflation. But in fact, the income from rising prices goes directly into the hands of some people, and this further increases the demand for consumer goods, causing more serious inflation. The cause of all this is two types of enterprises and the double-track economic system. Let's analyze it as the follows.

First, under the double-track price system before 1988, the state controlled the prices of energy resources, communications and raw and finished materials. Even when there were shortage, the state tried to supply these commodities at low prices to state-owned enterprises. But most of the energy resources and raw and finished materials offered to state-owned enterprises at these low prices went into the market through official and private speculation, and were sold at high prices, the income going into the private pockets. This stimulated the demand for consumer goods, and caused the non-basic industrial sector to raise the prices of consumer goods.

If the control of the prices of means of production is completely set free, or the state raises the prices in a planned way, what would happen? Just what happened after 1988 when state-owned enterprises were burdened with serious deficits. Even if the state could raise more revenue, it would have to subsidize these deficit enterprises with most of the new income. Even operating at a deficit, state-owned enterprises were still able to raise wages. This, of course, did nothing to restrain inflation.

Second, could we raise the tax rates to reduce the profits of the non-basic industrial sector and thereby prevent it from expanding? It is impossible to implement such a policy because of the existence of the dual enterprise system.

First of all, we can say that this policy is meaningless for most state-owned enterprises because they are under the state's monopoly for income and expenditures. The increased tax from this source will amount to a subsidy.

Thus this policy is mainly applied to new and developing enterprises. But this method of raising tax rates is directly contrary to the idea of expanding the autonomy of enterprises and enlivening the economy. For example, at present some large and medium-sized state-owned enterprises taking the lead in enlivening the economy by the adoption of the contracting system and the assets operation responsibility system rely on fired tax rates. As to non-state enterprises, their operational conditions remain much inferior. No doubt the raising of tax rates will further strangle their development. At present, we are applying the policy of tax reduction in order to attract foreign investment.

Third, in reality, the existence of factors, such as official speculators and government merchants with unhealthy tendency, makes it more difficult for the state to regulate the economy by applying tax policy. Raising the tax rates is effective only for those enterprises operating by legitimate means, but not effective for enterprises operating by illegal means. This dampens the enthusiasm of enterprises. The purpose of raising tax rates is to redress the differences in income and distribution. These differences are caused by the abuse of power for personal gain and an as yet incomplete adoption of the double-track market economic system. The problem is that the existence of the double-track system, with two types of enterprises, along with other non-economic factors, cannot guarantee a unified tax rate. On the other hand, it is impossible to carry out macro-control by an across-the-board tax hike.

What has been mentioned above can be proved by central financial revenue statistics. Since 1984, the proportion of the state financial revenue in the national income has been gradually reduced. Furthermore, the proportion of the capital construction investment in financial revenue has also been reduced in a sustained way, while financial subsidies and other expenses have increased.

From this analysis we can see that the reason for structural dislocation and inflation is the existence of two types of enterprises, and the non-coordination of two sets of regulation mechanisms. The only way to solve this contradiction is to quicken the economic structural reform, and the emphasis should be put on promoting comprehensive market-regulation mechanisms and the development of new enterprises. In the case of structural dislocation and inflation, the macroeconomic policy runs contrary to this direction, i.e., reducing unscheduled investment by administrative means will result in the protection of large and medium-sized state enterprises and the restriction of the establishment and development of new enterprises.

Now let's analyze the monetary retrenching policy as the main means of retrenching. Before 1984, when structural dislocation occurred, the state applied mainly administrative directives and financial policies to restrict investment scale and the unscheduled development of enterprises, such as the retrenching policy of 1980-1981. Since 1984, reform of the financial system has caused new enterprises to develop step by step; because the capital of these enterprises come mainly from bank loans. It is difficult to determine their development scale by administrative order since they are not restricted by state planning and the volume of investment funds. So monetary policy has become the main measure of state macroeconomic control. When serious inflation and an over-heated economy appeared in 1985 and 1988, the state applied an intense monetary retrenching policy in order to readjust structural dislocation. This monetary policy was similar to previous administrative directives, but the results were worse. Previous administrative retrenching was used to stop production and merge and change products according to economic benefits to trade, departments, and enterprises. But the monetary retrenching policy sought to sternly control and reduce unscheduled loans with one clean cut. Since the capital resources of new and developing enterprises came mainly from bank loans, this monetary retrenching policy seriously hindered their development. Township enterprises went bankrupt one after another, and many flourishing enterprises also found themselves in a predicament because of capital shortage. Under this circumstance of a serious shortage of credit funds, the interest rates for unscheduled credit funds as well as black market interest rates shot up. This coexistence of several kinds of interest rates seriously twisted market price mechanisms. Besides, these circumstances resulted in a suspension of the credit and debt chain of enterprises. All these factors caused market mechanism regulation to be paralyzed. Since 1984, the national economy has been jointly regulated by both planning and market mechanisms, so the disfunction of market mechanisms is bound to cause serious problems.

An important point we should stress here is the coexistence of the two types of enterprises. A new and important fact of economic life is that these new and developing enterprises are more efficient and more vigorous than state-owned enterprises. So the method of retrenching unscheduled credit was introduced just to strangle the efficient new and developing enterprises while protecting inefficient state-owned enterprises. An important cause of structural dislocation was that inefficient enterprises consumed great quantities of energy resources and raw materials, but they did not contribute tax revenue to the state. This resulted in a decrease of financial income and insufficient investment in the basic industrial sector. under normal circumstances, a retrenching policy should make full use of market competitive mechanisms which eliminate low-efficiency enterprises and foster superior enterprises. This means that the prices and interest rates of all kinds of enterprises should be raised, causing the low-efficiency enterprises to collapse. But with the coexistence of two types of enterprises, it is very difficult to regulate prices and interest rates. The effect of raising prices has been analyzed, along with an analysis of interest rates. When differential interest rates are used to control unscheduled investment, the high interest rate will be added to the product price as a cost. This only results in inflation. By the same token, when a unified interest rate is applied, state-owned enterprises will be in deficit, and its fiscal burden will be heavier. This is the very reason why interest rates cannot play a role in regulating the national economy.

The serious results of the monetary retrenching policy have been borne out in the economy, greatly reducing production. Because output value and the economic growth rate have declined, the state's financial income has also largely been reduced and expenses for subsidizing the deficit have increased. The reason for this proportional structural dislocation has been the reduction of the state's financial income, and the reduction of investment in the basic industrial sector. People always say, "Reform needs money." So the reduction of the economic growth rate and financial income is the most dangerous threat to the success of the state's macrocontrol policies. In fact, the application of the monetary retrenching policy lasted a very short time —only half a year. Then the state put in more money in order to stimulate the economy. That is why the cyclical fluctuation lasted only a very short time during 1984-85. But it was very difficult to eliminate the results of the monetary retrenching policy in a short time. The results made the economy turn to the planned economy again, and made the government protect state-owned enterprises and monopolize the market. The market sluggishness and retrogression of reform during 1989-91 were direct reasons for the standstill of market mechanisms. Though the state had augmented the money supply again and again, economic recovery remained very slow.

During the transitional process from a double-track system to a market system, supporting reforms for the enterprises and financial and banking systems play a very important role in controlling economic fluctuation and retaining sustained and steady economic development. This important role has been revealed in the state's new reorganization of the economy this year.

One of the main objectives of China's economic reform is to make enterprises become economic entities operating independently and taking full responsibility for its own profits and losses, and to radiate economic vitality. Therefore, a series of reform measures have been applied to expand the autonomy of enterprises, such as a bonus-stimulation system, wages tied to performance, profit retention linking to achievements, the contract system, the rental system, etc. Reform of the property-right system was applied in order to construct and organize joint-stock enterprises. Its important policy objective is to strengthen the autonomy in enterprise operations and reduce the state's administrative interference. It should be said that this is completely correct for enterprise reform, and an essential prerequisite for forming a market-competitive environment which will eliminate enterprises that cannot compete successfully. Successful enterprises can attract capital by augmenting stocks or issuing bonds with higher interest rates, but underachieving enterprises will be sifted out because of the limited amount of available capital. But why is furthering the enterprise's autonomy regarded as "unauthorized speculative loans?" And why is it sternly restricted or prohibited? The reason is that reform of the financial and banking systems has not been accompanied by reform in the enterprise system.

While the investing power and fund-raising power of enterprises is being expanded, China's banks still implement a policy of "quota management" on loans, i.e., each year the amount of loans granted by each bank is appraised and decided for the next year. This is a kind of borrowing plan. Meanwhile, the state also has a general estimate of investments for the coming year (or years) and decides loan quotas. All this is closely related to investment estimates for the entire country. For investment in some large key projects which exceeds the state's financial ability, the state may solve the problem by setting an appropriate amount for the national debt. According to the calculation of the government, the money supply then will not be increased over normal limits. But because of the enterprise's implementation of the fund-raising and investment authority, it is difficult for the government to estimate the fund-raising potentiality of numerous scattered enterprises by the joint-stock system and bonds in a high-growth economy. Under the loan "quota management" system, the fund-raising activities touched off by the implementation of the enterprise's operation power has exerted great influence on China's economy. The concrete manifestations of this are as follows.

First, a considerable amount of money has gone from bank deposits into enterprise stocks and bonds, and further into practical investment, so bank deposits have been reduced. At the same time bank loans are still being granted according to the original quotas. This means the money supply has increased, thus exacerbating inflation.

Second, since the interest rate on state treasury bonds is fairly low, few are willing to buy treasury bonds. This means that the capital source for the state's major projects cannot be guaranteed. But most of the major projects are industries urgently needed for the development of the national economy.

Because of this situation, in order to control inflation and guarantee the carrying out of the readjustment of the industrial structure, the state must institute a new round of retrenchment, i.e., the state must cut credits by a wide margin, apportion treasury bonds, and strictly restrict the fund raising and investing activities of the enterprises. But the results have not been good. Macroeconomic fluctuations have thereby occurred, and the enterprise's powers over operation and investment have also been affected.

Thus it can be seen that when the reform of the enterprise system suitable to a market economy has been carried out to a certain degree, the relevant reform of the banking and financial systems must also be carried out at the same time, otherwise it is difficult to maintain a steady balance of economic development and economic operations. Under the present circumstances, how can we pass through the period of transition to a market economy and maintain this balance?

II. Present Focal Points and Difficulties During the Transition to a Market Economy

As mentioned above, at present the main problem in operating the double-track system is the coexistence of two kinds of enterprises and two sets of regulations, and lack of full support for reform which seriously obstructs the regulating function of market mechanisms. Now the focal point of reform is to completely eliminate the state's protection of state-owned enterprise and to establish a perfect macrocontrol mechanism.

1. Reform of State-Owned Enterprises

As the above analysis demonstrates, state-owned enterprises are divided into two parts. One part is the basic industrial sector, such as energy resources, communications, raw materials, etc. The output value of the industrial sector accounts for about 50 percent of that of state-owned enterprises, but the number of these enterprises in the industrial sector is very small. Since the basic industrial sector requires large investment, and achieves results slowly, it is basically invested in and operated by the state. For the time being, non-state enterprises don't have the ability to invest in basic industries. Therefore, the focus of reform of these enterprises is mainly to change their operational mechanisms so they are gradually able to enter the market. Since these enterprises are the focal point of state investment, it is impossible to sever them completely from state planning. Therefore, the main reform task at present is to give managers of these enterprises more autonomy by separating management rights from ownership, and organizing an entrepreneur stratum composed of technical managerial experts. Let entrepreneurs manage these state-owned enterprises. The other category of state-owned enterprises is the non-basic industrial sector, including some new and developing enterprises that take the lead in reform. Both the products and operational scope of these enterprises coincide with those of township enterprises and foreign-invested enterprises. These enterprises are the present focus of reform. The following measures should be adopted to reform these enterprises. The direction of reform should be to completely cut the state's ties to administrative management, with the state no longer offering capital (loans with low interests) and deficit subsidies to enterprises. Bankruptcy laws should also be resolutely implemented. And losing enterprises must be allowed to fire workers.

During the process of preparing enterprises for entry into the market, the greatest difficulty we face is the property rights of state-owned assets. The assets of enterprises cannot be evaluated in market terms because of the lack of market competition and a securities market at present. Therefore, the reform of enterprise property rights can be divided into two phases.

The first phase is to prepare enterprises for the market by normalizing the property rights of state-owned assets, and adopting stock and contracting systems to end administrative interference in enterprises. After the stock and contract systems have been formed, the administrative organs will no longer appoint enterprise managers. All these measures will promote the formation of an entrepreneurial stratum. During this process, the value of assets is not completely decided by the market, so the problem of underestimating assets may arise. But the present stock and contract systems allow the state to retain certain ownership, and this has laid the foundation for evaluating enterprise assets completely according to market value. The difference is that managerial rights will be given to entrepreneurs, and the managers will not be appointed or selected by the government. This is the method that is now applied to some township enterprises, and state-owned enterprises in Shenzhen, Guangdong, and other places. Except for some especially large enterprises, enterprises should be encouraged to adopt the stock system. Applying the strategy of purchasing all kinds of stocks and entering the security market, enterprise assets will have a better chance of being evaluated by the market, and various kinds of ownership systems can be implemented for enterprise assets.

Through these reforms, a preliminary competitive market can be formed. After the competitive market has been formed, we can implement complete competition of the survival of the fittest for enterprises by making use of the securities market and the system of annexation of enterprises so as to appraise their assets. All this will lay the foundation for the second phase of reform.

The objective of the second phase of reform is to make property rights clear and definite and further transform the state's management functions. Clear and definite property rights are a necessary condition for market mechanisms to fully develop their function. At present, the development of township enterprises is restricted to a large extent by vague property rights. The state should gradually sell the assets of the non-basic industrial sector to individual persons through the market in order to recover capital and increase investment in the basic industrial sector, thus making the proportion of the output value of the basic industrial sector approach 40 percent of the national economic output value. This is determined by China's economic development at its present stage. As a budding developing country, China can quicken the speed of development by introducing foreign advanced technology. It can be said that the pace of introducing technology for the processing and consumer goods industries is now comparatively rapid, with market mechanisms playing an effective regulating role. This allows the initiative of managers and technicians to be brought into play, regulating their products and tailoring them to demand. This may cause basic industries to experience shortages and a surplus of demand. Increasing investment in the basic industrial sector is the most important factor for economic development and structural balance at present. On the one hand, private enterprises don't have the ability to invest, and on the other hand, the state lacks efficient management in the non-basic industrial sector. Therefore, in order to change the state's function completely and transform the system to a market economy, one important step the state must take is to draw capital from the non-basic industrial sector, and invest it in the basic industrial sector.

2. Perfecting the Market System and Macrocontrol Mechanisms

The greatest problem we face in building and perfecting the market economy is how to form a complete system incorporating state macrocontrol. The Incompatible reforms of the 1980s sent the macroeconomic structure out of control, and brought about a return to planned administrative control again. The present macroeconomic situation has made the problem more severe. The problem urgently needing solution at present is how to maintain current high economic growth through further reform, and at the same time strengthen macrocontrol without following the same old road.

There are two objectives for maintaining sustained and steady economic operations and development: First, reinforcing the bottleneck industries and rectifying the dislocation of the industrial structure; second, keeping price levels comparatively stable. The first of these is important to rectify the delayed effects of economic development; the second is an important measure for preventing short-term economic fluctuation. According to the present realities of structural reform and economic development, we can do these two things at the same time to achieve the first goal. First of all, we may accelerate the decontrol of prices for the products and service of bottleneck industries so that they may realize rational profit rates. Based on this, the capital problem can be solved by applying the shareholding system to raise funds from the entire society, not just from government investment.* At the same time, the tax rates need to be readjusted according to macrocontrol. If necessary, for example when serious inflation threatens, tax rates may be raised by a large margin. Meanwhile, financial subsidies should be reduced so that more capital can be invested in basic industries. This is an important requirement for guaranteeing the state macrocontrol and the long and stable growth of the economy. A unitary tax rate should be formed

---

* It is not difficult to do this. The bottleneck industries mean insufficient supply. This is the basis for their prices to rise. In fact, many bottleneck industries are basic industries which are monopolistic. They may even be able to obtain monopoly-size profits.

gradually, and all sorts of preferential policies reduced, especially tax reduction policies formulated by local governments at different levels.

Will this financial retrenching policy restrict the development of new enterprises such as township enterprises and private enterprises, and result in a shrinking economy? It is obvious that raising tax rates will restrict the development of new enterprises. But it may help the state-owned enterprises now operating at a deficit. The introduction of new technology has accelerated, and at this time wages can be kept low through assuring the existence of a surplus labor force. Hence the development of new enterprises will not be greatly influenced.

Keeping prices relatively stable will guarantee that the money supply will not be excessively expanded. When the reform of the enterprise system has been carried out, the financial and banking systems must get rid of many measures featuring the planned economy to suit the market economy. For example, it is a pressing matter at the moment to turn quota management on bank credit into management on asserts and liabilities. All this can play an important role in retaining a stable money supply. Besides, the degree of control on interest rates should be further loosened. This will allow interest rates to reflect the price of capital more accurately. A unitary interest rate should be formed to meet market economy standards. This can be accomplished by regulating interest rates to control the money supply. This method may prevent the unitary form of monetary retrenching, and make enterprises really follow the road of selecting the superior and eliminating the inferior—striving for existence in competition. The above-mentioned may seem a platitude because people long for interest rates to act as a means of macrocontrol. The problem at present is that if the financial system does not take the lead in reform, conditions cannot be created for the reform of enterprises and for the perfection of the market. And it will also result in retrogression of reform in other areas. The reason why reform of the financial system did not achieve successful results is enterprises. Now the development of new and developing enterprises has created favorable conditions for the reform of the financial system. If the state makes up its mind to cast off the burden of losing state enterprises, and turns its sights to new and developing enterprises, then surely conditions will be favorable for the reform of the financial system. This means that some state-owned enterprises will face difficulties because of high interest rate and an insufficient capital supply, but this will not influence the entire economy. But if we give up financial reform and regulation of interest rates, and adopt a monetary retrenching policy in unitary form, this policy will be riskier than before. The objective of the banking system for further reform is to establish real commercial banks. The bank loan requirements for enterprises will be placed under strict evaluation—taking full responsibility for their own profits and losses. By doing so, a capital allocation environment of survival of the fittest will be formed. At the same time, we may make use of some policy-related banks to meet some necessary "policy loan" demands by the government.

An important step for the reform of the financial system is to speed up the establishment and perfection of the financial system in the area of stocks and the securities market. The function of stocks and securities market is not only raising funds, they can also evaluate enterprise assets in a real capital market. The value of assets cannot be evaluated without it. Now people worry about the development of the securities market, because it is obvious that some problems exist in the management of this market. On the other hand, many problems exist at the stock market, which can only be solved through the further development of the stock market. Since the securities market is not fully developed, we should bring the function of banks into full play so as to remedy this defect. Reorganization and annexation of enterprises should be encouraged through investment companies organized by specialized banks. For example, specialized banks may annex or auction those enterprises which are unable to repay loans because of deficits, or may control the annexation of enterprises from behind the scene and offer capital support, aimed at eliminating losing enterprises, supporting new and developing enterprises, and fostering an entrepreneur stratum through weakening property rights.

3. Reform of the Administrative Management System

Through weakening the property right relations to promote the reform of enterprises, an important accompanying measure is the reform of the present administrative management system. At present we have no alternative but to apply measures to weaken the property right relations, with the objective of switching to a market economy by fostering an entrepreneur stratum. But the present administrative management system has formed a serious threat to such reform. Some people will make use of their rights to set up false companies, and appropriate state assets so as to suppress real entrepreneurs and exterminate the entrepreneurial spirit. Therefore, great effort should be made to cut down all kinds of management organs so that their administrative power over assets and power to appoint enterprise managerial staffs will be reduced. Administrative power over assets should be centralized in the State Assets Administrative Bureau, and the power of staff appointments should gradually be transferred to the board of directors, or managers will be determined through tendering. An entrepreneurial stratum is formed through competition. Therefore, it is important to form a competitive environment which will produce entrepreneurs. But multiple administrative organs form a monopoly over managerial staff. When managerial staff and managers of enterprises devote their energies to cultivating good relations with others and obtaining wealth through non-economic channels, it will no longer stimulate people to create wealth and obtain private benefits through the application of new technology and knowledge.

In short, certain conditions have led China to switch to a market economic system. So long as we can accelerate the reform of administrative management and support reform of the economic system by building an honest and clean government, and guarantee to some extent the financial income of the state, we can carry reform forward more rapidly.

Difficulties and Countermeasures in the Transition from a Planned Economy to a Market Economy
—For the International Symposium on "The Market Economy and China"

Lü Zheng
Vice-president of the Institute of Industrial Economy,
the Chinese Academy of Social Sciences

At the end of 1978, China embarked on an historic transition from a planned economy to a market economy. The past 15 years of reform has seen great changes taking place in the mode of running the Chinese economy. These changes are best demonstrated by the following aspects:

1) After introducing the contract responsibility system with remuneration linked to output based on the household into the rural areas, the mode of agricultural production shifted from a collective economy to a private economy, allowing the agricultural labor force to flow freely into non-agricultural industries nationwide.

2) Various types of non-state-owned enterprises grew rapidly, forming a structure of coexistence and competition with the state-owned economy.

3) The majority of state-owned enterprises have, on the whole, freed themselves from subsidiary positions, and are gradually moving towards autonomy.

4) Breakthroughs have been achieved in the reform of the price system and in the shaping of the price mechanism. At present, the price of over 95 percent of consumer goods and the price of over 80 percent of means of production are determined

by the market.

5) The market system for the key productive elements such as goods, labor, capital, technology and information has primarily been established.

6) Market regulation has played a dominant role in various economic activities from fixed assets investment to the fields of production and circulation.

7) The Chinese economy has opened its door wider to the outside world. It has adopted the ongoing principles of the international market and is using the experience of the capitalist market economy in macrocontrol, and economic management.

The above changes demonstrate that the Chinese economic system has, on the whole, shifted away from the traditional planned economy, and has now entered the market economy. However, to transfer completely from a planned economy to a market economy, there are still many deep-rooted difficulties to be faced. The following paragraphs are devoted to analyzing several important problems emerging in the process of China's transition.

I. Problems Associated with State-Owned Enterprises Assuming Responsibility for Their Own Profits and Losses

Since 1980, the fundamental idea and practice of reforming state-owned enterprises has been aimed at expanding their autonomy. This process has undergone roughly four stages: During the first stage, from 1979 to 1982, the state shared profits with enterprises in order to give enterprises more financial power. The second stage, from 1983 to 1986, saw an attempt to standardize the distribution relationship between the state and enterprises, and a tax system was introduced into enterprises to replace the profit sharing method. The third stage was from 1987 to 1991, when a profit contract responsibility system was implemented in an all-round way in enterprises. In the fourth stage, from 1992 to the present, on the basis of continuing the contract responsibility system, enterprises began to change their management mechanism according to the demands of the market economy. These reform measures have, to a certain extent, expanded the autonomy of state-owned enterprises and strengthened their vitality. But up to the present, the majority of state-owned enterprises have not achieved substantial progress in this transition of systems. Due to obscure property-rights relations in state-owned enterprises, the degree of an enterprise's autonomy mainly depends on the extent of the loosening of control by the government administrative organizations at various levels. Also, the problem of the soft restraint on state-owned enterprises' budgets under the traditional system has not yet been solved. In reality, these enterprises do not assume the risks of the market in assets management. If an enterprise suffers a loss, the state will eventually cover this loss. Market pressures and the incentive mechanisms have not been formed yet to push enterprises to reduce cost, and to stimulate technological progress. The goal pursued by enterprise managers is to maximize short-term wages, bonus and welfare. Practice shows that stressing the expansion of enterprise autonomy instead of establishing a mechanism of self-responsibility for profits and losses, especially self-responsibility for losses, is counterproductive to adaptation to the demands of the market economy.

The past practices of reform did not allow state-owned enterprises to be responsible for losses, and it is also not feasible at the present to set up a unified model. A realistic measure is to carry out classified reform of state-owned enterprises. That is, allowing different types of enterprises to adopt different ways of assuming responsibility for losses.

The first type of enterprises are a small group of large state-run infrastructure industries such as railways, post and telecommunications, energy, raw and finished materials, and petrochemicals. These enterprises will continue to implement an overall contract responsibility system throughout. The base and proportion of profit are fixed in the contract for a certain period of time and the enterprise can keep the surplus or be responsible for the losses. Besides, enterprises should also be responsible for protecting and increasing the value of their assets.

The second type of enterprises are those competitive state-owned ones, which mainly take the form of shareholding system, so as to realize the separation of government and enterprises, the separation of ownership and management, and assure that enterprises are wholly responsible for market risks, profits and losses. When an enterprise's assets cannot compensate for its debt, the enterprise will go bankrupt according to low. At present, the real problem facing the implementation of the shareholding system in state-owned enterprises is deciding who represents the property right of the state-owned shares and who should be responsible for the profits and losses of operating this part of the state-owned property.

Whether the enterprises are of the overall contract responsibility or of the shareholding system variety, the selection of their managers must introduce the competitive mechanism of the market. That is, to adhere to the rule of keeping the superior and discarding the inferior, to employ capable managers with handsome salaries, and to fire those who perform poorly. It also means linking the performance of enterprises closely to material benefits, social status, and the reputations of their managers. Likewise, the performance of an enterprise should also be related to employee income, welfare and continued employment.

The third type of enterprises are a large number of the small-sized state-owned enterprises. Through the measure of transfer with compensation, such as auction or long-term lease, these enterprises will become collective or individual ones. Via transfer with compensation, the state recoups its original capital. If the capital assessment is done fairly, the problem of draining state-owned property will not exist.

Generally speaking, to successfully change from the planned economy to the market economy, we must focus on reform of state-owned enterprises. Only when these enterprises have been transformed will they be able to institute a new management mechanism.

II. Transformation of Governmental Functions

The traditional planned economy has created unwieldy governmental organization. The government's economic-control function consists not only of making economic plans and the rules of the economic operations, but also of directly guiding and participating in the productive activities of enterprises. The past 15 years of reform have witnessed a great change in the government's economic-control functions, i.e., it has moved from direct control and participation to indirect control and interference. However, this change is not thorough, and is still unadaptable to the demands of a market economy. The difficulties of this transition of governmental functions are as follows:

First, at present there is no clear and operable target model defining the government's economic-control function.

Second, there are no effective measures for dealing with the layoff of surplus government employees.

As to the definition of governmental functions, there is a comparatively prevailing view that since China is a developing country it should adopt a market economy of the government-dominant-type in its transition to the market economy. At present, the conditions are not yet ripe for following the market economic system of the Western developed countries. Of course, we do not reject learning from the effective methods and successful experiences of these countries. What we need to do now is to solve the problem of how to allow the market to play a basic role in the distribution of resources and how to define the government's dominant role in economic operations. The two must then be combined together under conditions of a market economy of the government-dominant-type.

When we say let the market play a basic role in the distribution of resources, we mean to include the following aspects:

1) The distribution of resources is dependent on economic benefit, that is, profit is the basic determinant of the distribution of resources.

2) The enterprise has autonomy in deciding the input and output of the productive factors, that is, what to produce and how to produce it. Within the jurisdiction of the law, the government should not intervene in the enterprise's autonomy.

3) Price mechanisms are the fundamental lever in guiding capital flow. Under the law of average profit margin in a market economy, resources can be distributed proportionately to various

sectors.

4) Proportionate market supply is automatically controlled by the price mechanism.

5) The competition mechanism and keeping the superior and discarding the inferior are the solid rule and common phenomena of the market operation. This mechanism is conducive to optimizing the distribution of resources.

6) The enterprise will be responsible for its own profits and losses, and assume market risks. The government will not subsidize the enterprise running at a loss.

These are the fundamental principles guiding the allocation of resources in the market economy. But as China is now in a transition period, the micro foundation of the market economy is still imperfect. The market system is still at the construction stage. Under this situation, it is unrealistic to indiscriminately copy the model of the mature market economy. Instead, we should, on the one hand, reform governmental organizations and their functions, and on the other hand, let the government play an effective role, so as to give impetus to establishing and perfecting the new market economic system.

But how can we allow the market to play a basic role in the distribution of resources and at the same time let the government play its dominant role? Some economists suggest that China learn from the Japanese experience and establish governmental organizations similar to those of Japan. These organizations guide, control and intervene in economic activities by using law and economic levers as well as various non-governmental intermediary organizations. Some economists prefer the system of the Republic of Korea. The government of the Republic of Korea controls and guides economic development by making the economic plans and implementing policies. There are still others advocating the German experience—using financial policy of the central bank to intervene and control economic operations.

In view of the Chinese reality and the reform of governmental organization and its functions, the Chinese government's role in managing and controlling the economy cannot copy the experience of any single country, but must examine everything and choose the best.

From the successful experience of Japan, Germany and South Korea in developing their economies rapidly after the Second World War, we notice that apart from establishing a market economy (especially an enterprise system which is initiative, competitive and creative), their governments' correct economic development policies and their effective control, guidance and intervention in economic affairs are also fundamental reasons for their successes. After China has turned to a market economy, the government will still need the following macrocontrol functions.

1) To work out economic development plans, including medium- and long-term economic development targets and strategy and to draw overall arrangements for productivity, choosing the leading industries, controlling the investment scale, and drafting targets and policies for the development of science and technology.

2) To guide and control the economy by using economic levers such as finance and fiscal policies and administrative means to ensure sustained, stable and coordinated development of the national economy.

3) To standardize market behavior and market order to guard against monopoly and unfair competition, and to prevent and punish illegal economic activities.

4) To complement market inadequacy and remedy market failures. The government should be responsible for running a public social welfare which does not totally rely on market mechanisms. The government should give financial and policy support to the construction of infrastructure like transportation and communication. The government should support basic science research and hi-tech industries which can have a long-term impact on economic development. The government should regulate national income distribution, set up and perfect a social security system, and, presupposing competition and efficiency, realize social equity.

After the government's economic function is changed from direct control to indirect control, it becomes necessary to streamline the unwieldy governmental organization established during the planned economy, and to reduce the number of government employees. The disposition of these surplus government employees is a glaring problem during this transition period. Practically, it is really difficult just to streamline the government drastically without finding some arrangements for those left unemployed. If this turns out to be just some superficial adjustment, it will not only add a heavy burden to state finances, but will also delay the transitional process. Facing a difficult choice, we suggest that the government take an unswerving policy with an explicit target of reform of governmental organization and its functions.

As for the surplus government employees, there are at present three feasible solutions: (1) Those originally engaged in investment in capital construction, materials supply, sales, and import and export administration in the government departments should be allowed to gradually transfer into economic entities; but they must be separated from government institutions, and be responsible for their own profits and losses; (2) some office workers may transfer directly to enterprises; (3) intermediary organizations between the government and enterprises, like trade associations, can be set up to provide service for both enterprises and the government. At the initial stage, the government may give them some necessary financial support. But they should not be considered government institutions or supported by the government over a long period of time. The existence and development of trade associations is mainly dependent on whether they can provide enterprises with effective and irreplaceable services.

III. The Problem of Reforming the Social Security System

Unemployment insurance and pensions and medical care are the three pillars of social security. The formation, development and perfection of this security system is connected not only to the social-economic system, but also to the level of the social productivity. It is unrealistic to establish a perfect and widespread social security system when the productivity level is not sufficiently high. Even in the developed countries, the ongoing social security and welfare systems have also been threatened by financial inadequancy. In fact, China's present social security system only covers wage earners in urban areas, and is unavailable in vast rural areas. Therefore, when we discuss reform of the social security system, we are only talking about the urban residents who represent only 30 percent of the total population.

1) The reform of unemployment insurance

The "iron rice bowl" system created by the planned economy has masked serious hidden unemployment in state-owned enterprises and other institutions. Generally, the surplus employees in the state-owned enterprises account for 25-30 percent of the total number of employees in those enterprises. In order to meet the needs of transition to a market economy, we must cut down on redundant personnel. On the positive side, unemployment will create pressure on every employee, thus creating employment competition which is conducive to raising the quality of work and increasing efficiency. From a negative point of view, unemployment is bound to cause some social instability. Under a market economy, being unemployed is undoubtedly agonizing, but inevitable. In the face of market competition, the enterprises must adhere to the principle that efficiency comes first. Only in this way can the economy develop rapidly, and consequently create more jobs. The government's responsibility is to create job opportunities by means of macroeconomic policy, and to provide the unemployed with the necessary social support, in order to maintain social stability.

The state-owned enterprises have some autonomy in personnel decisions, but it is still very rare for an enterprise to fire employees based on productivity and market competition. There are now 150 million wage earners in urban areas in China. If we take 5 percent of each person's monthly income for the unemployment fund, we would collect 12-14 billion yuan a year for the entire country. With this money, we can provide 5-6 percent of the unemployed in urban areas with the necessary social support. Furthermore, the establishment of the mechanism of an unemployment insurance system will help to raise economic efficiency and maintain social stability.

2) The reform of the pension system

The pension system in urban areas relies on the units in which the pensioners worked before their retirement, and in rural areas it depends on traditional family care. Urban retirees receive pensions from their original work units, while rural elderly are supported by their children. The main disadvantages of a work unit-supported system are (1) A drain on the state's financial resources; (2) unfair sharing of the pension burden among old and new enterprises; (3) risks of pensioners losing their pensions when an enterprise runs at a loss or goes bankrupt. In rural areas, with the change from traditional productive methods and in farmers' ethics, as well as the family planning policy, some elderly farmers who can no longer work are left without any care. Therefore, we must change the old pension system.

Pension reform in China will gradually be socialized, and at the same time will encourage traditional family care for the elderly. To socialize pensions means that pension funding should be shared among the state, enterprises and employees, and accumulated by various insurance fund organizations. Once an employee retires, he will sever all economic ties to his original unit, and turn to the local specialized pension institution for his pension. The pension fund organizations will ensure that the accumulated funds increase in value by investing in state bonds and such like. Similarly, with economic development, the rural areas will gradually set up their own socialized pension systems.

3) The reform of the medical care system

In today's China there are 32 million staff in government institutions, and 140 million workers in enterprises enjoying free medical care. In rural areas, 15 percent of the country's administrative villages have cooperative medical care. With an increase in the aging population and the rising costs of medical care, free medical care in urban areas has become a heavy burden on the government and on enterprises, and has led to some serious waste. This free medical care provided by the state and enterprises must be reformed. So far, reform in this area has been very slow and has not yielded many results. That is because this reform involves the welfare of more than 100 million employees and their relatives. In this sensitive situation, neither the government nor enterprises has ventured to take drastic steps to reform this system. Of course, the employees must bear a part of the cost of medical care when they go to see the doctor or get the medicine. But the amount borne by the employees is so small as to be almost symbolic. To establish a socialized medical care system, we have to go through a process of initiation, development, consolidation and perfection. With our economic development still at a relatively low level, we cannot expect to establish a medical care system equal to that of the developed countries overnight. In the early stages we can only adopt a structure of coexistence between the old and the new medical care systems. We are now considering maintaining the old free medical care system for employees over the age of 40, but the proportion the individual employee pays should be raised. As for employees under the age of 40, reform will have them contribute to the insurance fund together with the state. This medical insurance fund will pay a fixed percentage of medical costs for the employees who have joined the fund, and the employees will pay the lion's share. It is our goal to set up a socialized medical care system within 20 years.

China has achieved remarkable progress in its transition toward a market economy. However, an arduous task remains to deepen the reform and set up a near-perfect socialist market economy system. This paper is only a brief analysis of some glaring difficulties during the current transition. Solving these difficulties will take time and is a gradual process. China's reform has entered a new and difficult stage. After more than 10 years of effort, greater achievement will be made, and it may be predicted that the new system of a socialist market economy with Chinese characteristics will take shape by early next century.

The Role of Futures Markets in the U.S. Economy and the Development of Futures Markets in China*

Merton H. Miller
Robert R. McCormick Distinguished Service
Professor Emeritus, University of Chicago

I have been asked to discuss the role of futures markets in the U.S. economy and the development of futures markets in China. This subject was presumably chosen by the sponsors of this Conference because they have observed the phenomenal growth of futures markets (and forward or over-the-counter derivative markets) throughout the world in recent years and are wondering whether China too should be participating in these developments. Some tentative first steps toward instituting futures markets have, in fact, already been taken, but there is still much hesitation by the authorities about pushing forward more vigorously. Their fear is that futures markets will simply lead to more speculation, of little or no social benefit to the Chinese economy. And that is the issue I want to address here: Concerns over speculation and futures markets. The technical side of futures markets and their regulation I leave to Professor Shen Hanyao of the Shanghai Economic Research Institute who will cover them in a paper to be presented later in this Conference.

Whenever I hear talk of speculation and futures exchanges, I am reminded of the hydraulic engineer from India who visited Holland and toured the famous Dutch canals. He was impressed with what he saw and he said that those must surely be the largest

* A talk presented at the International Conference on Market Economy and China, held in Beijing, China, September 19, 1993.

irrigation canals in the whole world. No, no, said his hosts. Those canals aren't for bringing the water *in*. They're for taking the water *out*!

And similarly for the U.S. futures exchanges like the Chicago Mercantile Exchange, or for your own fledgling futures markets like Shanghai Metal Futures Exchange. They are built not for the gamblers, but for the people who *don't* want to gamble.

Consider, for example, a modest-size petroleum distributor buying refined products such as heating oil from one or several petroleum refineries and selling the heating oil to local retail customers. Once the heating oil has been bought and put in storage tanks, the company will normally buy fire insurance on those tanks and their contents. Of course, an oil company big enough, with many such tank farms spread over the whole world, could afford to self-insure. But a company with only one set of tanks can't take that chance. A fire in the yard would destroy the business. *Not* buying insurance under those conditions would be gambling—gambling that no fire will occur.

But fire is not the only hazard the distributor faces. There is also price risk on the inventory stored in the tanks. Suppose the distributor has borrowed money from a bank to buy the inventory; and suppose the price of heating oil suddenly drops by 50 percent. The prices the distributor can collect from its retail customers will also fall by the same amount. The competition from other dealers will see to that. The distributor won't be able to pay back the bank loan, and the business will be destroyed just as surely as if there had been a fire.

Fortunately, however, distributors *can* insure themselves against a disastrous price fall just as easily as against a disastrous fire. They can simply take a short position in heating oil futures contracts. If the price of heating oil falls, they will lose money on their inventory. But they will *make* money on their futures contract. On balance, there will be no *net* loss and they will be able to repay the bank. In fact, most banks in the U.S. wouldn't even *lend* them the money unless they had first agreed to hedge that inventory by taking a short position in futures or the equivalent.

The need for hedging—or nongambling as it might be called —is easiest to visualize in the case of physical commodities like oil or metals, but it's equally important for those in the financial services industry. Consider, for example, a commercial bank or an investment bank that maintains an inventory of government bonds for resale to its customers. Changes in interest rates can produce swings in the values of those bonds so large that few banks would be willing to serve as distributors and market-makers unless they hedge their position with treasury-bond futures. In fact, so crucial to the distribution process for government bonds has the futures exchanges in the U.S. become that our Treasury Department has been known to postpone its scheduled auctions if they happen to come when the futures exchanges are closed for a holiday.

So much then for the demand for hedging, or for nongambling as I have called it. But, of course, as I need hardly remind you, hedging doesn't *eliminate* risk. It merely *transfers* it from those who don't want it to those who do.

And who might they be? Some of them, and these days, in fact, *most* of them, are firms and institutions in a different phase of the distribution cycle. My petroleum products distributor was worried that prices might fall. So he took an offsetting short position in futures. But an airline company that has already posted its fares is worried that prices of the petroleum products it uses in such large quantities may *rise*. So it will take a long position in futures. And similarly for financial products. Pension funds that want to *buy* government bonds, but won't have the money coming in until later in the year can hedge against a rise in bond prices—that is against a fall in interest rates—by taking a long position in bond futures, even as the underwriters distributing the bonds are taking short positions.

And that is why the real economic function of futures markets has come increasingly to be seen as that of providing a low cost, efficient way of bringing together people with offsetting risks. I do not mean to suggest, of course, that the participants in futures markets consist entirely of hedgers seeking to avoid risk. The two sides of the inventory risk equation balance approximately, but not exactly, and certainly not at every moment in time. When an imbalance *does* develop, someone from outside the regular inventory process must be induced to step in to fill the gap. These people have come to be called speculators—a term that, quite unjustifiably in my view, has very negative connotations.

How different the role of speculator might have been seen if they had only been given a more dignified name. The garbage collectors in many cities—and that is certainly a socially useful function—have recognized this and insist on being called "sanitary engineers." By the same token, the speculators on the exchanges could be called "insurance providers" or "liquidity providers," for that is what they do. They might even be called "market stabilizers" since successful speculation actually reduces price volatility, despite widespread misconceptions to the contrary.

If speculators, and the futures markets on which they operate, are doing so much social good, why is their reputation so bad? There are several reasons. Part of their bad repute reflects the general prejudice, found all through history, against middlemen —people who just move goods and services from one place to another—as opposed to people who actually make things. Part of their negative image, particularly in the U.S. and Japan, can be traced to the competition that financial futures offer to the older, more established stock—brokerage industry. A pension fund, for example, seeking to change its equity exposure, would find that the adjustment could be done five times as cheaply with futures as with the underlying securities. In the U.S., an accommodation between the competing sectors was reached eventually by inter-marriage, as it were. The big stock brokerage firms are now also big in futures brokerage as well. But that hasn't happened in Japan because the futures business there, at least until recently, was mainly left to foreign, especially U.S. financial service firms. The Japanese firms concentrated on their own protected market of Japanese stock buyers where they had an overwhelming advantage. Hence the competitive rivalry between the two sectors still continues in Japan, and complaints by stockbrokers there about the market volatility induced by futures have become a propaganda weapon in the struggle. No serious scientific basis for such charges have ever been established, however, either in Japan or the U.S.

Turning from those countries to China, I would have to add that some of the prejudice against futures markets I have encountered here arises from seeing them as gambling casinos, which is certainly understandable since some of your gambling casinos have been deliberately made to look like futures markets, complete with TV screens showing current transaction price on the U.S. exchanges, and use technical futures terms like "margins" for the stages of the bet. But there is an important difference between gambling casinos and true futures markets. Futures markets deal with risks that already exist, risks that must be borne by someone. But the risks in a gambling casino are entirely artificial. They wouldn't exist if somebody didn't spin the wheel, or throw the dice or deal the cards.

And that property of gambling casinos, in fact, is actually an argument for *encouraging* futures markets. The economic authorities of many countries in this part of the world must realize that their people are going to gamble no matter what the authorities say or do. Isn't it better to let people do their gambling on legitimate futures markets where that gambling can be turned to social benefit by providing businesses with cheaper insurance?

Do futures markets of the kind I have been describing have a place in a "socialist market economy"? That depends, of course, on what those terms actually mean in practice. If the "socialist" part were to mean, for example, that all the many state-owned and state-operated businesses were regarded merely as divisions of one grand state-owned conglomerate enterprise, then there would really be no need for a separate, outside risk-transfer or risk-management industry. The price risks noted in my illustrations would all be internalized. Any losses to the state's heating-oil distributor from a price fall would be offset by the higher profits of the state's airline company. State ownership on a large scale, in fact, has sometimes been defended precisely as a low-cost way of dealing with economic risks—of "diversifying" them away, so to speak.

But socializing or internalizing risks in this way also has drawbacks, as many American conglomerates have learned to their sorrow in recent years. Managers tend to function much more effectively when they have to bear the consequences for any losses suffered by their divisions. Exceptions cannot normally be made for losses stemming from price fluctuations without jeopardizing the whole compensation program. But if the managers are to bear the risks, they must also have the right, and the opportunity, to deal with those risks in ways they find cost-effective. For many such risks, the most cost-effective form of insurance, as I have suggested, would be hedging them via futures contracts.

To make the futures route cost-effective for the managers of firms in China, large-scale futures exchanges along American lines with hundreds of floor brokers and traders and thousands of square meters of trading floors are not required. Thanks to the personal computer revolution, levels of transactions too small to support a trading floor can now be handled electronically at reasonably low cost, leaving open the possibility of sketching to a trading-floor, open-outcry system when volume builds up sufficiently. No concern need be entertained, moreover, that the relative cheapness of computerized exchanges would lead to a wasteful proliferation of such exchanges, all trading the same products. The dynamics of liquidity in futures trading are such that all the business in any one contract will quickly gravitate to a single exchange, regardless of how many exchanges may enter the race initially.

Although the "socialist" component of "market socialism" may or may not be compatible with futures markets, depending on how much autonomy is granted to the managers of the state-owned firms, there can be no equivocation on the "market" component. For futures markets to have a role, prices must be free to move. In any market in which the government is fixing prices (and prices, in this sense, cover interest rates and foreign exchange rates), there is, by definition, no price risk. That doesn't mean, of course, that there is no risk; merely that the risk is transformed from a price risk to a supply risk or delivery risk for which futures markets, by themselves, cannot provide protection. But then again, as history shows, neither can anything else.

In sum, paradoxical as it may sometimes seem, the best way to cope with price fluctuations is not to suppress them. Let the market prices fully and accurately reflect the truth about supply and demand in the market, however painful that truth may be. Just make sure that those not willing to risk those pains can at least get insurance against them.

The Chinese Economy in the 21st Century

Lawrence J. Lau*
Department of Economics, Stanford University

I. Abstract

China has been one of the fastest growing countries since it began economic reform in 1979, achieving an average annual growth rate of real gross domestic product of approximately 9 percent. In 1992, the Chinese economy grew by 13.2 percent. In the first half of 1993, the Chinese economy grew at an annual rate in excess of 14 percent. This growth rate is unsustainable—in the face of material shortages and supply bottlenecks such as energy, transportation and communication—in the long run. The question is: What is the likely growth path of the Chinese economy in the next century?

While there are indeed many structural problems in the Chinese economy—insufficient infrastructure; over as well as under regulation; an antiquated financial system; the lack of a clearly specified set of business laws; and the widespread practice of government agencies (and universities) directly operating business enterprises on the side—the long-run fundamentals are quite sound. The thesis is advanced that Chinese economic growth during the next two to three decades will be largely driven

---

* The author is Kwoh-Ting Li, professor of Economic Development, Department of Economics, and co-director, Asia/Pacific Research Center, Stanford University. This paper is prepared for presentation at the International Conference on the Market Economy, Beijing, September 18-22, 1993. The author is grateful for discussions with Moses Abramovitz, Lawrence Klein and Roberto Mariano. An earlier version of this paper was presented at the Conference of the Asia Securities Industry Institute, Seoul, August 2-3, 1993. Responsibility for any errors remains with the author.

by the dynamics of its internal demand rather than by the growth of exports.

Using an econometric model of the Chinese economy developed jointly by the Institute of Quantitative and Technical Economics of the Chinese Academy of Social Sciences and the Department of Economics, Stanford University, projections are obtained between 1993 and 2020. It is found that after an initial period of adjustment, the Chinese economy will continue to grow at a steady pace of approximately 8 percent per annum, on average, between now and the year 2020, based on the assumption that the economic reform policies and marketization will continue. It is anticipated that the fast-growing Chinese economy will become a major engine of growth for the economies of East and Southeast Asia, through its consumption, investment, and raw material demands.

II. The Factors That Affect Long-Term Development

The Appearance of the Domestic Market

China's economic development is different from that of Japan, Taiwan and the Republic of Korea; because China has a potentially huge domestic market. It is extremely easy for China to obtain the large-scale economy that other countries were too far behind to catch up during their development. Under this situation, it is indispensable for China to have infrastructure communication, energy and transportation, to realize marketization and continue to adopt the policy of opening to the outside world.

Redeciding the Development Orientation of the State-Owned Sector

Over the next quarter century the state-owned sector in China will move away from light manufactures and will concentrate increasingly on infrastructure such as communication, energy and transportation, and on pioneer industries with high capital and technology requirements and high risks. While it will continue to grow in absolute terms, it will shrink relatively to the non-state-owned sector (foreign and joint-venture enterprises, township enterprises, collective enterprises and even private enterprises). However, the relative shrinkage of the state-owned sector may not necessarily involve large-scale privatization. In fact, it will come about through both the much faster growth of the more efficient non-state sector and its gradual absorption of the more inefficient state-owned enterprises.

Continued High Rate of Saving

The Chinese saving rate will continue to be high until around 2020 because of the demographics and because of the lag between the growth of income and the change in consumption patterns. However, beginning in approximately the second decade, the saving rate will begin to come down slowly.

Stability of the Economic Policy

One important question is whether the current economic policies of opening to the outside world and reform will continue with a transfer of power—the so-called succession problem. This author is quite confident that the next generation of Chinese leaders will continue to follow the line of Mr. Deng Xiaoping in the post-Deng era. This is primarily because these policies have worked, and therefore enjoy widespread support despite complaints about inequalities of distribution, and at this stage cannot easily be reversed. Anyone who visited China prior to 1979 and then sees China today would be absolutely astounded at the progress that has been made. Also, there is no credible alternative to the current set of economic policies. The progress realized to-date has led to expectations that have been rising fast—people expect economic progress to continue until they catch up with Hong Kong and Taiwan, thus putting enormous pressure on their leaders to perform. And their performance will be measured in terms of growth in the real standard of living. Unlike the first-generation of leaders who led the revolution and founded the People's Republic of China, and thus earned their right to govern, the next generation of leaders will need to prove themselves. All of these considerations point to the necessity and inevitability of the continuation of the reform and open policies initiated by Mr. Deng. While temporary reversals cannot be entirely ruled out, I am also convinced of the current leadership's commitment to continuing the twin policies of reform and opening to the outside world.

Potential Problems

(1) Government/Business Relations

Everyone in China is now in business in one way or another. The roles of the government official and the business executive are frequently embodied in the same person. While dual jobs, necessitated by the low salaries, are not uncommon in developing countries, this commingling of government and business is unusual and leads to conflicts of interest and abuses. This is a problem that must be tackled soon. A clean separation is the best solution.

(2) Central/Local Relations

Central-local relations need to be resolved, especially in regard to the division of the revenue base. Also important are such issues as local trade barriers and fiscal (monetary) policies, which should not, in general, be permitted.

(3) Fiscal Reform

The central government needs increased revenue to undertake infrastructural investment so as to create a single unified market and equalize the level of development throughout the country.

On the whole, the positive factors far outweigh the negative. Moreover, since the beginning of economic reform, there has been a significant shift in the attitude of the people. They now seem more ready to take charge of their own destinies, more responsive to incentives, and more willing to work hard. The entrepreneurial spirit has returned. Given the proper macroeconomic environment and competitive markets, the Chinese economy is poised to grow and advance.

III. The United States in the Late 19th Century

The development experience of the United States in the late 19th and early 20th centuries provides a good comparison for China. That particular era also happened to be the fastest-growing period ever for the U.S. economy ever. The United States used imported capital and technology from Europe (principally from the United Kingdom, but also from the Netherlands and Germany) to build up its infrastructure and to get its industries started. However, growth was mostly based on internally generated demand. Exports were (and still are) a relatively small proportion of the GNP of the United States. This is not to say that foreign trade, capital and technology were not important to the United States, they were. However, once the process of economic growth began, it was mostly fueled by internally generated demand.

The Chinese economy is now in a similar situation. Without the open policy, the dynamic growth and transformation of the Chinese economy would not have occurred. But once the process of economic growth begins, the previously dormant internal demand eventually takes over as the major impetus for further growth. This also fits well with the objective circumstances—the world market is not ready to absorb the exports of another Guangdong Province, let alone 10 or more of them. Thus, by necessity, China must begin to take advantage of its huge internal market in order to continue rapid economic growth.

In Fig. 3.1, the real GNP of the United States between 1870 and 1990 is plotted against time. It has, on the whole, an upward trend. In Fig. 3.2, the annual rate of growth of real GNP of the United States for the sub-period 1870-1914 is plotted. It shows that during this period, at least up to 1900, there were many years of very robust growth, exceeding 10 percent per annum. In particular, the period 1870-1890 has been identified by Abramovitz and David (1973) as the fastest growing period in U.S. history, with real GNP growing at an average annual rate of 5.5 percent. In Fig. 3.3, the real GNP per capita is plotted against time. It shows that per capita real GNP in 1870 was slightly above U.S.$ 2,000 in 1990 prices, implying a standard of living approximately comparable to that in China today in terms of purchasing power parity. During this period, however, the implicit GNP deflator was mostly declining. The annual rate of change of the implicit GNP deflator is plotted in Fig. 3.4.

In Fig. 3.5, the merchandise exports and imports of the

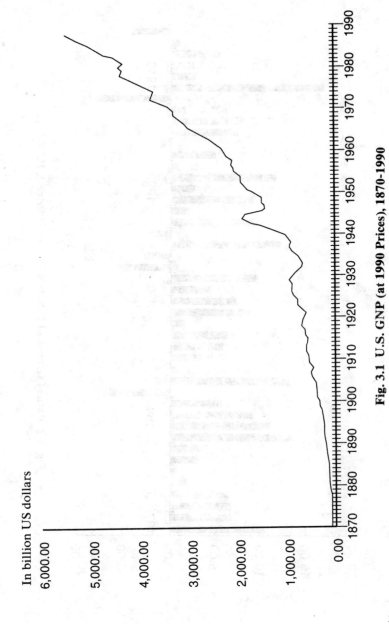

Fig. 3.1 U.S. GNP (at 1990 Prices), 1870-1990

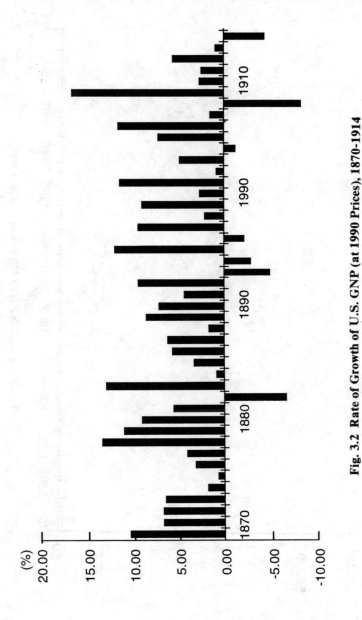

Fig. 3.2 Rate of Growth of U.S. GNP (at 1990 Prices), 1870-1914

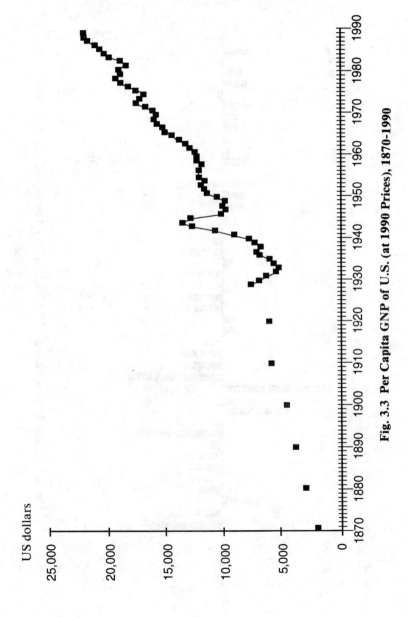

US dollars

Fig. 3.3 Per Capita GNP of U.S. (at 1990 Prices), 1870-1990

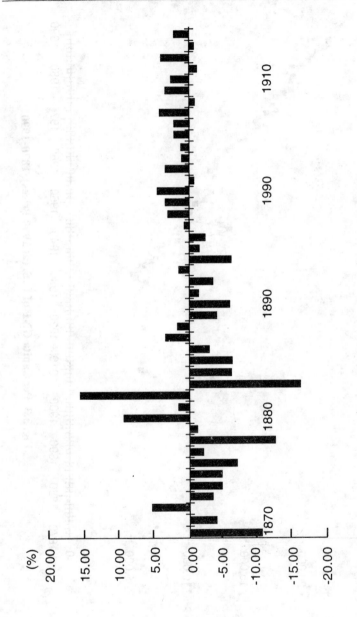

Fig. 3.4 Annual Rate of Change of the Implicit GNP Deflator of U.S. 1870–1914

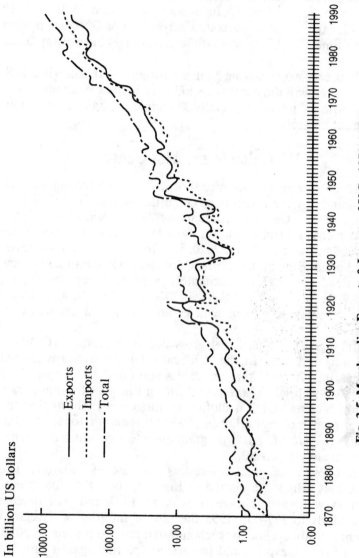

Fig. 3.5 Merchandise Exports & Imports of U.S., 1870-1990

In billion US dollars

— Exports
····· Imports
—·— Total

United States in current prices are plotted against time (on a logarithmic scale). Fig. 3.6 focuses on the period 1870-1914. In Fig. 3.7, exports and imports as a percentage of GNP are plotted against time. Fig. 3.7 shows that the percentages have always been low.

It is also worth noting that according to Abramovitz, U.S. economic growth during this period may be mostly attributed to the growth in inputs, especially "tangible capital," rather than technical progress.

IV. China in the 21st Century

Using an econometric model of the Chinese economy developed jointly by the Institute of Quantitative and Technical Economics of the Chinese Academy of Social Sciences and the Department of Economics, Stanford University, projections are obtained between 1993 and 2020. It is found that after an initial period of adjustment, the Chinese economy will continue to grow at a steady pace of approximately 8 percent per annum, on average, between now and the year 2020, based on the assumption that the economic reform policies and marketization will continue.

In Fig. 4.1, China's real gross domestic product (GDP) is plotted against time. In Fig. 4.2, real GDP per capita is plotted against time. It shows that per capita real GDP will surpass US$ 3,000 in 1990 prices by the year 2020. In Fig. 4.3, the annual rate of growth of real GDP is plotted against time. It shows that the rate of growth of real GDP in 1993 will remain strong, approximately 13 percent, but will gradually decline until it reaches approximately 8 percent.

A question of great interest is the rate of inflation. The projections, which are plotted in Fig. 4.4, show that the rate of inflation will have reached a peak in 1993 and will decline significantly in 1994. In 1995 the rate of inflation will begin a slow but steady decline to reach approximately 6 percent in 2020.

In Fig. 4.5, exports and imports are plotted against time. In Fig. 4.6, exports and imports are plotted as a percentage of

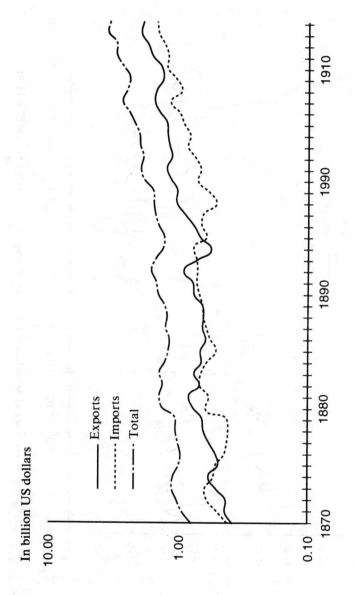

Fig. 3.6 Merchandise Exports & Imports of U.S., 1870-1914

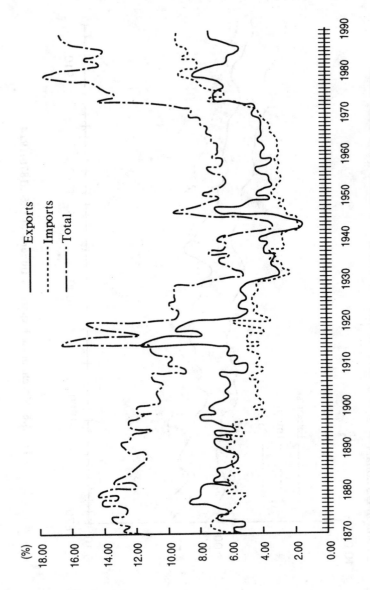

Fig. 3.7 Percentage of Merchandise Exports & Imports in GNP of U.S., 1870–1990

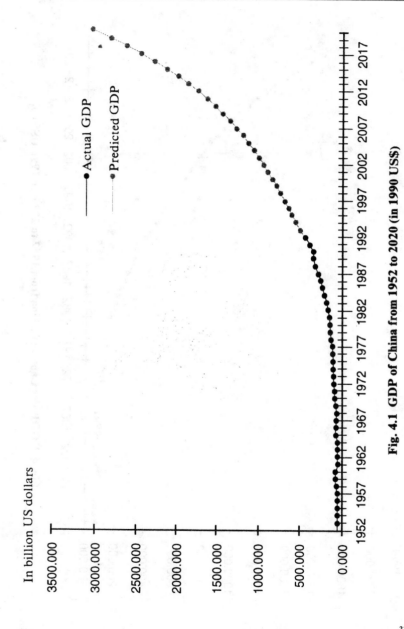

Fig. 4.1 GDP of China from 1952 to 2020 (in 1990 US$)

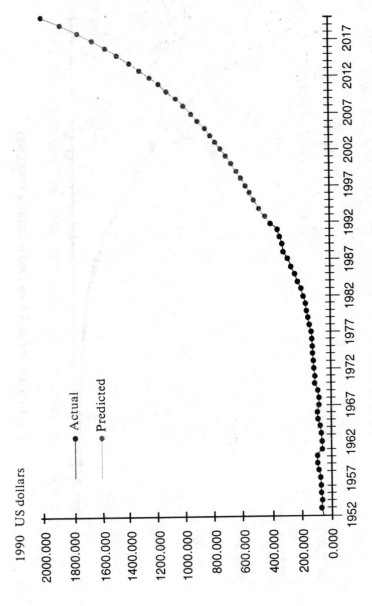

Fig. 4.2 GDP Per Capita of China from 1952 to 2020 (in 1990 US$)

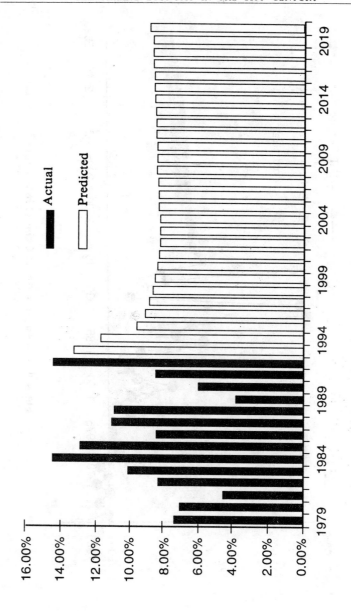

Fig. 4.3 Annual Growth Rate of China from 1979-2020

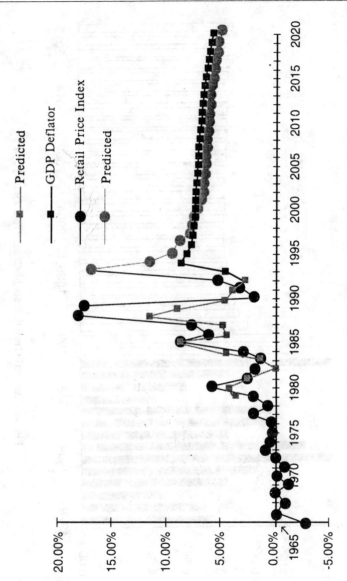

Fig. 4.4 Rates of Inflation of China (1965-2020)

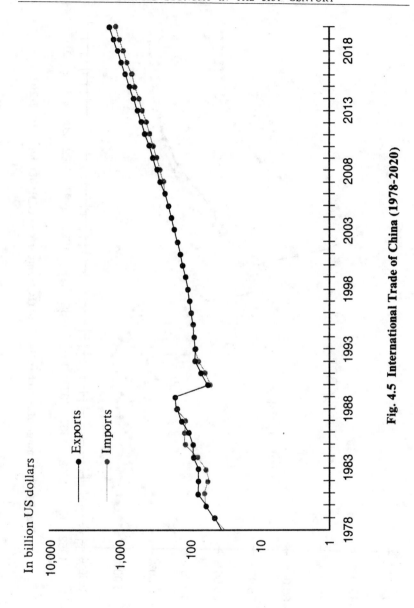

Fig. 4.5 International Trade of China (1978-2020)

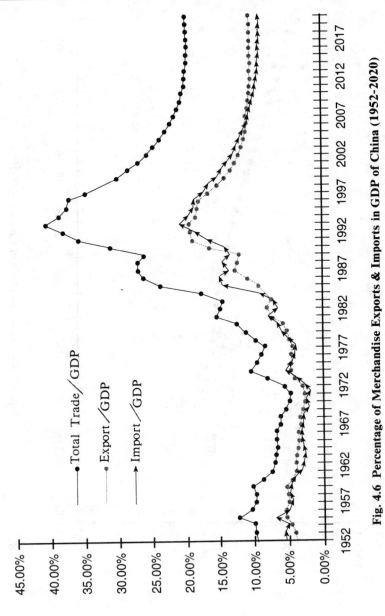

Fig. 4.6 Percentage of Merchandise Exports & Imports in GDP of China (1952-2020)

current GDP. It can be seen from Fig. 4.6 that the export and import shares were traditionally quite low. They rose to a peak in early 1990s but are projected to decline to approximately 10 percent of GDP in the 21st Century, reflecting the importance of internal growth.

Finally, in Fig. 4.7 the saving rate of China is plotted against time. It shows that the saving rate will remain approximately constant at a high value between 35 and 40 percent. It is anticipated that the fast-growing Chinese economy will become a major engine of growth for the economies of East and Southeast Asia, through its consumption, investment, and raw material demands.

V. China in the World Economy

In Fig. 5.1 we compare the current and projected future real GNPs of China with those of the United States, the European Community, Japan and several other Asian economies for the three years 1990, 2000 and 2020. We find that by the year 2020, Chinese real GNP will reach approximately half the level of the then U.S. real GNP, and will have become an important actor in the world economy in absolute terms. Fig. 5.2 compares the real GNP of selected countries and regions in per capita terms. It shows that while there will be significant improvement, China will continue to lag behind the developed countries, as well as the newly industrialized countries of East Asia, in terms of per capital real GNP. Chinese real GNP per capita will have surpassed US$ 3,000. It will take another 10-15 years, some time between 2030 and 2035, before the per capita real GNP of China reaches US$ 10,000 in 1990 prices, the line of division between developed and developing countries. As the Chinese economy grows, total trade as a percentage of GNP will fall continuously to approximately 20 percent in 2020, or comparable in order of magnitude to that of the United States.

VI. Concluding Remarks

I am often asked whether the mainland of China will develop

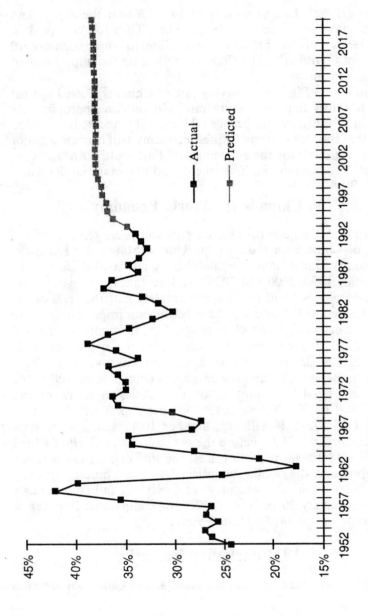

Fig. 4.7 Saving Rate of China (in percent)

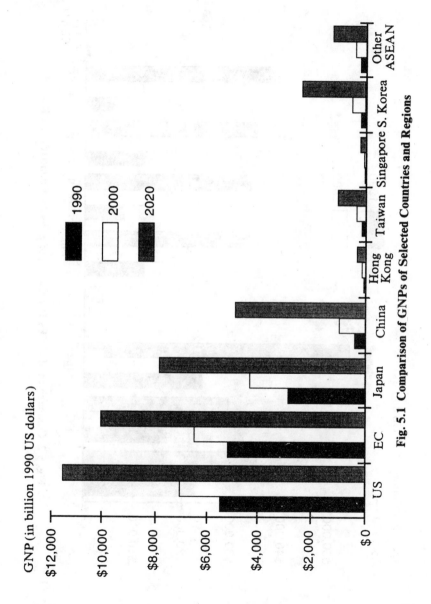

GNP (in billion 1990 US dollars)

Fig. 5.1 Comparison of GNPs of Selected Countries and Regions

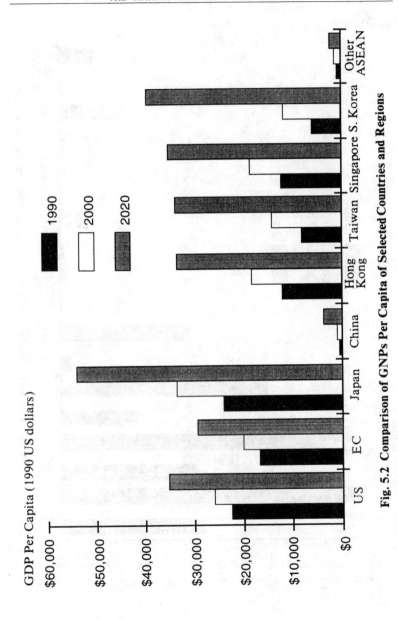

Fig. 5.2 Comparison of GNPs Per Capita of Selected Countries and Regions

in the same way as the four Little Dragons—Hong Kong, Singapore, South Korea and Taiwan. My answer is always no. There is no way China can ever achieve the same level of exports, on a per capita basis, as these four economies. There are simply not enough customers in the rest of the world. This does not mean, however, that the policy of opening to the outside world is wrong or useless. It is useful in bringing in not only technology and capital but most important of all a new outlook, attitude and behavior—a new way of doing things in organization, production, marketing and service, as well as new challenges and competition, leading to renewal and continual improvement.

The mainland of China does have two major advantages over these four economies: relative abundance of natural resources and an enormous domestic market. With the potentially huge domestic market, China can readily take advantage of scale economies, without having to rely on the export market. In fact, future Chinese economic development is likely to be more similar to that of the United States in the late 19th and early 20th centuries. There, imported capital and technology initially played a leading role. Subsequently, as the domestic market developed, the dynamic interactions of internal demands were able to sustain continual economic growth. The foreign sector, while pivotal in getting American economic development started, was never a dominant part of the U.S. economy, as it is for Japan and Taiwan.

The U.S. experience suggests that for a large economy such as China's, once the process of economic development gets started and gathers enough momentum, it can become internally self-sustaining. A bootstrap strategy that does not work for much smaller economies may work in China. The extent of the Chinese market allows the specialization and division of labor that generates added economic value without regard to the export market. As a result, Chinese economic development will eventually be much less dependent on the cyclical fortunes of the other economies. The boom of 1992 shows that it is possible for concerted actions prompted by a common expectation to move the economy into fast-forward again. If every one believes that the economy will be growing rapidly and acts accordingly, the economy will in fact grow rapidly, provided that the initial productive capacity is in place. Mr. Deng Xiaoping's southern visit provided precisely the signal for the convergence of public expectations.

In order to maximize the benefits of China's unique advantage in having a huge domestic market, the central government must pursue the development of infrastructural links and at the same time resolutely outlaw tangible and intangible internal trade barriers within China. By concentrating on infrastructural investments and restraining inefficient enterprises from wasting new sources, China will be able to increase the efficiency of its new investment. By taking care that inflation and the budget deficit do not get out of control, China will be able to moderate its boom and bust cycles and stay on a smooth but rapid growth path. Then, with its huge domestic market, it may potentially become the next engine of growth not only for Asia but also for the rest of the world.

References

Abramovitz, M. and P. A. David (1973), "Reinterpreting Economic Growth: Parables and Realities," *American Economic Review*, 63:428-439.

Lewis, C., assisted by K. T. Schlotterbeck (1938), *America's Stake in International Investments*, Washington, D.C.: The Brookings Institution.

The Modern Market and Small Production Peasant Households
—New Idea About Handling Relations Between Peasants and the Market

Liu Fuyuan
Academic Secretary and Research
Fellow of the Scientific Research Bureau of
the Chinese Academy of Social Sciences

Relations between peasants and the market has aroused the wide interest of the people. Theoreticians have proposed many ways of showing peasants the road to the market. I think in studying this question we should change our way of thinking and use the theory of the market economy to solve the problem of peasants vis-a-vis the market. We should no longer use the old ways of thinking in discussing how the government should guide and organize peasants into the market, and we should hold the government responsible for the peasants' gains and losses in the market. The government should stand outside the market to cultivate and regulate the market so that the market splits up peasants, and peasants learn to swim in the course of swimming. It is not for the government to run study courses before they swim.

I. What Kind of Peasants Should Be Guided, and What Kind of Market They Should Enter

In the traditional relationship, the Chinese peasants have always been involved in the market one way or the other. Especially in recent years, the government has changed the policy of state monopoly for purchase and marketing of grain, cotton, etc. and has opened the rural market, and most commodity farm products are marketed and sold by peasants themselves. These peasants cultivate small plots, produce small quantities of farm produce, and most of them also have other jobs. This kind of market is the rural fair, or the commodity economy market of small production. The peasants and markets of this kind already coexist. Without peasants of this kind, there is no market of this kind, and without a market, there are no peasants of this kind.

Now, China plans to establish a modern market economic system, but this type of market is not yet in existence. How shall we talk about entering this market? The modern market economy is the sum total of the relationships of exchange among the commodity producers in the form of enterprises rather than the sum total of the relationships of the exchange among small producers. The main part of the market is the complete commodity producer motivated by profit, and its quantity of production is large enough to ensure that profits are larger than the cost of labor. The traditional self-sufficient small peasants who do not have this ability are not the main part of the market economy, because they sell at their own doorways or at the rural fairs a small quantity of their surplus goods the value of which is barely enough to meet their expenditures and consumption. If the self-sufficient small peasant households for whom "to sell is to buy" are organized, if the big companies are combined with the small peasant households, the marketing costs will almost consume all available farm surplus. Since there is a large gap in economic forces between big companies and small peasant households, transactions between them cannot be equal, and peasants get the worst of it.

Organizing and guiding peasants into the market is an attractive slogan. But what counts is that the main part of the market must be modern peasant households who are engaged in large-scale farming and whose production is motivated by profit. Why did we replace the organization of peasants in cooperatives with collectivization? Precisely because it is very difficult or even impossible to organize small peasant households as the main body of the cooperatives. What we collectivized was not peasant households or peasants, but rather farm laborers. The members of these collective economic units joined the cooperatives and collective economic organizations not as economic entities or in the capacity of peasant households, but rather in the capacity of farm laborers. Once these farm laborers participate in the collective economy, their labor will become a component part of the collective labor of the collective economy. Their original household economy no longer existed. Therefore, the consequences of organizing small peasant households is inevitably self-negation of the small peasant economy and small peasant households. The labor and means of production integrated in the families were disintegrated, and reintegrated into the collectives. However, a real cooperative economy is a combination of economic entities, but a collective economy is a combination of its laborers. Small peasant households do not have the primary conditions for cooperation. Therefore, to get peasants organized must inevitably mean collectivization and the negation of the existence of the household economy. At present, those who want to enter the market are small peasant households by the hundreds of thousands, their production scale half the size of what it was before, and their numbers doubled. To get these small peasant households organized in a simple way to enter the market economy will end either in giving it up halfway or re-collectivization. Although collectivization was objectively the model for the development of Chinese agriculture with minimum cost, it is now an out-moded idea after decades of disturbances and the economic reforms of recent years. The new pattern of the rural economy has made it impossible for most rural areas to develop their collective economies alone. Therefore, it is impossible for all peasant households and agricultural laborers to directly enter the market economy with their old social status and capacities. They must first transform before they can enter the market economy.

II. Entering the Market After Transformation

The market is forcing peasant households to transform with

its strong attractions and pressures. Some of them will gradually rise to become enterprise farms, while the greater number of them will be transferred to non-agricultural trades in the cities. The annual tide of migrating peasant workers is a reflection of their efforts to seek a new economic role. Spontaneous collectivization has never been peasants' own choice. Government guidance or coercion are now impossible or come too late. We have only one choice: Letting market transform peasants, then temper and educate them so they will gradually enter the market through cooperation on a voluntary basis. This is the only road, no matter what it costs.

The process of transformation and restructuring peasants into the market is in fact to rely on the pressures of market competition and the law of value to discourage small production and lead peasants away from this economic niche. Those who remain in the countryside will then become peasant households in the true sense, working on an expanded production scale. These peasant households will enter the new market through social cooperation. This is the inevitable road for the development of the market economy and the transition from the traditional market of small producers to the modern market economy. If we are truly bent on the market economy, and are not just professing love of what we fear, we should not be afraid of the transformation of the peasants, nor should we expect that all peasants will increase their income and enter the market happily and comfortably after the market is fully opened. The market economy is a process of continued transformation and integration of producers. Some people will enter the market as owners of enterprise farms, and some will enter the market as owners of their own labor. The former purchase the means of production and labor and sell their products on the market, while the latter sell their labor and buy means of subsistence on the market. This is the optimum allocation of resources and the law of the operation of the market economy.

The transformation of peasants by the market will place surplus agricultural labor on the market. The urbanization of the population will make labor power a commodity, changing the status of most peasants, changing some peasants into workers and wage-earners while a small number of peasants become entrepreneurs in various trades. The concentration of the means of production, production on a large scale, separation of the small producers from the means of production, money turned into capital, labor turned into a commodity—these are the inevitable results of the formation and development of a market economy. To guide peasants into this market, the primary thing is to use the difference in income between peasants and workers, and between workers and business people caused by the market structure, to direct surplus rural labor away from the farms and villages and into the urban and rural labor market.

Another important aspect in guiding peasants into the market economy is making land a commodity, and putting the right to the use of land on the market. We shall regulate the circulation and concentration of land through market mechanisms and improve utilization of land resources. In order to do this, we must not encourage privatization, but rather see that land becomes a commodity under conditions of public ownership. The essence of making land a commodity under public ownership is to make the right to the use of land a commodity, and to use land rent to regulate the use of land. First of all, it is essential to strengthen public property land ownership rights, abolish the de facto eternal tenant system, use changes in land rent rates to force households doing farm work and other jobs simultaneously to give up the farmland and expand the scale of using the land as much as possible through competition by bidding.

While transforming peasants through the market, the government should provide economic and non-economic macro conditions allowing peasants to change their status and leave their native places to seek new jobs. The communities should compensate properly for the migration of the peasants who part with the farmland for life. They have been masters of the public means of production and have contributed their labor to the land from generation to generation. When they depart from their communities, they should be given reasonable compensation based on land rent and land price. If the communities do not have the financial power, the government should purchase the land they leave behind. This new state-owned land then can be put under the management of the communities, or under the management of the State Bureau of Land Administration or the state-owned land sales corporations. The land should be rented to skilled farmers with the rent paid to the state. The communities can use the money from leasing land to pay compensation to peasants who leave their native places. The peasant households who stay on the farmland should constantly raise their level of specialization and socialization, increase the production of commodity goods gradually, and develop farms managed like enterprises. Only such peasant households and farms are qualified to enter the market economy and to become the main body of the market. Only this makes it easier for them to form cooperatives and unite in the sphere of production to compete with industrial and commercial enterprises, leaving no room for small merchants and pedlars to profit from them.

III. The Government's Role in the Process of Guiding Peasants into the Market

The process of guiding peasants into the market is in fact a process of cultivating the new main part of the market and new peasants. It is also a process of changing the mode of agricultural production. The government's stress should be on changing its own function to create appropriate macro environments for the formation and development of rural economic organizations, and to create a policy environment for integrating peasants. To change the government's function, it is most important that the government will no longer restrict peasants from going to cities, but abolish urban and rural residence restrictions, abolish the residence restrictions in all cities, develop the urban and rural labor market, and create favorable conditions for the relocation of rural surplus labor in cities and towns.

In the course of guiding peasants into the market, the government should take protective measures for agriculture in order to avoid drastic highs and lows. The governments of the Western market-oriented countries all take protective measures for agriculture, without exception. We hold that it is essential to make clear why agriculture is protected, to what degree, and what the goals are. Protecting peasants as a policy goal of the government is subordinate to the government's economic plan and development strategy. In the face of more than 200 million small peasant households, we should not take the protection of the 200 million small peasant households as our policy goal in the course of making the transition to the market economy. We should decide on a policy of only protecting specialized households. By only protecting specialized households, is it possible to protect agriculture and guide peasants into the market economy. We should give full play to the market mechanism, allow the market to transform households doing both farmwork and other jobs, and gradually concentrate the land in the hands of specialized households so that these households will develop into enterprise farms. In accordance with the laws of the market economy, at least two thirds of the 200 million small peasant households in China should gradually leave the land. As a result of government protection and the development of the agricultural support industries, the number of small peasant households has not dropped and the land not been concentrated while the size of peasant households becomes smaller and smaller. On the contrary, the number of peasant households has continued to increase, farmland is more scattered than ever, and the cost-profit rate of agricultural produce is far greater than that of non-agricultural industries. All this is abnormal. It is contrary to the development of the market economy and the change in the mode of production. It should be admitted that our present protection goals are contradictory to the overall socioeconomic development strategy.

The government should decide protection goals on the basis of the present situation of rural economic development and the present level of market development. For example, in grain production at present, the goal of protection should be to keep a safe grain supply above the warning line. So long as market fluctuations do not endanger the supply, the government should not take macrocontrol measures, but allow the market mechanism to regulate products and industries. At present, as long as the grain-producing counties and specialized households (the scope for the specialized households can be larger, all households with the commodity rate of food grains higher than 50 percent can be counted as specialized households) are protected, the warning line for a safe grain supply can be protected. After the households doing both farm work and other jobs are restructured, the actual strength of the specialized households will be increased to raise the safety coefficient for the grain supply. With progress in the urbanization of the population and in carrying on production on an enterprise scale, the protection goals should be gradually reduced so far as peasant households are concerned. When the market economic system is virtually formed, the goals of protection should apply to the agricultural enterprises whose production is carried out on a proper scale, and should be to ensure that these enterprises acquire an average profit under normal production conditions. Taking correct protection goals is an essential condition for guiding peasants into the market, forcing the households not under protection to give up farmland, and speeding up their transfer to non-agricultural trades and cities.

In recent years, prices for farm produce have been weak, and the agricultural income of peasants rose slowly or even dropped a bit. Peasants did not know how to cope with this situation, and the people engaged in agricultural economic administration and study were laden with anxieties. At various discussions and seminars, people appealed to the government to attach importance to agriculture and grain production and take new measures to protect peasants. Some scholars argued that the steps taken in reforming the grain supply, purchase system and price control were too drastic. I hold that if the government is urged to take new measures to cope with the present situation in production and circulation in the absence of the above-mentioned strategic thoughts, it will be very difficult to take effective countermeasures that will not run contrary to regulations.

I believe that the present difficulties in rural areas are inevitable and normal in the period of transition from the dual system to the single system, and there is no cause for alarm. In the transition to the market economy, neither peasants nor the government will have an easy and comfortable time, and problems are unavoidable. The difficulties at present are a bit too large because of delays in opening the grain market. I once wrote an article saying that the grain market should have been gradually opened by around 1985 without changing prices or the dual system, and that it should gradually move closer to the single system. In recent years, reform has been at the crossroads, no substantial reform measures have been adopted, and the stress has been placed on increasing purchasing prices for the fixed quotas in an attempt to move the fixed purchasing prices closer to the market prices. The result has been that, just like walking in the moonlight, I walk while the shadow walks, and the shadow also walks when I walk. Now more than 1,000 counties have lifted the control over prices. Why have so many counties decided to lift price controls in just a little more than one year? To be frank, it was a matter of casting away a burden. The earlier the grain market is opened, the more initiative the government has and the earlier it can reduce its financial burden. For peasants, the opening of the market created pressure and became a disaster in the market because of agricultural overproduction. Now that it is opening there is nothing to worry about, as it must be opened sooner or later. As long as it is opened, there is pressure on peasants, and the earlier it is opened, the greater the pressure. For many years, peasants were not at all impressed by government protection. In their minds, the government did not give them any protection, but took too much from them. Now that the market is opened, and the government no longer takes anything from them, peasants begin to understand the importance of dependence on the government, and acknowledge government protection. When government protection was offered, they did not express their gratitude nor respect for the government. However, when they lose this protection, they find it precious. So some peasants and theoreticians began to ask for government protection. In their minds, even the purchase of grains at fixed prices with which they were not satisfied in the past, became acceptable. They no longer complain about the wide gap in prices between agricultural and industrial products. I think all this is understandable. What is more important is what attitude the government should take toward it. I think that the government's most reasonable attitude is to observe things soberly for some years instead of taking any new protective measures hastily. The government should let peasants face the world and brave the storm in the course of developing the market mechanism, and give due play to market mechanisms. Don't regulate, but rather remove the obstacles to market regulation. Don't interfere with the income of peasants and the fluctuations of the grain market. Without fluctuations, there is no market. Fluctuation is market regulation. Market fluctuations and drops in peasants' income are indications that market mechanisms are readjusting the structure. If the government takes measures at this time to check market fluctuations, and artificially raises peasants' income, this is the reverse of regulations applying to the industrial structure and demonstrates a fear of the market economy.

The government should have a clear understanding of the characteristics of the present rural economic pattern in China. The more than 200 million small peasant households and the scattered distribution of the support-agriculture industries have formed a very stable rural economic structure that has led to the slow rise in agricultural income, and has enabled the agricultural population to gain extra income from non-agricultural enterprises. This has made an increase in grain production difficult to obtain. It has also made the grain production relatively stable, and made large drops in grain production impossible. The 200 million or so peasant households containing a rural population of more than 900 million must first of all produce enough food for their own consumption, and this portion of overall supply is unaffected by market fluctuations. Grains as commodities are the result of turning surplus goods into commodities. With the surplus grain from rural people totaling 900 million to meet the needs of the remaining 200 million people, some market fluctuations will not cause large shortages in the grain supply. Even if there are slight shortages, the government can easily meet an emergency through imports. Looking back over the history of the development of the grain economy in recent years, we can clearly see that grain price fluctuations have been constant and difficult to avoid, and were caused by weather, not by economic factors. The changes in acreage sown were chiefly caused by an adjustment in the industrial structure and the lack of mechanisms for concentrating the land, not by insufficient protection from the government. The chief cause of weak prices was the normal, periodic and relative overproduction in the course of developing the national economy, not the opening of the market or a cutback in state grain purchases. In short, fluctuations in the grain market are caused by many complicated factors, but we should distinguish the main factors from the secondary, and the normal from the abnormal. With this understanding, the government should remain calm, observe the situation soberly, and allow the market to regulate supply spontaneously. Impatient measures to counter regulation should not be taken, but rather the opportunity should be seized to accumulate the regulating forces. When it is time for the government to regulate the market, it will be able to smoothly solve the problems which the market cannot. This is called what the government should not do and what it should do. In regulating the market, government action must not only be well-timed, but also take into consideration the dynamics of degree. Opportunity and momentum are both essential for effective action.

The day-to-day work of the government does not include coping with market fluctuations, but rather solving the root causes of fluctuations; not building dams, but opening canals. The so-called macrocontrol means to solve the contradictions between total supply and total demand. Solving these contradictions means removing the non-economic causes of obstacles to market regulation, namely, the transfer of capital and the allocation of resources among the various departments. These non-economic causes are often the result of problems within departments and governmental policies at different levels. Now, the government organs, functions and policies that suited the traditional economic operations should be transformed into government organs, functions and policies that fit the operations of the market economy. To speed up these changes, the most important element at present is smoothing out the relationship between the government and the market, and between the government and enterprises and peasants. Norms for market operations must be established, non-economic factors for drops in peasant income must be eliminated and the sharpening of social contradictions in rural areas must be ameliorated. Resolute measures must be taken in this respect to prevent the loss of peasant income so that peasants can set their minds on the development of production, positively meet the demands of the market and regulate crop cultivation and employment structure in a way that will further their own economic interests.

In short, the present relationship between peasants and the market should be dissolved and peasants should be guided into the market economy. The government should spare no effort to eliminate non-economic factors that prevent peasants from entering the market, readjust the industrial structure in a macro way and create a new macro and policy environments for the formation of the market of factors, the urbanization of population and the organization of production enterprises.

Two Catch-up Models:
The Chinese and the Japanese

Shinyasu Hoshino
President of the National Institute
for Research Advancement, Tokyo, Japan

The Chinese economy developed to a remarkable extent in the 1980s, and this has attracted considerable attention because it demonstrates the significance of the "socialist market economy" policy which China has been pursuing since the late 1970s. As the nations of the former Soviet Union and the rest of Eastern Europe attempt to make the transition to a market economy through so-called "shock therapy," the achievements of Chinese gradualism are now being appreciated. One approach for analyzing the Chinese economy is to compare and examine the change from a command planned economy to a market economy from the viewpoint of whether gradualism or radicalism works best. However, the capitalist market economy also has various models. These include the original English model, the German-U.S. model following England, the Japanese "catch-up" model based on high economic growth after World War II, and the Korean model which followed Japan. Each of these countries has found its own path to development depending on their historical circumstances and natural endowments.

E. H. Carr, in his "Nationalism and After," pointed out that one of the characteristics of the 20th century nation-state is that the main purpose of national policy is not just to maintain order or execute official affairs in a narrow sense, but to contribute to the welfare of its citizens and improve their standard of living. This socialization of state goals leads to an emphasis on mass economic demands. National policy is targeted at raising average income levels and creating opportunities for employment, with the example of other countries' successes used to justify policy. The policies of socialist nations can be considered as one type of model of the mass-oriented state. In addition, the goal of a economic reform in these circumstances is to promote high levels of economic growth while allocating the gains achieved as equitably as possible. In other words, the goal of national policy is economic development with full employment, increasing levels of income, and the even spread of an improved standard of living. All nations would agree with these goals.

Both Japan and China are realizing success in accomplishing these economic goals with the aim of catching up to the living standard enjoyed in the advanced nations. Indeed, both China and Japan have comprehensively addressed their policies to the goal of achieving just that.

Japan set the goal of doubling its GNP in 10 years between 1960 to 1970 by introducing the "Doubling National Income Plan." In fact, national income increased more than threefold during that period, and the average annual growth rate of GNP (adjusted for inflation) for the high economic growth period (1955-70) was 10 percent, and in the 1966-69 boom period was as high as 11.8 percent. The Chinese economy has achieved results comparable to the high economic growth period in Japan. The average annual growth rate of GNP (adjusted for inflation) for 1980-89 was 9.4 percent, in 1992 GNP growth was 12.8 percent and 13.9 percent for the first half of 1993.

In addition, the Ikeda Cabinet, which announced the Income Doubling Plan, also adopted a growth-oriented policy of first expanding the size of the pie as much as possible and then allocated the pieces as equitably as possible. In the process of high economic growth, many types of people gradually started to consider themselves members of the middle class, and today Japan is a middle-class mass society. In 1992, Deng Xiaoping said, "taking a socialist road means gradually making the whole of society rich." The idea of joint prosperity can be described as follows: First of all, promoting development in specific regions satisfying certain conditions, and then promoting development elsewhere. Early-developing regions will lead the development of the other regions, and finally the whole country will become rich." This policy is being implemented in China, and a growth-oriented policy is being pursued which aims equality.

Thus, it seems that the Chinese and Japanese models have had a similar intention behind their policy goals. Yet, I would like to examine the sustainability of Chinese economic development by comparing the Chinese model (from 78 to present), which is steadily achieving success, with the Japanese model in the period of high economic growth (1955-70), with special attention paid to the differences. To ensure accuracy, detailed explanations are required. Here, however, I would like to examine the main outline of differences between the two economic systems, even at the expense of a slight sacrifice of accuracy.

I. Economic Systems

1. Differences in the Ownership of Corporate Assets

In Japan, most corporations are privately owned joint-stock companies. There are approximately 1.5 million companies in Japan. Most of them are joint-stock companies with about 2,000 large and medium-sized companies whose stocks are listed on the Tokyo stock exchange. Japanese companies are established and operated in accordance with the general principles of civil and corporate law, and are regulated according to anti-trust law and individual law such as the Electricity Enterprises Act.

In China, there are various forms of ownership such as those owned by the people (state-owned), group-owned, and privately owned, but the major economic role is played by state-owned and group-owned corporations. There are about 10,000 large and medium-sized state-owned companies and a little less than 19 million township-owned enterprises, both of which assume primary responsibility for industrial production and the supply of services. Although the share of production accounted for by state-owned corporations is gradually decreasing, they still dominate the basic production sector. In order to promote efficient production, most state-owned corporations rely on contracts and are making efforts to separate the nation's proprietary rights over assets from the management rights of those who operate the companies.

2. The Separation of Ownership and Management

In discussions of the joint-stock company, the separation of ownership and management is usually emphasized. In the youthful era of capitalist entrepreneurs such as Rockefeller and Carnegie, managers owned stocks and at the same time demonstrated excellent management ability, so ownership and management of companies was unified in this period. However, the general public became stockholders as the joint-stock company system matured, and there occurred a separation of the stockholders' control of a company through their proprietary rights and the right of managers to manage as appointees of the stockholders. Managers improve the economic performance of their firms for the sake of the stockholders, and are able to prolong their terms in office by increasing dividends, for which they in turn receive remuneration. If they fail to make wise managerial decisions, they will be dismissed by the stockholders. In joint-stock companies in the United States, this separation between ownership and management is quite established. There are several characteristics of this system which need to be discussed. First, in order to achieve this type of system, a firm must experience the ascendancy of stockholders. However, management tends to lose its long-term perspective due to the necessity of achieving short-term results to please dividend-conscious stockholders. This can lead to a lack of investment in technological innovation. Thus, another characteristic is that entire companies are often available for sale, and can be acquired to compensate for the weaknesses in the existing firm. In this way, a strategic combination of corporate holdings built through mergers and acquisitions can increase the company's productivity and profitability. The final characteristic of the joint-stock company system in the U.S. is the existence of institutions to monitor both the issuance of and transaction in stocks, and the accuracy of the reporting of corporate results by the company.

The Japanese joint-stock company system is quite different

from that of the United States. First, two thirds of the company's shares are held by other firms in an interlocking relationship, and the stocks held by individual investors account for less than one third of the shares in most firms. Capital for investment is more often secured through bank loans than stocks issuance. Second, the president, as the chief executive officer of the company, has more power than shareholders or the board of directors, and has real control of the company. Third, although the president is officially appointed at the shareholders meeting, in fact, there are cases in which an individual who has no shares is selected as president, usually a company employee. Fourth, mergers and acquisitions are often blocked by interlocking shareholding. Fifth, management can create a long-term corporate strategy and make aggressive investment in technological innovation and new fields with the aim of becoming first in the industry. Finally, the financial reporting or companies is monitored by banks. It is this system which led to the high economic growth rates of the Japanese economy.

In the Chinese economy, a system based on contracts is developing year by year, and the separation between ownership and management is progressing. In order to institutionalize these changes, the contracting of tasks by enterprises should be based on the guarantee that the nation, as a "shareholder," will receive a "dividend," while managers are left with the authority to operate their enterprises and take managerial responsibility. This seems to be a model of separation between ownership and management similar to the U.S.-type joint-stock company system. In the case of state-owned enterprises in China, it may be necessary to promote further separation of government and corporate management by imposing severer restrictions on enterprise budgets to achieve greater managerial independence and responsibility for enterprise profit and loss. Although I will discuss it again later, the basic point is to establish a mechanism through which managers can exercise their abilities so that innovation will be promoted for the long-term, as technological development proceeds. In this way, improvements in productivity through investment in new advanced facilities will be

351

possible. From this point of view, the existing contract system seems to be too short-term focused.

A higher level of ability is demanded from Chinese managers than Japanese managers. A Japanese manager is appreciated when displaying an animal drive to lead the company to attainment of the largest market share in the industry. On the other hand, the Chinese manager is required not only to possess this animal drive to achieve, but also must maintain a high ethical standard as a public servant. This is also applicable to the administrative officials who control ownership of corporate assets.

3. Employee Welfare

In Japan, a universal social security system has been established and all citizens can join the national pension, national health insurance, and unemployment insurance plans. On the other hand, most companies have private pension plans and make retirement payments. Some companies even own hospitals for their employees and members of their families. The extent of such fringe benefits varies by company, and there is a tendency for the best companies to offer the best fringe benefits. Thus, partly because of the lifetime employment system, employees tend to have a sense of commitment to the group bound by the same fate to their companies and this strengthens their sense that the company is "my company."

In China, there is a system which has been sustained since the era of the planned economy aspect, in which enterprises are responsible for the welfare of employees. In this aspect, Chinese corporations seem to have much in common with Japanese companies. However, in strengthening the independent nature of corporate management it may be necessary to separate welfare from the enterprise to a degree, and create a universal system accessible to the general public. At that point, the additional fringe benefits provided by the enterprise will strengthen the sense of a common fate which derives from belonging to the same company. This is very important because state-owned enterprises in basic industries have a strong need to promote long-term technological development, and retaining excellent employees is a prerequisite for doing so.

4. The Relationship Between Enterprises and the Government

In Japan, competition among companies grew fierce after the postwar dissolution of *zaibatsu*, the big financial combines, and the prevention of private monopolies through anti-monopoly legislation. From the viewpoint of international competitiveness, the government, centering on the Ministry of International Trade and Industry, guided this competition among companies in specific directions by selectively allocating the acquisition of new technology and financial resources. This guidance was based on a government-determined economic plan which served as general market research. Companies have participated in the planning process, and therefore the plan itself creates a national consensus. In addition, this process has a strong educational impact on all citizens by highlighting economic prospects.

In China, competition among regions is growing fierce partly because of the contract system. This competition is desirable because it is expected that development will spread to every region one after another, based on the success of reform and openness. Thus, competition may be a driving force for economic development. There are various types of corporations in China such as state-owned enterprises, township enterprises, and foreign-invested enterprises (joint venture, limited partnership, and pure enterprise with foreign capital) and it is essential to cultivate and foster a corporate style suitable to each region. On the other hand, excessive regionalism "often leads to extreme protection of corporations belonging to a region, closing of the market, and prevention of the flow of goods, funds, materials, and people out of the region" (Sekiguchi, Zhu Shaowen, and Uekusa, *Reform of the Economic System in China*, Chapter 8). In order to promote the reforms required for economic efficiency and long-term development, such as removal of excess and duplicate investment as well as mobilization of production capabilities of state-owned companies into fields where greater growth is expected, it is necessary to share finance between central and local governments and to further promote the independence of enterprise management.

II. Industrial Policy

1. The Japanese Experience

It is the area of industrial policy that the clearest differences between Japan and China are demonstrated. Japanese policy aims at economic self-sufficiency and completion of all industries, while Chinese policy aims at reform and openness. I would like to examine these policies in detail. First, I will examine Japanese industrial policies after 1955.

The main tasks of industrial policy from 1955 to 1960 was to promote economic independence, the development of heavy and chemical industries, and exports so that Japan could cope with economic globalization. When Japan joined GATT in 1955, movement in the direction of the liberalization of trade was set as national policy. However, it was only after 1960 that a full-scale liberalization policy began to be adopted. The goal was to increase the liberalization rate to 80 percent in three years in accordance with the General Principles for the Liberalization of Trade and Foreign Exchange. In 1963, Japan received a recommendation from the IMF to terminate its Article 8 status and consequently joined the OECD. As a result, opening of Japanese industry to international competition could not be avoided in the period from 1960 to 1965. Such pressure for openness played an important role in the promotion of an advanced industrial structure.

The shift to a more advanced industrial structure promoted the rationalization of important basic industries and the growth of new industries based on innovative technologies. A typical example of the former is the second rationalization plan for the steel industry. In accordance with this plan, new integrated steel plants were constructed one after another, and labor productivity was dramatically improved as costs were drastically reduced. In both quality and quantity, Japan achieved top level status in the steel industry.

Other major industrial fields saw similar changes:

(1) Automobile industry: Domestic automobile production was fostered by limitations on imports and protected by high

Customs duties. After 1959, automobiles were mass-produced.

(2) Synthetic fiber industry: In accordance with the Five-year Plan for Fostering Synthetic Fibers, preferential treatment in terms of finance and taxes, as well as research assistance, was provided. The number of production facilities increased dramatically from 1955 to 1960.

(3) Petrochemical industry: In accordance with the Countermeasures for Fostering the Petrochemical Industry, subsidies, preferential treatment in taxation, and authorization for the introduction of technologies were provided. By 1960, four petrochemical complexes were in operation.

(4) Synthetic rubber industry: The Japan Synthetic Rubber Co. Ltd., financed by the government, was established in 1957 to promote the domestic production of synthetic rubber.

(5) Electronics industry: In accordance with the Temporary Measures for the Promotion of the Electronics Industry (1957), R & D and rationalization of production was promoted. By giving aid mainly to the electronics components industry, the basis for the growth of the electronics industry as a whole was established.

(6) Others: Temporary Measures for the Promotion of the Machine Industry (1956) to modernize the machine industry and the promotion for the Aircraft Industry Act (1958) which promoted domestic production of airplanes.

Major reforms undertaken to promote industrial rationalization included financing from the Japan Development Band, a preferential treatment system of rationalized and automated facilities in major industries, the allocation of restricted materials and imports based on the Foreign Exchange Control Act of 1949, and the measures promoting the selective introduction of foreign technologies based on the Foreign Capital Act of 1950. On the other hand, political measures like import restrictions and Customs protection were also used to promote industries, and in the cases of the synthetic rubber and airplane industries, public policy corporations were created.

Here I would like to restate and elaborate upon the Japanese experience with industrial policy. There was excessive competition among companies in early postwar Japan due to *zaibatsu* dissolution and economic democratization. In order to limit the costs of bankruptcy and unemployment caused by such excessive competition, while keeping the competitive energies created in such an environment, industrial policy was created to guide the Japanese economy through a shift in industrial structure to industries where productivity improvements and future consumer markets could be expected. The case I have raised show that this industrial policy included: (1) selection of industries for emphasis, that it, selecting promising industries by forecasting technology and demand; (2) indicative planning based on sharing important information with industries and firms, so that they would have a common recognition of prices, the availability of technology, macroeconomic forecasts, and forecasts for the industry; (3) promotion of technological advance through efforts to improve productivity and reduce costs by promoting the selective introduction of foreign technology and R & D to enhance international competitiveness; and (4) restrictions on excessive price competition through the establishment of price cartels authorized by the government.

2. Characteristics of the Chinese Approach to Reform and Liberalization

The Chinese national economy began as a dual economy which included a modern industrial sector and a traditional agricultural sector, or stated differently, capital intensive cities and labor intensive agricultural villages. This dualistic structure became more pronounced during the 1950s due to development strategies centered on heavy chemical industries and the family registry system which limited the mobility of labor.

The reform and liberalization policies introduced in the late 1970s were first aimed at an improvement in agricultural productivity. By the early 1980s, the growth rate of agriculture superseded that of the industrial sector. This can be attributed to the contract system introduced in the agricultural sector. In the industrial sector, however, liberalization has been pursued by foreign-invested enterprises, state-owned enterprises have accepted technology transfer through contracts, and efforts to separate management from ownership are continuing. Particularly noteworthy is rapid industrial growth in the special economic zones, as well as the speedy development of the township-owned enterprises closely related to the development of agricultural villages and city industries. All in all, industrial development in China so far is truly remarkable.

Now, I will attempt to evaluate the mechanisms of development up to the present. First, Chinese industrial development owes much to its advantages in labor costs in today's interdependent economic relations. Liberalization policies have invited an influx of foreign capital into China which has combined with cheap labor to enhance international competitiveness. In addition, export industries enjoy favorable tax status in the special economic zones. Thus, advantages for export industries, in addition to low labor cost, makes China attractive to foreign capital. Further, since employee salaries in such businesses are better than average Chinese wages, overall income levels are raised. The rise in income levels increases the domestic demand which further influences the development of commerce and other industries. In a similar way, the township enterprises are also showcases of Chinese development through their combination of surplus labor in agricultural villages with industrial development.

Currently, labor-intensive industries are leading economic recoveries in Central European countries such as Poland and the Czech Republic. In these countries, prices went up in the process of "shock therapy," but wages have lagged behind. This effectively reduced the cost of labor, which in turn gave an advantage to their export industries aimed at the Western European market. However, as in the case of China, large and medium-sized state-owned enterprises have not yet recovered their competitiveness in labor intensive production, and remain a problem.

The problem for the Chinese economy, which has demonstrated rapid growth in agriculture, light industry and processing industry, is that it will eventually have to shift to more capital intensive industry. Even in labor-intensive industries, advantages arising from cheap labor cost will eventually disappear as the economy grows. I propose that what China needs now might be some sort of industrial policy.

The second characteristic of Chinese economic development is the introduction of foreign enterprises and technology transfer through liberalization. There has been a remarkable influx of foreign corporations into China in the automobile and telecommunication industries. Mr. Deng Xiaoping expressed the view in 1992 that "we should allow more of all foreign-invested, and there is nothing to be afraid of. As far as we can keep ourselves calm, we do not need to fear anything. We have many advantages. We have large and medium-sized state-owned enterprises, and we also have township-owned businesses. What is more important is the fact that we have political leadership." He goes on to point out that "we have to let foreign corporations earn a certain amount of their share. Still, the state can recover part of it as tax, and at the same time, we can gain information as well as develop markets." *Business Week* (May 17, 1993), in comparing Japan and China, states that "although China will be an economic superpower in size, it won't compete as directly with the U.S. or European technology-based industries as Japan does. Instead, its strength will be mostly in light manufacturing and low-tech industries. And unlike the *keiretsu* of Japan, the new Chinese corporation will be more open to foreign participation."

I am puzzled by this argument. First, I do not believe that China will end up as just a base for foreign corporations. It will shift to a more advanced industrial structure which will enable it to achieve independent technological development. Another possible scenario is that China may utilize foreign enterprises as a driving force in its own economic growth. This way, economic growth will be realized far more rapidly than through the independent growth of Chinese enterprises. The foreign transplanting process will be controlled by a strong political leadership maintaining its policy line of a "socialist market economy," as Mr. Deng Xiaoping suggests. This way, China will form a large and rapidly growing open market with a population of 1.2 billion —which is more than the population of the U.S., Japan and EC combined—without becoming a colony. However, this probably will not be China's scenario of the choice.

This leads us to the second problem. Although *Business*

Week gives China credit for not competing with the West at present and for the relative ease with which foreign corporation can locate there, such an attitude will no longer be valid when China absorbs technology and emerges as a high-tech country. This is exactly what China should be attempting to achieve and is what China has to achieve to reach an advanced level of industrialization. In order to do so, I believe it is central that China rationalize its large to medium-sized state-owned enterprises and cultivate new fields through technological innovation. These undertakings are closely related to China's macroeconomic management.

III. Macroeconomic Policy

First, we have to talk about finance. In the Japanese economy, a major portion of tax revenue consists of individual income tax and corporate income tax. Individuals are taxed progressively while corporate income fluctuates drastically according to economic performance at any given time. Therefore, Japan enjoyed a consistent natural increase in tax revenues during its high-growth era and the fiscal balance continued to be in the black. In other words, tax revenue increased naturally because the actual growth rate was greater than the forecasted figures with which tax revenue needs were estimated. Such a tax structure can assist stabilization in periods of economic fluctuation. At the same time, surplus tax revenue was available for the improvement of infrastructure. Indeed, sustaining a high growth rate for an extended period of time requires that infrastructure improvements keep pace with the advance of industrialization.

In the case of the Chinese economy, however, the central government's budget has remained in the red despite rapid growth. The major cause of the deficit is the need of the national budget to support state-owned enterprises. The deficits of the state-owned enterprises, as already stated, is due to soft budget restrictions, administrative interference, and defects in the system of payment to the authorities, among others. Efforts to improve the situation have repeatedly been attempted. However, under the current budget deficit, China cannot afford to both cover the deficits of state-owned enterprises and pay for improvements in social infrastructure. China has no choice but to rely on foreign assistance in dealing with these problems. It is imperative to establish a mechanism that will provide a favorable economic cycle centered on sound financing.

One option for China to consider is progressive taxation according to income level. Initially, it will be difficult to target individuals as the basis for taxation, and therefore incomes will have to be taxed at the enterprise level, where salaries could be taxed progressively. In any case, it is fundamentally important to establish a mechanism by which an automatic increase in tax revenue is produced when the economy is expanding at a rate higher than forecasts predict.

Second, we must address the improvement of state-owned enterprises, but this depends on the kind of basic industrial policy China adopts. One possible method would be to eliminate unproductive state-owned enterprises as much as possible. In this event, competition with the foreign-invested enterprises and township enterprises will be more vigorous. On the other hand, if an independent and complete industrial structure is to be built, Japanese industrial policy will serve as a model. Careful examination and preparation are required for the successful application of either policy.

Third, reform of the financial system must be addressed. Introduction of the stock ownership system is one of the methods for securing funds, but stock corporations and the socialist market economy fundamentally contradict each other. Ownership by stockholders and shared ownership by all the people, which is the basis for socialism or collective ownership, are incompatible, and moreover, will lead to a decay of socialist political structures. Therefore, banks will have to monitor enterprise efficiency. It is desirable to have an improved financial system where the central bank is separated from other general banks, and commercial banks are separated from policy-related financial institutions. Policy-oriented financial institutions are expected to play a major role in promoting the active rationalization of state-owned enterprises. At the same time, it is imperative to establish an independent central bank which can fully control the amount of monetary flow and a tax revenue structure which can function to stabilize economic fluctuations. Orthodox financial policies should be adopted to create corporate financing that will sensitively respond to central bank interest and reserve rate policies.

Finally, I need to mention some of the other issues that will have to be addressed in the actual adaptation of economic control using macroeconomic policies. They include measures against the disparity of the dualistic economy, and social security policies toward the unemployed and elderly. Unfortunately, I will have to leave these to a discussion on another occasion.

Anyhow, there is no question that China is now facing a crucial crossroad at which it must decide what kind of industrial policy it will adopt in order to promote the sustainable development of the Chinese economy.

Constraints of Foreign Currency in the Process of Economic Development from the Japanese Experience

Yoshio Matsunaga
Professor at the Waseda University

I. The Japanese Experience in the 1960s

The Japanese experience found that a great volume of foreign currency is necessary for rapid economic development.

Japan also fell into frequent foreign currencies difficulties in the period of high speed economic growth of the 1960s. It was said that the constraining factor for Japanese economic growth was the balance of payments. This obstacle to Japanese economic growth was called the wall of the balance of payments.

Japan's foreign reserves were almost two billion dollars in those days and many said that at least the amount of three months' imports are always required as holdings. But the Japanese external reserves were frequently below this amount. In this case, the Japanese economy had to brake the speed of economic growth.

In those days, I was making an effort to resolve theoretically the optimum volume of external reserves necessary for the Japanese economy. To this purpose I was thinking, first of all, how to make clear the structure of the Japanese balance of payments.

As a result of trial and error, the formula for the elements of the balance of payments which I succeeded in developing was as follows.

$$dI \leq \frac{s}{m}dX$$

This formula was developed from the Keynesian multiplier theory, so this formula is not peculiar to the Japanese economy alone. It is useful for any country, including China.

In this formula,

1. dI on the left side is the increase of total investments within a country. It includes investments not only for modernization in various forms, but also for construction of social overhead capital. No doubt, investment for social overhead capital and for modernization of equipment is indispensable for the economic growth of every country.

The more investment made possible by optimal combinations and a sustainable pace, the greater a country's economic development. Such investments increase production capacity and productivity, as well as the international competitiveness of the country.

2. The increase of such investments is limited to the right side of the above formula. If dI is larger than the right side of the formula, the balance of payments is in deficit, and the country will fall into difficulties with its international reserves. In the 1960s, as Japanese holdings of international reserves were low, and the Japanese exchange rate was fixed, Japan continued to run a balance of payments deficit for a long period. In other words, how much investment is possible, and how much growth rate is sustainable are completely bound by the right side of the formula in the medium or long term.

Now, dX, which consists of the right side of the formula, shows the increase of exports. The larger the increase of exports, the more domestic investments are possible without risking a shortage of foreign reserves. And s, also on the right side, is a country's marginal propensity to save, according to the Keynesian definition. In other words, s is the ratio of the increase of saving against the increase of income. Roughly speaking, s is the savings ratio. And the larger the value of s, the more domestic investment is possible without causing a shortage of foreign reserves.

Finally, m, another element of the right side, is the marginal propensity to import. That is, m is the country's approximate rate of dependence on imports (Imports / GNP). As m is the denominator of the right side, the smaller m is, the larger the right side becomes. So, when m is small, the country is able to invest more in modernization and development without risking a shortage of foreign reserves.

3. In the 1960s, Japan had developed almost without dependence on foreign capital such as external borrowing. Basically, Japan had been financing the necessary volumes of foreign currencies only from exports. Therefore, basically the right side of the above formula limited the annual growth rates of the Japanese economy.

But now, almost all developing countries, including China, have greater access to foreign capital. Now, they can use many opportunities for external borrowing and direct investment from advanced countries. If we consider these possibilities, the formula limiting domestic investment, as mentioned above, can be amended as follows. As a matter of fact, the boundary conditions will be mitigated.

$$dI \leqq \frac{s}{m}dX + \frac{s + m}{m}dB$$

In this formula, dB, which is newly introduced, is the increase in external borrowing. According to this amendment, the formula is mitigated by

$$\frac{s + m}{m}dB$$

Even in this case, a higher s (the savings ratio) is better, and a lower m (ratio of dependence on imports) is better for maximizing investments and sustaining a higher economic growth rate. The functions of s and m are exactly the same as in the previous formula.

II. Success of the Japanese Economy

In the mid-1960s, I was trying to theoretically resolve the optimum holdings of international reserves, and for this purpose, as the first step, I wanted to grasp the characteristics of the

Japanese balance of payments, and I succeeded in creating the above formulas. After this, I got strongly excited with respect to the following two points.

First of all, as already explained by my formulas, those formulas themselves are "the ceiling for the balance of payments," which was said in those days to be very low.

And secondly, it became clear that the Japanese balance of payments ceiling was increasing very fast against the usual perception, after I checked the values of dX, s and m which appear in my formulas. I had the feeling that I was touching the secret essence of Japanese economic growth.

Japanese exports were increasing at a speed two or three times that of other developed countries. And the ratio of savings in Japanese household was also two or three times the value of that in other countries. The Japanese ratio of savings in households was about 18 percent of disposable income. In the United States or Britain, this ratio was 5 to 6 percent, and in Germany and France about 10 percent.

Finally, the Japanese ratio of dependence on imports (m) was only half or below half of European countries. The Japanese ratio was about 9 percent, and the European ratio was about 20 percent or more.

As I previously noted, the possible volumes of domestic investment without foreign reserve difficulties depend upon the values of dX, s and m. The larger values of dX and s, and the smaller the value of m, the greater the potential for economic growth. The Japanese economy in the 1960s was experiencing favorable conditions in all three points.

The balance of payments ceiling, and bounding Japanese economic growth had been increasing very rapidly as compared with other major countries. In fact, since domestic investments were increasing more rapidly than the ceiling, the Japanese balance of payments was actually running a deficit. But the reason the Japanese economy could sustain high-speed economic growth in the long-run was that this ceiling was increasing very rapidly.

Investments on top of investments rapidly brought more

modernized equipment into Japanese firms, and made Japanese international competitiveness stronger. As a result, there was a rapid increase of exports, and this increase enhanced the ceiling even more.

Continuing investments brought not only an increase in productivity, but also increased Japanese production capacity, and as a result there was a high rate of economic growth without inflation. In the latter half of the 1960s, a "ceiling of labor-shortage" newly appeared as a lower ceiling. So consumer prices began to rise more rapidly, while wholesale prices remained surprisingly stable. The average annual rate of increase of this price-level was only 1 percent during the 1960s. This stability can be attributed to large-scale investments and efficiency during this period.

III. Suggestions for the Chinese Economy

It is desirable for China to keep the above formula in mind during the process of modernization and a move toward the market economy. And China should make efforts to enhance this ceiling as much as possible. Japan's high economic growth rate in the 1960s has brought today's prosperous Japanese economy, but high growth rates themselves ended as a new labor-shortage ceiling appeared. But, in the case of China, this labor-shortage ceiling is perhaps far higher than that of Japan. So in the case of China, the ceiling of balance of payments will be the most important boundary of economic growth over the long haul.

The high economic growth rate of the 1960s in Japan broke down also because of pollution at the same time the labor-shortage appeared. But today, because of the bitter experience of those days, technologies to aid in the reduction of pollution have advanced considerably. Now, such advanced technologies are available to China and other developing countries. After all, the most anxious boundary for China will surely be the ceiling of the balance of payments.

Recently in Japan, the increase of exports, (dX) in my formula, has become much weaker. For instance, the rate of increase for Japanese exports from 1986 to 1991 was only 49.4 percent, compared with a 68.4 percent average for developed countries and 71.8 percent for total world exports.

Recently, the increase of Japanese exports has fallen below the world average. But in spite of this deterioration in exports, the Japanese balance of trade surplus remains very large and has been growing very rapidly. This raises the following questions. How important are the roles of the other two elements, that is, the roles of the savings ratio (s) and the ratio of dependence on imports (m)?

In the case of Japan, it is not necessary to enhance the ceiling of balance of payments because the inducements for domestic investment and the potential power of economic growth are now considerably weakened. Rather, Japan must try to bring down this ceiling as far as possible in order to reduce its trade surplus for international cooperation. Japan also should reduce its savings ratio and increase the ratio of dependence on imports.

In contrast, China must try to increase exports and at the same time enhance the national savings rate and bring down the rate of dependence on imports. And if China is able to show persuasive, sustainable high rates of economic development, much of the foreign capital, whether direct investments or indirect external loans, will naturally flow into the country. And as a result, sustainable high rates of growth become surer without foreign reserve difficulties. It is desirable to draw up concrete programs for the enhancement of the ceiling of the balance of payments, and to point them out clearly.

IV. International Competitiveness of Japanese Products

It is natural that the increase in Japanese exports has significantly weakened recently. Adjustments in the exchange rates have occurred often since the first adjustment in 1971. But in spite of these adjustments, it is a mystery why some Japanese industrial products even now have dominate positions in the world market. What are the elements of such successful Japanese competitiveness?

Several years ago, while visiting a Korean automobile factory, I had some critical thoughts about Japanese competitiveness. At this time the price of the most popular car in Korea was being sold at an unimaginably cheap price for domestic customers. But that night I discovered the essence of the competitiveness of Japanese manufactures in the bathroom of a Korean hotel where we stayed. One of the wall's electric socket was distorted, and the wallpaper, here and there, was blistered. If Japanese craftsmen had done this work such shoddiness would never happen.

In Japan, not only electricians and wallpaper craftsmen, but also almost every factory worker is able to do their work with great skill. So in Japan, very reliable products are made. Japanese products are hard to break and their appearance, too, is finished finely and precisely. In this way, Japanese manufactured products remain strongly competitive in spite of their high cost.

This is a very important point for China, too. It is not enough to produce manufactured goods cheaply by using cheap labor. It is also necessary to make reliable goods for the world market. This is not necessarily related to the modernization of equipment and the creation of infrastructures. It is rather a problem of the attitude of the workers in their factories. It is also a problem of education. And this point is necessary not only for the enhancement of the Chinese ceiling of the balance of payments, but also for lowering the ratio of China's dependence on imports.

V. Enhancement of Savings Ratio

In Japan, the high ratio of household savings has contributed to raising the Japanese ceiling of the balance of payments. However, now that the potential power of Japan's economic growth has been considerably weakened, this high ratio is one of the causes of the trade surplus.

In the case of Japan, the main reason for the high savings ratio is, I think, to be found in Japan's particular situation. Therefore, the Japanese case may not be appropriate for China or other countries.

I think that this high savings ratio is based on Japan's unique constitution. In Japan, the national constitution strictly limits the military budget to within 1 percent of the GNP. By this limitation, the government's financial burden becomes that much slighter, and as a result the tax rate is held in check.

In fact, tax burden against national income is very slight in Japan as compared with other major developed countries. And this is also true to direct personal income tax. In my judgement, the high Japanese savings ratio depends upon this low rate of personal income tax.

Even if a Japanese individual does not have a strong desire to save, the income tax deducted from his personal income is so small that more money (more saving) is left in his hand. Though I have been considering the reasons for the high Japanese savings ratio in many ways, the above is my conclusion.

Therefore, I cannot recommend the Japanese model for China or other countries with respect to the savings ratio.

However, I have heard that the people of China have always had a strong mind to save. The ratio of savings in Taiwan, for example, is very high. And the Korean ratio is also very high. These facts suggest the importance of the role of saving. It may be essential to arrange the financial and stock markets in such a way as to promote savings in the mind of the public.

VI. Bringing Down the Ratio of Import Dependence

Though the Japanese experience may not be appropriate for China or other countries, perhaps there is a trade-off relationship between the value of the savings ratio and the value of the direct personal tax burden against personal income. Having a trade-off relationship with the savings ratio, according to my investigations, is the direct tax, and not the indirect tax.

Japan has been adopting a taxation system inclining toward direct taxes, but in spite of this inclination, the Japanese personal direct tax burden remains lower than other major countries. And this makes Japan's savings ratio higher. From this consideration,

I can suggest that China adopt a taxation system inclined toward indirect taxes while also making direct taxes lower.

As for the savings ratio, my suggestions have been stated above. But as for dependence on imports, some suggestions may be possible.

Even now, Japanese dependence on imports is very low in comparison with other advanced countries. For instance, this value in 1990 was only 7.9 percent of the GNP. And this low ratio is one of the reasons for Japan's trade surplus. The question is why is Japan's dependence on imports so very low.

Many reasons may be considered. But according to my thinking, the most influential factor is the economic size of the country. That is, the size of its GNP. To put it another way, it is the size of the domestic market.

Almost all developing countries regulate imports because of foreign reserve difficulties or the necessity to foster their infant industries. So their dependence on imports might become low. For this reason, I tried to compare the values of this ratio among the advanced countries. Apparently we are able to isolate a co-relationship between GNP size and import dependence.

The two countries with the largest GNP, the United States and Japan, both have extremely low ratios of import dependence. On the other hand, very small advanced countries like Belgium, the Netherland and Switzerland have the highest import ratios. And medium-size countries like Germany, Britain, France, and Italy have import ratios of about 20 percent, in the medium range.

Perhaps the reason of this co-relationship is as follows. In the modern developed world, the demands of people are considerably diversified and individual markets are greatly subdivided. For this reason small countries cannot produce many commodities on a sufficiently competitive scale because of their very small domestic markets. Now in advanced countries, when people want to buy a car, one will select a sportscar and another will select a station wagon. In this situation, small countries cannot efficiently produce each commodity. As a result, these countries are oblized to import them from other countries.

On the other hand, in those countries with large domestic markets, either sportscar or station wagon can be produced efficiently. And very large countries like Japan have many automobile manufacturers such as Toyota, Nissan, Honda, Mitsubishi, Mazda, Suzuki and others able to coexist each other. In these countries, many companies work hard in a broad range of industries to be more competitive and stronger, so the country becomes less and less dependent on imports.

In the case of China with its extremely large population, there is a great possibility to become less import-dependent like Japan and the United States, after the Chinese economy has developed and the income level of its people has been raised to some extent. In China, many enterprises could co-exist, compete with each other, and enhance each other's competitiveness in a very broad range of industries. China has great potential for achieving this. The problem is how to realize such potential.

Korea has not so large a population, and for this reason Korean dependence on imports is rather high. But until quite recently we did not see imported goods in the Korean domestic consumer's market. It should be understood that Korea has severely regulated imports in order to save foreign currencies and, at the same time, to protect their infant industries.

Such Korean procedures seem also to be necessary for the modern Chinese economy. This point itself directly bears on import-dependence and at the same time will contribute to constructing a stable economy without balance of payment difficulties in the future.

At this point in time, China, with its huge population, unquestionably has far greater possibilities than other developing countries. China is able to proceed with an import substitution policy in many fields, not only for consumer goods but also for productive goods. China also should be able to foster plural enterprises which compete with each other because of the very large potential domestic market.

The important point is, I think, to provide healthy conditions for competition and to carefully select those fields which truly require foreign currencies. It is necessary to carefully select those fields that ought to rely on imports in the present Chinese economy. By this procedure, China will be able to avoid anxiety about a foreign currency deficit and to construct complementary, competitive, and extensive production networks. It would seem that the areas which allow the use of foreign currencies for export industries should proceed carefully. Besides the preferential right to use foreign currencies, other efficient methods for promoting exports should be considered. For example, some optimum adjustments in the exchange rate should make export itself more profitable. Japan also used a central management system of foreign currencies in the process of its development. The key point is to use foreign currencies as efficiently as possible.

The Regionalization of the Asian Economy and Its Impact on China's Development

Francois Gipouloux
Research fellow of the National Center
for Scientific Research, France, and
the Maison Franco-Japonaise, Tokyo

Introduction

Regionalization in Asia is not a new phenomenon. In its economic and cultural dimensions, it has been pervasive throughout a long history.[1] But during the last century regionalization was frozen first by colonialism—both Western and Japanese—and then by a command economy, especially in China.

As in other regions in the world, East Asia did not escape the partition of economic areas created by nearly two decades of uninterrupted growth. The entire region, however, is far from constituting an homogeneous entity due to historical, cultural and social reasons which are not addressed in this paper. At least three trends are, nevertheless, generating a greater synergy: Intensification of trade, enhancement of an intra-regional network of investment, and an identification with common cultural values inherited from the sinicization of East Asia. Let us just mention the vitality of the debate on the resilience of Confucianism is contemporary societies, or the concept of a sphere of Chinese written characters and their relationship with what may be termed an oriental alternative for economic development.

Regionalization has, however, specific effects on the dynamics of growth in the region in relation to Chinese economic development.

I. Toward a Japan-Centered Production System in Asia

1. Three Important Changes Occurred in the Early 1990s

1) Asian new industrialized economies gradually shifted to an economic growth led by domestic demand. Growth of domestic markets stimulated the demand for consumer goods such as automobiles and also promoted a move toward tertiary activities.

2) Trade is expanding between New Industrialized and Economic Sectors (NIES) and other Asian countries despite ongoing strong ties with Japan. In 1990, Chinese exports to NIES was over 52 percent. The Association of Southeast Asia Nations (ASEAN) provides another example. Although exports among ASEAN countries still plays a minor role, exports to Asian NIES increased dramatically and comprises more than 30 percent of the total.

3) At the same time, large new industrialized corporations as well as medium-sized industries are expanding their investment abroad, mainly in ASEAN countries and China, to cope with manpower shortages and soaring labor costs at home. This last move tends to create a strongly interrelated industrial network in East Asia.

Japanese scholars as well as officials from government agencies have put the emphasis on the emergence of a multi-layer structure with Japan at the center, while NIES, ASEAN countries and coastal areas of China form the outer layers. Watanabe Toshio for instance, has analyzed the mechanism of economic growth which, starting from the NIES, is spreading to ASEAN countries and coastal areas of China.[2] This dynamics of growth, fueled by Japanese capital and technology, has worked out as long as the U.S. market played the role of main absorber of Asian goods. However, the U.S. market has now contracted and Asian economies will face serious market access problems. One could logically ask whether Japan can replace the U.S. as the major absorber of Asian goods, as Japan, since the Plaza agreement in particular, has set up a dense network of intertwined trade and investment flow throughout Asia. Nevertheless, there is no statistical evidence that Japan is becoming a regional absorber of Asian goods. This striking imbalance is undoubtly the main source of concern and resentment by other Asian countries, and one of the most serious issues undermining the future of a more integrated system for East Asian economies.

Aware of this difficulty, other Japanese scholars argue that intra-regional trade could substitute for the lack of extensive access to the Japanese market. Although intra-Asian trade had greatly expanded during the last decade, it remains to be seen whether the scale of China-NIES or NIES-ASEAN trade can take over the role formerly played by the U.S. market. Moreover, a similar orientation toward exports among several East Asian economies make intra-regional competition likely to intensify.

2. An East Asian Economic Corridor as an Alternative?

Closer regional cooperation often means development of direct links within smaller, mainly geographical entities striving for more collective economic gains. Mega-regions could provide an interesting analytical tool for exploring the process of economic interdependence in East Asia.

The Sea of Japan, the Yellow Sea, or the South China Sea, to mention only a few examples, will certainly become regional clusters for further integration. Is it, however, relevant to talk about the emergence of a new regional entity in East Asia which could henceforth be referred to as the East Asian Economic Corridor where localized economic zones could develop "face to face" relationships?

There are, however, some conceptual difficulties in assessing the process of regionalization in East Asia. Asian cross-regional areas are not cohesive in terms of economic structure, industrial specialization, innovation or research infrastructure. The lack of infrastructures, the institutional difficulties hampering personnel exchanges, and demographic imbalances must be kept in mind. Not to mention the per capita income level or population and geographical size.[3]

3. The Division of Chinese Economic Areas

Moreover, economic regionalization is poised to have consequences on the major economic entities. China illustrates this point. When one looks at China as a market, the country is obviously immense. One of the first visible effects of a decade of economic reforms and openness in China has been the split between three clear-cut economic areas: Coastal provinces, central China, and remote western and border areas. This process has caused upheaval in the traditional vision of Chinese economic geography, where the north/south split along the Yangtze River was prominent. Now, a two-fold split is clearly visible: Meridian lines divide China into east, center and west. A new north/south line separates the coastal provinces, up to Shandong, from the northern coastal provinces, mainly north of Hubei and Liaoning. The dynamics of Chinese development is also proceeding along several geographic or geopolitical lines: Coastal areas, valleys and borders. The trend toward the division of national territory into loosely interrelated economic areas is likely to continue. Looking at China as a huge national entity divided into provinces, which are mainly administrative entities, is misleading. Several strategic locations for economic development are emerging, centered around cities, ports and river harbors. Hong Kong/Guangzhou; Shanghai/Nanjing; Beijing/Tianjin; Chengdu/Chongqing; and Wuhan, the large inland port where the east-west run of the Yangtze River crosses the north/south railway's axis. The striking fact is that these urban-centered economic areas are roughly equidistant, 100-200 kilometers.

This new configuration of economic areas reminds some of the divisions which have been a perennial feature throughout Chinese history.[4] It could also have political implications. Seen from a long historical perspective, China reveals the alternating emergence, hegemony and decline of several strategic and economic regions which have played major political roles: the Wei valley, the lower Yellow River valley, the lower reaches of the Yangtze River and the Sichuan Basin. China has never been a unified market, and today can only attain this objective through a combination of heterogeneous factors such as infrastructure programs, legal framework, the rehabilitation of an entrepreneurial image, etc.

China is also following different patterns of economic development. At least two can be identified: An export-oriented pattern in Guangdong Province, and a domestic private-sector-based pattern in the Yangtze valley of Zhejiang and Jiangsu provinces. Although the merits of Guangdong are obvious, there are some doubts about the generalization of an export-oriented strategy to the whole country. First, in the initial stage of its development, Guangdong Province has benefited from unique government features, and is heavily dependent upon overseas capital. How can other regions of China emulate Guangdong in attracting Hong Kong capital, since they lack a direct relationship with the territory? Second and more importantly, world economy is witnessing dramatic changes. During the 1960s and 1970s, i.e. at the time of their highest growth, the Four Little Dragons benefited from an enormous market provided by the United States. During this period, Taiwan and the Republic of Korea depended on the U.S. market for 30 percent to 50 percent of their exports. In 1992, China's exports to the United States accounted for only 8 percent (or 20 percent if indirect exports through Hong Kong are included) and will have great difficulty going beyond this ratio due to the sharpening of Sino-US friction over trade issues.

On the other hand, despite an agriculturally weighted economy, a large manpower surplus and scarce natural resources, Zhejiang and Jiangsu provinces have also adopted bold market economy mechanisms. But both provinces have made township and privately owned enterprises the driving force of their economic growth.

In both cases however, the most dynamic units of the economic structure since the beginning of the reform have appeared in the coastal areas, not in the heartland of traditional industries of inland China nor in Shanghai, both of which received huge amounts of investment from the state in the past. In this new configuration of geo-economic entities, Shanghai belongs to the north, even though it is located at the mouth of the Yangtze River.

4. The New Relationship Between Core and Periphery

Regionalization also causes new factors to appear in the relationship between core and periphery. From an historic point of view, Owen Lattimore has convincingly showed how in the case of China peripheral elements were highly innovative and contributed to a radical modification of political institutions and territorial structures in the center and in the state organization.[5] Such an approach could be fruitful in studying the current situation in China as well as other areas of East Asia. Far from strengthening a former center/periphery structure, the regionalization process produces new divisions. What role do local operators plays in bottom-up or local to local, versus top-down integration? In the case of China, are we witnessing the reconquest of the center by the periphery?

5. Cities and Harbors Instead of the National State as New Clusters for Economic Development

In its extreme developments, the globalization-regionalization process seems thus to lead the system of international economic relations back to what the French historian Fernand Braudel has analyzed in his authoritative work *Material Civilization and Capitalism*. In this respect, cities and great harbors could become once again the main poles for the world economy, and could encompass the same richness found in the maritime republics, the Italian cities of Genoa, Venice and Amalfi, and the Baltic cities at the end of the medieval era.

Once again today, the large cities and great metropolises are concentrated areas of financial activity, research centers, renowned educational institutions, and communications hubs. In these functions, the city is not limited to municipality, but embraces a wide range of activities and interest which are metropolitan as well as regional. It is necessary however, that exchanges between cities not be restricted to formal channels or national initiatives, but display increasing direct contact and links without passing through capital cities. The same could be said in the case of harbors activities. Ports, especially in East Asia, are evolving from general products and commodity flow toward specialized functions and value-added activities.

As knowledge resources and knowledge infrastructure become increasingly important in the creation of wealth, new forms of cities development are emerging.

II. The Re-Asianization of Japan

Japan is obviously taking advantage of the growing interdependence of East Asian economies. In 1991, she traded more with the Four Little Dragons[6] than with the European Community, and more with East Asia than with the United States.[7] As a result of earlier Japanese direct investment, Japan's surplus with East Asia has continued to grow since 1990. Except for China and Indonesia, East Asian countries are all running a deficit in their commercial exchanges with Japan. Although Japanese direct investment has declined since 1990 in overall terms, it has increased in Asia. According to statistics released by the Ministry of Finance, Japanese direct investment in Asia surged 8.2 percent in fiscal year 1992, making Asia's share of total Japanese investment 18.8 percent, up from 14.3 percent one year earlier. This makes its investment in Europe (US$ 7.06 billion) and in Asia (US$ 6.43 billion) roughly equivalent. Significantly, Japanese foreign direct investment in Asia is concentrated in the manufacturing sector. This trend has had important economic consequence.

1. Dependence upon Japanese Capital Goods

As far as the Four Little Dragons are concerned, dependence on Japan is striking and becoming worse. In 1992, Taiwan's deficit vis a vis Japan—US$ 12.9 billion—was, when expressed on a per capita basis, three times America's deficit with Japan. Korea's case is similarly revealing. Korean dependency upon Japanese capital goods and intermediate products can be traced back to the beginning of the 1970s. From 1984 to 1987 this dependency deepened with the take-off of Korean exports. Since 1989, imports from Japan aimed at acquiring automation equipment to substitute for costly manpower, and expensive consumer goods to satisfy the needs of better-off consumers. The mechanism underlying Korean dependency on Japan is thus two-fold. In order to remain competitive, export policy has to rely on quality improvements obtained through the import of sophisticated equipment. Second, the export-promotion policy has caused a shortage in the supply of domestically produced intermediate goods and components. The great amount of parts and components required by export industries are not available on the domestic market. This critical discontinuity between export-oriented sectors and intermediate-goods producers results in increased imports, and thus a deepening dependence on Japan.[8]

Generally speaking, Japan is still the key supplier of capital goods and intermediate products to Asian countries. Especially in the case of machinery, ASEAN's dependence on imports from Japan increased greatly after 1985 to account for about 40 percent of all their machinery imports in 1990. The same goes for NIES. During 1986-1988, machinery imports from Japan account for more than 40 percent of their total machinery imports. Moreover, dependence on parts imported from Japan is still high, above 10 percent, for both NIES and ASEAN countries. As a comparison, the ratio of Japan's parts imports from the rest of the world —against its nominal GNP in the manufacturing sector—is below 2 percent.

2. The Two Strategies of Japanese Firms

There are thus clearly visible differences in the pattern of division of labor in East Asia. During the second half of the 1980s, Japan, taking advantage of its cheap labor costs, succeeded in transforming East Asia into a productive base for goods aimed at U.S. and European markets. Many observers argued that the expansion of Japan's foreign investment would lead to a sharp decline in exports. The reverse has occurred. The consequence of high Japanese investment overseas was the transformation of Asia into a productive base, but it also induced a strong demand for high value-added parts and industrial supplies for Japan. According to the MITI, Japanese subsidiaries overseas are now registering sales close to US$ 200 million. The so-called diversion effect from outward foreign direct investment is weak.

During 1992, Japan's exports (in terms of U.S. dollars) grew by 8.0 percent. But exports to Southeast Asia registered an increase of 11.7 percent and exports to China grew by 39.1 percent. It became obvious that foreign firms had become consumers, then distributors of exports from Japan. Such a trend strengthened dependence on Japanese technology.

Beginning with the second *endaka* in 1993, a new trend of Japanese economic expansion in East Asia aimed at taking control of the fastest-growing markets. The first surge of Japanese FDI has helped create an emerging middle class eager to buy Japanese products. China is a case in point, illustrating the overlapping of these different strategies.

The first strategy was to utilize China as a production base. Labor costs in Shenzhen, considered the place where labor costs rose dramatically, are still one tenth of those in Japan (US$ 90-130 per month), and land rent is still low. However, a further expansion of FDI in China depends on the development of a broad spectrum of supporting industries: Component manufacturing, tool making, and a raw-materials processing industry. For foreign investors operating in China, as well as in other Asian countries, the further raising of local content ratio requested by the host country requires the localization of more sophisticated components. However, raw materials for these items are often special steel, casting material, etc. Suppliers able to meet both quality and volume requirements are virtually nonexistent.

Japanese enterprises' second strategy in China is market-oriented expansion. In 1990, per capita GNP in Beijing and Liaoning Province was more than US$ 800, compared with US$ 715 in the Philippines. This tremendous potential of a market of some 200 to 400 million consumers has induced Japanese companies such as Hitachi, Sony and Sanyo to launch a growing number of joint ventures in consumer electronics,[9] and others to investment in distribution and services. The Yaohan group, for instance, plans to open 1,000 supermarkets in China by the year 2010.

Continental and maritime Asia now offers a new and growing crowd of consumers. Already industrialists, Japanese corporations can continue as merchants, provided they set up an appropriate network of commercial outlets. There are at least two advantages to such a strategy:

1) Commerce involves less risk of nationalization than industry. Merchandizing affords long-term prospects, and can succeed even where the life cycle of industrial experience has proved to

be rather short.

2) Economic progress in Asia works as a political stabilizer. Moreover, a growing affluence in other Asian countries will help check the immigration flow from there into Japan. From that point of view, one may ask whether the best consumers are those in Asia rather than in America.

3. The Role of Japanese Multinational Firms in East Asia

Interestingly, a growing number of Japanese affiliates established in Asian countries procure a substantial portion of their equipment from local joint ventures—including Japanese corporations—or by importing from Japanese joint ventures in other Asian countries. According to a survey by MITI more than 60 percent of Japan's machinery imports, on a value basis, from the Asian NIES and ASEAN countries are procured from Japanese machinery-industry affiliates based in those regions.

Analyses conducted among several large Japanese companies in Asia identified significant elements of their strategy. Firms activities outside the national frontiers are generally analysed in terms of property control.[10] Such an analysis presents the advantage of easy delimitation of foreign firms in the host country. However, this does not take into account the totality of the phenomenon. There is, in effect, a multitude of links between Japanese and Asian firms which are not included in the framework of property rights. As S. Tokunaga pointed out, whenever Japanese firms dominate raw material, components, semifinished products and machinery and equipment supply, they see no interest in controlling the local firms:

As long as they possess exclusive technological advantages, Japanese firms can build up international intracompany production networks without ownership in relation to Asian firms. The export of capital goods to local firms without ownership has a stronger potential for establishing subcontracting ties between Japanese and local firms than FDI with majority ownership. In the transfer of technology, or transplanting part of the production process to developing Asian countries, Japanese firms aggressively pursue the acquisition of majority ownership of their local production facilities.[11]

Three consequences may be noted:

1. Majority ownership in FDI becomes a crucial strategy for private companies to prevent local firms from becoming competitive in their home markets.

2. Logistics, in this context, constitutes a governing element of strategy, since it forces marketing discipline and is a critical extension of production flexibility.

3. Asia is more and more strongly integrated into Japan's industrial structure.

Conclusion

1) East Asia is now a region of concentrated high growth, expanding markets, and substantial investment potential—saving rate is still high despite strong growth. However, what we are experiencing in Asia is no longer a bilateral or government to government relationship, but a complex network of multilateral relations where trade, capital, technology and expertise are deeply intertwined. Hong Kong, Singapore, Shanghai, Dalian, Pusan, Kitakyushu, and Fukuoka to mention only a few cities, are becoming clusters in a more interdependent and densely interconnected Asian network.

2) Japanese corporations will continue to play a very important role in this area. One has to recognize that Japanese corporations are still in the initial phases of globalization. Japanese production abroad is only 7-8 percent of their total production, compared to 20 percent for the United States and European countries. Moreover, Japanese FDI, especially in Asia, is at the crossroads and has to find a self-regulating mechanisms because, as the result of the "export and invest" strategy of Japanese corporation, there is a risk that Asia will become too export-oriented and too dependent on external markets. This trend could provoke protectionist moves in the United States and Europe, especially at a time when those countries are plagued with high levels of unemployment. In this regard, the cost of capital, or the rate of return on investment should be considered an appropriate regulation tool. There is now a necessity to pay a higher equity

capital costs by gradually dissolving interlocking shares.

3) A common complaint from recipient countries of Japanese FDI concerns the reluctance of Japanese corporations to transfer technology. This issue is a very complicated one. But generally speaking, Japanese corporations have to go beyond mere exploitation of low labor costs. They also have to contribute higher income levels locally, so that an increasing share of local production can be absorbed locally. In this regard, an appropriate interface between the parent company and the local affiliates must be found.

4) Whether there are the regional entities in East Asia capable of developing alternative institutional frameworks or not? If the question of a necessity of cooperation is often raised in East Asia, its objective remain unclear: to lift barriers which are still barring economic exchanges in East Asia? To harmonize technological norms and financial regulations? To simplify tariffs duties and fiscality for foreign investment? Among all these issues, whether the management of trade frictions with the other main trade partners of the area as a whole—United States and Europe—is the major point or not?

5) Are we heading toward a Chinese commercial empire in East Asia, as a counterweight to the Japanese presence in the region? Two networks are operating in East Asia: the Japanese and the Chinese. In the long run, the strong influence of the network of Chinese overseas may force the Japanese to share economic leadership in East Asia with China, and Japan will have to change its political relationship with the rest of Asia in order to secure its growing economic presence in the region.

Notes

1. Cf. Hamashita Takeshi *China-Centered World Order in Modern Times: Tribute Trade System in Modern Asia,* University of Tokyo Press, 1990.
2. Watanabe Toshio: *Asia, Its Growth and Agony,* East-West Center, Hawaii University Press, 1992.
3. Cf. Lim Jung-duk. "Industrial Restructuring for the Development of the Yellow Sea Rimland," Kim Wonbae (ed.) *Report on Regional Development in the Yellow Sea Rim.* East West Center Population Institute, Honolulu, Ha-

waii, 1991.

4. Cf. the pioneering work of Chi Ch'ao-ting, *Economic Areas in Chinese History,* London, 1926.

5. Cf. Owen Lattimore: "The Periphery as a Locus of Innovation," Jean Gottann (ed.) *Center and Periphery: Spatial Variations in Politics,* Beverly Hills, London: Sage, 1980.

6. Japan-EC trade (1991): US$: 90.95; NIES/CEE trade (1991): US$: 94.16; NIES: the Republic of Korea, Taiwan, Singapore, Hong Kong.

7. Japan/USA trade (1991): US$: 144.85, Japan/East Asia trade (1991): US$: 169.15; East Asia: ASEAN 4 (Thailand, Malaysia, Indonesia, Philippines), NIES 4, China.

8. Cf. Kasai Nobuyuki, "The Age of Japan-Korea Symbiosis and the Economy of the Pan-Yellow-Sea Rimland," *East Asian Economic Perspectives*, IC-SEAD, Kitakyushu, March 1992.

9. According to Hitachi officials, camcorders, with a market estimated at 500,000 units in two years, are set to become the most popular entertainment device in China, following color TV sets and videocassete recorders. cf. *Japan Times,* 7. 9. 1993.

10. On this particular point cf. Aoki Takeshi: "Japanese FDI and the Forming of Networks in the Asian Pacific Region"; Chen Jian'an: "Japanese Firms with Direct Investment in Asia and Their Management," Tokunaga Shojiro (ed.), *Japan Foreign Investment and Asia Economic Interdependence,* Tokyo University Press, Tokyo 1992. On the period from 1970 to the present, see also Dennis J. Encarnation: *Rivals Beyond Trade: America versus Japan in Global Competition.* Cornell University Press, Ithaca and London, 1992.

11. Tokunaga Shojiro, *Japan Foreign Investment* ... op. cit. p. 43.

The Growth and Standardization of China's Futures Markets

Shen Hanyao
President of the Shanghai
Economic Development Institute

As the socialist market economy replaces China's planned economy, futures trading is becoming more and more attractive to governments at all levels, and enterprises and investors with its special charm, unique trading methods and potentially important role in the national economy. At present, developing various kinds of futures markets has become one of the growing economic fashions.

With the emergence of national metal, petroleum, coal and chemical futures markets and large wholesale markets encompassing futures trading mechanisms, various functions of this market, such as its size, pricing, and low risk have now taken an initial shape. However, due to the delay in formulating laws and regulations on futures trading, and the abrupt rise of futures markets all over the country, overspeedy growth and irregular operations have appeared in China's futures trading.

Therefore, it is a pressing matter for China to sum up the experiences and lessons on futures trading and the development of the futures market, work out necessary laws and regulations, strengthen macrocontrol, standardize futures trading and perfect the futures business.

I. The Expansion of China's Futures Market

1. The Necessity for the Expansion of China's Futures Market
Futures markets develop after a commodity economy has

attained a certain level. Now the futures market has become an indispensable component of a highly developed modern market system and is playing various roles in the development and operation of the market economy.

As the traditional planned economy is being transformed into the socialist market economy, introducing "futures mechanism," developing futures trading, and establishing the futures market have become an objective demand of economic development.

1) Switching the economic structure requires a new market form and regulations to replace the traditional planned distribution methods and regulations.

In recent years, with the gradual deepening of economic structural reform, the varieties and quantity of agricultural and sideline products and the means of production originally regulated according to the state's plan have been drastically decreased from 256 varieties to 17. For instance, except for tobacco, which is still a monopolized commodity, and cotton with its fixed purchasing quotas, all agricultural products are regulated by the market. The quantity of materials and commodities under unified state distribution has also dropped sharply. For instance, steel products within the category of state-monopolized distribution made up 77.1 percent in 1979, and fell to 36.5 percent in 1992. Timber under state unified distribution accounted for 85 percent in 1979, and this percentage decreased to 19.3 percent in 1992. Cement earmarked for unified distribution amounted to 35.7 percent, and this figure was reduced to 8.2 percent in 1992.

More than 90 percent of the materials required by production enterprises in the coastal areas and below the prefecture and city levels, and over 75 percent of the materials needed by important large state-owned enterprises are now purchased on the market. A large number of enterprises have been directly pushed into the market during this transformation of the economic system. Therefore it is urgent to establish new market forms with complete functions and to adopt corresponding regulation and control measures.

2) Sharp price fluctuations urgently need new stabilizing

mechanisms.

In the course of freeing controls over the market and along with the dramatic changes in the relations between market supply and demand, the market prices of some important means of production, and agricultural and sideline products affecting the national economy and people's livelihood have correspondingly experienced sharp rises and declines. For instance, in 1985 a kilo of rice cost 0.68 yuan. This price rose suddenly to 1.8 yuan in 1988 and dropped back to one yuan in 1991, the price fluctuation range exceeding 160 percent. This was also true for prices relating to the means of production. For example, between 1980 and 1990, the price of one ton of aluminum ingots rose from 7,500 yuan to 16,000 yuan, and finally stabilized at 8,800 yuan or so.

The sharp rise and fall of prices have caused great losses for producers, operators, and consumers alike. Take grain production as an example. In recent years, the amount of grain exchanged on the market has reached several hundred million tons. On the spot market prices are restricted by production cost, supply and demand, their own production characteristics (such as climate and seasons) and other factors, frequently leading to sharp price fluctuation. Consequently, the production of grain has been wavering in periodic fluctuations, giving birth to a vicious cycle (difficult to sell grain—difficult to purchase grain—and back to hard to sell grain again).

One important reason for this situation is the unhealthy growth of China's market and an imperfect market system. As a result, the market lacks mechanisms for shifting price risks and forecasting future prices. Spot transactions and the market decide the circulation prices of commodities, but they cannot predicate the relation between supply and demand and the tendencies of price changes. Producers and consumers who lack price guidance can only do business according to immediate prices, and have to take tremendous risks because of changing prices. So, since price risks cannot be transferred, the state financial sector has to carry the burden of risk by allocating a large amount of money annually as price subsidies. Hence there is a heavier and heavier financial burden on the state.

We can see that economic structural reform and an expansion of the market economy in China are in urgent need of a new and stable mechanism which will not only provide guidance for enterprises in formulating price policies, but will also enable enterprises to avoid price risks.

3) A larger market with greater circulation needs to be formed to promote the effective allocation of resources.

China's economic development has always been restricted by insufficient natural resources. Under the traditional planned economy, the government distributed natural resources through planned allocations and administrative interferences. Because of changes in the economic structure, enterprises must obtain various materials required for production through the open market. The expansion of market supply and demand, especially the sharp rise of supply and demand resulting from the expansion of capital construction in recent years, has produced a tense state in all aspects of the nation's economy. For instance, in 1992 investments in fixed assets increased by 37.6 percent, and shot up quickly again this year. Consequently, the shortage of natural resources becomes more serious daily; and the materials required by important industries, especially metal and construction materials, are in short supply, giving birth to the black market. This rampant black market has distorted the allocation of natural resources. It is therefore necessary to establish a new and larger market system with greater circulation, which, through centralized exchange and public price bidding, will promote the reasonable allocation of insufficient resources, and through the gathering effects of a larger market will induce a greater circulation of materials and commodities between domestic and international markets.

2. China's Futures Markets in Practice

At present, China's futures markets may be arranged into the following three categories:

1) Large wholesale markets with futures trading mechanisms which handle commodities through spot transactions or forward contracts.

2) Markets with exchange mechanism which deal with some

trading commodities by forward contracts, and with some commodities by signing standard futures contracts.

3) Fairly standardized futures markets which do business through standard futures contracts.

Since October 12, 1990 when the Zhengzhou Wholesale Grain Market, the first in China with a futures trading mechanism, began operations, national and regional futures trading markets of various types or large exchange markets with futures trading mechanism have grown up rapidly within a short period of time. Some examples are Shenzhen Nonferrous Metal Exchange House, Shanghai Metal Exchange House, Yantai China Chemical Materials Exchange Market, Northeast China Petrochemical Exchange House, Nanjing Petroleum Exchange House, Tianjin Petrochemical Center, Shanghai Coal Exchange House, Shanghai Meat Commodity Wholesale Market, Shanghai Grain and Oil Exchange House, Shanghai Agricultural Materials Exchange Market, Shanghai Chemical Exchange, Shanghai Petroleum Exchange, Shanghai Stock Exchange House, and Shanghai Foreign Exchange Futures Market. The commodities handled by the futures trading markets include nonferrous metal, petroleum products, chemical products, coal, grain and edible oil products, iron and steel products, foreign exchange, treasury bills, and other commodity and financial futures.

Though futures trading in China has a short history, it already has displayed strong vitality. Futures trading mechanisms and market functions have already appeared.

1) The price discovering mechanism and price guiding roles also have been initially formed, and prices for a portion of trading commodities have become the authoritative prices.

The futures market, which is completely decided by market supply and demand, gathers together many factors to finally form a unified trading price through public bidding or centralized competitive bidding. The final price then reflects the changes in domestic and international quotations.

The formation of the price discovering mechanism of the futures market enables prices to truly reflect the supply and demand of commodities, thus providing a long-term price guide.

Operators of enterprises may reasonably arrange production and operations according to the changes in future prices reflected in futures contract and thereby effectively reduce short-term actions and short-sighted decisions.

The most prominent example is the Shanghai Metal Exchange House, well-known as the most competitive market. As it concentrates the main production enterprises and consumption circulation enterprises of China's nonferrous metal trade, its market prices produced through centralized competitive bidding have become the national authoritative prices. Since it began operations on May 28, 1992, its prices have experienced rises and declines time and again, truly displaying the changes in domestic supply and demand, the price changes of the relevant products on the international market, and changes in the domestic exchange rates. This exchange house's fluctuating prices are more sensitive and a few steps ahead of the price changes of other exchange houses. Hence it plays the role of forecasting future prices. Since its establishment, Zhengzhou Wholesale Grain Market has initially played the role of a national grain wholesale market. With the constant expansion of the market, its prices have become the guiding grain market prices for the entire country, thus exerting important influence on reducing the sharp fluctuation of grain prices and on controlling grain prices on the market.

2) The functions of hedging and avoiding price risks have gradually developed.

One of the basic economic functions of the futures market is its price-risk control mechanism. The most commonly used trading method for avoiding price risks is hedging, that is, futures contracts for buying or selling goods of the same quantity in the spot market by adopting contrary trading orientation, hoping that within a certain time period, the actual price risks brought about by the price changes at the spot market will be compensated or reduced to a minimum through selling or purchasing futures contracts.

With the deepening of economic structural reform, control over the prices of various materials has gradually relaxed. And operators of enterprises are becoming more and more sensitive to price risks. With hedging, enterprises may lock in profits or production costs. In the early days of the adoption of futures trading, many operators did not know that price risks may be avoided with hedging, whose main trading purpose is the settlement of physical goods, resulting in a low switch rate for the contracts. But with the expansion of futures trading, more and more enterprises have adopted hedging through the futures market, reflecting their ability to lock in profits or production costs and thereby avoid risks. According to Shanghai Metal Exchange House statistics, in its early days the total volume of settled physical goods made up 86 percent of their total trade volume; one year later, this figure was reduced to about 7.9 percent.

3) The gathering effects of a larger market with greater circulation has become evident.

The futures market, known for its fair, just and transparent trading methods, adopts a membership system and standardizes trading behavior through concentrated trading, public bidding and unified settlement to avoid shortcomings in the course of the implementation of contracts and payment.

The normalization of trading on the futures market has also improved the circulation of resources. In the futures market, an optimized allocation of resources is formed by selling and purchasing contracts, price bidding, and the best utilization of resources. In addition, the futures market allocates resources within a large market, thus forming a circulation of materials within domestic markets and between domestic and international markets.

Meanwhile, the futures market practices highly concentrated trading and radiates in all directions through member companies, brokerages, and the mass media which disseminates information to enhance the gathering effects of a large market.

For instance, Shanghai Metal Exchange House traded 2.06 million tons of copper, aluminum, zinc, tin and nickel within a half year of its inauguration, with business volume exceeding 33.4 billion yuan. The highest business volume per day reached 1.12 billion yuan, involving a total of more than 19,000 business contracts. In 1993, daily business volume increased sharply, with the first three months averaging 1.57 billion yuan a day, and increasing to 5.3 billion yuan on April 24. Member enterprises of this exchange house engage in bulk sales on their own and also serve as agents doing business for clients. More than 600 enterprises all over the country now conduct business at the exchange house through their agents. As a member of the Shanghai Metal Exchange House, the Shanghai Materials and Trade Center has served as agent for more than 100 clients, involving a total business volume of two billion yuan.

II. Some Problems in the Development of Futures Trading

The following problems have appeared in China's futures trading market:

1) Futures markets have appeared like a swarm of bees in some places, creating a situation in which each place trades on its own, employing separated markets.

Since October 1990 when Zhengzhou Wholesale Grain Market was established, the futures craze has become more and more prevalent. Within a few years, futures markets have sprung up like bamboo shoots after a spring rain throughout the country. Now China has several dozen large futures markets (or other markets with futures mechanisms), including over 30 prefectural markets, and over a dozen national markets. In addition, markets of various types are being founded engaging in trading cotton, construction materials and petrochemical products.

Some worrisome problems have appeared during this excessive development of China's futures markets.

The first is blind growth. Some comrades of some regions and departments began to found these markets before they even knew what futures are, which commodities could be traded as futures, what the nature and rules of the futures market are, or how they should be operated and managed. In addition, they traded in futures with commodities that could easily spoil such as watermelons, Chinese herbal medicines, and aquatic products.

The second problem is the repeated founding of futures markets of the same kind. Since some comrades believe that the market economy means a free market, they repeatedly constructed them regardless of necessary government planned management, macrocontrol, and the local subjective and objective conditions for setting up such a market. For instance, nonferrous metal exchange houses of different sizes have been set up in Shenzhen, Shanghai and Beijing; petroleum exchange houses have been founded in Shanghai and Nanjing; and other regions are preparing for the establishment of futures market of the same kind. The redundant founding of futures markets, which is now in the ascendant, will surely bring hidden troubles to the expansion of this market.

The third problem is the establishment of separate markets which do business on their own. Some comrades developed or organized futures markets with a traditional planned economic modes to obtain high profits. Therefore, some regions and departments, proceeding from their own interests, established futures markets and formed separated sectors characterized by isolation and exclusiveness, so that the gathering effects of the large futures markets could not be brought into full play. Some futures markets founded in a hurry held a grand opening ceremony, but then had great difficulties continuing in business.

2) Trading behavior in the futures market is not standardized.

Futures markets in China have developed without indispensable unified laws and regulations. Though each futures exchange house and market has worked out its own "trading regulations," "articles of association" or "interim regulations on administration" in the course of organizing various kinds of exchange houses and national markets, it is still very difficult to restrict and standardize trading behavior without authoritative and unified regulations.

For instance, a large futures market in Shanghai introduced some control mechanisms when it was first founded. Within half a year after its inauguration however, only 49 percent of its original membership was still doing business there. When trading, the representatives of the member units ignored the relevant regulations and still clung to their old business practices. Abnormal trading phenomenal often appeared, such as the delivery of goods before the signing of a contract.

Some so-called exchange houses still lack the necessary systems, technologies, and management required for real futures trading. For instance, standardized futures contracts up to international standards are a rarity; a perfected settlement system is still not in existence; and a lack of business experience makes for risky dealing. Therefore the futures markets can only handle spot trade or long-term contracts rather than engage in real futures trading. However, as spot trade or long-term contracts are restricted, and some rules are applied, they must be revised to meet realistic demands. Only this way can wrong market trading behavior be corrected and price risks put under control.

3) Futures trading and futures market policies must be rectified.

In these early days of the futures market, the administrative departments must adopt necessary policies and measures to promote the formation and development of the market.

For instance, the regulations formulated by some exchange houses in Shanghai specify that within the exchange houses spot contracts are allowed to be sold, control over prices lifted, member units may serve as agents and collect commissions, and profits and losses incurred may be offset from enterprise's profits. Nonmember units may authorize member units to do business on the market free of the restrictions of their original business scope and status, and financial enterprises may do business as member units. These policies and regulations stress opening up the market and have effectively made the market brisk. However, sometimes the regulations of exchange houses are not identical with the existing regulations of the administrative departments in charge. For instance, the exchange houses allow member units to offset losses incurred from their profits. This was approved by financial regulations of the Shanghai Municipal Government. However, some member units out of Shanghai find it difficult to implement these regulations because they are restricted by local financial policies.

In addition, each locality adopts different policies to promote the cultivation and development of the market. Some places try to attract customers with preferential policies such as reduction of or exemption from taxes. They vie with each other by offering ever-more preferential treatment. Such measures will not promote fair and just competition in the futures market, but will lead to the loss of tax revenue for the state.

4) Methods of managing futures markets are not unified.

Ways of managing the futures markets are not unified. In general, there are two management methods. First, a market or an exchange house is managed with interim management regulations and self-formulated trading practices. Second, the departments for industry and commerce and prices are in charge of the management of a market or an exchange house. At present, most futures markets in China, and markets with futures mechanisms are self-managed. However in practice the problem often appears as to whether transregional business contracts should adopt the regulations of the trading market or those of the administration regulations of the departments for industry and commerce and price control as the criterion.

5) The national and regional futures markets lack a large numbers of independent and public broker companies.

The existing national and regional futures markets now lack large number of broker companies to serve as go-betweens. In general, the futures markets have full power members providing agent services. They do so according to the clients' wishes and keep separate business accounts. This seems unjust because they are engaged in their own trade while acting as agents for outside clients. If things continue this way, contradictions will appear and disputes between competing economic interests will occur.

6) Various types of underground and non-standardized futures brokers now exist.

With the growth of futures trading in recent years, various forms of underground futures brokers have emerged all over the country, especially in the coastal areas of southeast China, some of them under the pretence of providing consulting services on futures, and some under the banner of offering investment advice. These underground brokers adopt immoral business methods with extra ordinary trading practices and incorrect operational targets. Consequently, they have caused serious damage to the expansion of the futures market and distorted the real meaning of that activity.

These underground broker companies are most typically gambling-type operations. Under the pretence of market quotations from the United States, Britain and Japan, they often attract customers by claiming they are in line with international futures market practices through Hong Kong and Taiwan futures markets. In essence, these brokers adopt illegal trading methods by making use of clients' sales information to gain profits rather than enter the futures market and actually deliver orders for goods. In addition, they not only collect high service fees, but often embezzle investors' deposits. Some underground brokers reprocess and recycle information so their clients only get out-of-date information or distorted material. In this way these brokers are engaged in fraudulent practices.

Though the founding of some futures consulting companies gained the approval of the relevant departments, they are often engaged in extra ordinary activities. For instance, some futures consulting companies were originally allowed to provide futures advice and do trading on their own; however, they also handle broker age business. Some of them lack the necessary transparency and regulations, so clients' complaints and legal disputes arise. The appearance of a futures company in a city usually goes something like this. The company mainly serves as an agent handling international futures in terms of Japanese and American market quotations. In the last 10-day period of March 1993, the price of red beans at the grain exchange house in Tokyo dropped sharply, and 160 of its customers were "caught," 38 of whom suffered losses because their valid deposits were lower than their support deposits. The losses varied from tens of thousands to several million Japanese yen, the highest hitting four million yen. This directly touched off problems for the company. The customer complaints asked if the sales sheets had entered the market and if the company had purposely guided them the wrong way. But the company maintained that the increase of the value of the Japanese yen and the export of agricultural products from the United States led to the sharp reduction in the prices of Japanese agricultural products, and in addition that the brokers and customers lacked a sense of risk, along with improper operations. The municipal government organized a special investigation group to help clear this up.

III. Strengthening Macrocontrol, Speeding up Regulations for Futures Trading, and Standardizing the Futures Trading Market

The practice of China's futures trading indicates that at its best the futures market has a price discovering mechanism, the function of avoiding risks, and gathering effects as a large market with a large circulation. Enterprises carry out hedging through futures trading to regularly avoid price fluctuations on the spot market. The state regulates supply and demand through the founding of the futures market to stabilize the economy. Futures trading has played an irreplaceable role in the development of the market economy and in the cultivation and perfection of the market system. However, due to the shortage of unified laws and regulations, abnormal phenomena have appeared, such as vying for the founding of futures markets in a blind way and adopting non-standard trading practices. Moreover, a group of underground brokers engaged in illegal trading was born, to which we must attach great importance, otherwise they will touch off unforeseen troubles.

To enable futures trading to develop in a healthy way, we should reinforce macrocontrol, speed up the formation of laws and regulations, and standardize futures trading markets.

1) A high-level unified administrative body with authority should be set up.

The futures markets in China, which sprang up abruptly under the administration of many organs and are separated from each other, have caused unfavorable influences on the formation of a national unified market. We think we may use the successful experiences of foreign governments to manage these markets by establishing a high-level authoritative futures administrative body which will standardize and coordinate the development of the market.

The United States strictly controls futures trading through an effective three-level administrative system. The highest level is the U.S. futures trading administrative committee, the leading group of which consists of five members nominated by the President and approved by the Senate. There are four departments under this committee: Economic Analysis, Trading Market, Legislation, and Supervision and Examination, consisting of about 700 employees. It not only supervises the code of conduct of each futures market, but also takes responsibility for examining and approving the futures contracts for the commodities that will soon come to market. Under special circumstances, if a market monopoly has appeared or will appear, or if other sudden events affect market prices that do not reflect the relations between supply and demand, the committee has the right to take urgent measures. The medium-level body is the U.S. National Futures Management Association. As a national trade management organization, its main responsibilities are as follows: a. reinforcing occupational morality and standardizing and implementing regulations for the protection of clients; b. examining and distinguishing eligible members from among professional futures personnel; c. auditing and supervising professional futures capital, finance and the implementation of the relevant regulations; d. providing arbitration on disputes involving futures trading; and e. disseminating information on futures trading among clients and members. The administrative regulations worked out by the futures market include standards for contracts, futures trading actions, and arbitration procedures.

We think a strict multilevel futures trading management system should be formed as soon as possible in accordance with China's actual circumstances and the progress of structural reforms. It is most important to change the situation in which the futures markets in China are managed by many organs, each handling things on its own. A unified and authoritative futures trading administrative committee attended by all departments in charge and approved by the National People's Congress should be set up. This committee should be responsible for regularly working out futures trading legislation and a unified program for the development of the future market, supervising all trading houses, and standardizing China's futures trading.

2) We should control the total amount, make rational arrangements and plan in a unified way.

The founding and development of a first-class futures market requires many subjective and objective conditions. The futures markets of other countries once suddenly appeared like a swarm of bees. For instance, the year 1898 witnessed the founding of nearly a hundred futures markets in Japan, but by 1938, a little over 20 of them had survived. In 1991, Russia set up 500 futures trading houses, and a year later, half of them had disappeared. Now the number of futures markets in advanced industrial countries such as Japan, Britain and Germany ranges from a few to more than a dozen. Even the United States, known for its advanced economy and flourishing futures trading in the world, has no more than 20 futures markets.

Within a short time period, more than several dozen national and regional futures markets, or exchange markets with futures mechanisms, were founded in China; and there is a tendency for more and more of them to be set up. Many Chinese of insight are worried about the quick increase in the number of these markets, which have also attracted attention from international markets. In particular, the U.S. futures community was shocked by this phenomenon. The U.S. National Futures Association said that the present futures trade in China is in disorder, and wished that the futures trade in China would develop on a healthy basis by perfecting laws and regulations and effective controls. U.S. futures circles now take a wait-and-see attitude.

We believe the current futures markets in China are overheated and should be put under restriction. Before a high-level national futures administrative committee is founded, a coordinating committee of all functional departments and under the leadership of the State Council should be set up to formulate a unified plan to control the number of futures markets through strict examination and approval. We should not set up these markets for some commodities where a national futures market already exists in order to avoid redundancy. We should also rationally establish national futures markets in appropriate places.

The practice and experiences of other countries have proved that the location of the markets is the key to a normally operating futures market. The location and conditions of futures markets, however, are often decided by factors such as natural resources, consumption, finance, telecommunications, and transportation. So the markets are mainly located in the following places. First, where commodities are produced. For instance, in the United States futures trading of agricultural and side-line products are mainly concentrated in Chicago and Kansas City because they are the central cities of the agricultural production areas of the midwestern United States. Second, they are located in circulation centers or collecting and distribution centers. For instance, the London Metal Exchange House is in London because London is the collecting and distributing center of imported nonferrous metals in Britain. Third, they are located in financial and trading centers. For example, New York is a U.S. futures trading center, because New York is one of the U.S. centers of banking and finance. Though the Shanghai Metal Exchange House was founded only a year ago, it has become the third largest nonferrous metal exchange house in the world due to many exceptional advantages. For instance, Shanghai is the largest industrial center in China and consumes more than 600,000 tons of nonferrous metals annually, making up one sixth of the nation's total consumption and ranking first in China in the consumption of nonferrous metals. In addition, Shanghai is China's major financial and trading center.

3) We should establish comprehensive futures markets and trade in a wide variety of commodities.

Restricted by the existing system, the national and regional futures markets and trading markets with futures trading mechanisms that have been founded are unitary or specialized markets. They are separated one from the other, causing an increase in trading costs.

Most foreign futures markets are comprehensive ones. For instance, the world-renowned Chicago Board of Trade (CBOT), a futures exchange house in Chicago, is engaged in trading crops and other agricultural products, gold, silver and other valuable metals, long- and medium-term government bonds, as well as other financial futures and relevant futures contracts. Some are located in one trading center, such as the U.S.'s New York Commodity Exchange Center in the World Trade Center. Its business halls cover an area of 22,500 square feet, larger than four basketball courts, in which coffee, sugar, cotton and commodity exchange houses are located and jointly use advanced telecommunications equipment and information networks. This not only helps reduce trading costs and is favorable for doing business, it also improves the mobility of futures commodity contracts for each trading house.

We think that with the deepening of economic structural reform the department's ownership eventually will be smashed. To improve the market's cohesive forces and reduce trading costs, we may set up an extra-large futures market in Shanghai where futures trading markets are concentrated. Two different kinds of developmental modes may be considered. First, on the basis of existing futures exchange houses, we may expand the comprehensive futures market. For instance, nonferrous metals, black metals and other relevant commodities may be traded at the Shanghai Metal Exchange House. The Shanghai Grain and Edible Oil Exchange House may be developed into an exchange for agricultural and side-line products of all grains, edible oils, cotton, and materials for farm use, all in one place. Agricultural and side-line products may enter the market simultaneously or may be sold at different subsidiaries of the exchange houses. Secondly, we may consider establishing large trading buildings to house several exchanges. This will help gather investments, adopt the most modernized equipment and install the four essential systems for standard international futures markets: A timely price-quotation system (including the price board and quoted prices of various futures commodities), a trading system, a telecommunications and discussion system (such as the global news, closing reports, economic targets and comments on specialized commodities), and a technical analysis system to improve the efficiency of market trade and the consulting and analyzing.

4) Standard futures contracts should be formulated and implemented as soon as possible.

The key to founding the futures market is to standardize futures contracts. In accordance with the development of foreign futures trade, true futures trading begins with a revolution in trading methods—that is, standardizing contracts.

The practice of futures trading in China has shown that some so-called futures trading according to contracts is actually spot purchases and sales. Due to different specifications and quality of trading commodities, different settlement places and difficulties in deciding the readjustment rates of relevant products, long-term contracts take larger price risks and have more difficulties for switch trade. Therefore, the prices prescribed by the long-term contracts cannot well represent the changes in supply and demand. In addition, small trading amounts in the market produce insufficient market mobility for long-term contracts.

We should discuss in great earnest how to standardize futures contracts as soon as possible, but the commodities designated to adopt standardized futures contracts should tally with the country's circumstances and actual demands. Because in the futures market, the inappropriate selection of commodities will lead to the failure of futures trading. Such historical lessons can be found in foreign futures markets and in those out of mainland China. For example, in 1976 Hong Kong founded a commodity futures exchange house. With the consideration that textiles are Hong Kong's main product, the futures exchange house first selected cotton as a trading commodity. However, Hong Kong is neither a cotton producer nor a cotton collecting and distributing center, so that the cotton futures business had long been slack. Eventually, the exchange house had to give up cotton futures trading in

1987.

5) An independent (or a relatively independent) accounting center should be established.

Foreign futures markets are often engaged in large businesses involving a wide variety of commodities. In order to improve accounting efficiency and reinforce control over trading risks, each futures market should set up an independent or relatively independent accounting company, with the responsibility of clearing accounts for the business of each broker every day, supervising the implementation of each due futures contract, controling the futures market risks through a strict deposit system, and guaranteeing the normal operations of the futures market.

At present, the Chinese futures markets have fairly poor accounting practices. With the constant emergence of standard futures contracts, futures switch trade will increase remarkably. Settling accounts by hand cannot meet the demands of large markets with great circulations. If we want to perfect and standardize futures trading, we must reinforce the capacity of controlling risks and set up relatively independent, strongly financed futures accounting companies. Before the founding of these accounting companies, we should strengthen control over risks in the existing letter-of-guarantee system and work out definite regulations on the scope and quota of the letter of guarantee. We should adopt the system of mortgage and letter of guarantee to put an end to the "trade without capital" if necessary.

6) The brokerage firms should be established.

The expansion of the futures markets cannot be separated from standardized broker companies because they complement each other. The futures market is characterized by concentration, and the brokerage firm, by strong radiation. Therefore we hold that the founding of futures markets should be under strict control and they should be rationally distributed. Futures brokerage firms should be developed on the basis of such standardization. We suggest that the relevant departments should take both control and development into consideration when formulating policy. Those underground brokerage firms which aim at profits, engage in illegal business and encroach on their clients' interests should be resolutely abolished. Futures consulting companies, the establishment of which was approved, but which are engaged in extra ordinary trade and have exceeded their business scope, should be under reinforced supervision and management. The eligible brokerage firms with operational and consulting abilities should be granted legal operational status so as to enhance the futures market and promote futures trading.

In order to foster and establish standardized futures brokers we suggest:

1. To ensure fairness and justice in futures trading and safeguard customer interests, a futures company should separate its own business from its activities as agents by founding a specialized broker company to serve as an agent for clients.

2. Brokerage firms at different levels should be established and they should serve as agents for different classes of business.

The first class should be a large, financially strong trans-market, comprehensive brokerage firm with great influence, which should stand in the place where many futures markets gather. To prevent a market monopoly and improve competitiveness and trading efficiency, two or three such large futures companies may be set up with approval of the state department in charge. They should have representation, strong economic strength, and the capacity to provide advice to numerous enterprises. Therefore, large brokerage firms should be composed of large or extra-large group corporations of different trades and should hold membership of a number of national markets which handle different futures commodities so as to improve operational efficiency, reduce trading costs, supply various hedging agent services for enterprises of various trades and avoid price risks. When conditions are mature, they can cooperate with large foreign brokerage firms which are also members of famous futures exchange houses themselves so as to provide consulting services to enterprises for their absorption of foreign resources, understanding of international quotations, and initiation of international business.

The second class should be unitary brokerage firms of various futures exchange houses. Separated from the original members with full powers, they are independently engaged in trust and agent business of futures commodities related to the exchange houses.

The third class consists of numerous small brokerage firms which may be engaged in agent services trusted by the first- or second-class brokerage firms.

Multi-level brokerage firms may help form multi-level risk acceptance mechanisms and attract a large amount of capital to the futures market to ensure the market's mobility.

7) Personnel specialized in futures trading should be trained.

The development of China's futures market badly needs a large number of professional personnel including market managers, broker consultants, price specialists, computer operators, etc. So the relevant departments should speed up the training of personnel specialized in futures trading. With reference to foreign futures trading qualification testing methods and in combination of the characteristics and demands of the Chinese futures market, we should organize qualification tests for futures trading so as to further train eligible personnel for the futures market.

Reform, Internationalization and Macroeconomic Instability

Ross Garnaut and *Guonan Ma*
The Australian National University

I. Introduction

China is now experiencing its fourth inflationary boom since reform began in 1978. The character and management of the fourth boom are affected significantly by the greater openness to the outside world, now a feature of the Chinese economy. Apart from efficiency, greater openness influences the short-term trade-off between rates of growth and degrees of macroeconomic instability.

This paper describes the relationship between growth and instability over the reform period, focusing particularly on the external sector. It notes the apparent deterioration in the trade-off between short-term growth and stability through the 1980s, which seems to have been arrested by the deepening of reform and by integration into the international economy since the inflationary episode of 1988-1989. It notes that instability associated with short-term spurts of growth recently has manifested more quickly in the deterioration of external accounts than in domestic inflation. This has had the practical effect of giving the authorities more time to adjust demand before being swamped by economic and political responses to instability. It concludes with some suggestions for further reform.

II. Changing Relationship Between Growth and Stability

Figure 1 shows that high annual growth rates of real GNP have been accompanied by sharp oscillations. Both the peak (13.6 percent in 1984) and trough (3.6 percent in 1989) growth rates occurred during the period following the accumulation of reform steps that were brought together in the 1984 plenum decisions on urban reform (Raby, 1991). There was an acceleration of inflation from 1984. Strong growth has tended to be accompanied by high inflation, most emphatically in the latter part of the 1980s. When growth has been sluggish, inflation has quickly subsided.

The recent inflationary episode, that is since 1992, has seen output growth levels close to the peak of 1984, associated with retail price inflation higher than in 1985 but well below the 1988 peak. Figure 2 shows that the single-year movement in trade balance seems set to be the largest ever in 1993 (over 5 percentage points of GDP).

Figure 2 shows that trade balance has tended to vary inversely with cyclical fluctuations in GNP growth, with some lags. Net exports, expressed as a percentage of GNP, decline when the economy expands rapidly, but increase quickly when growth slows down. The ratio of net exports to total output has fluctuated a great deal, with the largest trough-to-peak and peak-to-trough variations each being about 6 percentage points of GNP. These movements are large enough to make the open policy a major element in the overall stability of China's economy.

To explore the possible changing relationship between growth and price stability in the 1980s, Figure 3 (a) plots the annual data and Figure 3 (b) the three-year moving averages for key macroeconomic variables (in Figure 3 (b), the moving average is identified by the third year of the period).

Figure 3 (a) suggests that the data from 1979 to 1990 fall into three sets. The first set, covering the years 1979 to 1984 suggests only a weak tendency toward higher inflation in years of strong growth. The year 1980 is unusual in this period for its high inflation. Inflation was low in 1982 and 1983 despite relatively

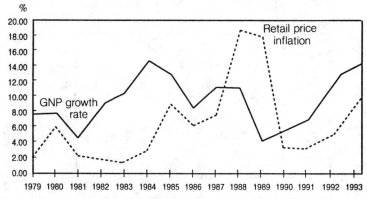

Note: 1993 is year of latest data.
Source: State Statistical Bureau (SSB) 1991.

Fig. 1 Annual GNP Growth and Inflation Rates (Percent, 1979-1993)

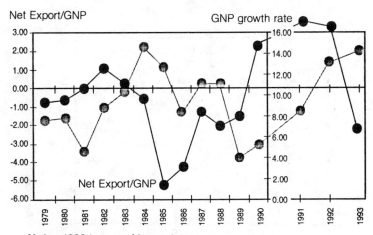

Note: 1993 is year of latest data.
Source: SSB 1993.

Fig. 2 Trade Balance and GNP Growth Rate (Percent, 1979-1993)

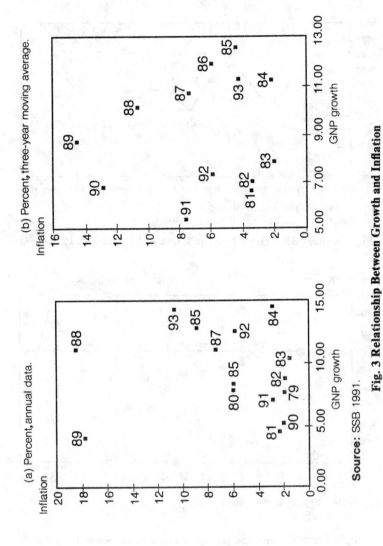

(a) Percent, annual data.

(b) Percent, three-year moving average.

Source: SSB 1991.

Fig. 3 Relationship Between Growth and Inflation

strong growth partly because of strong non-inflationary agricultural expansion. These early years preceded urban price reform, and reflected the continued efficacy of the old controls on prices.

The second set of data covers the years 1985-1987 when major urban state enterprise and price reforms unfolded. There appears to have been an increase in the rate of inflation associated with any given rate of growth—a worsening trade-off between growth and price stability. This period may have been influenced by the release, through price reforms, of previously accumulated and suppressed inflationary pressures. New factors emerging in the reform process began to play an important role.

Then, 1988 and 1989 reveal a sharp deterioration in the relationship between growth and price increases: Growth that was high, but within range for the decade, generated exceptionally high inflation. For any given growth-rate, inflation was considerably higher than in the earlier period. This is a clear indication that as the economy became more responsive to market pressures, the existing economic policy had not yet succeeded in establishing an effective new framework of macroeconomic management to replace the weakened old command controls.

In 1990 and 1991, the relationship between growth and inflation was consistent with both the patterns of the early 1980s and of 1985-1987, with moderate growth associated with relatively low inflation. The return of high growth and high inflation in 1992 suggests a more favorable trade-off than in the late 1980s, although not so favorable as in the early 1980s: A pattern similar to 1985-1987.

The annual data may obscure important lagged relationships between output growth and inflation. Figure 3 (b) explores this possibility (in the crudest of manners) using three-year moving averages. These data reveal two broad curves relating output growth to inflation. The first curve covers the period from 1981 to 1984. There is no sign of a deteriorating trade-off between growth and inflation in this period. The second curve starting in 1985, however, shows a rapid deterioration, with the three-year moving average inflation rate being higher and growth rate being lower for each year from 1985 to 1989. Interestingly, 1990 and

1991 seem to fall within the curve describing the experiences of the early 1980s. 1992 fell between the curves of the early 1980s and mid-1980s, and 1993 seems to be on the mid-1980s curve. (Note that in Figure 3 (b), "1985" refers to the three years up to and including 1985.)

Overall, the data are consistent with the propositions that the trade-off between growth and price stability deteriorated through the 1980s; and that this deterioration was arrested and partly reversed in the early 1990s. It is also consistent with the proposition that with greater integration into the international economy, in the 1990s instability was reflected relatively more in fluctuations in external accounts and relatively less in fluctuations in the rate of increase in prices.

III. Causes of Instability

We have published elsewhere an account of the causes of economic instability in China in the reform period (Garnaut and Ma, 1993).

The immediate sectorial origins of instability in output and demand growth varied over time. Agriculture played a major role in production fluctuations during the early 1980s, while changes in industrial output dominated fluctuations subsequently. The large, early contribution of agriculture to growth resulted from a series of supply shocks induced by institutional and pricing policy changes. The origin of the strong agricultural growth of the early 1980s in improving supply conditions made this a macroeconomic golden age, in which high rates of growth were compatible with considerable price stability and moderate external deficits. The relative contribution of fluctuations in industrial output was greater later in the decade, when it was closely associated with fluctuations in demand, and a less favorable trade-off between growth and inflation.

On the demand side, investment was the leading source of increased aggregate demand in the first, second and current inflationary episodes, and consumption the leading source in the third episode of 1987 and 1988.

It is obviously true that fluctuations in demand were associated closely with fluctuations in monetary growth. But it is more interesting to examine the origins of monetary expansion, which varied over time.

During the lead-up to the first inflationary episode in 1979 and 1980, official fiscal deficits surged to 5 percent of GNP, and in addition extensive use was made of bank loans in place of budgetary appropriations to finance investment in state enterprises. Subsequently, in the austerity program of 1981, traditional administrative measures were used to slash state investment, and to depress consumer demand by forced sales of treasury bonds.

During 1982-1984, there was an explosion of investment demand, fuelled by the interaction of decentralized enterprise decision-making, the political leadership's high ambitions for growth, and the availability of bank credit. Trade balance was allowed to deteriorate markedly in order to dampen excess demand.

Command controls, including access to credit, were again principal instruments for controlling demand from mid-1986. Credit controls took the main weight of deflation. This was followed by relaxation from mid-1986, setting the stage for the third inflationary episode.

It is notable that official budget deficits, while fairly high in the first inflationary episode, have not played the central role in generating macroeconomic instability that it has in many developing and transitional economies. The budget deficit has remained below 3 percent of GNP since 1983, although there have been signs of an upward trend in recent years. Deficit financing by the central bank has not been a major source of monetary expansion (generally less than 1 percent of GNP). Monetizing the formal budget deficit has not been the decisive factor in the expansion of the money supply.

The real source of inflationary pressure has been the blurred distinction between monetary and fiscal spheres, which gives rise to disguised monetization of public-sector deficits, not captured by the formal budgetary process (Ma 1992). Disguised monetization occurs through mounting arrears in payments by government and state enterprises; undisclosed state enterprises financial losses; pressures on state banks to finance parafiscal operations; a huge overhang of non-performing state-bank loans; and triangular debt among state enterprises. Some sources of disguised monetization have been reduced over time, but there has been a tendency for this to be followed by expansion of other sources. The untangling of triangular debt, for example, required a massive injection of bank credit.

It follows that public sector deficits, broadly defined, have been the major cause of monetary instability.

IV. Instability and the Open Policy

As the share of exports and imports in GNP and the share of foreign borrowing in the financing of public debt and fixed investment have increased, there has been more potential for interaction between the external sector and domestic macroeconomic performance (Table 1).

A number of arguments have been advanced to the effect that the greater openness of China's economy has contributed to greater instability and inflationary pressures in the 1980s. One argument is that as the importance of trade in China's economy increased, international price fluctuations and inappropriate policy responses induced domestic price instability. Export of primary commodities is considered to have worsened the domestic shortage of raw materials and dampened manufacturing profits. Several major *yuan* devaluations in the 1980s are thought by some observers to have pushed up the overall domestic price level through higher prices for imported merchandise. Finally, the decentralized trading system and the export-oriented development strategy are said to have caused the excess export of Chinese goods and services.

None of these arguments stand up to close scrutiny. The declining relative importance of primary goods in both exports and imports (Table 2) indicates that any impact of trade on domestic material shortages diminished during the reform process. Net imports of commodities rose in the inflationary episode of the late 1980s. Even the direct price effects were not all in one direction: Unfavorable price movements for some traded goods were balanced by favorable changes in others, for instance wool and wheat prices reduced by subsidized sales from the United States. However, the terms of trade worsened in the 1980s due to a decline in international oil prices which might have presented difficulties for macroeconomic management.

Excessive export could not have generated inflation because for most of the 1980s China experienced a trade deficit, especially in expansionary episodes from 1984 (Figure 2 and Table 1). Although export subsidies could add to fiscal difficulties, they are related to the over-valued exchange rate, and their recent abolition means they will not present major problems in the future. The wide variations in trade balance moving against changes in total output must have helped reduce overall output fluctuations. The finding by Khor (1991) that broad money leads imports is additional evidence that trade plays a stabilizing role in relation to excess aggregate demand.

Table 1 in combination with Figure 1 suggests a weakening of the association between fluctuations in output growth and inflation as integration into the international economy deepened in the early 1990s. Simultaneously, there was a strengthening of the association between fluctuations in output growth and the trade deficit (Figure 2).

The anti-inflationary impact of international economic integration can be demonstrated at the sectorial level by reference to recent experience with metals used in industrial production. The demand boom of 1992 and early 1993 drove the domestic market price of steel up by around 70 percent, in some cases to double the international price at the swap market exchange rate. The liberalization of steel imports eased the inflationary pressure, especially in coastal areas with greater access to foreign exchange. In the first half of 1993, China's steel imports were 3.6 times as high as in the corresponding period of 1992, and exceeded by a wide margin the full year's imports in 1992. It is expected that steel imports will account for 17 percent of domestic consumption in 1993—a ratio far in excess of any period since the inflationary

415

boom of 1984 and 1985. At the same time, China's relatively low steel exports fell by 68 percent in the first half of 1993, providing an additional stabilizing influence.

Table 1   Importance of External Factors (%)

Year GNP	Ratio of imports plus exports to GNP	Share of external borrowing in budget deficit financing	Net exports as a percentage of
1980	12.8	14.2	-0.6
1981	15.4	42.1	0.0
1982	14.9	-7.5	1.1
1983	14.8	6.0	0.3
1984	17.3	16.0	-0.6
1985	24.2	5.2	-5.2
1986	26.6	27.3	-4.3
1987	27.3	26.6	-1.3
1988	27.3	37.3	-2.1
1989	26.1	35.6	-1.6
1990	32.0	37.8	2.4
1991	36.4	-	2.2

Note: External borrowing refers to borrowing net of retiring debt outstanding.

Sources: SSB 1990 and 1991; SSB 1990b.

Table 2   Changing Structure of Trade (%)

Year	Exchange rate (US$=100)	Share of primary goods in imports	Share of primary goods in exports	Oil revenue in exports
1980	149.84	34.8	50.2	22.0
1981	170.50	36.5	46.6	22.1
1982	189.25	39.6	45.0	22.0
1983	197.57	27.2	43.3	19.5

1984	232.70	19.0	45.7	21.8
1985	293.67	12.5	50.6	24.8
1986	345.28	13.2	36.4	10.4
1987	372.21	16.0	33.5	10.2
1988	372.21	18.2	30.3	7.1
1989	376.59	19.9	28.7	6.7
1990	478.37	18.5	25.6	6.9
1991	532.0	17.0	22.5	5.5

Source: SSB 1991; SSB 1990b.

Table 3   Official and Secondary Market Exchange Rates, 1978-1992
(yuan/US$)

Year	Official exchange rate	Secondary market exchange rate
1978	1.68	-
1979	1.55	-
1980	1.50	-
1981	1.70	3.08
1982	1.89	3.08
1983	1.98	3.08
1984	2.29	3.08
1985	2.93	3.23
1986	3.43	5.00
1987	3.72	5.70
1988	3.72	6.32
1989	3.76	5.91
1990	4.78	5.75
1991	5.32	5.90
1992	5.51	6.50

Sources: Gao (1993); Zhang (1992); and *Far Eastern Economic Review,* June 17, 1993.

A similar set of adjustments has been occurring with copper, aluminum and other industrial inputs. Copper exports fell by 69 percent and imports rose by 20 percent in the first half of 1993, over the corresponding period in 1992. Aluminum exports fell by 45 percent and imports rose by 104 percent. In both cases domestic were higher than international prices in 1993.

Macroeconomic instability has been manifested relatively less in inflation and more in external deficits as the trade share of output has increased. There are good reasons to see this shift in the manifestation of instability as helpful to economic management. One reason is that the authorities have more time to adjust to external than to domestic inflationary pressures, before they are overwhelmed by destabilizing political and policy responses. A second reason is that inflation is more likely to be compounded by loss of community confidence in monetary assets, with large and uncontrollable effects.

There is no conclusive evidence that the greater openness of China's economy had a net adverse effect on domestic stability in the 1980s. Indeed, the variations in net exports have been significantly stabilizing over the past decade. Liberalization of the trade regime could increase this effect in the future, contributing to the loosening of supply bottlenecks and to the improvement of productive efficiency.

V. Reform of Trade and Exchange Rate Regimes

It is clear that there is a close interrelationship between reforms related to international economic integration and the maintenance of macroeconomic stability. The role of variations in net exports in offsetting the inflationary impact of demand surges will be affected by reform of the trade and exchange rate regimes.

The huge, deflationary reduction in net exports in 1993 was partly the result of market forces operating within the existing trade and payments regime, and partly the result of explicit relaxations of the control of imports. The latter represents an important systemic reform, which happens to be helpful to macroeconomic stabilization. It can be taken further in the current or subsequent inflationary episodes, but its contribution is not capable of continual repetition unless trade liberalization is reversed—a development that would be seriously damaging to China's market-oriented reform, international economic relations and economic growth.

It follows that in any future inflationary episodes the stabilizing role of the external sector will be felt proportionately more through normal market mechanisms, and may be felt less immediately and less powerfully. This may mean that excess demand will again be manifested more strongly in increases in domestic price levels, reducing the time the authorities will have available for macroeconomic stabilization if severe economic and political dislocation is to be avoided.

The lesson is clear: There is no alternative to rapid progress of financial market and enterprise reform directed at the control of both open and disguised public-sector deficits in a market economy.

The variations in net exports through fluctuations in domestic demand will also be affected by reforms in the trade and payments regimes. The easing of controls on access to and use of foreign exchange through the current boom has accelerated and increased net exports in the same manner as the liberalization of trade. As with trade liberalization, there would be costs to market-oriented reform, foreign economic relations, and growth from any retreat into tighter exchange controls. Some of the external sector's contributions to stabilization in the current inflationary episode can therefore be expected to be weaker in the future.

There has been a significant shift in the relative importance of the fixed and floating elements of the Chinese exchange rate regime over the past two years. Access to the swap market has been extended considerably. The World Bank has estimated that 80 percent of exports are now subject to the swap market rate.

The boom in domestic demand and the widening access to the swap market led to rapid and large depreciation of the floating exchange rate. The widening access to the swap market was helpful for efficient resource allocation, domestically and internationally. In itself, it diminished the stabilizing effect of foreign trade on domestic demand: Some portion of excess domestic demand that would have overflowed into increased net imports at the fixed official exchange rate was reflected instead in a higher swap market rate, and greater incentives for import competitiveness and export production.

It is important for efficient resource allocation in an increasingly market-oriented economy that the easing of the current inflationary boom be associated with movements toward unification of the exchange rate regime. In practice, this must inevitably mean further liberalization of access to the swap market, and unification within a floating exchange rate. In itself, this may diminish the stabilization role of the external sector in relation to fluctuations in domestic demand driven by public deficits. It will be necessary to maintain controls on state enterprise access to foreign exchange until they are subject to genuinely hard budget constraints. These factors will add to the importance and urgency of reforms in managing fluctuations in domestic demand, and particularly public deficits, in the framework of a market economy.

VI. Conclusions

Over the 15 years of Chinese economic reform there has been a tendency to macroeconomic instability, including four important inflationary episodes. There has been a powerful tendency for periods of more rapid growth to be associated with higher inflation and increased net imports.

After the period of high growth driven by the expansion of agricultural supply in the early 1980s, there was a tendency for the trade-off between growth and inflation to deteriorate, particularly between 1984 and 1989. The deterioration was arrested and partially reversed in the early 1990s.

Fluctuations in output since the early 1980s have been driven by variations in domestic demand, themselves fueled by public deficits, especially deficits that are not apparent in the official public accounts. The increasing openness of the Chinese economy to foreign trade has diminished the variations in rates of growth associated with fluctuations in demand, most powerfully in the current inflationary episode. This has assisted macroeconomic management by giving the authorities more time to bring demand under control before being overwhelmed by political and economic reactions to inflation.

The continued strengthening of economic efficiency and foreign economic relations and sustained rapid growth require extension of liberalization of China's trade, payments and foreign exchange regimes. In itself, this may weaken the stabilizing role of variations in net exports through fluctuations in demand. This reality increases the urgency and importance of reforms to control fluctuations in demand at their source—the open and disguised public sector deficits that have led to periodic surges in money creation.

Appendix:

Major Statistical Figures on China's National Economy and Social Development in 1996*

In 1996, China's gross domestic production (GDP) reached 6,779.5 billion yuan, a 9.7 percent increase over 1995, including: 1,355 billion additional value in primary industries, a 5.1 percent increase; 3,314.8 billion yuan in secondary industries, a 12.3 percent increase; and 2,109.7 billion yuan in tertiary industries, an 8 percent increase. GDP per capita came to 5,569 yuan; and total social labor productivity, 9,902 yuan. In 1996, China produced 490 million tons of grain, a 5 percent increase over 1995; 22 million tons of oil-bearing crops, a 1.7 percent decrease over the previous year; 4.2 million tons of cotton, a 11.7 percent decrease; 5.8 million tons of meat, a 10.3 percent increase; and 28 million tons of aquatic products, a 11.2 percent increase. In 1996, China's total energy production (converted into standard coal) stood at 1.26 billion tons, a 4.6 percent increase over 1995; and China produced 1.38 billion tons of raw coal, a 4.5 percent increase over the previous year; 158 million tons of raw oil, a 5.3 percent increase; generated 1,075 billion kwh of electric power, a 6.7 percent increase; turned out 101.1 million tons of steel, a 6.0 percent increase; 490 million tons of cement, a 3.2 percent increase; 3.01 million tons of ethylene, a 25.4 percent increase; 26.6 million tons of chemical fertilizer (converted into 100 percent content), a 4.4 percent increase; 1.49 million automobiles, a 2.6 percent increase; 19.34 million program-controlled telephone exchanges, an 18.3 percent increase; 21.09 million color television sets, a 2.5 percent increase; and 9.28 million household refrigerators, a 1.0 percent increase. The total social retail sales volume of consumer goods in 1996 reached 2,461.4 billion yuan, a rise of

---

* From the 1996 Statistics Report on the National Economy and Social Development by the State Statistical Bureau of the People's Republic of China.

19.4 percent over the previous year. The year's retail prices of consumer goods grow by 6.1 percent, with the range of increase dropping by 8.7 percentage points. The residents' consumer prices in 1996 grew by 8.3 percent, with the range of increase dropping by 8.8 percentage points. The total import and export volume in 1996 came to 289.9 billion US dollars, or an increase of 3.2 percent over the previous year, of which total export volume came to 151.1 billion US dollars, or a 1.5 percent increase, and total import volume, 138.8 billion US dollars, or a 5.1 percent rise. In 1996, 55.27 billion US dollars in foreign funds were actually utilized by China, a 14.2 percent increase, including 42.35 billion US dollars of direct investment by foreign business, a 12.2 percent increase; tourism generated 10.2 billion US dollars of foreign currency, a 16.8 percent increase. The deposits balance of all financial institutions came to 6,859.6 billion yuan, a 27.3 percent increase; and the balance of various loans, 6,115.7 billion yuan, a 21.2 percent increase.

The amount of cash flow was 880.2 billion yuan, a 11.6 percent increase over the previous year; national foreign currency reserves were 105 billion US dollars; and insurance income was 75.6 billion yuan, a 20.5 percent increase.

There were 3.02 million college students, 2.656 million students in the colleges and universities for adults, 16,200 postgraduates, 17.8 million high school students, including 10.1 million students in secondary vocational schools, 50.48 million junior middle school students, and 136.15 million primary school students. In 1996, China had 2,641 public libraries, 1,205 museums, and 3,600 archives, 1,238 broadcasting stations, 880 TV stations, and 189,000 public health institutions with 3.1 million beds. China had a population of 1.22 billion with average life expectancy being 70.80 years. Per capita income in cities and towns that could be budgeted was 4,839 yuan, a 13 percent increase; and per capita expendable income, 4,377 yuan, a 12.4 percent increase. Per capita net income in rural areas stood at 1,926 yuan, a 22 percent increase. The total employed for the entire nation registered 688.5 million. Annual average wages for workers and staff in cities and towns across the country hit 6,210 yuan, a 12.9

percent increase. Newly built residential houses in urban areas covered an area of 360 million square meters, and those in rural areas, 760 million square meters.